BIBLE VERSES

PSALM 34 VERSE 1

A PSALM OF PRAISE AND TRUST

I will bless the Lord at all times;

his praise shall continually be in my mouth.

PSALM 41 VERSE 1

Psalm of the compassionate

Blessed Is he that considereth the poor:

The Lord will deliver him in time of trouble.

GOD BLESS AMERICA

"FREEDOM IS NOT BY CHANCE BUT BY CHOICE"

"TO CLEAR AWAY THE LEGACY OF INEQUALITY"

43rd Pres. of U.S.A George w. Bush

TABLE OF CONTENTS

WORDS OF WISDOM

"Live as if you were to die tomorrow and learn as if you were to live forever"
By Mahatma Gandhi.

"Mastering others requires force, Mastering the self needs strength." Tao Te Ching

"Knowing others is wisdom. Knowing the self is enlightenment." Tao Te Ching

Every morning in Africa, a gazelle wakes up knowing it must run

faster than the lion or be killed.

Every morning, a lion awakens knowing it must outrun the

slowest gazelle or starve to death.

It doesn't matter if you are a lion or a gazelle. When the sun

comes up, you'd better be running. Reference from, "How to Win any Argument" by Robert Mayer

"The parallelism is that in a modern day society a job is still seen as the object of the hunt or prey, if we land the job we essentially kill the prey which is symbolic of the job. Accomplishing the various tasks on the jobs is dividing up the kill {prey} which provides the means of putting food on the table and providing a roof over your head, it is still analogous of the cave man days of hunting for food to survive." James Watson

FORETHOUGHT

"A LAWYER IS EITHER A SOCIAL ENGINEER OR A PARASITE ON SOCIETY"
Charles Hamilton Houston (September 3, 1895 – April 22, 1950)

"JUSTICE IS NOT BLIND AS LONG AS IT CAN BE SEEN THROUGH THE WALLS OF INJUSTICE"

A GUIDE TO REPRESENTING YOURSELF IN COURT

SPECIAL THANKS

FOR ALL THE EMPLOYEES WORKING AT OFFICE DEPOT IN JACKSONVILLE, FL

FOR BEING SO PATIENT WITH ME WITH THE CREATION OF THE BOOK COVER,

IT WAS A CHALLENGING TASK TO ACCOMPLISH, BUT WE DID IT TOGETHER

WITH HELP OF THE LORD AND YOUR PATIENCE.

THANKS BRIAN, CASSIE, AND SARAH, YOUR HELP WILL BE FOREVER

APPRECICATED, AND REMEMBERED.

Dedication

To all my teachers who instilled in me confidence, and self-esteem that I could accomplish anything if I put my mind to it, especially Mr. Jackson my six grade teacher, and to my Father Lee Watson who always said while I was in the company of his friends, "this is my son and I am so proud of him." Those words resonate with me even now as I sit here and write this book and it was those words that always made me feel loved when they were said by my Father while I was in the company of his friends.

ALSO DEDICATED IN MEMORY OF SUPREME COURT JUSTICE ANTONIN GREGORY SCALIA

Antonin Gregory Scalia (March 11, 1936 – February 13, 2016) was an Associate Justice of the Supreme Court of the United States, who served for 29 years, from 1986 until his death. As the longest-serving justice on the Court, Scalia became the Senior Associate Justice. He was appointed to the Court by U.S. President Ronald Reagan in 1986.

SOME OF HIS PROFOUNDS WORDS AND SAYINGS WHILE SITTING ON THE BENCH

Life is too short to pursue every human act to its most remote consequences; "for want of a nail, a kingdom was lost" is a commentary on fate, not the statement of a major cause of action against a blacksmith.

"Frequently an issue of this sort will come before the Court clad, so to speak, in sheep's clothing: the potential of the asserted principle to effect important change in the equilibrium of power is not immediately evident, and must be discerned by a careful and perceptive analysis. But this wolf comes as a wolf."

Morrison v. Olsen, 487 U.S. 654, 699 (1988) (dissenting

The story is told of the elderly judge who, looking back over a long career, observes with satisfaction that, *when I was young, I probably let stand some convictions that should have been overturned, and when I was old I probably set aside some that should have stood; so overall, justice was done.* I sometimes think that is an appropriate analogy to this Court's constitutional jurisprudence, which alternately creates rights that the Constitution does not contain and denies rights that it does.

Compare Roe V. Wade, 410 U.S. 113 (1973) (right to abortion does exist) with Maryland v. Craig, 497 U.S. 836 (1990) (right to be confronted with witnesses, U.S. Const., Amdt. 6, doesnot).

Board of Ed. of Kiryas Joel v. Grumet (1994) (dissenting)

"Individuals who have been wronged by unlawful racial discrimination should be made whole; but under our Constitution there can be no such thing as either a creditor or a debtor race." "That concept is alien to the Constitution's focus upon the individual . . .

To pursue the concept

of racial entitlement - even for the most admirable and benign of purposes - is to reinforce and preserve for future mischief the way of thinking that produced race slavery, race privilege and race hatred. In the eyes of government, we are just one race here. It is **American.**"

"The main business of a lawyer is to take the romance, the mystery, the irony, the ambiguity out of everything he touches."

"Have the courage to have your wisdom regarded as stupidity"

"In law school, I never understood [antitrust law]. I later found out, in reading the writings of those who now do understand it, that I should not have understood it because it did not make any sense then."

"The story is told of the elderly judge who, looking back over a long career, observes with satisfaction that, when I was young, I probably let stand some convictions that should have been overturned, and when I was old I probably set aside some that should have stood; so overall, justice was done. I sometimes think that is an appropriate analogy to this Court's constitutional jurisprudence, which alternately creates rights that the Constitution does not contain and denies rights that it does."

"The Court's reliance upon *stare decisis* can best be described as contrived. It insists upon the necessity of adhering not to all of *Roe*, but only to what it calls the 'central holding.'
It seems to me that *stare decisis* ought to be applied even to the doctrine of *stare decisis*, and I confess never to have heard of this new, keep-what-you-want-and -throw-away-the-rest version."

HOW TO REPRESENT YOURSELF
IN COURT
AGAINST 3 BAD BEARS
And Win A Settlement

WRITTEN BY
JAMES WATSON

Introduction

The legal premise of my case with Equifax, Experian and Trans Union was the allegedly errors made by all three CRA's on my consumer credit file while I was trying to improve my credit score in June of 2011. all CRA's at the same time allegedly duplicated seven creditors on my consumer credit report, and unwilling to admit that those errors prevent me from obtaining credit cards and other consumer credit from creditors.

The idea of this book came to me when we were ordered by the court to have a case management conference. The Gave us the option on having this case management conference by telephone Since the defendant's since Lawyers were not located in the Jacksonville area. While speaking to them via telephone it suddenly came to me that Defendant's lawyers tone of voice, demeanor, and behavior on the telephone where similar to the three little Bears story I read as a child. So I thought how good it would be if I could provide samples of the papers I filed with the Courts so others can get an ideal and see how to file their papers or Pleadings in Court from some sample I filed in my case.

The book is not only to help Pro se's in filing their Pleadings but it would help the court's system ease their case load because Pro se would have a better perspective of what Pleading to in Court against the Defendants, which ultimately should case the heavy load of our federal Judges.

If most Pro se's would file correct format Pleadings either by following samples in this book or by following other lawyers Pleadings, I believe they would receive the benefit of doubt from the Courts because although they are representing themselves as Pro se's, they still are required to performed the equally as well as Attorneys.

Coincidently after I settled my case someone called me asking for advice on the nuts and bolts on what they should do in his case, in which he had just filed in the Federal Court, as I can recall I think his name was John.

The FCRA is one of the most complex and comprehensive Statute ever written by U.S. Congress. With the high cost of legal representation and very few lawyers willing to taking cases either pro bono or on a contingency basis, it was time to give some people a helping hand in representing themselves in court. by providing them with these samples Pleadings, which will allow them to do a better job and just maybe do a good enough job to either settle their cases out of Court or try a winning case by jury trial.

This book neither gives legal advice, but is a how to guide book showing how I filed my Pleading in the Courts system. The highest compliment a person or Lawyer can receive from someone in the Court's system is when they say," he certainly knows his way around the court," or in my instance one of Defendant's Lawyers asked me how do you know all this information? I replied, "I read." **"READERS MAKES LEADERS"**

If there is one thing I can't overly emphasize enough, is the defendant's lawyers are going to <u>have years of experience and host of professional support. It would wise for you get as much support as you can if you travel down this road. Good Luck</u>

STATISTICS OF PRO SE SELF REPRESENTATION
IN THE COURT SYSTEM

Samuel Johnson, once said, "Attorneys who represents themselves in Court are criticize by the Community" His most prominent famous saying is "An Attorney who represented himself is a fool for a client," The truth is that saying still resonates deep in society even today.

The right to represent oneself in a Legal action has long been a recognized in the United States and predates the ratification of the Constitution, as stated in Section 35 of the Judiciary Act of 1789, 1 Stat. 73, 92, enacted by the first Congress of United States.

The U.S. Judiciary Act, the code of Conduct for the United States Judges, the Federal Rules of Civil Procedure, the Federal Rules of Criminal Procedure, the Federal Rules of Evidence and the Federal Rules of Appellate Procedure address the right of the self-represented litigants in several places.

Pro se self-representation is not unique but does present a Challenge for claimants in the Legal system. The state of Louisiana Court of Appeals track the results of pro se appeals compared to represented appeals. In The year 2000, 7% of civil appeals submitted to the Court by pro se were granted, compared to 46% of writ submitted by their legal counsel.

The comparison in criminal cases the ratio is such i.e. 34% of pro se writs were granted, compared to 45% of writ Submitted by counsel.

A study conducted of pro se felony Defendants found and concluded that pro se representing themselves were not ill served by the decision to represent themselves nor were they mentally ill.

In state Court pro se's charge with felonies were significantly better than, their represented counterparts, of the two hundred or more studied outcome provided just under 50% of the Pro se felons were convicted of any charge. For those with representation by legal Counsel in state Court defendants by contrast a total of 75% were convicted of a charge. Only 26 percent of pro se defendants ended up with a felony conviction, while 63 percent of their counterparts were convicted of Felonies in federal Court

Some Notable Pro Se Litigants

Edward C. Lawson, a Black American civil rights activist was a Pro se defendants' in Kolender v. Lawson (461 U.S. 352, 1983) in which the U.S Supreme Court rule that a police officer could not arrest a citizen merely for refusing to present an ID.

Robert Kearns was the inventor of the intermittent windshield wipers, in which he Represented himself as a Pro se litigant who sue both Chrysler and ford companies and won. His legal story was the subject of the movie Flash of Genius.

Jim Traficant, was a former U.S. Representative from Ohio, who representative himself as a pro se in a Racketeer influence and Corrupt Organization Act case in1983, and was acquitted of all charges.

Now because of my settlement in 2014 with all three CRA's you can add my name to that list of Notable Pro Se litigants, **James Watson.**

CHANGE NEEDED BY CONSUMERS ON CRA's REPORTING OF INFORMATION

Due to the abusive nature of the CRAs toward consumers in the 1970's Congress began looking at ways to curve this abuse with the passing of legislature to help consumer deal with disputes they had on their credit files. With continuous uproar from how consumer where been treated by the CRAs Congress revisit the FCRA. The FCRA's amendments included in the Fair and Accurate Credit Transactions Act of 2003 ("FACT Act"),[5 and] how the courts have interpreted the FCRA in response to consumers moving against the CRAs for sending out inaccurate credit information and/ or failing to correct inaccurate credit information. The Consumer Credit Reporting Reform Act of 1996 ("CCRA') is also discussed, because it added two important tools for consumers: the availability of statutory damages and the requirement that deleted information cannot be reinserted into the credit report without notice and verification, (Emphasis added reinsertion is still taking place today). With the passing of the FCRA on April 25, 1971, the FCRA provided some relief for consumers who could prove an injury caused by false or inaccurate credit reports by CRAs. For Consumers to fully appreciate the purpose and significance of the FCRA and its amendments, it is imperative to examine the legal landscape that existed prior to the FCRA and its amendments. At common law, credit b u r e a u s had overly extreme limited responsibilities for reporting errors, and when sued for defamation, a

CRA was able to raise a defense of conditional privilege.

Although the common law provided no real solution against CRAs for reporting false information on consumer credit it sowed the seed for common law holding to hold CRAs accountable for errors in consumer's credit reports. See an English case, *Toogood v.* Spyring, and all related cases.

Summary of
Rights

Para informacion, en *espanol, visitewww.ftc.gov/ credit oescribes ala FTCConsumer Response* Center, *Room 130-A 600 Pennsylvania Ave.N.W., Washington, D.C. 20580.*

A Summary of Your Rights Under the Fair Credit Reporting Act

The federal Fair Credit Reporting Act (FCRA) promotes the accuracy, fairness. and privacy of information in the files of consumer reporting agencies. There are many types of consumer reporting agencies, including credit bureaus and specialty agencies (such as agencies that sell information about check writing histories. Medical records. And rental history records). Here is a summary of your major rights under the FCRA. For more information, including information about additional rights, go to www.ftc.gov/credit or write to: Consumer Response Center, Room 130-A, Federal Trade Commission, 600 Pennsylvania Ave. NW., Washington, D.C.20580.

- You must be told If Information in your file has been used against you. Anyone who uses a credit report or another type of consumer report to deny your application forced, insurance, or employment· or to take another adverse action against you must tell you, and must give you the name, address, and phone number of the agency that provided the information.

- You have the right to know what is in your file. You may request and obtain all the information about you in the files of a consumer reporting agency (your"file disclosure"). You will be required to provide proper identification, which may include your Social Security Number in many cases. the disclosure will be free. You are entitled to a free file disclosure if:
  - a person has taken adverse action against you because of information in your credit report;
  - you are the victim of Identity theft and place a fraud alert in your file;
  - your file contains inaccurate information as a result of fraud;
  - you are on public assistance;
  - you are unemployed but expect to apply for employment within 60 days.

  In addition, by September 2005 all consumers will be entitled to one free disclosure every 12 months upon request from each nationwide credit bureau and from nationwide specialty consumer reporting agencies. See www.ftc.gov/ccredit for additional information.

- You have the right to ask for a credit score. Credit scores are numerical summaries of your credit- worthiness based on information from credit bureaus. You may request accredit score from consumer reporting agencies that create scores or distribute scores used in residential real property loans. but you will have to pay for it. In some mortgage transactions. you will receive credit score information for free from the mortgage lender.

You have the right to dispute Incomplete or inaccurate, Information. If you identify

information in your file that is incomplete or inaccurate, and report it to the consumer reporting agency, the agency must investigate unless your dispute is frivolous. See www.ftc.gov/credit for

- Consumer reporting agencies must correct or delete inaccurate, incomplete, or unverifiable I information. Inaccurate, incomplete or unverifiable information must be removed or corrected, usually within 30 days. However, the consumer reporting agency is not required to remove accurate derogatory information from your file unless it is outdated (as described below) or cannot be verified. A consumer reporting agency may continue to report information it has verified as accurate.

- Consumer reporting agencies may not report outdated negative Information. In most cases, a consumer reporting agency may not report negative Information that is more than seven years old. or bankruptcies that are more than 10 years old.

- Access to your file Is limited. A consumer reporting agency may provide information about you only to people with a valid need. usually to consider an application with a creditor, insurer, employer, landlord, or other business. The FCRA specifies those with a valid need for access.

- You must give your consent for reports to be provided to employers. A consumer reporting agency may not give out information about you to your employer, or a potential employer, without your written consent given to the employer. Written consent generally is not required in the trucking industry. For more information, go to www.ftc.gov/credit.

- You may limit "prescreened" offers of credit and insurance you get based on information in your credit report. Unsolicited "prescreened" offers for credit and insurance must include a toll-free phone number you can call if you choose to remove your name and address from the lists these offers are based on. You may opt-out with the nationwide credit bureaus at 1-888-567-8688.

- You may seek damages from violators. If a consumer reporting agency, or. in some cases, a user of consumer reports or a furnisher of information to a consumer reporting agency violates the FCRA, you may be able to sue in state or federal court.

- Identity theft victims and active duty military personnel have additional rights.

A SUMMARY OF YOUR RIGHTS UNDER THE FAIR CREDIT REPORTING ACT, CONTINUED...

States may enforce the FCRA, and many states have their own consumer reporting laws. In some cases, you may have more rights under state law. For more Information, contact your state or local consumer protection agency or your state Attorney General.

Federal enforcers are:

TYPE OF BUSINESS:	CONTACT:
Consumer reporting agencies, creditors and others not listed below	Federal Trade Commission: Consumer Response Center · FCRA Washington, DC 20580 1·877·382·4357
National banks, federal branches/agencies of foreign banks (word "National" or initials "N.A." appear in or after bank's name)	Office of the Comptroller of the Currency Customer Assistance Group 1301 McKinney Street, Suite 3450 Houston, TX 77010·9050 800·613·6743
Federal Reserve System member banks (except national banks, And federal branches/agencies of foreign banks)	Federal Reserve Consumer Help PO Box 1200 Minneapolis, MN 55480 202-452·3693
Savings associations and federally chartered savings banks (word "Federal" or initials "F.S.B." appear in federal institution's name)	Office of Thrift Supervision Consumer Complaints Washington, DC 20552 800·842·6929
Federal credit unions (words "Federal Credit Union" appear in institution's name)	National Credit Union Administration 1775 Duke Street Alexandria, VA 22314 703·519·4600
State chartered banks that are not members of the Federal Reserve System	Federal Deposit Insurance Corporation Consumer Response Center, 2345 Grand Avenue, Suite 100 Kansas City, Missouri 64108-2638 1·877-275·3342
Air, surface, or rail common carriers regulated by former Civil Aeronautics Board or Interstate Commerce Commission	Department of Transportation, Office of Financial Management Washington, DC 20590 202·366-1306
Activities subject to the Packers and Stock Yards Act, 1921	Department of Agriculture Office of Deputy Administrator. GIPSA Washington, DC 20250 202·720·7051

Florida resident

As of July 1, 2006 you have a right to place a "security freeze" on your consumer report, which will prohibit a consumer reporting agency from releasing any information in your consumer report without your express authorization. A security freeze must be requested in writing by certified mail to a consumer reporting agency. The security freeze is designed to prevent credit loans, and services from being approved in your name without your consent. You should be aware that using a security freeze to control access to the personal and financial information in your consumer report may delay, interfere with, or prohibit the timely approval of any subsequent request or application you make regarding a new loan, credit, mortgage, insurance, government services or payments, rental housing, employment, investment, license, cellular telephone, utilities, digital signature, Internet credit card transaction or other services, including an extension of credit at point of sale. When you place a security freeze on your consumer report, you will be provided a personal identification number or password to use if you choose to remove the freeze on your consumer report or authorize the release of your consumer report for a designated period of time after the security freeze is in place. To provide that authorization, you must contact the consumer reporting agency and provide all of the following:

The personal identification number or password. Proper identification to verify your identity.
Information specifying the period of time for which the report shall be made available.
Payment of a fee authorized by this section of the Florida Statutes.

A consumer reporting agency must authorize the release of your consumer report no later than 3 business days after receiving the above information.

A security freeze does not apply to a person or entity, or its affiliates, or collection agencies acting on behalf of the person or entity, with which you have an existing account. That requests information in your consumer report for the purposes of reviewing or collecting the account. Reviewing the account includes activities related to account maintenance, monitoring, credit line increases, and account upgrades and enhancements.

You have the right to bring a civil action against anyone, including a consumer reporting agency, who fails to comply with the provisions of Sec. 501.005, Florida Statutes, which governs the placing of a consumer report security freeze on your consumer report.

SUING YOUR CREDITORS AND CRA's

Who	Why	Precedent/Law	Fine
Creditor if they report your credit history inaccurately Chase Manhattan	Defamation Financial injury By the Court	US Court of Appeals, ninth Circuit, No.00-15946, Nelson vs.	Extent of Damage Incurred By the wronged Party as deemed
Creditors if you Dispute a debt, The FCRA And they fail to Report it as Disputed to the Credit bureaus	Protection under The FCRA	FCRA Section 623	$1000
Creditors if they Pull your credit file Without Permissible Purpose	Injury to your Credit report and Credit Score	FCRA Section 604 (A)(3)	$1000
Credit bureau if they refuse to Correct information After being Provided proof Trans Union Corporation US Court of Appeal for the Third Circuit Court Case 115 F.3d 220 June 9, 1997, Filed (D.C. No. 95-cv-01743)	Defamation Willful Injury	FCRA Section 623 Cushman v.	Extent of Damages Incurred By the wronged Party, as deemed By the Courts
Credit bureaus if They reinsert a Removed item from Your credit report Without notifying You in writing Within 5 business Days	Consumer protection afforded by the FCRA	FCRA Part (A) (5) (B)(a)	$1000

Credit bureaus if They fail to Respond to your Written disputes Within 30 days (a 15-day extension May be granted if	Consumer protection afforded by the	FCRA 611 Part (A) (1)	$1000
They receive Information from The creditor within The first30 days)			
Collection Agency Can Not be Both Purchaser and 'assignee' It's one or the Other	Protection under the FDCPA	Gearing v. Check Brokerage Corp 233 F. 3d 469 (7th Cir. 2000)	$1000
Misrepresentations By the collector About Themselves or the Debt Are actionable Regardless Of intent	Protection under the FDCPA	Gearing v. Check Brokerage Corp Cacace v. Lucas 775 F. Supp. 502, 505 (D. Com. 1990)	$1000
Creditors or Collection Agencies, and Credit bureaus if They try "Re-Age" your account By updating the date of last activity On your credit Report in the hopes Of keeping negative Information on your account longer	Consumer protection afforded by the FCRA	FCRA Section 605 (c) Running of the reporting period	$1000
If you dispute a Debt, the collection Agency fails to Report it disputed To the credit Bureaus	Protection under the FDCPA	FDCPA Section 807(8)	$1000
Collection Agencies if they do Not validate your	Consumer protection afforded by the	FDCPA Section 809(b)	$1000

27

Debt yet continue To pursue Collection activity (file for judgments, Call or write you)	FDCPA	FTC opinion letter Cass from
Collection Agencies if you Have sent them a Cease and desist Letter and they still Call you	Consumer protection afforded by the FDCPA	FDCPA $1000 Section 8059 (c)
Collection Agencies if they Have not validated Your debt and they Still continue to Report to the credit Bureaus	Consumer protection afforded by the FDCPA	$1000 FDCPA Section 809(b) FTC opinion letter Cass from Lefevre
Collection Agencies if they - Cash a post-dated Date on the check Cost you money by making you Accept collect calls Or COD mail- Take or threaten to take any Personal property Without a judgment	Consumer protection FDCPA	FDCPA 808 $1000 Section
If collector calls You after 9 PM at Night or before 8 AM	Consumer Protection afforded by the	FDCPA Section $1000 805. (a)(1)
Calls you at your Place of Employment if the Debt Collector Knows or has Reason to know That your employer Prohibits the Consumer from Receiving such Communication.	Consumer protection afforded by the FDCPA	FDCPA $1000 805. (a)(3)

Call any third part About your debt Like friends, Neighbors, Relatives, etc. However, they can Contact your Attorney a Consumer Reporting agency, The creditor, or the Attorney of the Creditor, or the Attorney of the Debt collector.	Consumer protection afforded by the FDCPA	FDCPA Section 805. (b)	$1000
The collection Agency cannot use Any kind of Harassment or Abuse	Consumer protection afforded by the FDCPA	FDCPA Section 806	$1000
Collector cannot Claim to garnish Your wages, seize Property or have You arrested	Consumer protection afforded by the FDCPA	FDCPA 807	$1000
Collector must live in a county in Which you lived When you signed The Original Contract for the Debt or where you	Consumer protection afforded FDCPA	FDPCA 811 (a) (2)	$1000 also a good ground for getting a Judgment vacated

Live at the time when they file the lawsuit
The use or threat of use violence or other criminal means harm the physical person,
Physical person, reputation, or property of any person
The use of obscene or profane language or language the natural consequence of
Which is to abuse the hearer or reader. (3) The publication of a list pf consumer who
Allegedly Refuse to pay debts except to a consumer reporting (4) The advertisement for
Sale of any debt to coerce.

Refer to the FDCPA AND FCRA ACTS

JONES DAY

January 16, 2014

VIA UPS

James Watson

Re: Jams Watson v. Experian Information
Solutions, et. al.

Dear Mr. Watson:

I am enclosing the settlement check in the amount of ... and a copy of the fully

executed Settlement Agreement.

Enclosure

Strasburger

ATTORNEYS AT LAW

January 15, 2014

VIA FEDERAL EXPRESS

Re: No. 3:12-cv-00552-UAMH-JBT (M.D of Fla.-Jacksonville Div.)
James L. Watson, Sr. v. Equifax, et al.

Dear Mr. Watson:

Enclosed please find Trans Union LLC's _____ in the amount...paid to the order of Plaintiff **James** L. Watson, in settlement of the **above referenced matter**.

I am providing the settlement check to you on the express condition that it not be negotiated or placed for payment until the Order of Dismissal with Prejudice has **been** entered by the Court.

Sincerely,

Alliison Reddoch

AR:
km

Enclosure

KING&SPALDING

January 14, 2014

VIA OVERNIGHT DELIVERY

James L. Watson

King & Spalding LLP 1

180 Peachtree Street

N.E. Atlanta, GA

30309-3521

Re: James L. Watson v. Equifax Information
Services LLC Case No.: 3: 12-cv-00552-UAMH-JBT

Dear Mr. Watson:

Enclosed please find a copy of the fully executed Settlement Agreement and
General Release regarding the above-referenced matter along with a settlement
check in the amount for _____.

Sincerely,

Pamela L. Sauls

IN THE UNITED STATES DISTRICT COURT
FOR THE MIDDLE DISTRICT OF FLORIDA
JACKSONVILLE DIVISION

JAMES L. WATSON

Plaintiff,

V.

CASE NO.3:12-CV-00552-UAMH-JBT

EQUIFAX, EXPERIAN, and TRANSUNION,

Defendants.

SETTLEMENT AGREEMENT AND RELEASE

This Settlement Agreement and Mutual Release ("Agreement") is made and entered into by James L. Watson ("Plaintiff) and Equifax Information Services LLC ("Equifax") as of December 19, 2013. Equifax is referred to herein as the "Defendant." Plaintiff and Defendant are collectively referred to herein as the "Parties."

FACTS

Plaintiff filed the above-captioned lawsuit in the United States District Court -Middle District of Florida ("the Lawsuit"). Plaintiff alleges that Defendant is liable for violations of the Fair Credit Reporting Act and inaccuracies associated with Plaintiffs credit reports published prior to the execution of this Agreement ("the Credit Reports").

The Parties now desire to resolve all disputes, asserted or unasserted and arising out of, any acts, failures to act, omissions, misrepresentations, facts, events, transactions, or occurrences described in the Lawsuit or related to the Credit Reports.

NOW THEREFORE, in consideration of the mutual promises, terms, and conditions contained herein; and for other good and valuable consideration hereby deemed received, the Parties agree as follows:

TERMS OF AGREEMENT

Defendant agrees to the total settlement amount redacted The settlement check shall be Made payable to James L. Watson, Sr., Pro Se Plaintiff.

Within five of the execution of this Agreement, Defendants agree to file a Motion to Dismiss with Prejudice, and proposed Order, or to file such other papers as are necessary to dismiss with prejudice his claims against Defendant. Except rights and obligations created by this Agreement, Plaintiff, his heirs, agents, privies, attorneys, insurance carriers, executors, administrators, and successors and assigns, hereby release and forever discharge Defendant and its agents, affiliates, servants, employees, officers, directors, shareholders, attorneys, privies, insurance carriers, predecessors, parents, subsidiaries, successors, and assigns from any and all debts, controversies, claims, demands, damages, actions, causes of action or suits of any kind or nature, including by contract, tort, statute, or otherwise, known or unknown, now existing and up to the date on which Plaintiff signs this Agreement including, without limitation, any obligations under the Fair Credit Reporting Act. This Agreement necessarily includes, but is not limited to, any and all claims, demands, damages, actions, causes of action or suits which are based directly or indirectly upon facts, events, transactions or occurrences related to or alleged, or embraced by the Lawsuit or the Credit Reports.

The Parties further agree that this Agreement has been fully read and understood by them, and that each of them has received independent legal advice from their respective attorneys as to the effect and import of its provisions. The Parties further agree that this Agreement is being entered into for the express purpose and intention of making and entering into a full and final compromise, adjustment and settlement of all claims which were or could have been asserted in the Lawsuit, whether or not referred to therein.

Plaintiff warrants and represents that there has been no assignment, sale or transfer, by operation of law or otherwise, of any claim, right, or interest released herein. Plaintiff agrees to indemnify, defend and hold harmless Equifax from any claim, liability, or expense which maybe incurred as a result of the assertion of any such claim, right, or interest by any person by reason of any such assignment, sale or transfer. This Agreement shall in no event be construed as or be deemed to be evidence of an admission or concession on the part of Defendant of any claim or any fault or liability or damages whatsoever. Defendant denies any and all wrongdoing of any kind whatsoever in connection with the Lawsuit and does not concede any infirmity in the defenses that each asserted or intended to assert. The Parties have reached the agreement reflected herein in order to avoid further expense, inconvenience and delay, and to dispose of extremely expensive, burdensome, and protracted litigation.

Without limiting the generality of the foregoing, Plaintiff acknowledges
That attached hereto as Exhibit A is his Equifax Consumer Credit Report as of December 18, 2013. Plaintiff hereby agrees that he will not initiate any legal action against Equifax based on the information currently contained in Exhibit A, and that Equifax may publish such information in the normal course of its business. pursuant to the Fair Credit Reporting Act and any other applicable federal and/or state laws.

The Parties agree that this Agreement constitutes a good faith settlement of the Lawsuit and acknowledge that it is entered into freely and voluntarily.

Unless otherwise required by law or court order, Plaintiff agrees to keep this Agreement confidential, except when necessary to assert a due legal right, or when his accountants or attorneys are privy to its contents in confidential communications. In the event Plaintiff is forced to file this Agreement with a court, he shall do so under seal so that the contents are not revealed beyond disclosure to duly authorized court personnel such as judges and court clerks or to taxing authorities, if necessary, or as otherwise ordered by the Court.

1 O. This Agreement constitutes the sole and entire agreement between Plaintiff and Equifax, and supersedes all prior agreements, negotiations, and discussions between the Parties, with respect to the subject matter covered in it. Plaintiff and Equifax each acknowledge that, in entering into this Agreement, they are not relying upon any representations or warranties made by anyone other than those terms and provisions expressly set forth in this Agreement. It is expressly understood and agreed that this Agreement may not be altered, amended, waived, modified or otherwise changed in any respect or particular whatsoever except by writing duly executed by authorized representatives of Plaintiff and Equifax, respectively. The Parties further acknowledge and agree that they will make no claims at any time or place that this Agreement has been orally supplemented, modified, or altered in any respect whatsoever.

This Agreement is being made in and shall be deemed to be performed in the State of Florida and shall be governed by, construed, and enforced in accordance with the laws of the State of Florida without giving effect to the provisions, policies, or principles thereof relating to choice of law or conflict of laws. Each of the Parties hereby consents to the jurisdiction of the federal courts located in the State of Florida with respect to any dispute relating to or arising out of this Agreement.

In any action to enforce the terms of this Agreement, including any action to recover damages for any violations of it, including the confidentiality provisions of paragraph 9 above, the prevailing party shall be entitled to recover its reasonable attorneys' fees and disbursements in addition to costs of suit.

Should any provision of this Agreement be held invalid or illegal, such invalidity or illegality shall not invalidate the whole of this Agreement, but, rather the Agreement shall be construed as if it did not contain the invalid or illegal part, and the rights and obligations of the Parties shall be construed and enforced accordingly.

Each Party has the requisite authority to enter into this agreement on their own behalf. This Agreement may be executed in counter parts signed on varying date.

Credit score ranges

FICO SCORE: 300-850
SCORE FROM EXPERIAN: 330-830
SCORE FROM EQUIFAX: 300-850
SCORE FROM TRANS UNION: 300-850
VANTAGE SCORE: 300-850

Credit reports are used to calculate consumers Fico or Vantage scores. Credit

scores are used to obtain such things as mortgages, car loans, credit cards

and other consumer credit, insurance, and employment. A poor credit

score can cost your thousands of dollars more than a person with a good credit

score for the same product. A consumer with a high credit score could receive an

interest rate that is half that of a consumer with a lower credit score

HOW CREDIT SCORES ARE DERIVE

35%- payment history
30%- amount owed
15%- length of credit history
10%-types of credit
10%- new credit

ACRONYM FOR HOW SCORES ARE DERIVED

PH=PAYING HISTORY

A=AMOUNT

L=LENGTH OF CREDIT HISTORY

T=Types of Credit

N=New Credit

Your credit score can drop if your credit card balance goes above 30% of your credit card limit e. g. if your credit Card limit is $10,000 and your balances goes to $7,100 which is 71% of that limit, your credit score may drop, there are many determining factors which would determine about how much it will decrease.

Section: [15 U.S.C. § 1681a]

          Subsection: (d) (2) (D) of section 603

              Paragraph (1) *In general.* The term "consumer report" means any written,

oral, or other communication of any information by a consumer reporting agency
bearing on a consumer's credit worthiness, credit standing, credit capacity, character,
general reputation, personal characteristics, or mode of living which is used or expected
to be used or collected in whole or in part for the purpose of serving as a factor in
establishing the consumer's eligibility for

              Subparagraph: (A) subject to section 624, any Clause (i) report containing

information solely as to transactions or experiences between the consumer and the

person

making the report;

   Subclause (I) made in connection with an application that was made by, or a

transaction that was initiated by, any consumer, or in connection with a review of an

account under section 604(a)(3)(F)(ii) [§ 1681b];

A PERFIT ILLUSTRATION IS SUBSECTION (K) OF SECTION 603

I suggest you first read the entire FCRA statute, then concentrate on the applicable

section or sections that applies to your issue or issues in dispute.

USING WORD ASSOCIATION TO HELP YOU REMEMBER SECTIONS OF THE FCRA AS INDICATED BELOW

§ 602. Congressional findings and statement of purpose [15 U.S.C. § 1681]

Associated word, "Congressional"

§ 603. Definitions; rules of construction [15 U.S.C. § 1681a], applicable to all

§ 604. Permissible purposes of consumer reports [15 U.S.C. § 1681b] boys need permission to Drive before age 18

§ 605. Requirements relating to information contained in consumer reports [15 U.S.C. § 1681c] Contain information in report; Both Contain and Cinco starts with a "C

§ 605A. Identity theft prevention; fraud alerts and active duty alerts [15 U.S.C. §1681c-1]

Crime of white collar workers against citizens

§ 605B. Block of information resulting from identity theft [15 U.S.C. §1681c-2] Blocking of information to prevent you from having a fit-acronym for (**from identity theft)**

§ 606. Disclosure of investigative consumer reports [15 U.S.C. §1681d]

Disclosure of investigative information on individual consumers

§ 607. Compliance procedures [15 U.S.C. §1681e]

Everyone must comply from 1997 with section 607=13

§ 608. Disclosures to governmental agencies [15 U.S.C. § 1681f] Federal Government agencies, or FAG-- Federal agencies of the Gov

§ 609. Disclosures to consumers [15 U.S.C. § 1681g] given out to consumers 1 freely every yr.

§ 610. Conditions and form of disclosure to consumers [15 U.S.C. § 1681h] Homeland security.

611. Procedure in case of disputed accuracy [15 U.S.C. § 1681i] Investigation of reinsertioner Disputes.

612. Charges for certain disclosures [15 U.S.C. § 1681j] Jingling Money out of consumersyour pockets

613. 613. Public record information for employment purposes [15 U.S.C. § 1681k] Kentucky Fried Kitchen Employment Hiring.

614. 614. Restrictions on investigative consumer reports [15 U.S.C. § 1681*l*] Looking and peeping does not exclude public information. 40

§ 615. Requirements on users of consumer reports [15 U.S.C. § 1681m] Many Users of

consumer reports.

§ 616. Civil liability for willful noncompliance [15 U.S.C. § 1681n] Noncompliance Willfully.

§ 617. Civil liability for negligent noncompliance [15 U.S.C. § 1681o] Oh, heck I just felt like

being Negligent Noncompliant.

§ 618. Jurisdiction of courts; limitation of actions [15 U.S.C. § 1681p]

Place where to file lawsuit or POJ, Place of Jurisdiction.

§ 619. Obtaining information under false pretenses [15 U.S.C. § 1681q] quack like a duck

but they are really foxes in disguise.

§ 620. Unauthorized disclosures by officers or employees [15 U.S.C. § 1681r] Reporting not
authorized.

§ 621. Administrative enforcement [15 U.S.C. § 1681s] Statutory administrated enforcement
-SAE acronym

§ 622. Information on overdue child support obligations [15 U.S.C. § 1681s-1] Slap with
failure to pay child support

§ 623. Responsibilities of furnishers of information to consumer reporting agencies

[15 U.S.C. § 1681s-2]

Secondary source Furnisher of information or the last letter of the word "Furnishers"
ending in "S"

§ 624. Affiliate sharing [15 U.S.C. § 1681s-3] Sharing information solicitation

§ 625. Relation to State laws [15 U.S.C. § 1681t] This Title and state applied laws- SAL

§ 626. Disclosures to FBI for counterintelligence purposes [15 U.S.C. § 1681u] Under

Investigation by FBI.

§ 627. Disclosures to governmental agencies for counterterrorism purposes

[15 U.S.C.§1681v] Victory to keep Homeland secure and safe or V-Day.

§ 628. Disposal of records [15 U.S.C. §1681w] – "Waste not want not," records.

§ 629. Corporate and technological circumvention prohibited [15 U.S.C.§1681x]

X Generation are smarter with computers.

ACRONYMS TO HELP YOU REMEMBER THE FCRA ACT

CWSCC=Credit worthiness, Standing, Credit, Capacity

UCR=Unfair credit Reporting

FACR=Fair accurate credit reporting

FIRP=Fairness, Impartiality, Respect to privacy

CAR=Confidentiality, accuracy, Relevancy

FEC=Fair, Equitable, credit

RICI=Reporting inaccurate credit information

JW=Judicial Law

CW=Common Law

ICR=investigative Consumer

Report CUF= consumer, user, Furnisher

POJ, Place of Jurisdiction

fit-acronym for **(from identity theft)**

THE FAIR CREDIT REPORTING ACT

As a public service, the staff of the Federal Trade Commission (FTC) has prepared the following complete text of the Fair Credit Reporting Act (FCRA), 15 U.S.C. § 1681 et seq. Although staff generally followed the format of the U.S. Code as published by the Government Printing Office, the format of this text does differ in minor ways from the Code (and from West's U.S. Code Annotated). For example, this version uses FCRA section numbers (§§ 601-629) in the headings. (The relevant U.S. Code citation is included with each section heading and each reference to the FCRA in the text.) Although the staff has made every effort to transcribe the statutory material accurately, this compendium is intended only as a convenience for the public and not a substitute for the text in the U.S. Code.

This version of the FCRA includes the amendments to the FCRA set forth in the Consumer Credit Reporting Reform Act of 1996 (Public Law 104-208, the Omnibus Consolidated Appropria-tions Act for Fiscal Year 1997, Title II, Subtitle D, Chapter 1), Section 311 of the Intelligence Authorization for Fiscal Year 1998 (Public Law 105-107), the Consumer Reporting Employment Clarification Act of 1998 (Public Law 105-347), Section 506 of the Gramm-Leach-Bliley Act (Public Law 106-102), Sections 358(g) and 505(c) of the Uniting and Strengthening America by Providing Appropriate Tools Required to Intercept and Obstruct Terrorism Act of 2001 (USA PATRIOT Act) (Public Law 107-56), the Fair and Accurate Credit Transactions Act of 2003 (FACT Act) (Public Law 108-159), Section 719 of the Financial Services Regulatory Relief Act of 2006 (Public Law 109-351), Section 743 (Div. D, Title VII) of the Consolidated Appropriations Act of 2008 (Public Law 110-161), the Credit and Debit Card Receipt Clarification Act of 2007 (Public Law 110-241), and Sections 205 and 302 of the Credit Card Accountability Responsibility and Disclosure (CARD) Act of 2009 (Public Law 111-24), the Consumer Financial Protection Act of 2010 (CFPA) (Title X of the Dodd-Frank Wall Street Reform and Consumer Protection Act, Public Law 111-203), and the Red Flag Program Clarification Act of 2010 (Public Law 111-203). The Commission website posted this document on **September 1, 2011.**

The provisions added to the FCRA by the FACT Act became effective at different times. In some cases, the provision includes its own effective date. In other cases, the FACT Act provides that the effective dates be prescribed by the FTC and Federal Reserve Board. See 16 CFR Part 602 (69 Fed. Reg. 6526; February 11, 2004) (69 Fed. Reg. 29061; May 20, 2004).

The provisions added to the FCRA by the CFPA became effective on July 21, 2011, the "designated transfer date" on which the Bureau of Consumer Financial Protection assumed certain duties specified by the CFPA.   See 75 Fed. Reg. 57252 (Sept. 20, 2010)

FCRA TABLE OF CONTENTS

§ 601. Short title

This title may be cited as the "Fair Credit Reporting Act".

§ 602. Congressional findings and statement of purpose [15 U.S.C. §1681]

Accuracy and fairness of credit reporting. The Congress makes the following findings:

The banking system is dependent upon fair and accurate credit reporting. Inaccurate credit reports directly impair the efficiency of the banking system, and unfair credit reporting methods undermine the public confidence which is essential to the continued functioning of the banking system.

An elaborate mechanism has been developed for investigating and evaluating the credit worthiness, credit standing, credit capacity, character, and general reputation of consumers.

Consumer reporting agencies have assumed a vital role in assembling and evaluating consumer credit and other information on consumers.

There is a need to insure that consumer reporting agencies exercise their grave responsibilities with fairness, impartiality, and a respect for the consumer's right to privacy.

Reasonable procedures. It is the purpose of this title to require that consumer reporting agencies adopt reasonable procedures for meeting the needs of commerce for consumer credit, personnel, insurance, and other information in a manner which is fair and equitable to the consumer, with regard to the confidentiality, accuracy, relevancy, and proper utilization of such information in accordance with the requirements of this title.

§ 603. Definitions; rules of construction [15 U.S.C. §1681a]

Definitions and rules of construction set forth in this section are applicable for the purposes of this title.

The term "person" means any individual, partnership, corporation, trust, estate, cooperative, association, government or governmental subdivision or agency, or other entity.

The term "consumer" means an individual.

Consumer Report

In general. The term "consumer report" means any written, oral, or other communication of any information by a consumer reporting agency bearing on a consumer's credit worthiness, credit standing, credit capacity, character, general reputation, personal characteristics, or mode of living which is used or expected to be used or collected in whole or in part for the purpose of serving as a factor in establishing the consumer's eligibility for credit or insurance to be used primarily for personal, family, or household purposes;

employment purposes; or

any other purpose authorized under section 604 [§ 1681b].

Exclusions. Except as provided in paragraph (3), the term "consumer report" does not include

subject to section 624, any

report containing information solely as to transactions or experiences between the consumer and the person making the report;

communication of that information among persons related by common ownership or affiliated by corporate control; or

communication of other information among persons related by common ownership or affiliated by corporate control, if it is clearly and conspicuously disclosed to the consumer that the information may be communicated among such persons and the consumer is given the opportunity, before the time that the information is initially communicated, to direct that such information not be communicated among such persons;

any authorization or approval of a specific extension of credit directly or indirectly by the issuer of a credit card or similar device;

any report in which a person who has been requested by a third party to make a specific extension of credit directly or indirectly to a consumer conveys his or her decision with respect to such request, if the third party advises the consumer of the name and address of the person to whom the request was made, and such person makes the disclosures to the consumer required under section 615 [§ 1681m]; or

a communication described in subsection (o) or (x).[1]

Restriction on sharing of medical information. Except for information or any communication of information disclosed as provided in section 604(g)(3), the exclusions in paragraph (2) shall not apply with respect to information disclosed to any person related by common ownership or affiliated by corporate control, if the information is–

medical information;

[1] Should be read as "(o) or (*y*)" because section 603(x) was re-designated as 603(y) in 2010 by the CFPA

an individualized list or description based on the payment transactions of the consumer for medical products or services; or

an aggregate list of identified consumers based on payment transactions for medical products or services.

The term "investigative consumer report" means a consumer report or portion thereof in which information on a consumer's character, general reputation, personal characteristics, or mode of living is obtained through personal interviews with neighbors, friends, or associates of the consumer reported on or with others with whom he is acquainted or who may have knowledge concerning any such items of information. However, such information shall not include specific factual information on a consumer's credit record obtained directly from a creditor of the consumer or from a consumer reporting agency when such information was obtained directly from a creditor of the consumer or from the consumer.

The term "consumer reporting agency" means any person which, for monetary fees, dues, or on a cooperative nonprofit basis, regularly engages in whole or in part in the practice of assembling or evaluating consumer credit information or other information on consumers for the purpose of furnishing consumer reports to third parties, and which uses any means or facility of interstate commerce for the purpose of preparing or furnishing consumer reports.

The term "file," when used in connection with information on any consumer, means all of the information on that consumer recorded and retained by a consumer reporting agency regardless of how the information is stored.

The term "employment purposes" when used in connection with a consumer report means a report used for the purpose of evaluating a consumer for employment, promotion, reassignment or retention as an employee.

The term "medical information" –

means information or data, whether oral or recorded, in any form or medium, created by or derived from a health care provider or the consumer, that relates to –

the past, present, or future physical, mental, or behavioral health or condition of an individual;

the provision of health care to an individual; or

the payment for the provision of health care to an individual.

does not include the age or gender of a consumer, demographic information about the consumer, including a consumer's residence address or e-mail address, or any other information about a consumer that does not relate to the physical, mental, or behavioral health or condition of a consumer, including the existence or value of any insurance policy.

Definitions Relating to Child Support Obligations

The "overdue support" has the meaning given to such term in section 666(e) of title 42 [Social Security Act, 42 U.S.C. § 666(e)].

The term "State or local child support enforcement agency" means a State or local agency which administers a State or local program for establishing and enforcing child support obligations.

Adverse Action

Actions included. The term "adverse action"

has the same meaning as in section 701(d)(6) of the Equal Credit Opportunity Act; and

means a denial or cancellation of, an increase in any charge for, or a reduction or other adverse or unfavorable change in the terms of coverage or amount of, any insurance, existing or applied for, in connection with the under- writing of insurance;

a denial of employment or any other decision for employment purposes that adversely affects any current or prospective employee;

a denial or cancellation of, an increase in any charge for, or any other adverse or unfavorable change in the terms of, any license or benefit described in section 604(a)(3)(D) [§ 1681b]; and

an action taken or determination that is

made in connection with an application that was made by, or a transaction that was initiated by, any consumer, or in connection with a review of an account under section 604(a)(3)(F)(ii)[§ 1681b]; and

adverse to the interests of the consumer.

Applicable findings, decisions, commentary, and orders. For purposes of any determination of whether an action is an adverse action under paragraph (1)(A), all appropriate final findings, decisions, commentary, and orders issued under section 701(d)(6) of the Equal Credit Opportunity Act by the Bureau or any court shall apply.

The term "firm offer of credit or insurance" means any offer of credit or insurance to a consumer that will be honored if the consumer is determined, based on information in a consumer report on the consumer, to meet the specific criteria used to select the consumer for the offer, except that the offer may be further conditioned on one or more of the following:

The consumer being determined, based on information in the consumer's application for the credit or insurance, to meet specific criteria bearing on credit worthiness or insurability, as applicable, that are established

before selection of the consumer for the offer; and

for the purpose of determining whether to extend credit or insurance pursuant to the offer.

Verification

that the consumer continues to meet the specific criteria used to select the consumer for the offer, by using information in a consumer report on the consumer, information in the consumer's application for the credit or insurance, or other information bearing on the credit worthiness or insurability of the consumer; or

of the information in the consumer's application for the credit or insurance, to determine that the consumer meets the specific criteria bearing on credit worthiness or insurability.

The consumer furnishing any collateral that is a requirement for the extension of the credit or insurance that was

established before selection of the consumer for the offer of credit or insurance; and

disclosed to the consumer in the offer of credit or insurance.

The term "credit or insurance transaction that is not initiated by the consumer" does not include the use of a consumer report by a person with which the consumer has an account or insurance policy, for purposes of

reviewing the account or insurance policy; or

collecting the account.

The term "State" means any State, the Commonwealth of Puerto Rico, the District of Columbia, and any territory or possession of the United States.

Excluded communications. A communication is described in this subsection if it is a communication

that, but for subsection (d)(2)(D), would be an investigative consumer report;

that is made to a prospective employer for the purpose of

procuring an employee for the employer; or

procuring an opportunity for a natural person to work for the employer;

that is made by a person who regularly performs such procurement;

that is not used by any person for any purpose other than a purpose described in subparagraph (A) or (B) of paragraph (2); and

with respect to which

the consumer who is the subject of the communication

consents orally or in writing to the nature and scope of the communication, before the collection of any information for the purpose of making the communication;

consents orally or in writing to the making of the communication to a prospective employer, before the making of the communication; and

in the case of consent under clause (i) or (ii) given orally, is provided written confirmation of that consent by the person making the communication, not later than 3 business days after the receipt of the consent by that person;

the person who makes the communication does not, for the purpose of making the communication, make any inquiry that if made by a prospective employer of the consumer who is the subject of the communication would violate any applicable Federal or State equal employment opportunity law or regulation; and

the person who makes the communication

discloses in writing to the consumer who is the subject of the communication, not later than 5 business days after receiving any request from the consumer for such disclosure, the nature and substance of all information in the consumer's file at the time of the request, except that the sources of any information that is acquired solely for use in making the communication and is actually used for no other purpose, need not be disclosed other than under appropriate discovery procedures in any court of competent jurisdiction in which an action is brought; and

notifies the consumer who is the subject of the communication, in writing, of the consumer's right to request the information described in clause (i).

The term "consumer reporting agency that compiles and maintains files on consumers on a nationwide basis" means a consumer reporting agency that regularly engages in the practice of assembling or evaluating, and maintaining, for the purpose of furnishing consumer reports to third parties bearing on a consumer's credit worthiness, credit standing, or credit capacity, each of the following regarding consumers residing nationwide:

Public record information.

Credit account information from persons who furnish that information regularly and in the ordinary course of business.

Definitions relating to fraud alerts.

The term "active duty military consumer" means a consumer in military service who–

is on active duty (as defined in section 101(d)(1) of title 10, United States Code) or is a reservist performing duty under a call or order to active duty under a provision of law referred to in section 101(a)(13) of title 10, United States Code; and

is assigned to service away from the usual duty station of the consumer.

The terms "fraud alert" and "active duty alert" mean a statement in the file of a consumer that –

notifies all prospective users of a consumer report relating to the consumer that the consumer may be a victim of fraud, including identity theft, or is an active duty military consumer, as applicable; and

is presented in a manner that facilitates a clear and conspicuous view of the statement described in subparagraph (A) by any person requesting such consumer report.

The term "identity theft" means a fraud committed using the identifying information of another person, subject to such further definition as the
      Bureau may prescribe, by regulation.
          See also 16 CFR Part 603.2 69 Fed. Reg. 63922 (11/03/04)

The term "identity theft report" has the meaning given that term by rule of the Bureau, and means, at a minimum, a report –
          See also 16 CFR Part 603.3

that alleges an identity theft; *69 Fed. Reg. 63922 (11/03/04)*

that is a copy of an official, valid report filed by a consumer with an appropriate Federal, State, or local law enforcement agency, including the United States Postal Inspection Service, or such other government agency deemed appropriate by the Bureau; and

the filing of which subjects the person filing the report to criminal penalties relating to the filing of false information if, in fact, the information in the report is false.

The term "new credit plan" means a new account under an open end credit plan (as defined in section 103(i) of the Truth in Lending Act) or a new credit transaction not under an open end credit plan.

(q)   Credit and Debit Related Terms

The term "card issuer" means –

a credit card issuer, in the case of a credit card; and

a debit card issuer, in the case of a debit card.

The term "credit card" has the same meaning as in section 103 of the Truth in Lending Act.

The term "debit card" means any card issued by a financial institution to a consumer for use in initiating an electronic fund transferred from the account of the consumer at such financial institution, for the purpose of transferring money between accounts or obtaining money, property, labor, or services.

The terms "account" and "electronic fund transfer" have the same meanings as in section 903 of the Electronic Fund Transfer Act.

The terms "credit" and "creditor" have the same meanings as in section 702 of the Equal Credit Opportunity Act.

The term "Federal banking agency" has the same meaning as in section 3 of the Federal Deposit Insurance Act.

The term "financial institution" means a State or National bank, a State or Federal savings and loan association, a mutual savings bank, a State or Federal credit union, or any other person that, directly or indirectly, holds a transaction account (as defined in section 19(b) of the Federal Reserve Act) belonging to a consumer.

The term "reseller" means a consumer reporting agency that--

assembles and merges information contained in the database of another consumer reporting agency or multiple consumer reporting agencies concerning any consumer for purposes of furnishing such information to any third party, to the extent of such activities; and

does not maintain a database of the assembled or merged information from which new consumer reports are produced.

The term "Commission" means the Federal Trade Commission.

The term "Bureau" means the Bureau of Consumer Financial Protection.

The term "nationwide specialty consumer reporting agency" means a consumer reporting agency that compiles and maintains files on consumers on a nationwide basis relating to--

medical records or payments;

residential or tenant history;

check writing history;

employment history; or

insurance claims.

Exclusion of Certain Communications for Employee Investigations

A communication is described in this subsection if--

but for subsection (d)(2)(D), the communication would be a consumer report;

the communication is made to an employer in connection with an investigation of–

suspected misconduct relating to employment; or

compliance with Federal, State, or local laws and regulations, the rules of a self-regulatory organization, or any preexisting written policies of the employer;

the communication is not made for the purpose of investigating a consumer's credit worthiness, credit standing, or credit capacity; and

the communication is not provided to any person except--

to the employer or an agent of the employer;

to any Federal or State officer, agency, or department, or any officer, agency, or department of a unit of general local government;

to any self-regulatory organization with regulatory authority over the activities of the employer or employee;

as otherwise required by law; or

pursuant to section 608.

Subsequent disclosure. After taking any adverse action based in whole or in part on a communication described in paragraph (1), the employer shall disclose to the consumer a summary containing the nature and substance of the communication upon which the adverse action is based, except that the sources of information acquired solely for use in preparing what would be but for subsection (d)(2)(D) an investigative consumer report need not be disclosed.

For purposes of this subsection, the term "self-regulatory organization" includes any self-regulatory organization (as defined in section 3(a)(26) of the Securities Exchange Act of 1934), any entity established under title I of the Sarbanes-Oxley Act of 2002, any board of trade designated by the Commodity Futures Trading Commission, and any futures association registered with such Commission.

§ 604. Permissible purposes of consumer reports [15 U.S.C. § 1681b]

In general Subject to subsection (c), any consumer reporting agency may furnish a consumer report under the following circumstances and no other:

In response to the order of a court having jurisdiction to issue such an order, or a subpoena issued in connection with proceedings before a Federal grand jury.

In accordance with the written instructions of the consumer to whom it relates.

To a person which it has reason to believe

intends to use the information in connection with a credit transaction involving the consumer on whom the information is to be furnished and involving the extension of credit to, or review or collection of an account of, the consumer; or

intends to use the information for employment purposes; or

intends to use the information in connection with the underwriting of insurance involving the consumer; or

intends to use the information in connection with a determination of the consumer's eligibility for a license or other benefit granted by a governmental instrumentality required by law to consider an applicant's financial responsibility or status; or

intends to use the information, as a potential investor or servicer, or current insurer, in connection with a valuation of, or an assessment of the credit or prepayment risks associated with, an existing credit obligation; or

otherwise has a legitimate business need for the information

in connection with a business transaction that is initiated by the consumer; or

to review an account to determine whether the consumer continues to meet the terms of the account.[2]

executive departments and agencies in connection with the issuance of government-sponsored individually-billed travel charge cards.[1]

---

[2] As written in the poorly drafted 2007 amendment that added section 604(a)(3)(G). Subsection (F)(ii) should end with "; or" instead of a period, and the text of subsection (G) should conform to the style of the rest of section 604(a)(3). An alternative would have been to add a new section 604(a)(7) allowing a permissible purpose for a consumer report "To executive departments and agencies ..."

In response to a request by the head of a State or local child support enforcement agency (or a State or local government official authorized by the head of such an agency), if the person making the request certifies to the consumer reporting agency that

the consumer report is needed for the purpose of establishing an individual's capacity to make child support payments or determining the appropriate level of such payments;

the paternity of the consumer for the child to which the obligation relates has been established or acknowledged by the consumer in accordance with State laws under which the obligation arises (if required by those laws);

the person has provided at least 10 days' prior notice to the consumer whose report is requested, by certified or registered mail to the last known address of the consumer, that the report will be requested; and

the consumer report will be kept confidential, will be used solely for a purpose described in subparagraph (A), and will not be used in connection with any other civil, administrative, or criminal proceeding, or for any other purpose.

To an agency administering a State plan under Section 454 of the Social Security Act (42 U.S.C. § 654) for use to set an initial or modified child support award.

To the Federal Deposit Insurance Corporation or the National Credit Union Administration as part of its preparation for its appointment or as part of its exercise of powers, as conservator, receiver, or liquidating agent for an insured depository institution or insured credit union under the Federal Deposit Insurance Act or the Federal Credit Union Act, or other applicable Federal or State law, or in connection with the resolution or liquidation of a failed or failing insured depository institution or insured credit union, as applicable.

Conditions for Furnishing and Using Consumer Reports for Employment Purposes.

Certification from user. A consumer reporting agency may furnish a consumer report for employment purposes only if

the person who obtains such report from the agency certifies to the agency that

the person has complied with paragraph (2) with respect to the consumer report, and the person will comply with paragraph (3) with respect to the consumer report if paragraph (3) becomes applicable; and

information from the consumer report will not be used in violation of any applicable Federal or State equal employment opportunity law or regulation; and

the consumer reporting agency provides with the report, or has previously provided, a summary of the consumer's rights under this title, as prescribed by the Bureau under section 609(c)(3) [§ 1681g].

Disclosure to Consumer.

In general. Except as provided in subparagraph (B), a person may not procure a consumer report, or cause a consumer report to be procured, for employment purposes with respect to any consumer, unless –

a clear and conspicuous disclosure has been made in writing to the con- sumer at any time before the report is procured or caused to be procured, in a document that consists solely of the disclosure, that a consumer report may be obtained for employment purposes; and

the consumer has authorized in writing (which authorization may be made on the document referred to in clause (i)) the procurement of the report by that person.

Application by mail, telephone, computer, or other similar means. If a consumer described in subparagraph (C) applies for employment by mail, telephone, computer, or other similar means, at any time before a consumer report is procured or caused to be procured in connection with that application –

the person who procures the consumer report on the consumer for employment purposes shall provide to the consumer, by oral, written, or electronic means, notice that a consumer report may be obtained for employment purposes, and a summary of the consumer's rights under section 615(a)(3); and

the consumer shall have consented, orally, in writing, or electronically to the procurement of the report by that person.

Scope. Subparagraph (B) shall apply to a person procuring a consumer report on a consumer in connection with the consumer's application for employment only if –

the consumer is applying for a position over which the Secretary of Transportation has the power to establish qualifications and maximum hours of service pursuant to the provisions of section 31502 of title 49, or a position subject to safety regulation by a State transportation agency; and

as of the time at which the person procures the report or causes the report to be procured the only interaction between the consumer and the person in connection with that employment application has been by mail, tele- phone, computer, or other similar means.

Conditions on use for adverse actions.

In general. Except as provided in subparagraph (B), in using a consumer report for employment purposes, before taking any adverse action based in whole or in part on the report, the person intending to take such adverse action shall provide to the consumer to whom the report relates –

a copy of the report; and

a description in writing of the rights of the consumer under this title, as prescribed by the Bureau under section 609(c)(3).[3]

Application by mail, telephone, computer, or other similar means.

If a consumer described in subparagraph (C) applies for employment by mail, telephone, computer, or other similar means, and if a person who has procured a consumer report on the consumer for employment purposes takes adverse action on the employment application based in whole or in part on the report, then the person must provide to the consumer to whom the report relates, in lieu of the notices required under subparagraph (A) of this section and under section 615(a), within 3 business days of taking such action, an oral, written or electronic notification–

that adverse action has been taken based in whole or in part on a consumer report received from a consumer reporting agency;

of the name, address and telephone number of the consumer reporting agency that furnished the consumer report (including a toll-free telephone number established by the agency if the agency compiles and maintains files on consumers on a nationwide basis);

that the consumer reporting agency did not make the decision to take the adverse action and is unable to provide to the consumer the specific reasons why the adverse action was taken; and

that the consumer may, upon providing proper identification, request a free copy of a report and may dispute with the consumer reporting agency the accuracy or completeness of any information in a report.

If, under clause (B)(i)(IV), the consumer requests a copy of a consumer report from the person who procured the report, then, within 3 business days of receiving the consumer's request, together with proper identification, the person must send or provide to the consumer a copy of a report and a copy of the consumer's rights as prescribed by the Bureau under section 609(c)(3).[3]

Scope. Subparagraph (B) shall apply to a person procuring a consumer report on a consumer in connection with the consumer's application for employment only if–

the consumer is applying for a position over which the Secretary of Transportation has the power to establish qualifications and maximum hours of service pursuant to the provisions of section 31502 of title 49, or a position subject to safety regulation by a State transportation agency; and

[3] The references in Sections 604(b)(3)(A) and 604(b)(3)(B) should be to Section 609(c)**(1)**, not (c)(3) that no longer exists as the result of Congress' re-organization of Section 609(c) in 2003 (FACT Act).

as of the time at which the person procures the report or causes the report to be procured the only interaction between the consumer and the person in connection with that employment application has been by mail, telephone, computer, or other similar means.

Exception for national security investigations.

In general. In the case of an agency or department of the United States Gov- ernment which seeks to obtain and use a consumer report for employment purposes, paragraph (3) shall not apply to any adverse action by such agency or department which is based in part on such consumer report, if the head of such agency or department makes a written finding that–

the consumer report is relevant to a national security investigation of such agency or department;

the investigation is within the jurisdiction of such agency or department;

there is reason to believe that compliance with paragraph (3) will –

endanger the life or physical safety of any person;

result in flight from prosecution;

result in the destruction of, or tampering with, evidence relevant to the investigation;

result in the intimidation of a potential witness relevant to the investigation;

result in the compromise of classified information; or

otherwise seriously jeopardize or unduly delay the investigation or another official proceeding.

Notification of consumer upon conclusion of investigation. Upon the conclusion of a national security investigation described in subparagraph (A), or upon the determination that the exception under subparagraph (A) is no longer required for the reasons set forth in such subparagraph, the official exercising the authority in such subparagraph shall provide to the consumer who is the subject of the consumer report with regard to which such finding was made –

a copy of such consumer report with any classified information redacted as necessary;

notice of any adverse action which is based, in part, on the consumer report; and

the identification with reasonable specificity of the nature of the investigation for which the consumer report was sought.

Delegation by head of agency or department. For purposes of subparagraphs (A) and (B), the head of any agency or department of the United States Government may delegate his or her authorities under this paragraph to an official of such agency or department who has personnel security responsibilities and is a member of the Senior Executive Service or equivalent civilian or military rank.

Report to the Congress. Not later than January 31 of each year, the head of each agency and department of the United States Government that exercised authority under this paragraph during the preceding year shall submit a report to the Congress on the number of times the department or agency exercised such authority during the year.

Definitions. For purposes of this paragraph, the following definitions shall apply:

The term "classified information" means information that is protected from unauthorized disclosure under Executive Order No. 12958 or successor orders.

The term "national security investigation" means any official inquiry by an agency or department of the United States Government to determine the eligibility of a consumer to receive access or continued access to classified information or to determine whether classified information has been lost or compromised.

Furnishing reports in connection with credit or insurance transactions that are not initiated by the consumer.

In general. A consumer reporting agency may furnish a consumer report relating to any consumer pursuant to subparagraph (A) or (C) of subsection (a)(3) in connection with any credit or insurance transaction that is not initiated by the consumer only if

the consumer authorizes the agency to provide such report to such person; or

(i)   the transaction consists of a firm offer of credit or insurance;

the consumer reporting agency has complied with subsection (e);

there is not in effect an election by the consumer, made in accordance with subsection (e), to have the consumer's name and address excluded from lists of names provided by the agency pursuant to this paragraph; and

the consumer report does not contain a date of birth that shows that the consumer has not attained the age of 21, or, if the date of birth on the consumer report shows that the consumer has not attained the age of 21, such consumer consents to the consumer reporting agency to such furnishing.

Limits on information received under paragraph (1)(B). A person may receive pursuant to paragraph (1)(B) only the name and address of a consumer;

an identifier that is not unique to the consumer and that is used by the person solely for the purpose of verifying the identity of the consumer; and

other information pertaining to a consumer that does not identify the relation- ship or experience of the consumer with respect to a particular creditor or other entity.

Information regarding inquiries. Except as provided in section 609(a)(5) [§1681g], a consumer reporting agency shall not furnish to any person a record of inquiries in connection with a credit or insurance transaction that is not initiated by a consumer.

Reserved.

Election of consumer to be excluded from lists.

In general. A consumer may elect to have the consumer's name and address excluded from any list provided by a consumer reporting agency under subsection (c)(1)(B) in connection with a credit or insurance transaction that is not initiated by the consumer, by notifying the agency in accordance with paragraph (2) that the consumer does not consent to any use of a consumer report relating to the consumer in connection with any credit or insurance transaction that is not initiated by the consumer.

Manner of notification. A consumer shall notify a consumer reporting agency under paragraph (1)

through the notification system maintained by the agency under paragraph (5); or

by submitting to the agency a signed notice of election form issued by the agency for purposes of this subparagraph.

Response of agency after notification through system. Upon receipt of notification of the election of a consumer under paragraph (1) through the notification system maintained by the agency under paragraph (5), a consumer reporting agency shall

inform the consumer that the election is effective only for the 5-year period following the election if the consumer does not submit to the agency a signed no- tice of election form issued by the agency for purposes of paragraph (2)(B); and

provide to the consumer a notice of election form, if requested by the consumer, not later than 5 business days after receipt of the notification of the election through the system established under paragraph (5), in the case of a request made at the time the consumer provides notification through the system.

Effectiveness of election. An election of a consumer under paragraph (1)

shall be effective with respect to a consumer reporting agency beginning 5 business days after the date on which the consumer notifies the agency in accordance with paragraph (2);

shall be effective with respect to a consumer reporting agency

subject to subparagraph (C), during the 5-year period beginning 5 business days after the date on which the consumer notifies the agency of the election, in the case of an election for which a consumer notifies the agency only in accordance with paragraph (2)(A); or

until the consumer notifies the agency under subparagraph (C), in the case of an election for which a consumer notifies the agency in accordance with paragraph (2)(B);

shall not be effective after the date on which the consumer notifies the agency, through the notification system established by the agency under paragraph (5), that the election is no longer effective; and

shall be effective with respect to each affiliate of the agency.

Notification System

In general. Each consumer reporting agency that, under subsection (c)(1)(B), furnishes a consumer report in connection with a credit or insurance transaction that is not initiated by a consumer, shall

establish and maintain a notification system, including a toll-free tele- phone number, which permits any consumer whose consumer report is maintained by the agency to notify the agency, with appropriate identification, of the consumer's election to have the consumer's name and address excluded from any such list of names and addresses provided by the agency for such a transaction; and

publish by not later than 365 days after the date of enactment of the Consumer Credit Reporting Reform Act of 1996, and not less than annually thereafter, in a publication of general circulation in the area served by the agency

a notification that information in consumer files maintained by the agency may be used in connection with such transactions; and

the address and toll-free telephone number for consumers to use to notify the agency of the consumer's election under clause (I).

Establishment and maintenance as compliance. Establishment and maintenance of a notification system (including a toll-free telephone number) and publication by a consumer reporting agency on the agency's own behalf and on behalf of any of its affiliates in accordance with this paragraph is deemed to be compliance with this paragraph by each of those affiliates.

Notification system by agencies that operate nationwide. Each consumer reporting agency that compiles and maintains files on consumers on a nationwide basis shall establish and maintain a notification system for purposes of paragraph (5) jointly with other such consumer reporting agencies.

Certain use or obtaining of information prohibited. A person shall not use or obtain a consumer report for any purpose unless

the consumer report is obtained for a purpose for which the consumer report is authorized to be furnished under this section; and

the purpose is certified in accordance with section 607 [§ 1681e] by a prospective user of the report through a general or specific certification.

Protection of Medical Information

Limitation on consumer reporting agencies. A consumer reporting agency shall not furnish for employment purposes, or in connection with a credit or insurance trans- action, a consumer report that contains medical information (other than medical contact information treated in the manner required under section 605(a)(6)) about a consumer, unless –

if furnished in connection with an insurance transaction, the consumer affirmatively consents to the furnishing of the report;

if furnished for employment purposes or in connection with a credit transaction –

the information to be furnished is relevant to process or effect the employment or credit transaction; and

the consumer provides specific written consent for the furnishing of the report that describes in clear and conspicuous language the use for which the information will be furnished; or

the information to be furnished pertains solely to transactions, accounts, or balances relating to debts arising from the receipt of medical services, products, or devises, where such information, other than account status or amounts, is restricted or reported using codes that do not identify, or do not provide information sufficient to infer, the specific provider or the nature of such services, products, or devices, as provided in section 605(a)(6).

Limitation on creditors. Except as permitted pursuant to paragraph (3)(C) or regulations prescribed under paragraph (5)(A), a creditor shall not obtain or use medical information (other than medical contact information treated in the manner required under section 605(a)(6)) pertaining to a consumer in connection with any determination of the consumer's eligibility, or continued eligibility, for credit.

Actions authorized by federal law, insurance activities and regulatory determinations. Section 603(d)(3) shall not be construed so as to treat information or any communication of information as a consumer report if the information or communication is disclosed –

in connection with the business of insurance or annuities, including the activities described in section 18B of the model Privacy of Consumer Financial and Health Information Regulation issued by the National Association of Insurance Commissioners (as in effect on January 1, 2003);

for any purpose permitted without authorization under the Standards for Individually Identifiable Health Information promulgated by the Department of Health and Human Services pursuant to the Health Insurance Portability and Accountability Act of 1996, or referred to under section 1179 of such Act, or described in section 502(e) of Public Law 106-102; or

as otherwise determined to be necessary and appropriate, by regulation or order, by the Bureau or the applicable State insurance authority (with respect to any person engaged in providing insurance or annuities).

> *Limitation on disclosure of medical information.* Any person that receives medical information pursuant to paragraph (1) or (3) shall not disclose such information to any other person, except as necessary to carry out the purpose for which the information was initially disclosed, or as otherwise permitted by statute, regulation, or order.

Regulations and Effective Date for Paragraph (2)

(A)[4] *Regulations required.* The Bureau may, after notice and opportunity for comment, prescribe regulations that permit transactions under paragraph (2) that are determined to be necessary and appropriate to protect legitimate operational, transactional, risk, consumer, and other needs (and which shall include permit- ting actions necessary for administrative verification purposes), consistent with the intent of paragraph (2) to restrict the use of medical information for inappropriate purposes. ***See also 12 CFR Parts 41/222/232/334/571/717***

70 Fed. Reg. 70664 (11/22/05)

> *Coordination with other laws.* No provision of this subsection shall be construed as altering, affecting, or superseding the applicability of any other provision of Federal law relating to medical confidentiality.

§ 605. Requirements relating to information contained in consumer reports [15 U.S.C. § 1681c]

> *Information excluded from consumer reports.* Except as authorized under subsection (b) of this section, no consumer reporting agency may make any consumer report containing any of the following items of information:

Cases under title 11 [United States Code] or under the Bankruptcy Act that, from the date of entry of the order for relief or the date of adjudication, as the case may be, antedate the report by more than 10 years.

---

[4] As written in section 1088(a)(4)(B) of the CFPA in 2010. The previous version of section 604(b)(5), added in 2003 by the FACT Act, contained two subsections (A) and (B). The latter stated that the rules required to be prescribed by the Federal financial agencies (not including the Commission) be finalized by June 4, 2004.

Civil suits, civil judgments, and records of arrest that from date of entry, antedate the report by more than seven years or until the governing statute of limitations has expired, whichever is the longer period.

Paid tax liens which, from date of payment, antedate the report by more than seven years.

Accounts placed for collection or charged to profit and loss which antedate the report by more than seven years.[5]

Any other adverse item of information, other than records of convictions of crimes which antedates the report by more than seven years.[5]

The name, address, and telephone number of any medical information furnisher that has notified the agency of its status, unless--

such name, address, and telephone number are restricted or reported using codes that do not identify, or provide information sufficient to infer, the specific provider or the nature of such services, products, or devices to a person other than the consumer; or

the report is being provided to an insurance company for a purpose relating to engaging in the business of insurance other than property and casualty insurance.

Exempted cases. The provisions of paragraphs (1) through (5) of subsection (a) of this section are not applicable in the case of any consumer credit report to be used in connection with

a credit transaction involving, or which may reasonably be expected to involve, a principal amount of $150,000 or more;

the underwriting of life insurance involving, or which may reasonably be expected to involve, a face amount of $150,000 or more; or

the employment of any individual at an annual salary which equals, or which may reasonably be expected to equal $75,000, or more.

Running of Reporting Period

In general. The 7-year period referred to in paragraphs (4) and (6)[6] of subsection (a) shall begin, with respect to any delinquent account that is placed for collection (internally or by referral to a third party, whichever is earlier), charged to profit and loss, or

---

[5] The reporting periods have been lengthened for certain adverse information pertaining to U.S. Government insured or guaranteed student loans, or pertaining to national direct student loans. See sections 430A(f) and 463(c)(3) of the Higher Education Act of 1965, 20 U.S.C. 1080a(f) and 20 U.S.C. 1087cc(c)(3), respectively.

[6] This provision, added in September 1996, should read "paragraphs (4) and *(5)*...." Prior Section 605(a)(6) was amended and re-designated as Section 605(a)(5) in November 1998. The current Section 605(a)(6), added in December 2003 and now containing no reference to any 7-year period, is obviously inapplicable.

subjected to any similar action, upon the expiration of the 180-day period beginning on the date of the commencement of the delinquency which immediately preceded the collection activity, charge to profit and loss, or similar action.

Effective date. Paragraph (1) shall apply only to items of information added to the file of a consumer on or after the date that is 455 days after the date of enactment of the Consumer Credit Reporting Reform Act of 1996.

Information Required to be Disclosed

Title 11 information. Any consumer reporting agency that furnishes a consumer report that contains information regarding any case involving the consumer that arises under title 11, United States Code, shall include in the report an identification of the chapter of such title 11 under which such case arises if provided by the source of the information. If any case arising or filed under title 11, United States Code, is withdrawn by the consumer before a final judgment, the consumer reporting agency shall include in the report that such case or filing was withdrawn upon receipt of documentation certifying such withdrawal.

Key factor in credit score information. Any consumer reporting agency that furnishes a consumer report that contains any credit score or any other risk score or predictor on any consumer shall include in the report a clear and conspicuous statement that a key factor (as defined in section 609(f)(2)(B)) that adversely affected such score or predictor was the number of enquiries, if such a predictor was in fact a key factor that adversely affected such score. This paragraph shall not apply to a check services company, acting as such, which issues authorizations for the purpose of approving or processing negotiable instruments, electronic fund transfers, or similar methods of payments, but only to the extent that such company is engaged in such activities.

Indication of closure of account by consumer. If a consumer reporting agency is notified pursuant to section 623(a)(4) [§ 1681s-2] that a credit account of a consumer was voluntarily closed by the consumer, the agency shall indicate that fact in any consumer report that includes information related to the account.

Indication of dispute by consumer. If a consumer reporting agency is notified pursuant to section 623(a)(3) [§ 1681s-2] that information regarding a consumer who was furnished to the agency is disputed by the consumer, the agency shall indicate that fact in each consumer report that includes the disputed information.

Truncation of Credit Card and Debit Card Numbers

In general. Except as otherwise provided in this subsection, no person that accepts credit cards or debit cards for the transaction of business shall print more than the last 5 digits of the card number or the expiration date upon any receipt provided to the cardholder at the point of the sale or transaction.

Limitation. This subsection shall apply only to receipts that are electronically printed, and shall not apply to transactions in which the sole means of recording a credit card or debit card account number is by handwriting or by an imprint or copy of the card.

Effective date. This subsection shall become effective –

3 years after the date of enactment of this subsection, with respect to any cash register or other machine or device that electronically prints receipts for credit card or debit card transactions that is in use before January 1, 2005; and

1 year after the date of enactment of this subsection, with respect to any cash register or other machine or device that electronically prints receipts for credit card or debit card transactions that is first put into use on or after January 1, 2005.

Notice of Discrepancy in Address

In general. If a person has requested a consumer report relating to a consumer from a consumer reporting agency described in section 603(p), the request includes an address for the consumer that substantially differs from the addresses in the file of the consumer, and the agency provides a consumer report in response to the request, the consumer reporting agency shall notify the requester of the existence of the discrepancy.

(2) Regulations

See also 16 CFR Part 641
72 Fed. Reg. 63771-72 (11/09/07)
74 Fed. Reg. 22640-41 (05/14/09)

Regulations required. The Bureau shall, in consultation with the Federal banking agencies, the National Credit Union Administration, and the Federal Trade Commission, prescribe regulations providing guidance regarding reasonable policies and procedures that a user of a consumer report should employ when such user has received a notice of discrepancy under paragraph (1).

Policies and procedures to be included. The regulations prescribed under subparagraph (A) shall describe reasonable policies and procedures for use by a user of a consumer report--

to form a reasonable belief that the user knows the identity of the person to whom the consumer report pertains; and

if the user establishes a continuing relationship with the consumer, and the user regularly and in the ordinary course of business furnishes information to the consumer reporting agency from which the notice of discrepancy pertaining to the consumer was obtained, to reconcile the address of the consumer with the consumer reporting agency by furnishing such address to such consumer reporting agency as part of information regularly furnished by the user for the period in which the relationship is established.

§ 605A. Identity theft prevention; fraud alerts and active duty alerts [15 U.S.C.§1681c-1]

One-call Fraud Alerts

Initial alerts. Upon the direct request of a consumer, or an individual acting on behalf of or as a personal representative of a consumer, who asserts in good faith a suspicion that the consumer has been or is about to become a victim of fraud or related crime, including identity theft, a consumer reporting agency described in section 603(p) that maintains a file on the consumer and has received appropriate proof of the identity of the requester shall –

include a fraud alert in the file of that consumer, and also provide that alert along with any credit score generated in using that file, for a period of not less than 90 days, beginning on the date of such request, unless the consumer or such representative requests that such fraud alert be removed before the end of such period, and the agency has received appropriate proof of the identity of the requester for such purpose; and

refer the information regarding the fraud alert under this paragraph to each of the other consumer reporting agencies described in section 603(p), in accordance with procedures developed under section 621(f).

> *Access to free reports.* In any case in which a consumer reporting agency includes a fraud alert in the file of a consumer pursuant to this subsection, the consumer reporting agency shall –

disclose to the consumer that the consumer may request a free copy of the file of the consumer pursuant to section 612(d); and

provide to the consumer all disclosures required to be made under section 609, without charge to the consumer, not later than 3 business days after any request described in subparagraph (A).

Extended Alerts

> *In general.* Upon the direct request of a consumer, or an individual acting on behalf of or as a personal representative of a consumer, who submits an identity theft report to a consumer reporting agency described in section 603(p) that maintains a file on the consumer, if the agency has received appropriate proof of the identity of the requester, the agency shall –

include a fraud alert in the file of that consumer, and also provide that alert along with any credit score generated in using that file, during the 7-year period beginning on the date of such request, unless the consumer or such representative requests that such fraud alert be removed before the end of such period and the agency has received appropriate proof of the identity of the requester for such purpose;

during the 5-year period beginning on the date of such request, exclude the consumer from any list of consumers prepared by the consumer reporting agency and provided to any third party to offer credit or insurance to the consumer as part of a transaction that was not initiated by the consumer, unless the consumer or such representative requests that such exclusion be rescinded before the end of such period; and

refer the information regarding the extended fraud alert under this paragraph to each of the other consumer reporting agencies described in section 603(p), in accordance with procedures developed under section 621(f).

Access to free reports. In any case in which a consumer reporting agency includes a fraud alert in the file of a consumer pursuant to this subsection, the consumer reporting agency shall –

disclose to the consumer that the consumer may request 2 free copies of the file of the consumer pursuant to section 612(d) during the 12-month period beginning on the date on which the fraud alert was included in the file; and

provide to the consumer all disclosures required to be made under section 609, without charge to the consumer, not later than 3 business days after any request described in subparagraph (A).

Active duty alerts. Upon the direct request of an active duty military consumer, or an individual acting on behalf of or as a personal representative of an active duty military consumer, a consumer reporting agency described in section 603(p) that maintains a file on the active duty military consumer and has received appropriate proof of the identity of the requester shall –

include an active duty alert in the file of that active duty military consumer, and also provide that alert along with any credit score generated in using that file, during a period of not less than 12 months, or such longer period as the Bureau shall deter- mine, by regulation, beginning on the date of the request, unless the active duty military consumer or such representative requests that such fraud alert be removed before the end of such period, and the agency has received appropriate proof of the identity of the requester for such purpose;

during the 2-year period beginning on the date of such request, exclude the active duty military consumer from any list of consumers prepared by the consumer reporting agency and provided to any third party to offer credit or insurance to the consumer as part of a transaction that was not initiated by the consumer, unless the consumer requests that such exclusion be rescinded before the end of such period; and
refer the information regarding the active duty alert to each of the other consumer reporting agencies described in section 603(p), in accordance with procedures developed under section 621(f).
See also 16 CFR Part 613.1 69 Fed. Reg. 63922 (11/03/04)

Procedures. Each consumer reporting agency described in section 603(p) shall establish policies and procedures to comply with this section, including procedures that inform consumers of the availability of initial, extended, and active duty alerts and procedures that allow consumers and active duty military consumers to request initial, extended, or active duty alerts (as applicable) in a simple and easy manner, including by telephone.

Referrals of alerts. Each consumer reporting agency described in section 603(p) that receives a referral of a fraud alert or active duty alert from another consumer reporting agency pursuant to this section shall, as though the agency received the request from the consumer directly, follow the procedures required under –

paragraphs (1)(A) and (2) of subsection (a), in the case of a referral under subsection (a)(1)(B);

paragraphs (1)(A), (1)(B), and (2) of subsection (b), in the case of a referral under subsection (b)(1)(C); and

paragraphs (1) and (2) of subsection (c), in the case of a referral under subsection (c)(3).

Duty of reseller to reconvey alert. A reseller shall include in its report any fraud alert or active duty alert placed in the file of a consumer pursuant to this section by another consumer reporting agency.

Duty of other consumer reporting agencies to provide contact information. If a consumer contacts any consumer reporting agency that is not described in section 603(p) to communicate a suspicion that the consumer has been or is about to become a victim of fraud or related crime, including identity theft, the agency shall provide information to the consumer on how to contact the Bureau and the consumer reporting agencies described in section 603(p) to obtain more detailed information and request alerts under this section.

Limitations on Use of Information for Credit Extensions

Requirements for initial and active duty alerts

Notification. Each initial fraud alert and active duty alert under this section shall include information that notifies all prospective users of a consumer report on the consumer to which the alert relates that the consumer does not authorize the establishment of any new credit plan or extension of credit, other than under an open-end credit plan (as defined in section 103(i)), in the name of the consumer, or issuance of an additional card on an existing credit account requested by a consumer, or any increase in credit limit on an existing credit account requested by a consumer, except in accordance with subparagraph (B).
Limitation on Users
In general. No prospective user of a consumer report that includes an initial fraud alert or an active duty alert in accordance with this section may establish a new credit plan or extension of credit, other than under an open-end credit plan (as defined in section 103(i)), in the name of the consumer, or issue an additional card on an existing credit account requested by a consumer, or grant any increase in credit limit on an existing credit account requested by a consumer, unless the user utilizes reasonable policies and procedures to form a reasonable belief that the user knows the identity of the person making the request.
Verification. If a consumer requesting the alert has specified a telephone number to be used for identity verification purposes, before authorizing any new credit plan or extension described in clause (i) in the name of such consumer, a user of such consumer report shall contact the consumer using that telephone number or take reasonable steps to verify the consumer's identity and confirm that the application for a new credit plan is not the result of identity theft.

Requirements for Extended Alerts

Notification. Each extended alert under this section shall include information that provides all prospective users of a consumer report relating to a consumer with –

notification that the consumer does not authorize the establishment of any new credit plan or extension of credit described in clause (i), other than under an open-end credit plan (as defined in section 103(i)), in the name of the consumer, or issuance of an additional card on an existing credit account requested by a consumer, or any increase in credit limit on an existing credit account requested by a consumer, except in accordance with subparagraph (B); and

a telephone number or other reasonable contact method designated by the consumer.

Limitation on users. No prospective user of a consumer report or of a credit score generated using the information in the file of a consumer that includes an extended fraud alert in accordance with this section may establish a new credit plan or extension of credit, other than under an open-end credit plan (as defined in section 103(i)), in the name of the consumer, or issue an additional card on an existing credit account requested by a consumer, or any increase in credit limit on an existing credit account requested by a consumer, unless the user contacts the consumer in person or using the contact method described in subparagraph (A)(ii) to confirm that the application for a new credit plan or increase in credit limit, or request for an additional card is not the result of identity theft.

§ 605B. Block of information resulting from identity theft [15 U.S.C.§1681c-2]

Block. Except as otherwise provided in this section, a consumer reporting agency shall block the reporting of any information in the file of a consumer that the consumer identifies as information that resulted from an alleged identity theft, not later than 4 business days after the date of receipt by such agency of –

appropriate proof of the identity of the consumer;

a copy of an identity theft report;

the identification of such information by the consumer; and

a statement by the consumer that the information is not information relating to any transaction by the consumer.

Notification. A consumer reporting agency shall promptly notify the furnisher of information identified by the consumer under subsection (a)--

that the information may be a result of identity theft;

that an identity theft report has been filed;

that a block has been requested under this section; and

of the effective dates of the block.

Authority to Decline or Rescind

In general. A consumer reporting agency may decline to block, or may rescind any block, of information relating to a consumer under this section, if the consumer reporting agency reasonably determines that –

the information was blocked in error or a block was requested by the con- sumer in error;

the information was blocked, or a block was requested by the consumer, on the basis of a material misrepresentation of fact by the consumer relevant to the request to block; or

the consumer obtained possession of goods, services, or money as a result of the blocked transaction or transactions.

Notification to consumer. If a block of information is declined or rescinded under this subsection, the affected consumer shall be notified promptly, in the same manner as consumers are notified of the reinsertion of information under section 611(a)(5)(B).

Significance of block. For purposes of this subsection, if a consumer reporting agency rescinds a block, the presence of information in the file of a consumer prior to the blocking of such information is not evidence of whether the consumer knew or should have known that the consumer obtained possession of any goods, services, or money as a result of the block.

Exception for Resellers

No reseller file. This section shall not apply to a consumer reporting agency, if the consumer reporting agency –

is a reseller;

is not, at the time of the request of the consumer under subsection (a), other- wise furnishing or reselling a consumer report concerning the information identified by the consumer; and

informs the consumer, by any means, that the consumer may report the identity theft to the Bureau to obtain consumer information regarding identity theft.

Reseller with file. The sole obligation of the consumer reporting agency under this section, with regard to any request of a consumer under this section, shall be to block the consumer report maintained by the consumer reporting agency from any subsequent use, if

the consumer, in accordance with the provisions of subsection (a), identifies, to a consumer reporting agency, information in the file of the consumer that resulted from identity theft; and

the consumer reporting agency is a reseller of the identified information.

Notice. In carrying out its obligation under paragraph (2), the reseller shall promptly provide a notice to the consumer of the decision to block the file. Such notice shall contain the name, address, and telephone number of each consumer reporting agency from which the consumer information was obtained for resale.

Exception for verification companies. The provisions of this section do not apply to a check services company, acting as such, which issues authorizations for the purpose of approving or processing negotiable instruments, electronic fund transfers, or similar methods of payments, except that, beginning 4 business days after receipt of information described in paragraphs (1) through (3) of subsection (a), a check services company shall not report to a national consumer reporting agency described in section 603(p), any information identified in the subject identity theft report as resulting from identity theft.

Access to blocked information by law enforcement agencies. No provision of this section shall be construed as requiring a consumer reporting agency to prevent a Federal, State, or local law enforcement agency from accessing blocked information in a consumer file to which the agency could otherwise obtain access under this title.

§ 606. Disclosure of investigative consumer reports [15 U.S.C. § 1681d]

Disclosure of fact of preparation. A person may not procure or cause to be prepared an investigative consumer report on any consumer unless

it is clearly and accurately disclosed to the consumer that an investigative consumer report including information as to his character, general reputation, personal character- istics and mode of living, whichever are applicable, may be made, and such disclosure

is made in a writing mailed, or otherwise delivered, to the consumer, not later than three days after the date on which the report was first requested, and

includes a statement informing the consumer of his right to request the additional disclosures provided for under subsection (b) of this section and the written summary of the rights of the consumer prepared pursuant to section 609(c) [§ 1681g]; and

the person certifies or has certified to the consumer reporting agency that

the person has made the disclosures to the consumer required by paragraph (1); and
the person will comply with subsection (b).

Disclosure on request of nature and scope of investigation. Any person who procures or causes to be prepared an investigative consumer report on any consumer shall, upon written request made by the consumer within a reasonable period of time after the receipt by him of the disclosure required by subsection (a)(1) of this section, make a complete and accurate disclosure of the nature and scope of the investigation requested. This disclosure shall be made in a writing mailed, or otherwise delivered, to the consumer not later than five days after the date on which the request for such disclosure was received from the consumer or such report was first requested, whichever is the later.

Limitation on liability upon showing of reasonable procedures for compliance with provisions. No person may be held liable for any violation of subsection (a) or (b) of this section if he shows by a preponderance of the evidence that at the time of the violation he maintained reasonable procedures to assure compliance with subsection (a) or (b) of this section.

Prohibitions

Certification. A consumer reporting agency shall not prepare or furnish investigative consumer report unless the agency has received a certification under subsection (a)(2) from the person who requested the report.

Inquiries. A consumer reporting agency shall not make an inquiry for the purpose of preparing an investigative consumer report on a consumer for employment purposes if the making of the inquiry by an employer or prospective employer of the consumer would violate any applicable Federal or State equal employment opportunity law or regulation.

Certain public record information. Except as otherwise provided in section 613 [§ 1681k], a consumer reporting agency shall not furnish an investigative consumer report that includes information that is a matter of public record and that relates to an arrest, indictment, conviction, civil judicial action, tax lien, or outstanding judgment, unless the agency has verified the accuracy of the information during the 30-day period ending on the date on which the report is furnished.

Certain adverse information. A consumer reporting agency shall not prepare or furnish an investigative consumer report on a consumer that contains information that is adverse to the interest of the consumer and that is obtained through a personal interview with a neighbor, friend, or associate of the consumer or with another person with whom the consumer is acquainted or who has knowledge of such item of information, unless

the agency has followed reasonable procedures to obtain confirmation of the information, from an additional source that has independent and direct knowledge of the information; or

the person interviewed is the best possible source of the information.

§ 607. Compliance procedures [15 U.S.C. § 1681e]

Identity and purposes of credit users. Every consumer reporting agency shall maintain reasonable procedures designed to avoid violations of section 605 [§ 1681c] and to limit the furnishing of consumer reports to the purposes listed under section 604 [§ 1681b] of this title. These procedures shall require that prospective users of the information identify themselves, certify the purposes for which the information is sought, and certify that the information will be used for no other purpose. Every consumer reporting agency shall make a reasonable effort to verify the identity of a new prospective user and the uses certified by such prospective user prior to furnishing such user a consumer report. No consumer reporting agency may furnish a consumer report to any person if it has reasonable grounds for believing that the consumer report will not be used for a purpose listed in section 604 [§ 1681b] of this title.

Accuracy of report. Whenever a consumer reporting agency prepares a consumer report it shall follow reasonable procedures to assure maximum possible accuracy of the information concerning the individual about whom the report relates.

Disclosure of consumer reports by users allowed. A consumer reporting agency may not prohibit a user of a consumer report furnished by the agency on a consumer from disclosing the contents of the report to the consumer, if adverse action against the consumer has been taken by the user based in whole or in part on the report.

Notice to Users and Furnishers of Information

Notice requirement. A consumer reporting agency shall provide to any person

who regularly and in the ordinary course of business furnishes information to the agency with respect to any consumer; or

to whom a consumer report is provided by the agency;
a notice of such person's responsibilities under this title.
See also 16 CFR 698, App G-H
69 Fed. Reg. 69776 (11/30/04)

Content of notice. The Bureau shall prescribe the content of notices under paragraph (1), and a consumer reporting agency shall be in compliance with this subsection if it provides a notice under paragraph (1) that is substantially similar to the Bureau prescription under this paragraph.

Procurement of Consumer Report for Resale
Disclosure. A person may not procure a consumer report for purposes of reselling the report (or any information in the report) unless the person discloses to the consumer reporting agency that originally furnishes the report
the identity of the end-user of the report (or information); and

each permissible purpose under section 604 [§ 1681b] for which the report is furnished to the end-user of the report (or information).

Responsibilities of procurers for resale. A person who procures a consumer report for purposes of reselling the report (or any information in the report) shall

establish and comply with reasonable procedures designed to ensure that the report (or information) is resold by the person only for a purpose for which the report may be furnished under section 604 [§ 1681b], including by requiring that each person to which the report (or information) is resold and that resells or provides the report (or information) to any other person

identifies each end user of the resold report (or information);

certifies each purpose for which the report (or information) will be used; and

certifies that the report (or information) will be used for no other purpose; and

before reselling the report, make reasonable efforts to verify the identifications and certifications made under subparagraph (A).

Resale of consumer report to a federal agency or department. Notwithstanding para- graph (1) or (2), a person who procures a consumer report for purposes of reselling the report (or any information in the report) shall not disclose the identity of the end-user of the report under paragraph (1) or (2) if –

the end user is an agency or department of the United States Government which procures the report from the person for purposes of determining the eligibility of the consumer concerned to receive access or continued access to classified information (as defined in section 604(b)(4)(E)(i)); and

the agency or department certifies in writing to the person reselling the report that nondisclosure is necessary to protect classified information or the safety of persons employed by or contracting with, or undergoing investigation for work or contracting with the agency or department.

§ 608. Disclosures to governmental agencies [15 U.S.C. § 1681f]

Notwithstanding the provisions of section 604 [§ 1681b] of this title, a consumer reporting agency may furnish identifying information respecting any consumer, limited to his name, address, former addresses, places of employment, or former places of employment, to a governmental agency.

§ 609. Disclosures to consumers [15 U.S.C. § 1681g]

Information on file; sources; report recipients. Every consumer reporting agency shall, upon request, and subject to 610(a)(1) [§ 1681h], clearly and accurately disclose to the consumer:

All information in the consumer's file at the time of the request except that--

if the consumer to whom the file relates requests that the first 5 digits of the social security number (or similar identification number) of the consumer not be included in the disclosure and the consumer reporting agency has received appropriate proof of the identity of the requester, the consumer reporting agency shall so truncate such number in such disclosure; and

nothing in this paragraph shall be construed to require a consumer reporting agency to disclose to a consumer any information concerning credit scores or any other risk scores or predictors relating to the consumer.

The sources of the information; except that the sources of information acquired solely for use in preparing an investigative consumer report and actually use for no other purpose need not be disclosed: Provided, that in the event an action is brought under this title, such sources shall be available to the plaintiff under appropriate discovery procedures in the court in which the action is brought.

(A)   Identification of each person (including each end-user identified under section 607(e)(1) [§ 1681e]) that procured a consumer report

for employment purposes, during the 2-year period preceding the date on which the request is made; or

for any other purpose, during the 1-year period preceding the date on which the request is made.

An identification of a person under subparagraph (A) shall include

the name of the person or, if applicable, the trade name (written in full) under which such person conducts business; and

upon request of the consumer, the address and telephone number of the person.

Subparagraph (A) does not apply if –

the end user is an agency or department of the United States Government that procures the report from the person for purposes of determining the eligibility of the consumer to whom the report relates to receive access or continued access to classified information (as defined in section 604(b)(4)(E)(i)); and

the head of the agency or department makes a written finding as prescribed under section 604(b)(4)(A).

The dates, original payees, and amounts of any checks upon which is based any ad- verse characterization of the consumer, included in the file at the time of the disclosure.

A record of all inquiries received by the agency during the 1-year period preceding the request that identified the consumer in connection with a credit or insurance transaction that was not initiated by the consumer.

If the consumer requests the credit file and not the credit score, a statement that the consumer may request and obtain a credit score.

Exempt information. The requirements of subsection (a) of this section respecting the disclosure of sources of information and the recipients of consumer reports do not apply to information received or consumer reports furnished prior to the effective date of this title except to the extent that the matter involved is contained in the files of the consumer reporting agency on that date.

Summary of Rights to Obtain and Dispute Information in Consumer Reports and to Obtain Credit Scores

See also 16 CFR Part 698, App F

Bureau Summary of Rights Required   ***69 Fed. Reg. 69776 (11/30/04)***

In general. The Bureau shall prepare a model summary of the rights of con- sumers under this title.

Content of summary. The summary of rights prepared under subparagraph shall include a description of –

the right of a consumer to obtain a copy of a consumer report under sub- section (a) from each consumer reporting agency;

the frequency and circumstances under which a consumer is entitled to receive a consumer report without charge under section 612;

the right of a consumer to dispute information in the file of the consumer under section 611;

the right of a consumer to obtain a credit score from a consumer reporting agency, and a description of how to obtain a credit score;

the method by which a consumer can contact, and obtain a consumer report from, a consumer reporting agency without charge, as provided in the regulations of the Bureau prescribed under section 211(c) of the Fair and Accurate Credit Transactions Act of 2003; and

the method by which a consumer can contact, and obtain a consumer report from, a consumer reporting agency described in section 603(w), as provided in the regulations of the Bureau prescribed under section 612(a)(1)(C).

Availability of summary of rights. The Bureau shall –

actively publicize the availability of the summary of rights prepared under this paragraph;

conspicuously post on its Internet website the availability of such summary of rights; and promptly make such summary of rights available to consumers, on request.

Summary of rights required to be included with agency disclosures. A consumer reporting agency shall provide to a consumer, with each written disclosure by the agency to the consumer under this section –

the summary of rights prepared by the Bureau under paragraph (1);

in the case of a consumer reporting agency described in section 603(p), a toll-free telephone number established by the agency, at which personnel are accessible to consumers during normal business hours;

a list of all Federal agencies responsible for enforcing any provision of this title, and the address and any appropriate phone number of each such agency, in a form that will assist the consumer in selecting the appropriate agency;

a statement that the consumer may have additional rights under State law, and that the consumer may wish to contact a State or local consumer protection agency or a State attorney general (or the equivalent thereof) to learn of those rights; and

a statement that a consumer reporting agency is not required to remove accurate derogatory information from the file of a consumer, unless the information is outdated under section 605 or cannot be verified.

Summary of Rights of Identity Theft Victims
See also 16 CFR Part 698, App E
69 Fed. Reg. 69776 (11/30/04)
In general. The Bureau, in consultation with the Federal banking agencies and the National Credit Union Administration, shall prepare a model summary of the rights of consumers under this title with respect to the procedures for remedying the effects of fraud or identity theft involving credit, an electronic fund transfer, or an account or transaction at or with a financial institution or other creditor.

Summary of rights and contact information. Beginning 60 days after the date on which the model summary of rights is prescribed in final form by the Bureau pursuant to paragraph (1), if any consumer contacts a consumer reporting agency and expresses a belief that the consumer is a victim of fraud or identity theft involving credit, an electronic fund transfer, or an account or transaction at or with a financial institution or other creditor, the consumer reporting agency shall, in addition to any other action that the agency may take, provide the consumer with a summary of rights that contains all of the information required by the Bureau under paragraph (1), and information on how to contact the Bureau to obtain more detailed information.

Information Available to Victims
In general. For the purpose of documenting fraudulent transactions resulting from identity theft, not later than 30 days after the date of receipt of a request from a victim in accordance with paragraph (3), and subject to verification of the identity of the victim and the claim of identity theft in accordance with paragraph (2), a business entity that has provided credit to, provided for consideration products, goods, or services to,

accepted payment from, or otherwise entered into a commercial transaction for consideration with, a person who has allegedly made unauthorized use of the means of identification of the victim, shall provide a copy of application and business transaction records in the control of the business entity, whether maintained by the business entity or by another person on behalf of the business entity, evidencing any transaction alleged to be a result of identity theft to –

the victim;

any Federal, State, or local government law enforcement agency or officer specified by the victim in such a request; or

any law enforcement agency investigating the identity theft and authorized by the victim to take receipt of records provided under this subsection.

Verification of identity and claim. Before a business entity provides any information under paragraph (1), unless the business entity, at its discretion, otherwise has a high degree of confidence that it knows the identity of the victim making a request under paragraph (1), the victim shall provide to the business entity –

as proof of positive identification of the victim, at the election of the business entity –

the presentation of a government-issued identification card;

personally identifying information of the same type as was provided to the business entity by the unauthorized person; or

personally identifying information that the business entity typically re- quests from new applicants or for new transactions, at the time of the victim's request for information, including any documentation described in clauses (i) and (ii); and

as proof of a claim of identity theft, at the election of the business entity –

a copy of a police report evidencing the claim of the victim of identity theft; and

a properly completed –

copy of a standardized affidavit of identity theft developed and made available by the Bureau; or

an affidavit of fact that is acceptable to the business entity for that purpose.

Procedures. The request of a victim under paragraph (1) shall –
be in writing;

be mailed to an address specified by the business entity, if any; and if asked by the business entity, include relevant information about any transaction alleged to be a result of identity theft to facilitate compliance with this section including –

if known by the victim (or if readily obtainable by the victim), the date of the application or transaction; and

if known by the victim (or if readily obtainable by the victim), any other identifying information such as an account or transaction number.

No charge to victim. Information required to be provided under paragraph (1) shall be so provided without charge.

Authority to decline to provide information. A business entity may decline to provide information under paragraph (1) if, in the exercise of good faith, the business entity determines that –

this subsection does not require disclosure of the information;

after reviewing the information provided pursuant to paragraph (2), the business entity does not have a high degree of confidence in knowing the true identity of the individual requesting the information;

the request for the information is based on a misrepresentation of fact by the individual requesting the information relevant to the request for information; or

the information requested is Internet navigational data or similar information about a person's visit to a website or online service.

Limitation on liability. Except as provided in section 621, sections 616 and 617 do not apply to any violation of this subsection.

Limitation on civil liability. No business entity may be held civilly liable under any provision of Federal, State, or other law for disclosure, made in good faith pursuant to this subsection.

No new recordkeeping obligation. Nothing in this subsection creates an obligation on the part of a business entity to obtain, retain, or maintain information or records that are not otherwise required to be obtained, retained, or maintained in the ordinary course of its business or under other applicable law.

Rule of Construction
In general. No provision of subtitle A of title V of Public Law 106-102, prohibiting the disclosure of financial information by a business entity to third parties shall be used to deny disclosure of information to the victim under this subsection.

Limitation. Except as provided in subparagraph (A), nothing in this subsec- tion permits a business entity to disclose information, including information to law enforcement under subparagraphs (B) and (C) of paragraph (1), that the business entity is otherwise prohibited from disclosing under any other applicable provision of Federal or State law.

Affirmative defense. In any civil action brought to enforce this subsection, it is an affirmative defense (which the defendant must establish by a preponderance of the evidence) for a business entity to file an affidavit or answer stating that–

the business entity has made a reasonably diligent search of its available business records; and

the records requested under this subsection do not exist or are not reasonably available.

Definition of victim. For purposes of this subsection, the term "victim" means a consumer whose means of identification or financial information has been used or transferred (or has been alleged to have been used or transferred) without the authority of that consumer, with the intent to commit, or to aid or abet, an identity theft or a similar crime.

Effective date. This subsection shall become effective 180 days after the date of enactment of this subsection.

Effectiveness study. Not later than 18 months after the date of enactment of this subsection, the Comptroller General of the United States shall submit a report to Congress assessing the effectiveness of this provision.

Disclosure of Credit Scores

In general. Upon the request of a consumer for a credit score, a consumer reporting agency shall supply to the consumer a statement indicating that the information and credit scoring model may be different than the credit score that may be used by the lender, and a notice which shall include –

the current credit score of the consumer or the most recent credit score of the consumer that was previously calculated by the credit reporting agency for a purpose related to the extension of credit;

the range of possible credit scores under the model used;

all of the key factors that adversely affected the credit score of the consumer in the model used, the total number of which shall not exceed 4, subject to paragraph (9);

the date on which the credit score was created; and

the name of the person or entity that provided the credit score or credit file upon which the credit score was created.

Definitions. For purposes of this subsection, the following definitions shall apply:

The term "credit score" –

means a numerical value or a categorization derived from a statistical tool or modeling system used by a person who makes or arranges a loan to predict the likelihood of certain credit behaviors, including default (and the numerical value or the categorization derived from such analysis may also be referred to as a "risk predictor" or "risk score"); and

does not include –

any mortgage score or rating of an automated underwriting system that considers one or more factors in addition to credit information, including the loan to value ratio, the amount of down payment, or the financial assets of a consumer; or

any other elements of the underwriting process or underwriting decision.

The term "key factors" means all relevant elements or reasons adversely affecting the credit score for the particular individual, listed in the order of their importance based on their effect on the credit score.

Timeframe and manner of disclosure. The information required by this subsection shall be provided in the same timeframe and manner as the information described in subsection (a).

Applicability to certain uses. This subsection shall not be construed so as to compel a consumer reporting agency to develop or disclose a score if the agency does not –

distribute scores that are used in connection with residential real property loans; or

develop scores that assist credit providers in understanding the general credit behavior of a consumer and predicting the future credit behavior of the consumer.

Applicability to credit scores developed by another person.

In general. This subsection shall not be construed to require a consumer re- porting agency that distributes credit scores developed by another person or entity to provide a further explanation of them, or to process a dispute arising pursuant to section 611, except that the consumer reporting agency shall pro- vide the consumer with the name and address and website for contacting the person or entity who developed the score or developed the methodology of the score.

Exception. This paragraph shall not apply to a consumer reporting agency that develops or modifies scores that are developed by another person or entity.

Maintenance of credit scores not required. This subsection shall not be construed to require a consumer reporting agency to maintain credit scores in its files.

Compliance in certain cases. In complying with this subsection, a consumer reporting agency shall –

supply the consumer with a credit score that is derived from a credit scoring model that is widely distributed to users by that consumer reporting agency in connection with residential real property loans or with a credit score that assists the consumer in understanding the credit scoring assessment of the credit behavior of the consumer and predictions about the future credit behavior of the consumer; and

a statement indicating that the information and credit scoring model may be different than that used by the lender.

Fair and reasonable fee. A consumer reporting agency may charge a fair and reasonable fee, as determined by the Bureau, for providing the information required under this subsection. ***See also 69 Fed. Reg. 64698 (11/08/04)***

Use of enquiries as a key factor. If a key factor that adversely affects the credit score of a consumer consists of the number of enquiries made with respect to a consumer report, that factor shall be included in the disclosure pursuant to paragraph (1)(C) without regard to the numerical limitation in such paragraph.

Disclosure of Credit Scores by Certain Mortgage Lenders

In general. Any person who makes or arranges loans and who uses a consumer credit score, as defined in subsection (f), in connection with an application initiated or sought by a consumer for a closed end loan or the establishment of an open end loan for a consumer purpose that is secured by 1 to 4 units of residential real property (hereafter in this subsection referred to as the "lender") shall provide the following to the consumer as soon as reasonably practicable:

Information Required under Subsection (f)

In general. A copy of the information identified in subsection (f) that was obtained from a consumer reporting agency or was developed and used by the user of the information.

Notice under subparagraph (D). In addition to the information provided to it by a third party that provided the credit score or scores, a lender is only required to provide the notice contained in subparagraph (D).

Disclosures in Case of Automated Underwriting System

In general. If a person that is subject to this subsection uses an automated underwriting system to underwrite a loan, that person may satisfy the obligation to provide a credit score by disclosing a credit score and associated key factors supplied by a consumer reporting agency.

Numerical credit score. However, if a numerical credit score is generated by an automated underwriting system used by an enterprise, and that score is disclosed to the person, the score shall be disclosed to the consumer consistent with subparagraph (c).

Enterprise defined. For purposes of this subparagraph, the term "enterprise" has the same meaning as in paragraph (6) of section 1303 of the Federal Housing Enterprises Financial Safety and Soundness Act of 1992.

Disclosures of credit scores not obtained from a consumer reporting agency. A person that is subject to the provisions of this subsection and that uses a credit score, other than a credit score provided by a consumer reporting agency, may satisfy the obligation to provide a credit score by disclosing a credit score and associated key factors supplied by a consumer reporting agency.

Notice to home loan applicants. A copy of the following notice, which shall include the name, address, and telephone number of each consumer reporting agency providing a credit score that was used:

"Notice To The Home Loan Applicant

"In connection with your application for a home loan, the lender must disclose to you the score that a consumer reporting agency distributed to users and the lender used in connection with your home loan, and the key factors affecting your credit scores.

"The credit score is a computer generated summary calculated at the time of the request and based on information that a consumer reporting agency or lender has on file. The scores are based on data about your credit history and payment patterns. Credit scores are important because they are used to assist the lender in determining whether you will obtain a loan. They may also be used to determine what interest rate you may be offered on the mortgage. Credit scores can change over time, depending on your conduct, how your credit history and payment patterns change, and how credit scoring technologies change.

"Because the score is based on information in your credit history, it is very important that you review the credit-related information that is being furnished to make sure it is accurate. Credit records may vary from one company to another.

"If you have questions about your credit score or the credit information that is furnished to you, contact the consumer reporting agency at the address and telephone number provided with this notice, or contact the lender, if the lender developed or generated the credit score. The consumer reporting agency plays no part in the decision to take any action on the loan application and is unable to provide you with specific reasons for the decision on a loan application.

"If you have questions concerning the terms of the loan, contact the lender."

Actions not required under this subsection. This subsection shall not require any person to –

explain the information provided pursuant to subsection (f);

disclose any information other than a credit score or key factors, as de- fined in subsection (f);

disclose any credit score or related information obtained by the user after a loan has closed;

provide more than 1 disclosure per loan transaction; or

provide the disclosure required by this subsection when another person has made the disclosure to the consumer for that loan transaction.

No Obligation for Content

In general. The obligation of any person pursuant to this subsection shall be limited solely to providing a copy of the information that was received from the consumer reporting agency.

Limit on liability. No person has liability under this subsection for the content of that information or for the omission of any information within the report provided by the consumer reporting agency.

Person defined as excluding enterprise. As used in this subsection, the term "person" does not include an enterprise (as defined in paragraph (6) of section 1303 of the Federal Housing Enterprises Financial Safety and Soundness Act of 1992).

Prohibition on Disclosure Clauses Null and Void

In general. Any provision in a contract that prohibits the disclosure of a credit score by a person who makes or arranges loans or a consumer reporting agency is void.

No liability for disclosure under this subsection. A lender shall not have liability under any contractual provision for disclosure of a credit score pursuant to this subsection.

§ 610. Conditions and form of disclosure to consumers [15 U.S.C. § 1681h]

In General

Proper identification. A consumer reporting agency shall require, as a condition of making the disclosures required under section 609 [§ 1681g], that the consumer furnish proper identification.

Disclosure in writing. Except as provided in subsection (b), the disclosures required to be made under section 609 [§ 1681g] shall be provided under that section in writing.

Other Forms of Disclosure

In general. If authorized by a consumer, a consumer reporting agency may make the disclosures required under 609 [§ 1681g]

other than in writing; and

in such form as may be

specified by the consumer in accordance with paragraph (2); and

available from the agency.

Form. A consumer may specify pursuant to paragraph (1) that disclosures under section 609 [§ 1681g] shall be made

in person, upon the appearance of the consumer at the place of business of the consumer reporting agency where disclosures are regularly provided, during normal business hours, and on reasonable notice;

by telephone, if the consumer has made a written request for disclosure by telephone;

by electronic means, if available from the agency; or

by any other reasonable means that is available from the agency.

Trained personnel. Any consumer reporting agency shall provide trained personnel to explain to the consumer any information furnished to him pursuant to section 609 [§ 1681g] of this title.

Persons accompanying consumer. The consumer shall be permitted to be accompanied by one other person of his choosing, who shall furnish reasonable identification. A consumer reporting agency may require the consumer to furnish a written statement granting permission to the consumer reporting agency to discuss the consumer's file in such person's presence.

Limitation of liability. Except as provided in sections 616 and 617 [§§1681n and 1681o] of this title, no consumer may bring any action or proceeding in the nature of defamation, invasion of privacy, or negligence with respect to the reporting of information against any consumer reporting agency, any user of information, or any person who furnishes information to a consumer reporting agency, based on information disclosed pursuant to section 609, 610, or 615 [§§ 1681g, 1681h, or 1681m] of this title or based on information disclosed by a user of a consumer report to or for a consumer against whom the user has taken adverse action, based in whole or in part on the report, except as to false information furnished with malice or willful intent to injure such consumer.

§ 611. Procedure in case of disputed accuracy [15 U.S.C. § 1681i]

Reinvestigations of Disputed Information

Reinvestigation Required

In general. Subject to subsection (f), if the completeness or accuracy of any item of information contained in a consumer's file at a consumer reporting agency is disputed by the consumer and the consumer notifies the agency directly, or indirectly through a reseller, of such dispute, the agency shall, free of charge, conduct a reasonable reinvestigation to determine whether the disputed information is inaccurate and record the current status of the disputed information, or delete the item from the file in accordance with paragraph (5), before the end of the 30-day period beginning on the date on which the agency receives the notice of the dispute from the consumer or reseller.

Extension of period to reinvestigate. Except as provided in subparagraph (c), the 30-day period described in subparagraph (A) may be extended for not more than 15 additional days if the consumer reporting agency receives information from the consumer during that 30-day period that is relevant to the reinvestigation.

Limitations on extension of period to reinvestigate. Subparagraph (B) shall not apply to any reinvestigation in which, during the 30-day period described in subparagraph (A), the information that is the subject of the reinvestigation is found to be inaccurate or incomplete or the consumer reporting agency determines that the information cannot be verified.

Prompt Notice of Dispute to Furnisher of Information

In general. Before the expiration of the 5-business-day period beginning on the date on which a consumer reporting agency receives notice of a dispute from any consumer or a reseller in accordance with paragraph (1), the agency shall provide notification of the dispute to any person who provided any item of information in dispute, at the address and in the manner established with the person. The notice shall include all relevant information regarding the dispute that the agency has received from the consumer or reseller.

Provision of other information. The consumer reporting agency shall prompt- ly provide to the person who provided the information in dispute all relevant information regarding the dispute that is received by the agency from the consumer or the reseller after the period referred to in subparagraph (A) and before the end of the period referred to in paragraph (1)(A).

Determination That Dispute Is Frivolous or Irrelevant

In general. Notwithstanding paragraph (1), a consumer reporting agency may terminate a reinvestigation of information disputed by a consumer under that paragraph if the agency reasonably determines that the dispute by the consumer is frivolous or irrelevant, including by reason of a failure by a consumer to provide sufficient information to investigate the disputed information.

Notice of determination. Upon making any determination in accordance with subparagraph (A)) that a dispute is frivolous or irrelevant, a consumer reporting agency shall notify the consumer of such determination not later than 5 business days after making such determination, by mail or, if authorized by the consumer for that purpose, by any other means available to the agency.

Contents of notice. A notice under subparagraph (B) shall include

the reasons for the determination under subparagraph (A); and

identification of any information required to investigate the disputed information, which may consist of a standardized form describing the general nature of such information.

> *Consideration of consumer information.* In conducting any reinvestigation under paragraph (1) with respect to disputed information in the file of any consumer, the consumer reporting agency shall review and consider all relevant information submitted by the consumer in the period described in paragraph (1)(A) with respect to such disputed information.

Treatment of Inaccurate or Unverifiable Information

In general. If, after any reinvestigation under paragraph (1) of any information disputed by a consumer, an item of the information is found to be inaccurate or incomplete or cannot be verified, the consumer reporting agency shall–

promptly delete that item of information from the file of the consumer, or modify that item of information, as appropriate, based on the results of the reinvestigation; and

promptly notify the furnisher of that information that the information has been modified or deleted from the file of the consumer.

Requirements Relating to Reinsertion of Previously Deleted Material

Certification of accuracy of information. If any information is deleted from a consumer's file pursuant to subparagraph (A), the information may not be reinserted in the file by the consumer reporting agency unless the person who furnishes the information certifies that the information is complete and accurate.

Notice to consumer. If any information that has been deleted from a consumer's file pursuant to subparagraph (A) is reinserted in the file, the consumer reporting agency shall notify the consumer of the reinsertion in writing not later than 5 business days after the reinsertion or, if authorized by the consumer for that purpose, by any other means available to the agency.

Additional information. As part of, or in addition to, the notice under clause (ii), a consumer reporting agency shall provide to a consumer in writing not later than 5 business days after the date of the reinsertion

a statement that the disputed information has been reinserted;

the business name and address of any furnisher of information contact- ed and the telephone number of such furnisher, if reasonably available, or of any furnisher of information that contacted the consumer reporting agency, in connection with the reinsertion of such information; and

a notice that the consumer has the right to add a statement to the consumer's file disputing the accuracy or completeness of the disputed information.

Procedures to prevent reappearance. A consumer reporting agency shall maintain reasonable procedures designed to prevent the reappearance in a consumer's file, and in consumer reports on the consumer, of information that is deleted pursuant to this paragraph (other than information that is reinserted in accordance with subparagraph (B)(i)).

Automated reinvestigation system. Any consumer reporting agency that com- piles and maintains files on consumers on a nationwide basis shall implement an automated system through which furnishers of information to that consumer reporting agency may report the results of a reinvestigation that finds incomplete or inaccurate information in a consumer's file to other such consumer reporting agencies.

Notice of Results of Reinvestigation

In general. A consumer reporting agency shall provide written notice to a consumer of the results of a reinvestigation under this subsection not later than 5 business days after the completion of the reinvestigation, by mail or, if authorized by the consumer for that purpose, by other means available to the agency.

Contents. As part of, or in addition to, the notice under subparagraph (A), a consumer reporting agency shall provide to a consumer in writing before the expiration of the 5-day period referred to in subparagraph (A)

a statement that the reinvestigation is completed;

a consumer report that is based upon the consumer's file as that file is revised as a result of the reinvestigation;

a notice that, if requested by the consumer, a description of the procedure used to determine the accuracy and completeness of the information shall be provided to the consumer by the agency, including the business name and address of any furnisher of information contacted in connection with such information and the telephone number of such furnisher, if reasonably available;

a notice that the consumer has the right to add a statement to the consumer's file disputing the accuracy or completeness of the information; and

a notice that the consumer has the right to request under subsection (d) that the consumer reporting agency furnish notifications under that subsection.

Description of reinvestigation procedure. A consumer reporting agency shall provide to a consumer a description referred to in paragraph (6)(B)(iii) by not later than 15 days after receiving a request from the consumer for that description.

Expedited dispute resolution. If a dispute regarding an item of information in a consumer's file at a consumer reporting agency is resolved in accordance with paragraph (5)(A) by the deletion of the disputed information by not later than 3 business days after the date on which the agency receives notice of the dispute from the consumer in accordance with paragraph (1)(A), then the agency shall not be required to comply with paragraphs (2), (6), and (7) with respect to that dispute if the agency

provides prompt notice of the deletion to the consumer by telephone;

includes in that notice, or in a written notice that accompanies a confirmation and consumer report provided in accordance with subparagraph (C), a statement of the consumer's right to request under subsection (d) that the agency furnish notifications under that subsection; and

provides written confirmation of the deletion and a copy of a consumer report on the consumer that is based on the consumer's file after the deletion, not later than 5 business days after making the deletion.

Statement of dispute. If the reinvestigation does not resolve the dispute, the consumer may file a brief statement setting forth the nature of the dispute. The consumer reporting agency may limit such statements to not more than one hundred words if it provides the consumer with assistance in writing a clear summary of the dispute.

Notification of consumer dispute in subsequent consumer reports. Whenever a statement of a dispute is filed, unless there are reasonable grounds to believe that it is frivolous or irrelevant, the consumer reporting agency shall, in any subsequent report containing the information in question, clearly note that it is disputed by the consumer and provide either the consumer's statement or a clear and accurate codification or summary thereof.

Notification of deletion of disputed information. Following any deletion of information which is found to be inaccurate or whose accuracy can no longer be verified or any notation as to disputed information, the consumer reporting agency shall, at the request of the consumer, furnish notification that the item has been deleted or the statement, codification or summary pursuant to subsection (b) or (c) of this section to any person specifically designated by the consumer who has within two years prior thereto received a consumer report for employment purposes, or within six months prior thereto received a consumer report for any other purpose, which contained the deleted or disputed information.

Treatment of Complaints and Report to Congress

In general. The Bureau shall –

compile all complaints that it receives that a file of a consumer that is maintained by a consumer reporting agency described in section 603(p) contains incomplete or inaccurate information, with respect to which, the consumer appears to have disputed the completeness or accuracy with the consumer reporting agency or otherwise utilized the procedures provided by subsection (a); and

transmit each such complaint to each consumer reporting agency involved.

> *Exclusion.* Complaints received or obtained by the Bureau pursuant to its investigative authority under the Consumer Financial Protection Act of 2010 shall not be subject to paragraph (1).

> *Agency responsibilities.* Each consumer reporting agency described in section 603(p) that receives a complaint transmitted by the Bureau pursuant to paragraph (1) shall –

review each such complaint to determine whether all legal obligations imposed on the consumer reporting agency under this title (including any obligation imposed by an applicable court or administrative order) have been met with respect to the subject matter of the complaint;

provide reports on a regular basis to the Bureau regarding the determinations of and actions taken by the consumer reporting agency, if any, in connection with its review of such complaints; and

maintain, for a reasonable time period, records regarding the disposition of each such complaint that is sufficient to demonstrate compliance with this subsection.

> *Rulemaking authority.* The Bureau may prescribe regulations, as appropriate to implement this subsection.

> *Annual report.* The Bureau shall submit to the Committee on Banking, Housing, and Urban Affairs of the Senate and the Committee on Financial Services of the House of Representatives an annual report regarding information gathered by the Bureau under this subsection.

Reinvestigation Requirement Applicable to Resellers

> *Exemption from general reinvestigation requirement.* Except as provided in para- graph (2), a reseller shall be exempt from the requirements of this section.

> *Action required upon receiving notice of a dispute.* If a reseller receives a notice from a consumer of a dispute concerning the completeness or accuracy of any item of information contained in a consumer report on such consumer produced by the

reseller, the reseller shall, within 5 business days of receiving the notice, and free of charge –

determine whether the item of information is incomplete or inaccurate as a result of an act or omission of the reseller; and

(i)   if the reseller determines that the item of information is incomplete or inaccurate as a result of an act or omission of the reseller, not later than 20 days after receiving the notice, correct the information in the consumer report or delete it; or

(ii)   if the reseller determines that the item of information is not incomplete or inaccurate as a result of an act or omission of the reseller, convey the notice of the dispute, together with all relevant information provided by the consumer, to each consumer reporting agency that provided the reseller with the information that is the subject of the dispute, using an address or a notification mechanism specified by the consumer reporting agency for such notices.

Responsibility of consumer reporting agency to notify consumer through reseller. Upon the completion of a reinvestigation under this section of a dispute concerning the completeness or accuracy of any information in the file of a consumer by a consumer reporting agency that received notice of the dispute from a reseller under paragraph (2) –

the notice by the consumer reporting agency under paragraph (6), (7), or (8) of subsection (a) shall be provided to the reseller in lieu of the consumer; and

the reseller shall immediately reconvey such notice to the consumer, including any notice of a deletion by telephone in the manner required under paragraph (8)(A).

Reseller reinvestigations. No provision of this subsection shall be construed as prohibiting a reseller from conducting a reinvestigation of a consumer dispute directly.

§ 612. Charges for certain disclosures [15 U.S.C. § 1681j]
See also 16 CFR Part 610
69 Fed. Reg. 35467 (06/24/04)
Free Annual Disclosure   *75 Fed. Reg. 9726 (03/03/10)*

Nationwide Consumer Reporting Agencies

In general. All consumer reporting agencies described in subsections (p) and
(w)) of section 603 shall make all disclosures pursuant to section 609 once during any 12-month period upon request of the consumer and without charge to the consumer.

Centralized source. Subparagraph (A) shall apply with respect to a consumer reporting agency described in section 603(p) only if the request from the consumer is made using the centralized source established for such purpose in accordance with section 211(c) of the Fair and Accurate Credit Transactions Act of 2003.

Nationwide Specialty Consumer Reporting Agency

In general. The Bureau shall prescribe regulations applicable to each consumer reporting agency described in section 603(w) to require the establishment of a streamlined process for consumers to request consumer reports under subparagraph (A), which shall include, at a minimum, the establishment by each such agency of a toll-free telephone number for such requests.

Considerations. In prescribing regulations under clause (i), the Bureau shall consider–

the significant demands that may be placed on consumer reporting agencies in providing such consumer reports;

appropriate means to ensure that consumer reporting agencies can satisfactorily meet those demands, including the efficacy of a system of staggering the availability to consumers of such consumer reports; and

the ease by which consumers should be able to contact consumer reporting agencies with respect to access to such consumer reports.

(iii)[7]   *Date of issuance.* The Bureau shall issue the regulations required by this subparagraph in final form not later than 6 months after the date of enactment of the Fair and Accurate Credit Transactions Act of 2003.

(iv)[7] *Consideration of ability to comply.* The regulations of the Bureau under this subparagraph shall establish an effective date by which each nation- wide specialty consumer reporting agency (as defined in section 603(w)) shall be required to comply with subsection (a), which effective date –

shall be established after consideration of the ability of each nationwide specialty consumer reporting agency to comply with subsection (a); and

shall be not later than 6 months after the date on which such regulations are issued in final form (or such additional period not to exceed 3 months, as the Bureau determines appropriate).

Timing. A consumer reporting agency shall provide a consumer report under para- graph (1) not later than 15 days after the date on which the request is received under paragraph (1).

---

[7] Subsections 612(a)(1)(C)(iii) and (iv) are obsolete. They relate to the to the issuance and effective dates of the "free report" rules that the 2003 FACT Act required the Commission to publish. The rules were published on time in June 2004 and updated in March 2010. The subsections appear as written, including 2010 amendments to the FCRA that changed "Commission" to "Bureau" (effective July 21, 2011) in several places in the FCRA.

Reinvestigations. Notwithstanding the time periods specified in section 611(a)(1), a reinvestigation under that section by a consumer reporting agency upon a request of a consumer that is made after receiving a consumer report under this subsection shall be completed not later than 45 days after the date on which the request is received.

Exception for first 12 months of operation. This subsection shall not apply to a consumer reporting agency that has not been furnishing consumer reports to third parties on a continuing basis during the 12-month period preceding a request under paragraph (1), with respect to consumers residing nationwide.

Free disclosure after adverse notice to consumer. Each consumer reporting agency that maintains a file on a consumer shall make all disclosures pursuant to section 609 [§ 1681g] without charge to the consumer if, not later than 60 days after receipt by such consumer of a notification pursuant to section 615 [§ 1681m], or of a notification from a debt collection agency affiliated with that consumer reporting agency stating that the consumer's credit rating may be or has been adversely affected, the consumer makes a request under section 609 [§ 1681g].

Free disclosure under certain other circumstances. Upon the request of the consumer, a consumer reporting agency shall make all disclosures pursuant to section 609 [§ 1681g] once during any 12-month period without charge to that consumer if the consumer certifies in writing that the consumer

is unemployed and intends to apply for employment in the 60-day period beginning on the date on which the certification is made;

is a recipient of public welfare assistance; or

has reason to believe that the file on the consumer at the agency contains inaccurate information due to fraud.

Free disclosures in connection with fraud alerts. Upon the request of a consumer, a consumer reporting agency described in section 603(p) shall make all disclosures pursuant to section 609 without charge to the consumer, as provided in subsections (a)(2) and (b)(2) of section 605A, as applicable.

Other charges prohibited. A consumer reporting agency shall not impose any charge on a consumer for providing any notification required by this title or making any disclosure required by this title, except as authorized by subsection (f).

Reasonable Charges Allowed for Certain Disclosures

In general. In the case of a request from a consumer other than a request that is covered by any of subsections (a) through (d), a consumer reporting agency may impose a reasonable charge on a consumer

for making a disclosure to the consumer pursuant to section 609 [§ 1681g], which charge shall not exceed $8;[8] and

shall be indicated to the consumer before making the disclosure; and

for furnishing, pursuant to 611(d) [§ 1681i], following a reinvestigation under section 611(a) [§ 1681i], a statement, codification, or summary to a person designated by the consumer under that section after the 30-day period beginning on the date of notification of the consumer under paragraph (6) or (8) of section 611(a) [§ 1681i] with respect to the reinvestigation, which charge

shall not exceed the charge that the agency would impose on each designated recipient for a consumer report; and

shall be indicated to the consumer before furnishing such information.

Modification of amount. The Bureau shall increase the amount referred to in para- graph (1)(A)(i) on January 1 of each year, based proportionally on changes in the Consumer Price Index, with fractional changes rounded to the nearest fifty cents.[8]

Prevention of Deceptive Marketing of Credit Reports

In general. Subject to rulemaking pursuant to section 205(b) of the Credit CARD Act of 2009, any advertisement for a free credit report in any medium shall prominently disclose in such advertisement that free credit reports are available under Federal law at AnnualCreditReport.com (or such other source as may be authorized under Federal law).

Television and radio advertisement. In the case of an advertisement broadcast by television, the disclosures required under paragraph (1) shall be included in the audio and visual part of such advertisement. In the case of an advertisement broadcast by television or radio, the disclosure required under paragraph (1) shall consist only of the following: "This is not the free credit report provided for by Federal law."

§ 613. Public record information for employment purposes [15 U.S.C. § 1681k]

In general. A consumer reporting agency which furnishes a consumer report for employment purposes and which for that purpose compiles and reports items of information on consumers which are matters of public record and are likely to have an adverse effect upon a consumer's ability to obtain employment shall

at the time such public record information is reported to the user of such consumer re- port, notify the consumer of the fact that public record information is being reported by the consumer reporting agency, together with the name and address of the person to whom such information is being reported; or

maintain strict procedures designed to insure that whenever public record information which is likely to have an adverse effect on a consumer's ability to obtain employment

---

[8] Pursuant to Section 612(f)(2), the Federal Trade Commission set the maximum charge at $11.00, effective January 1, 2011. See 75 Fed. Reg. 80817 (Dec. 23, 2010). The Bureau will set the charge for 2012 and later years.

is reported it is complete and up to date. For purposes of this paragraph, items of pub- lic record relating to arrests, indictments, convictions, suits, tax liens, and outstanding judgments shall be considered up to date if the current public record status of the item at the time of the report is reported.

Exemption for national security investigations. Subsection (a) does not apply in the case of an agency or department of the United States Government that seeks to obtain and use a consumer report for employment purposes, if the head of the agency or department makes a written finding as prescribed under section 604(b)(4)(A).

§ 614. Restrictions on investigative consumer reports [15 U.S.C. § 1681*l*]
Whenever a consumer reporting agency prepares an investigative consumer report, no adverse information in the consumer report (other than information which is a matter of public record) may be included in a subsequent consumer report unless such adverse information has been verified in the process of making such subsequent consumer report, or the adverse information was received within the three-month period preceding the date the subsequent report is furnished.

§ 615. Requirements on users of consumer reports [15 U.S.C. § 1681m]

Duties of users taking adverse actions on the basis of information contained in consumer reports. If any person takes any adverse action with respect to any consumer that is based in whole or in part on any information contained in a consumer report, the person shall

provide oral, written, or electronic notice of the adverse action to the consumer;

provide to the consumer written or electronic disclosure

of a numerical credit score as defined in section 609(f)(2)(A) used by such per- son in taking any adverse action based in whole or in part on any information in a consumer report; and

of the information set forth in subparagraphs (B) through (E) of section 609(f)(1);

provide to the consumer orally, in writing, or electronically

the name, address, and telephone number of the consumer reporting agency (including a toll-free telephone number established by the agency if the agency compiles and maintains files on consumers on a nationwide basis) that furnished the report to the person; and

a statement that the consumer reporting agency did not make the decision to take the adverse action and is unable to provide the consumer the specific reasons why the adverse action was taken; and

provide to the consumer an oral, written, or electronic notice of the consumer's right

to obtain, under section 612 [§ 1681j], a free copy of a consumer report on the consumer from the consumer reporting agency referred to in paragraph (3), which notice shall include an indication of the 60-day period under that sec- tion for obtaining such a copy; and

to dispute, under section 611 [§ 1681i], with a consumer reporting agency the accuracy or completeness of any information in a consumer report furnished by the agency.

Adverse Action Based on Information Obtained from Third Parties Other than Consumer Reporting Agencies

In general. Whenever credit for personal, family, or household purposes involving a consumer is denied or the charge for such credit is increased either wholly or partly because of information obtained from a person other than a consumer reporting agency bearing upon the consumer's credit worthiness, credit standing, credit capacity, character, general reputation, personal characteristics, or mode of living, the user of such information shall, within a reasonable period of time, upon the consumer's writ- ten request for the reasons for such adverse action received within sixty days after learning of such adverse action, disclose the nature of the information to the consumer. The user of such information shall clearly and accurately disclose to the consumer his right to make such written request at the time such adverse action is communicated to the consumer.

Duties of Person Taking Certain Actions Based on Information Provided by Affiliate

Duties, generally. If a person takes an action described in subparagraph (B) with respect to a consumer, based in whole or in part on information described in subparagraph (c), the person shall

notify the consumer of the action, including a statement that the consumer may obtain the information in accordance with clause (ii); and

upon a written request from the consumer received within 60 days after transmittal of the notice required by clause (i), disclose to the consumer the nature of the information upon which the action is based by not later than 30 days after receipt of the request.

Action described. An action referred to in subparagraph (A) is an adverse action described in section 603(k)(1)(A) [§ 1681a], taken in connection with a transaction initiated by the consumer, or any adverse action described in clause (i) or (ii) of section 603(k)(1)(B) [§ 1681a].

Information described. Information referred to in subparagraph (A)

except as provided in clause (ii), is information that

is furnished to the person taking the action by a person related by common ownership or affiliated by common corporate control to the person taking the action; and bears on the credit worthiness, credit standing, credit capacity, character, general reputation, personal characteristics, or mode of living of the consumer; and

does not include

information solely as to transactions or experiences between the consumer and the person furnishing the information; or

information in a consumer report.

      Reasonable procedures to assure compliance. No person shall be held liable for any violation of this section if he shows by a preponderance of the evidence that at the time of the alleged violation he maintained reasonable procedures to assure compliance with the provisions of this section.

Duties of Users Making Written Credit or Insurance Solicitations on the Basis of Information Contained in Consumer Files

In general. Any person who uses a consumer report on any consumer in connection with any credit or insurance transaction that is not initiated by the consumer, that is provided to that person under section 604(c)(1)(B) [§ 1681b], shall provide with each written solicitation made to the consumer regarding the transaction a clear and conspicuous statement that

information contained in the consumer's consumer report was used in connection with the transaction;

the consumer received the offer of credit or insurance because the consumer satisfied the criteria for credit worthiness or insurability under which the consumer was selected for the offer;

if applicable, the credit or insurance may not be extended if, after the consumer responds to the offer, the consumer does not meet the criteria used to select the consumer for the offer or any applicable criteria bearing on credit worthiness or insurability or does not furnish any required collateral;

the consumer has a right to prohibit information contained in the consumer's file with any consumer reporting agency from being used in connection with any credit or insurance transaction that is not initiated by the consumer; and

the consumer may exercise the right referred to in subparagraph (D) by notifying a notification system established under section 604(e) [§ 1681b].

Disclosure of address and telephone number; format. A statement under paragraph (1) shall –

include the address and toll-free telephone number of the appropriate notification system established under section 604(e); and

be presented in such format and in such type size and manner as to be simple and easy to understand, as established by the Bureau, by rule, in consultation with the Federal Trade Commission, Federal banking agencies and the
National Credit Union Administration.

See also 16 CFR Part 642 16 CFR Part 698 App A
70 Fed. Reg. 5022 (01/31/05)

Maintaining criteria on file. A person who makes an offer of credit or insurance to a consumer under a credit or insurance transaction described in paragraph (1) shall maintain on file the criteria used to select the consumer to receive the offer, all cri- teria bearing on credit worthiness or insurability, as applicable, that are the basis for determining whether or not to extend credit or insurance pursuant to the offer, and any requirement for the furnishing of collateral as a condition of the extension of credit or insurance, until the expiration of the 3-year period beginning on the date on which the offer is made to the consumer.

Authority of federal agencies regarding unfair or deceptive acts or practices not affected. This section is not intended to affect the authority of any Federal or State agency to enforce a prohibition against unfair or deceptive acts or practices, including the making of false or misleading statements in connection with a credit or insurance transaction that is not initiated by the consumer.

See also 16 CFR Part 681
Red Flag Guidelines and Regulations Required   ***72 Fed. Reg. 63772-74 (11/09/07)***
74 Fed. Reg. 22640-41 (05/14/09)

Guidelines. The Federal banking agencies, the National Credit Union Administration, the Federal Trade Commission, the Commodity Futures Trading Commission, and the Securities and Exchange Commission shall jointly, with respect to the entities that are subject to their respective enforcement authority under section 621 –

establish and maintain guidelines for use by each financial institution and each creditor regarding identity theft with respect to account holders at, or custom- ers of, such entities, and update such guidelines as often as necessary;

prescribe regulations requiring each financial institution and each creditor to establish reasonable policies and procedures for implementing the guidelines established pursuant to subparagraph (A), to identify possible risks to account holders or customers or to the safety and soundness of the institution or customers; and

prescribe regulations applicable to card issuers to ensure that, if a card issuer receives notification of a change of address for an existing account, and within a short period of time (during at least the first 30 days after such notification is received) receives a request for an additional or replacement card for the same account, the card issuer may not issue the additional or replacement card, un- less the card issuer, in accordance with reasonable policies and procedures –

notifies the cardholder of the request at the former address of the card- holder and provides to the cardholder a means of promptly reporting incorrect address changes;

notifies the cardholder of the request by such other means of communication as the cardholder and the card issuer previously agreed to; or

uses other means of assessing the validity of the change of address, in accordance with reasonable policies and procedures established by the card issuer in accordance with the regulations prescribed under subparagraph (B).

Criteria

In general. In developing the guidelines required by paragraph (1)(A), the agencies described in paragraph (1) shall identify patterns, practices, and specific forms of activity that indicate the possible existence of identity theft.

Inactive accounts. In developing the guidelines required by paragraph (1)(A), the agencies described in paragraph (1) shall consider including reasonable guidelines providing that when a transaction occurs with respect to a credit or deposit account that has been inactive for more than 2 years, the creditor or financial institution shall follow reasonable policies and procedures that provide for notice to be given to a consumer in a manner reasonably designed to reduce the likelihood of identity theft with respect to such account.

Consistency with verification requirements. Guidelines established pursuant to para- graph (1) shall not be inconsistent with the policies and procedures required under section 5318(l) of title 31, United States Code.

Definitions. As used in this subsection, the term "creditor" –

means a creditor, as defined in section 702 of the Equal Credit Opportunity Act (15 U.S.C. 1691a), that regularly and in the ordinary course of business

obtains or uses consumer reports, directly or indirectly, in connection with a credit transaction;

furnishes information to consumer reporting agencies, as described in section 623, in connection with a credit transaction; or

advances funds to or on behalf of a person, based on an obligation of the person to repay the funds or repayable from specific property pledged by or on behalf of the person;

does not include a creditor described in subparagraph (A)(iii) that advances funds on behalf of a person for expenses incidental to a service provided by the creditor to that person; and

includes any other type of creditor, as defined in that section 702, as the agency described in paragraph (1) having authority over that creditor may determine appropriate by rule promulgated by that agency, based on a determination that such creditor offers or maintains accounts that are subject to a reasonably foreseeable risk of identity theft.

) Prohibition on Sale or Transfer of Debt Caused by Identity Theft

In general. No person shall sell, transfer for consideration, or place for collection a debt that such person has been notified under section 605B has resulted from identity theft.

Applicability. The prohibitions of this subsection shall apply to all persons collecting a debt described in paragraph (1) after the date of a notification under paragraph (1).

Rule of construction. Nothing in this subsection shall be construed to prohibit –

the repurchase of a debt in any case in which the assignee of the debt requires such repurchase because the debt has resulted from identity theft;

the securitization of a debt or the pledging of a portfolio of debt as collateral in connection with a borrowing; or

the transfer of debt as a result of a merger, acquisition, purchase and assumption transaction, or transfer of substantially all of the assets of an entity.

Debt collector communications concerning identity theft. If a person acting as a debt collector (as that term is defined in title VIII) on behalf of a third party that is a creditor or other user of a consumer report is notified that any information relating to a debt that the person is attempting to collect may be fraudulent or may be the result of identity theft, that person shall

—

notify the third party that the information may be fraudulent or may be the result of identity theft; and

upon request of the consumer to whom the debt purportedly relates, provide to the consumer all information to which the consumer would otherwise be entitled if the consumer were not a victim of identity theft, but wished to dispute the debt under provisions of law applicable to that person.

Duties of Users in Certain Credit Transactions

In general. Subject to rules prescribed as provided in paragraph (6), if any person uses a consumer report in connection with an application for, or a grant, extension, or other provision of, credit on material terms that are materially less favorable than the most favorable terms available to a substantial proportion of consumers from or through that person, based in whole or in part on a consumer report, the person shall provide an oral, written, or electronic notice to the consumer in the form and manner required by regulations prescribed in accordance with this subsection.

Timing. The notice required under paragraph (1) may be provided at the time of an application for, or a grant, extension, or other provision of, credit or the time of communication of an approval of an application for, or grant, extension, or other provision of, credit, except as provided in the regulations prescribed under paragraph (6).

Exceptions. No notice shall be required from a person under this subsection if–

the consumer applied for specific material terms and was granted those terms, unless those terms were initially specified by the person after the transaction was initiated by the consumer and after the person obtained a consumer re- port; or

the person has provided or will provide a notice to the consumer under sub- section (a) in connection with the transaction.

Other notice not sufficient. A person that is required to provide a notice under sub- section (a)) cannot meet that requirement by providing a notice under this subsection.

Content and delivery of notice. A notice under this subsection shall, at a minimum –

include a statement informing the consumer that the terms offered to the consumer are set based on information from a consumer report;

identify the consumer reporting agency furnishing the report;

include a statement informing the consumer that the consumer may obtain a copy of a consumer report from that consumer reporting agency without charge;

include the contact information specified by that consumer reporting agency for obtaining such consumer reports (including a toll-free telephone number established by the agency in the case of a consumer reporting agency described in section 603(p)); and

include a statement informing the consumer of –

a numerical credit score as defined in section 609(f)(2)(A), used by such person in making the credit decision described in paragraph (1) based in whole or in part on any information in a consumer report; and

the information set forth in subparagraphs (B) through (E) of section 609(f)(1).

See also 16 CFR Part 610

(6) Rulemaking   **75 Fed. Reg. 2724 (01/15/10)**

Rules required. The Bureau shall prescribe rules to carry out this subsection.

Content. Rules required by subparagraph (A) shall address, but are not limited to –

the form, content, time, and manner of delivery of any notice under this subsection;

clarification of the meaning of terms used in this subsection, including what credit terms are material, and when credit terms are materially less favorable;

exceptions to the notice requirement under this subsection for classes of persons or transactions regarding which the agencies determine that notice would not significantly benefit consumers;

a model notice that may be used to comply with this subsection; and

the timing of the notice required under paragraph (1), including the circumstances under which the notice must be provided after the terms offered to the consumer were set based on information from a consumer report.

Compliance. A person shall not be liable for failure to perform the duties required by this section if, at the time of the failure, the person maintained reasonable policies and procedures to comply with this section.

Enforcement

No civil actions. Sections 616 and 617 shall not apply to any failure by any person to comply with this section.

Administrative enforcement. This section shall be enforced exclusively under section 621 by the Federal agencies and officials identified in that section.

§ 616. Civil liability for willful noncompliance [15 U.S.C. § 1681n]

In general. Any person who willfully fails to comply with any requirement imposed under this title with respect to any consumer is liable to that consumer in an amount equal to the sum of

(A)   any actual damages sustained by the consumer as a result of the failure or damages of not less than $100 and not more than $1,000; or

(B)   in the case of liability of a natural person for obtaining a consumer report under false pretenses or knowingly without a permissible purpose, actual damages sustained by the consumer as a result of the failure or $1,000, whichever is greater;

such amount of punitive damages as the court may allow; and

in the case of any successful action to enforce any liability under this section, the costs of the action together with reasonable attorney's fees as determined by the court.

Civil liability for knowing noncompliance. Any person who obtains a consumer report from a consumer reporting agency under false pretenses or knowingly without a permissible purpose shall be liable to the consumer reporting agency for actual damages sustained by the consumer reporting agency or $1,000, whichever is greater.

Attorney's fees. Upon a finding by the court that an unsuccessful pleading, motion, or other paper filed in connection with an action under this section was filed in bad faith or for purposes of harassment, the court shall award to the prevailing party attorney's fees reasonable in relation to the work expended in responding to the pleading, motion, or other paper.

Clarification of willful noncompliance. For the purposes of this section, any person who printed an expiration date on any receipt provided to a consumer cardholder at a point of sale or transaction between December 4, 2004, and the date of the enactment of this subsection but otherwise complied with the requirements of section 605(g) for such receipt shall not be in willful noncompliance with section 605(g) by reason of printing such expiration date on the receipt.

§ 617. Civil liability for negligent noncompliance [15 U.S.C. § 1681o]

In general. Any person who is negligent in failing to comply with any requirement imposed under this title with respect to any consumer is liable to that consumer in an amount equal to the sum of

any actual damages sustained by the consumer as a result of the failure; and

in the case of any successful action to enforce any liability under this section, the costs of the action together with reasonable attorney's fees as determined by the court.

Attorney's fees. On a finding by the court that an unsuccessful pleading, motion, or other paper filed in connection with an action under this section was filed in bad faith or for purposes of harassment, the court shall award to the prevailing party attorney's fees reasonable in relation to the work expended in responding to the pleading, motion, or other paper.

§ 618. Jurisdiction of courts; limitation of actions [15 U.S.C. § 1681p]

An action to enforce any liability created under this title may be brought in any appropriate United States district court, without regard to the amount in controversy, or in any other court of competent jurisdiction, not later than the earlier of (1) 2 years after the date of discovery by the plaintiff of the violation that is the basis for such liability; or (2) 5 years after the date on which the violation that is the basis for such liability occurs.

§ 619. Obtaining information under false pretenses [15 U.S.C. § 1681q]

Any person who knowingly and willfully obtains information on a consumer from a consumer reporting agency under false pretenses shall be fined under title 18, United States Code, imprisoned for not more than 2 years, or both.

§ 620. Unauthorized disclosures by officers or employees [15 U.S.C. § 1681r]

Any officer or employee of a consumer reporting agency who knowingly and willfully provides information concerning an individual from the agency's files to a person not authorized to receive that information shall be fined under title 18, United States Code, imprisoned for not more than 2 years, or both.

§ 621. Administrative enforcement [15 U.S.C. § 1681s]

Enforcement by Federal Trade Commission.

In General. The Federal Trade Commission shall be authorized to enforce compliance with the requirements imposed by this title under the Federal Trade Commission Act (15 U.S.C. 41 et seq.), with respect to consumer reporting agencies and all other persons subject thereto, except to the extent that enforcement of the requirements imposed under this title is specifically committed to some other Government agency under any of subparagraphs (A) through (G) of subsection (b)(1), and subject to subtitle B of the Consumer Financial Protection Act of 2010, subsection (b). For the purpose of the exercise by the Federal Trade Commission of its functions and powers under the Federal Trade Commission Act, a violation of any requirement or prohibition imposed under this title shall constitute an unfair or deceptive act or practice in commerce, in violation of section 5(a) of the Federal Trade Commission Act (15 U.S.C. 45(a)), and shall be subject to enforcement by the Federal Trade Commission under section 5(b) of that Act with respect to any consumer reporting agency or person that is subject to enforcement by the Federal Trade Commission pursuant to this subsection, irrespective of whether that person is engaged in commerce or meets any other jurisdictional tests under the Federal Trade Commission Act. The Federal Trade Commission shall have such procedural, investigative, and enforcement powers, including the power to issue procedural rules in enforcing compliance with the requirements imposed under this title and to require the filing of reports, the production of documents, and the appearance of witnesses, as though the applicable terms and conditions of the Federal Trade Commission Act were part of this title. Any person violating any of the provisions of this title shall be subject to the penalties and entitled to the privileges and immunities provided in the Federal Trade Commission Act as though the applicable terms and provisions of such Act are part of this title.

Penalties

Knowing Violations. Except as otherwise provided by subtitle B of the Consumer Financial Protection Act of 2010, in the event of a knowing violation, which constitutes a pattern or practice of violations of this title, the Federal Trade Commission may commence a civil action to recover a civil penalty in a district court of the United States against any person that violates this title. In such action, such person shall be liable for a civil penalty of not more than $2,500 per violation.[9]

Determining Penalty Amount. In determining the amount of a civil penalty under subparagraph (A), the court shall take into account the degree of culpability, any history of such prior conduct, ability to pay, effect on ability to continue to do business, and such other matters as justice may require.

Limitation. Notwithstanding paragraph (2), a court may not impose any civil penalty on a person for a violation of section 623(a)(1), unless the person has been enjoined from committing the violation, or ordered not to commit the violation, in an action or proceeding brought by or on behalf of the Federal Trade Commission, and has violated the injunction or order, and the court

[9]Pursuant to the Federal Civil Penalties Inflation Adjustment Act of 1990, the Federal Trade Commission increased the maximum civil penalty to $3,500 per violation. See 74 Fed. Reg. 857 (Jan. 9, 2009).

may not impose any civil penalty for any violation occurring before the date of the violation of the injunction or order

Enforcement by Other Agencies.

In General. Subject to subtitle B of the Consumer Financial Protection Act of 2010, compliance with the requirements imposed under this title with respect to consumer reporting agencies, persons who use consumer reports from such agencies, persons who furnish information to such agencies, and users of information that are subject to section 615(d) shall be enforced under –section 8 of the Federal Deposit Insurance Act (12 U.S.C. 1818), by the appropriate Federal banking agency, as defined in section 3(q) of the Federal Deposit Insurance Act (12 U.S.C. 1813(q)), with respect to –any national bank or State savings association, and any Federal branch or Federal agency of a foreign bank; any member bank of the Federal Reserve System (other than a national bank), a branch or agency of a foreign bank (other than a Federal branch, Federal agency, or insured State branch of a foreign bank), a commercial lending company owned or controlled by a foreign bank, and any organization operating under section 25 or 25A of the Federal Reserve Act; and any bank or Federal savings association insured by the Federal Deposit Insurance Corporation (other than a member of the Federal Reserve System) and any insured State branch of a foreign bank;

the Federal Credit Union Act (12 U.S.C. 1751 et seq.), by the Administrator of the National Credit Union Administration with respect to any Federal credit union;

subtitle IV of title 49, United States Code, by the Secretary of Transportation, with respect to all carriers' subject to the jurisdiction of the Surface Transportation Board;

the Federal Aviation Act of 1958 (49 U.S.C. App. 1301 et seq.), by the Secretary of Transportation, with respect to any air carrier or foreign air carrier subject to that Act;

the Packers and Stockyards Act, 1921 (7 U.S.C. 181 et seq.) (except as provided in section 406 of that Act), by the Secretary of Agriculture, with respect to any activities subject to that Act;

the Commodity Exchange Act, with respect to a person subject to the jurisdiction of the Commodity Futures Trading Commission;

the Federal securities laws, and any other laws that are subject to the jurisdiction of the Securities and Exchange Commission, with respect to a person that is subject to the jurisdiction of the Securities and Exchange Commission; and

subtitle E of the Consumer Financial Protection Act of 2010, by the Bureau, with respect to any person subject to this title.

Incorporated Definitions. The terms used in paragraph (1) that are not defined in this title or otherwise defined in section 3(s) of the Federal Deposit Insurance Act (12 U.S.C. 1813(s)) have the same meanings as in section 1(b) of the International Banking Act of 1978 (12 U.S.C. 3101).

State Action for Violations

Authority of states. In addition to such other remedies as are provided under State law, if the chief law enforcement officer of a State, or an official or agency designated by a State, has reason to believe that any person has violated or is violating this title, the State –

may bring an action to enjoin such violation in any appropriate United States district court or in any other court of competent jurisdiction;

subject to paragraph (5), may bring an action on behalf of the residents of the State to recover

damages for which the person is liable to such residents under sections 616 and 617 [§§ 1681n and 1681o] as a result of the violation;

in the case of a violation described in any of paragraphs (1) through (3) of section 623(c) [§ 1681s-2], damages for which the person would, but for section 623(c), be liable to such residents as a result of the violation; or

damages of not more than $1,000 for each willful or negligent violation; and

in the case of any successful action under subparagraph (A) or (B), shall be awarded the costs of the action and reasonable attorney fees as determined by the court.

Rights of federal regulators. The State shall serve prior written notice of any action under paragraph (1) upon the Bureau and the Federal Trade Commission or the appropriate Federal regulator determined under subsection (b) and provide the Bureau and the Federal Trade Commission or appropriate Federal regulator with a copy of its com- plaint, except in any case in which such prior notice is not feasible, in which case the State shall serve such notice immediately upon instituting such action. The Bureau and the Federal Trade Commission or appropriate Federal regulator shall have the right –

to intervene in the action; upon so intervening, to be heard on all matters arising therein;

to remove the action to the appropriate United States district court; and to file petitions for appeal.

Investigatory powers. For purposes of bringing any action under this subsection, nothing in this subsection shall prevent the chief law enforcement officer, or an official or agency designated by a State, from exercising the powers conferred on the chief law enforcement officer or such official by the laws of such State to conduct investigations or to administer oaths or affirmations or to compel the attendance of witnesses or the production of documentary and other evidence.

Limitation on state action while federal action pending. If the Bureau, the Federal Trade Commission, or the appropriate Federal regulator has instituted a civil action or an administrative action under section 8 of the Federal Deposit Insurance Act for a violation of this title, no State may, during the pendency of such action, bring an action under this section against any defendant named in the complaint of the Bureau, the Federal Trade Commission, or the appropriate Federal regulator for any violation of this title that is alleged in that complaint.

Limitations on State Actions for Certain Violations

Violation of injunction required. A State may not bring an action against a person under paragraph (1)(B) for a violation described in any of paragraphs (1) through (3) of section 623(c), unless

the person has been enjoined from committing the violation, in an action brought by the State under paragraph (1)(A); and

the person has violated the injunction.

Limitation on damages recoverable. In an action against a person under para- graph (1)(B) for a violation described in any of paragraphs (1) through (3) of section 623(c), a State may not recover any damages incurred before the date of the violation of an injunction on which the action is based.

Enforcement under other authority. For the purpose of the exercise by any agency referred to in subsection (b) of this section of its powers under any Act referred to in that subsection, a violation of any requirement imposed under this title shall be deemed to be a violation of a requirement imposed under that Act. In addition to its powers under any provision of law specifically referred to in subsection (b) of this section, each of the agencies referred to in that subsection may exercise, for the purpose of enforcing compliance with any requirement imposed under this title any other authority conferred on it by law.

Regulatory Authority

In General. The Bureau shall prescribe such regulations as are necessary to carry out the purposes of this title, except with respect to sections 615(e) and 628. The Bureau may prescribe regulations as may be necessary or appropriate to administer and carry out the purposes and objectives of this title, and to prevent evasions thereof or to facilitate compliance therewith. Except as provided in section 1029(a) of the Consumer Financial Protection Act of 2010, the regulations prescribed by the Bureau under this title shall apply to any person that is subject to this title, notwithstanding the enforcement authorities granted to other agencies under this section.

Deference. Notwithstanding any power granted to any Federal agency under this title, the deference that a court affords to a Federal agency with respect to a determination made by such agency relating to the meaning or interpretation of any provision of this title that is subject to the jurisdiction of such agency shall be applied as if that agency were the only agency authorized to apply, enforce, interpret, or administer the provisions of this title The regulations prescribed by the Bureau under this title shall apply to any person that is subject to this title, notwithstanding the enforcement authorities granted to other agencies under this section.

Coordination of Consumer Complaint Investigations

In general. Each consumer reporting agency described in section 603(p) shall develop and maintain procedures for the referral to each other such agency of any consumer complaint received by the agency alleging identity theft, or requesting a fraud alert under section 605A or a block under section 605B.

Model form and procedure for reporting identity theft. The Bureau, in consultation with the Federal Trade Commission, the Federal banking agencies, and the National Credit Union Administration, shall develop a model form and model procedures to be used by consumers who are victims of identity theft for contacting and informing creditors and consumer reporting agencies of the fraud.
See also 70 Fed.Reg. 21792 (04/27/05)

Annual summary reports. Each consumer reporting agency described in section 603(p) shall submit an annual summary report to the Bureau on consumer complaints received by the agency on identity theft or fraud alerts.

Bureau regulation of coding of trade names. If the Bureau determines that a person described in paragraph (9) of section 623(a) has not met the requirements of such paragraph, the Bureau shall take action to ensure the person's compliance with such paragraph, which may include issuing model guidance or prescribing reasonable policies and procedures, as necessary to ensure that such person complies with such paragraph.

Enforcement by Federal Trade Commission.

In General. The Federal Trade Commission shall be authorized to enforce compliance with the requirements imposed by this title under the Federal Trade Commission Act (15 U.S.C. 41 et seq.), with respect to consumer reporting agencies and all other persons subject thereto, except to the extent that enforcement of the requirements imposed under this title is specifically committed to some other Government agency under any of subparagraphs (A) through (G) of subsection (b)(1), and subject to subtitle B of the Consumer Financial Protection Act of 2010, subsection (b). For the purpose of the exercise by the Federal Trade Commission of its functions and powers under the Federal Trade Commission Act, a violation of any requirement or prohibition imposed under this title shall constitute an unfair or deceptive act or practice in commerce, in violation of section 5(a) of the Federal Trade Commission Act (15

U.S.C. 45(a)), and shall be subject to enforcement by the Federal Trade Commission under section 5(b) of that Act with respect to any consumer reporting agency or person that is subject to enforcement by the Federal Trade Commission pursuant to this subsection, irrespective of whether that person is engaged in commerce or meets any other jurisdictional tests under the Federal Trade Commission Act. The Federal Trade Commission shall have such procedural, investigative, and enforcement powers, including the power to issue procedural rules in enforcing compliance with the requirements imposed under this title and to require the filing of reports, the production of documents, and the appearance of witnesses, as though the applicable terms and conditions of the Federal Trade Commission Act were part of this title. Any person violating any of the provisions of this title shall be subject to the penalties and entitled to the privileges and immunities provided in the Federal Trade Commission Act as though the applicable terms and provisions of such Act are part of this title.

Penalties

Knowing Violations. Except as otherwise provided by subtitle B of the Consumer Financial Protection Act of 2010, in the event of a knowing violation, which constitutes a pattern or practice of violations of this title, the Federal Trade Commission may commence a civil action to recover a civil penalty in a district court of the United States against any person that violates this title. In such action, such person shall be liable for a civil penalty of not more than $2,500 per violation.[9]

Determining Penalty Amount. In determining the amount of a civil penalty under subparagraph (A), the court shall take into account the degree of culpability, any history of such prior conduct, ability to pay, effect on ability to continue to do business, and such other matters as justice may require.

Limitation. Notwithstanding paragraph (2), a court may not impose any civil penalty on a person for a violation of section 623(a)(1), unless the person has been enjoined from committing the violation, or ordered not to commit the violation, in an action or proceeding brought by or on behalf of the Federal Trade Commission, and has violated the injunction or order, and the court

[9]Pursuant to the Federal Civil Penalties Inflation Adjustment Act of 1990, the Federal Trade Commission increased the maximum civil penalty to $3,500 per violation. See 74 Fed. Reg. 857 (Jan. 9, 2009).

may not impose any civil penalty for any violation occurring before the date of the violation of the injunction or order

Enforcement by Other Agencies.

In General. Subject to subtitle B of the Consumer Financial Protection Act of 2010, compliance with the requirements imposed under this title with respect to consumer reporting agencies, persons who use consumer reports from such agencies, persons who furnish information to such agencies, and users of information that are subject to section 615(d) shall be enforced under –

section 8 of the Federal Deposit Insurance Act (12 U.S.C. 1818), by the appropriate Federal banking agency, as defined in section 3(q) of the Federal Deposit Insurance Act (12 U.S.C. 1813(q)), with respect to –

any national bank or State savings association, and any Federal branch or Federal agency of a foreign bank;

any member bank of the Federal Reserve System (other than a national bank), a branch or agency of a foreign bank (other than a Federal branch, Federal agency, or insured State branch of a foreign bank), a commercial lending company owned or controlled by a foreign bank, and any organization operating under section 25 or 25A of the Federal Reserve Act; and

any bank or Federal savings association insured by the Federal Deposit Insurance Corporation (other than a member of the Federal Reserve System) and any insured State branch of a foreign bank;

the Federal Credit Union Act (12 U.S.C. 1751 et seq.), by the Administrator of the National Credit Union Administration with respect to any Federal credit union;

subtitle IV of title 49, United States Code, by the Secretary of Transportation, with respect to all carriers' subject to the jurisdiction of the Surface Transportation Board;

the Federal Aviation Act of 1958 (49 U.S.C. App. 1301 et seq.), by the Secretary of Transportation, with respect to any air carrier or foreign air carrier subject to that Act;

the Packers and Stockyards Act, 1921 (7 U.S.C. 181 et seq.) (except as provided in section 406 of that Act), by the Secretary of Agriculture, with respect to any activities subject to that Act;

the Commodity Exchange Act, with respect to a person subject to the jurisdiction of the Commodity Futures Trading Commission;

the Federal securities laws, and any other laws that are subject to the jurisdiction of the Securities and Exchange Commission, with respect to a person that is subject to the jurisdiction of the Securities and Exchange Commission; and

subtitle E of the Consumer Financial Protection Act of 2010, by the Bureau, with respect to any person subject to this title.

Incorporated Definitions. The terms used in paragraph (1) that are not defined in this title or otherwise defined in section 3(s) of the Federal Deposit Insurance Act (12 U.S.C. 1813(s)) have the same meanings as in section 1(b) of the International Banking Act of 1978 (12 U.S.C. 3101).

State Action for Violations

Authority of states. In addition to such other remedies as are provided under State law, if the chief law enforcement officer of a State, or an official or agency designated by a State, has reason to believe that any person has violated or is violating this title, the State –

may bring an action to enjoin such violation in any appropriate United States district court or in any other court of competent jurisdiction;

subject to paragraph (5), may bring an action on behalf of the residents of the State to recover

damages for which the person is liable to such residents under sections 616 and 617 [§§ 1681n and 1681o] as a result of the violation;

in the case of a violation described in any of paragraphs (1) through (3) of section 623(c) [§ 1681s-2], damages for which the person would, but for section 623(c), be liable to such residents as a result of the violation; or

damages of not more than $1,000 for each willful or negligent violation; and

in the case of any successful action under subparagraph (A) or (B), shall be awarded the costs of the action and reasonable attorney fees as determined by the court.

Rights of federal regulators. The State shall serve prior written notice of any action under paragraph (1) upon the Bureau and the Federal Trade Commission or the appropriate Federal regulator determined under subsection (b) and provide the Bureau and the Federal Trade Commission or appropriate Federal regulator with a copy of its com- plaint, except in any case in which such prior notice is not feasible, in which case the State shall serve such notice immediately upon instituting such action. The Bureau and the Federal Trade Commission or appropriate Federal regulator shall have the right –

to intervene in the action;

upon so intervening, to be heard on all matters arising therein;

to remove the action to the appropriate United States district court; and to file petitions for appeal.

Investigatory powers. For purposes of bringing any action under this subsection, nothing in this subsection shall prevent the chief law enforcement officer, or an official or agency designated by a State, from exercising the powers conferred on the chief law enforcement officer or such official by the laws of such State to conduct investigations or to administer oaths or affirmations or to compel the attendance of witnesses or the production of documentary and other evidence.

Limitation on state action while federal action pending. If the Bureau, the Federal Trade Commission, or the appropriate Federal regulator has instituted a civil action or an administrative action under section 8 of the Federal Deposit Insurance Act for a violation of this title, no State may, during the pendency of such action, bring an action under this section against any defendant named in the complaint of the Bureau, the Federal Trade Commission, or the appropriate Federal regulator for any violation of this title that is alleged in that complaint.

Limitations on State Actions for Certain Violations

Violation of injunction required. A State may not bring an action against a person under paragraph (1)(B) for a violation described in any of paragraphs (1) through (3) of section 623(c), unless

the person has been enjoined from committing the violation, in an action brought by the State under paragraph (1)(A); and

the person has violated the injunction.

Limitation on damages recoverable. In an action against a person under para- graph (1)(B) for a violation described in any of paragraphs (1) through (3) of section 623(c), a State may not recover any damages incurred before the date of the violation of an injunction on which the action is based.

Enforcement under other authority. For the purpose of the exercise by any agency referred to in subsection (b) of this section of its powers under any Act referred to in that subsection, a violation of any requirement imposed under this title shall be deemed to be a violation of a requirement imposed under that Act. In addition to its powers under any provision of law specifically referred to in subsection (b) of this section, each of the agencies referred to in that subsection may exercise, for the purpose of enforcing compliance with any requirement imposed under this title any other authority conferred on it by law.

Regulatory Authority *In General.* The Bureau shall prescribe such regulations as are necessary to carry out the purposes of this title, except with respect to sections 615(e) and 628. The Bureau may prescribe regulations as may be necessary or appropriate to administer and carry out the purposes and objectives of this title, and to prevent evasions thereof or to facilitate compliance therewith. Except as provided in section 1029(a) of the Consumer Financial Protection Act of 2010, the regulations prescribed by the Bureau under this title shall apply to any person that is subject to this title, notwithstanding the enforcement authorities granted to other agencies under this section.

Deference. Notwithstanding any power granted to any Federal agency under this title, the deference that a court affords to a Federal agency with respect to a determination made by such agency relating to the meaning or interpretation of any provision of this title that is subject to the jurisdiction of such agency shall be applied as if that agency were the only agency authorized to apply, enforce, interpret, or administer the provisions of this title The regulations prescribed by the Bureau under this title shall apply to any person that is subject to this title, notwithstanding the enforcement authorities granted to other agencies under this section.

Coordination of Consumer Complaint Investigations

In general. Each consumer reporting agency described in section 603(p) shall develop and maintain procedures for the referral to each other such agency of any consumer complaint received by the agency alleging identity theft, or requesting a fraud alert under section 605A or a block under section 605B.

Model form and procedure for reporting identity theft. The Bureau, in consultation with the Federal Trade Commission, the Federal banking agencies, and the National Credit Union Administration, shall develop a model form and model procedures to be used by consumers who are victims of identity theft for contacting and informing
creditors and consumer reporting agencies of the fraud.
See also 70 Fed.Reg. 21792 (04/27/05)
Annual summary reports. Each consumer reporting agency described in section 603(p) shall submit an annual summary report to the Bureau on consumer complaints received by the agency on identity theft or fraud alerts.

> *Bureau regulation of coding of trade names.* If the Bureau determines that a person described in paragraph (9) of section 623(a) has not met the requirements of such paragraph, the Bureau shall take action to ensure the person's compliance with such paragraph, which may include issuing model guidance or prescribing reasonable policies and procedures, as necessary to ensure that such person complies with such paragraph.

§ 622. Information on overdue child support obligations [15 U.S.C. § 1681s-1]

Notwithstanding any other provision of this title, a consumer reporting agency shall in-clude in any consumer report furnished by the agency in accordance with section 604 [§ 1681b] of this title, any information on the failure of the consumer to pay overdue support which

is provided

to the consumer reporting agency by a State or local child support enforcement agency; or

to the consumer reporting agency and verified by any local, State, or Federal government agency; and
antedates the report by 7 years or less.

§ 623. Responsibilities of furnishers of information to consumer reporting agencies

[15 U.S.C. § 1681s-2]

Duty of Furnishers of Information to Provide Accurate Information

Prohibition

Reporting information with actual knowledge of errors. A person shall not furnish any information relating to a consumer to any consumer reporting agency if the person knows or has reasonable cause to believe that the information is inaccurate.

Reporting information after notice and confirmation of errors. A person shall not furnish information relating to a consumer to any consumer reporting agency if

the person has been notified by the consumer, at the address specified by the person for such notices, that specific information is inaccurate; and

the information is, in fact, inaccurate.

No address requirement. A person who clearly and conspicuously specifies to the consumer an address for notices referred to in subparagraph (B) shall not be subject to subparagraph (A); however, nothing in subparagraph (B) shall require a person to specify such an address.

Definition. For purposes of subparagraph (A), the term "reasonable cause to believe that the information is inaccurate" means having specific knowledge, other than solely allegations by the consumer, that would cause a reasonable person to have substantial doubts about the accuracy of the information.

Duty to correct and update information. A person who

regularly and in the ordinary course of business furnishes information to one or more consumer reporting agencies about the person's transactions or experiences with any consumer; and

has furnished to a consumer reporting agency information that the person determines is not complete or accurate, shall promptly notify the consumer reporting agency of that determination and provide to the agency any corrections to that information, or any additional information, that is necessary to make the information provided by the person to the agency complete and accurate, and shall not thereafter furnish to the agency any of the information that remains not complete or accurate.

Duty to provide notice of dispute. If the completeness or accuracy of any information furnished by any person to any consumer reporting agency is disputed to such person by a consumer, the person may not furnish the information to any consumer reporting agency without notice that such information is disputed by the consumer.

Duty to provide notice of closed accounts. A person who regularly and in the ordinary course of business furnishes information to a consumer reporting agency regarding a consumer who has a credit account with that person shall notify the agency of the voluntary closure of the account by the consumer, in information regularly furnished for the period in which the account is closed.

Duty to Provide Notice of Delinquency of Accounts

In general. A person who furnishes information to a consumer reporting agency regarding a delinquent account being placed for collection, charged to profit or loss, or subjected to any similar action shall, not later than 90 days after furnishing the information, notify the agency of the date of delinquency on the account, which shall be the month and year of the commencement of the delinquency on the account that immediately preceded the action.

Rule of construction. For purposes of this paragraph only, and provided that the consumer does not dispute the information, a person that furnishes information on a delinquent account that is placed for collection, charged for profit or loss, or subjected to any similar action, complies with this paragraph, if –

the person reports the same date of delinquency as that provided by the creditor to which the account was owed at the time at which the commencement of the delinquency occurred, if the creditor previously reported that date of delinquency to a consumer reporting agency;

the creditor did not previously report the date of delinquency to a consumer reporting agency, and the person establishes and follows reasonable procedures to obtain the date of delinquency from the creditor or another reliable source and reports that date to a consumer reporting agency as the date of delinquency; or

the creditor did not previously report the date of delinquency to a consumer reporting agency and the date of delinquency cannot be reasonably obtained as provided in clause (ii), the person establishes and follows reasonable procedures to ensure the date reported as the date of delinquency precedes the date on which the account is placed for collection, charged to profit or loss, or subjected to any similar action, and reports such date to the credit reporting agency.

Duties of Furnishers Upon Notice of Identity Theft-Related Information

Reasonable procedures. A person that furnishes information to any consumer reporting agency shall have in place reasonable procedures to respond to any notification that it receives from a consumer reporting agency under section 605B relating to information resulting from identity theft, to prevent that person from refurnishing such blocked information.

Information alleged to result from identity theft. If a consumer submits an identity theft report to a person who furnishes information to a consumer reporting agency at the address specified by that person for receiving such reports stating that information maintained by such person that purports to relate to the consumer resulted from identity theft, the person may not furnish such information that purports to relate to the consumer to any consumer reporting agency, unless the person subsequently knows or is informed by the consumer that the information is correct.

Negative Information

Notice to Consumer Required

In general. If any financial institution that extends credit and regularly and in the ordinary course of business furnishes information to a consumer reporting agency described in section 603(p) furnishes negative information to such an agency regarding credit extended to a customer, the financial institution shall provide a notice of such furnishing of negative information, in writing, to the customer.

Notice effective for subsequent submissions. After providing such notice, the financial institution may submit additional negative information to a consumer reporting agency described in section 603(p) with respect to the same transaction, extension of credit, account, or customer without providing additional notice to the customer.

Time of Notice

In general. The notice required under subparagraph (A) shall be provided to the customer prior to, or no later than 30 days after, furnishing the negative information to a consumer reporting agency described in section 603(p).

Coordination with new account disclosures. If the notice is provided to the customer prior to furnishing the negative information to a consumer reporting agency, the notice may not be included in the initial disclosures provided under section 127(a) of the Truth in Lending Act.

Coordination with other disclosures. The notice required under subparagraph (A) –

may be included on or with any notice of default, any billing statement, or any other materials provided to the customer; and

must be clear and conspicuous.
                    See also 12 CFR Part 222, App B

Model Disclosure   ***70 Fed. Reg. 33281 (06/15/04)***

Duty of Bureau. The Bureau shall prescribe a brief model disclosure that a financial institution may use to comply with subparagraph (A), which shall not exceed 30 words.

Use of model not required. No provision of this paragraph may be construed to require a financial institution to use any such model form prescribed by the Bureau.

Compliance using model. A financial institution shall be deemed to be in compliance with subparagraph (A) if the financial institution uses any model form prescribed by the Bureau under this subparagraph, or the financial institution uses any such model form and rearranges its format.

Use of notice without submitting negative information. No provision of this paragraph shall be construed as requiring a financial institution that has provided a customer with a notice described in subparagraph (A) to furnish negative information about the customer to a consumer reporting agency.

Safe harbor. A financial institution shall not be liable for failure to perform the duties required by this paragraph if, at the time of the failure, the financial institution maintained reasonable policies and procedures to comply with this paragraph or the financial institution reasonably believed that the institution is prohibited, by law, from contacting the consumer.

Definitions. For purposes of this paragraph, the following definitions shall apply:

The term "negative information" means information concerning a customer's delinquencies, late payments, insolvency, or any form of default.

The terms "customer" and "financial institution" have the same meanings as in section 509 Public Law 106-102.

Ability of Consumer to Dispute Information Directly with Furnisher
See also 16 CFR Part 660.4
74 Fed. Reg. 31484 (07/01/09)

In general. The Bureau, in consultation with the Federal Trade Commission, the Federal banking agencies, and the National Credit Union Administration, shall prescribe regulations that shall identify the circumstances under which a furnisher shall be required to reinvestigate a dispute concerning the accuracy of information contained in a consumer report on the consumer, based on a direct request of a consumer.

Considerations. In prescribing regulations under subparagraph (A), the agencies shall weigh —

the benefits to consumers with the costs on furnishers and the credit reporting system;
the impact on the overall accuracy and integrity of consumer reports of any such requirements;
whether direct contact by the consumer with the furnisher would likely result in the most expeditious resolution of any such dispute; and

the potential impact on the credit reporting process if credit repair organizations, as defined in section 403(3) [15 U.S.C. §1679a(3)], including entities that would be a credit repair organization, but for section 403(3)(B)(i), are able to circumvent the prohibition in subparagraph (G).

Applicability. Subparagraphs (D) through (G) shall apply in any circumstance identified under the regulations promulgated under subparagraph (A).

Submitting a notice of dispute. A consumer who seeks to dispute the accuracy of information shall provide a dispute notice directly to such person at the address specified by the person for such notices that –

identifies the specific information that is being disputed;

explains the basis for the dispute; and

includes all supporting documentation required by the furnisher to substantiate the basis of the dispute.

Duty of person after receiving notice of dispute. After receiving a notice of dispute from a consumer pursuant to subparagraph (D), the person that provided the information in dispute to a consumer reporting agency shall –

conduct an investigation with respect to the disputed information;

review all relevant information provided by the consumer with the notice;

complete such person's investigation of the dispute and report the results of the investigation to the consumer before the expiration of the period under section 611(a)(1) within which a consumer reporting agency would be required to complete its action if the consumer had elected to dispute the information under that section; and

if the investigation finds that the information reported was inaccurate, promptly notify each consumer reporting agency to which the person furnished the inaccurate information of that determination and provide to the agency any correction to that information that is necessary to make the information provided by the person accurate.

Frivolous or Irrelevant Dispute

In general. This paragraph shall not apply if the person receiving a notice of a dispute from a consumer reasonably determines that the dispute is frivolous or irrelevant, including –

by reason of the failure of a consumer to provide sufficient information to investigate the disputed information; or

the submission by a consumer of a dispute that is substantially the same as a dispute previously submitted by or for the consumer, either directly to the person or through a consumer reporting agency under subsection (b), with respect to which the person has already performed the person's duties under this paragraph or subsection (b), as applicable.

Notice of determination. Upon making any determination under clause (i) that a dispute is frivolous or irrelevant, the person shall notify the consumer of such determination not later than 5 business days after making such determination, by mail or, if authorized by the consumer for that purpose, by any other means available to the person.

Contents of notice. A notice under clause (ii) shall include--

the reasons for the determination under clause (i); and

identification of any information required to investigate the disputed information, which may consist of a standardized form describing the general nature of such information.

Exclusion of credit repair organizations. This paragraph shall not apply if the notice of the dispute is submitted by, is prepared on behalf of the consumer by, or is submitted on a form supplied to the consumer by, a credit repair organization, as defined in section 403(3), or an entity that would be a credit repair organization, but for section 403(3)(B)(i).

Duty to provide notice of status as medical information furnisher. A person whose primary business is providing medical services, products, or devices, or the person's agent or assignee, who furnishes information to a consumer reporting agency on a consumer shall be considered a medical information furnisher for purposes of this title, and shall notify the agency of such status.

Duties of Furnishers of Information upon Notice of Dispute

In general. After receiving notice pursuant to section 611(a)(2) [§ 1681i] of a dispute with regard to the completeness or accuracy of any information provided by a person to a consumer reporting agency, the person shall

conduct an investigation with respect to the disputed information;

review all relevant information provided by the consumer reporting agency pursuant to section 611(a)(2) [§ 1681i];

report the results of the investigation to the consumer reporting agency;

if the investigation finds that the information is incomplete or inaccurate, re- port those results to all other consumer reporting agencies to which the person furnished the information and that compile and maintain files on consumers on a nationwide basis; and if an item of information disputed by a consumer is found to be inaccurate or incomplete or cannot be verified after any reinvestigation under paragraph (1), for purposes of reporting to a consumer reporting agency only, as appropriate, based on the results of the reinvestigation promptly–

modify that item of information;

delete that item of information; or

permanently block the reporting of that item of information.

Deadline. A person shall complete all investigations, reviews, and reports required under paragraph (1) regarding information provided by the person to a consumer re- porting agency, before the expiration of the period under section 611(a)(1) [§ 1681i] within which the consumer reporting agency is required to complete actions required by that section regarding that information.

Limitation on liability. Except as provided in section 621(c)(1)(B), sections 616 and 617 do not apply to any violation of –

subsection (a) of this section, including any regulations issued thereunder;

subsection (e) of this section, except that nothing in this paragraph shall limit, expand, or otherwise affect liability under section 616 or 617, as applicable, for violations of subsection (b) of this section; or

subsection (e) of section 615.

Limitation on enforcement. The provisions of law described in paragraphs (1) through of subsection (c) (other than with respect to the exception described in paragraph (2) of subsection (c)) shall be enforced exclusively as provided under section 621 by the Federal agencies and officials and the State officials identified in section 621.
Accuracy Guidelines and Regulations Required
See also 16 CFR Part 660
74 Fed. Reg. 31484 (07/01/09)
Guidelines. The Bureau shall, with respect to persons or entities that are subject to the enforcement authority of the Bureau under section 621 –

establish and maintain guidelines for use by each person that furnishes information to a consumer reporting agency regarding the accuracy and integrity of the information relating to consumers that such entities furnish to consumer reporting agencies, and update such guidelines as often as necessary; and

prescribe regulations requiring each person that furnishes information to a consumer reporting agency to establish reasonable policies and procedures for implementing the guidelines established pursuant to subparagraph (A).

Criteria. In developing the guidelines required by paragraph (1)(A), the Bureau shall-

identify patterns, practices, and specific forms of activity that can compromise the accuracy and integrity of information furnished to consumer reporting agencies;

review the methods (including technological means) used to furnish information relating to consumers to consumer reporting agencies;

determine whether persons that furnish information to consumer reporting agencies maintain and enforce policies to ensure the accuracy and integrity of information furnished to consumer reporting agencies; and

examine the policies and processes that persons that furnish information to consumer reporting agencies employ to conduct re investigations and correct inaccurate information relating to consumers that has been furnished to consumer reporting agencies.
See also 16 CFR Parts 680, 698 Appx C
§ 624. Affiliate sharing [15 U.S.C. § 1681s-3]
72 Fed. Reg. 61455-64 (10/30/07)
74 Fed. Reg. 22639-40 (05/14/09)
Special Rule for Solicitation for Purposes of Marketing

Notice. Any person that receives from another person related to it by common ownership or affiliated by corporate control a communication of information that would be a consumer report, but for clauses (i), (ii), and (iii) of section 603(d)(2)(A), may not use the information to make a solicitation for marketing purposes to a consumer about its products or services, unless--
it is clearly and conspicuously disclosed to the consumer that the information may be communicated among such persons for purposes of making such solicitations to the consumer; and
the consumer is provided an opportunity and a simple method to prohibit the making of such solicitations to the consumer by such person.

Consumer Choice

In general. The notice required under paragraph (1) shall allow the consumer the opportunity to prohibit all solicitations referred to in such paragraph, and may allow the consumer to choose from different options when electing to prohibit the sending of such solicitations, including options regarding the types of entities and information covered, and which methods of delivering solicitations the consumer elects to prohibit.

Format. Notwithstanding subparagraph (A), the notice required under para- graph (1) shall be clear, conspicuous, and concise, and any method provided under paragraph (1)(B) shall be simple. The regulations prescribed to implement this section shall provide specific guidance regarding how to comply with such standards.

Duration

In general. The election of a consumer pursuant to paragraph (1)(B) to prohibit the making of solicitations shall be effective for at least 5 years, beginning on the date on which the person receives the election of the consumer, unless the consumer requests that such election be revoked.

Notice upon expiration of effective period. At such time as the election of a consumer pursuant to paragraph (1)(B) is no longer effective, a person may not use information that the person receives in the manner described in para- graph (1) to make any solicitation for marketing purposes to the consumer, unless the consumer receives a notice and an opportunity, using a simple method, to extend the opt-out for another period of at least 5 years, pursuant to the procedures described in paragraph (1).

Scope. This section shall not apply to a person –

using information to make a solicitation for marketing purposes to a consumer with whom the person has a pre-existing business relationship;

using information to facilitate communications to an individual for whose benefit the person provides employee benefit or other services pursuant to a contract with an employer related to and arising out of the current employment relationship or status of the individual as a participant or beneficiary of an employee benefit plan;

using information to perform services on behalf of another person related by common ownership or affiliated by corporate control, except that this sub- paragraph shall not be construed as permitting a person to send solicitations on behalf of another person, if such other person would not be permitted to send the solicitation on its own behalf as a result of the election of the consumer to prohibit solicitations under paragraph (1)(B);

using information in response to a communication initiated by the consumer;

using information in response to solicitations authorized or requested by the consumer; or
if compliance with this section by that person would prevent compliance by that person with any provision of State insurance laws pertaining to unfair discrimination in any State in which the person is lawfully doing business.

No retroactivity. This subsection shall not prohibit the use of information to send a solicitation to a consumer if such information was received prior to the date on which persons are required to comply with regulations implementing this subsection.

Notice for other purposes permissible. A notice or other disclosure under this section may be coordinated and consolidated with any other notice required to be issued under any other provision of law by a person that is subject to this section, and a notice or other disclosure that is equivalent to the notice required by subsection (a), and that is provided by a person described in subsection (a) to a consumer together with disclosures required by any other provision of law, shall satisfy the requirements of subsection (a).

User requirements. Requirements with respect to the use by a person of information received from another person related to it by common ownership or affiliated by corporate control, such as the requirements of this section, constitute requirements with respect to the exchange of information among persons affiliated by common ownership or common corporate control, within the meaning of section 625(b)(2).

Definitions. For purposes of this section, the following definitions shall apply:

The term "pre-existing business relationship" means a relationship between a person, or a person's licensed agent, and a consumer, based on–

a financial contract between a person and a consumer which is in force;

the purchase, rental, or lease by the consumer of that person's goods or services, or a financial transaction (including holding an active account or a policy in force or having another continuing relationship) between the consumer and that person during the 18-month period immediately preceding the date on which the consumer is sent a solicitation covered by this section;

an inquiry or application by the consumer regarding a product or service offered by that person, during the 3-month period immediately preceding the date on which the consumer is sent a solicitation covered by this section; or

any other pre-existing customer relationship defined in the regulations implementing this section.

The term "solicitation" means the marketing of a product or service initiated by a person to a particular consumer that is based on an exchange of information described in subsection (a), and is intended to encourage the consumer to purchase such product or service, but does not include communications that are directed at the general public or determined not to be a solicitation by the regulations prescribed under this section.

§ 625. Relation to State laws [15 U.S.C. § 1681t]

In general. Except as provided in subsections (b) and (c), this title does not annul, alter, affect, or exempt any person subject to the provisions of this title from complying with the laws of any State with respect to the collection, distribution, or use of any information on consumers, or for the prevention or mitigation of identity theft, except to the extent that those laws are inconsistent with any provision of this title, and then only to the extent of the inconsistency.

General exceptions. No requirement or prohibition may be imposed under the laws of any State

with respect to any subject matter regulated under

subsection (c) or (e) of section 604 [§ 1681b], relating to the prescreening of consumer reports;

section 611 [§ 1681i], relating to the time by which a consumer reporting agency must take any action, including the provision of notification to a consumer or other person, in any procedure related to the disputed accuracy of information in a consumer's file, except that this subparagraph shall not apply to any State law in effect on the date of enactment of the Consumer Credit Reporting Reform Act of 1996;

subsections (a) and (b) of section 615 [§ 1681m], relating to the duties of a person who takes any adverse action with respect to a consumer;

section 615(d) [§ 1681m], relating to the duties of persons who use a consumer report of a consumer in connection with any credit or insurance transaction that is not initiated by the consumer and that consists of a firm offer of credit or insurance;

section 605 [§ 1681c], relating to information contained in consumer reports, except that this subparagraph shall not apply to any State law in effect on the date of enactment of the Consumer Credit Reporting Reform Act of 1996;

section 623 [§ 1681s-2], relating to the responsibilities of persons who furnish information to consumer reporting agencies, except that this paragraph shall not apply

with respect to section 54A(a) of chapter 93 of the Massachusetts Annotated Laws (as in effect on the date of enactment of the Consumer Credit Reporting Reform Act of 1996); or

with respect to section 1785.25(a) of the California Civil Code (as in effect on the date of enactment of the Consumer Credit Reporting Reform Act of 1996);

section 609(e), relating to information available to victims under section 609(e);

section 624, relating to the exchange and use of information to make a solicitation for marketing purposes; or

section 615(h), relating to the duties of users of consumer reports to provide notice with respect to terms in certain credit transactions;

with respect to the exchange of information among persons affiliated by common ownership or common corporate control, except that this paragraph shall not apply with respect to subsection (a) or (c)(1) of section 2480e of title 9, Vermont Statutes Annotated (as in effect on the date of enactment of the Consumer Credit Reporting Reform Act of 1996);

with respect to the disclosures required to be made under subsection (c), (d), (e), or (g) of section 609, or subsection (f) of section 609 relating to the disclosure of credit scores for credit granting purposes, except that this paragraph –

shall not apply with respect to sections 1785.10, 1785.16, and 1785.20.2 of the California Civil Code (as in effect on the date of enactment of the Fair and Accurate Credit Transactions Act of 2003) and section 1785.15 through section 1785.15.2 of such Code (as in effect on such date);

shall not apply with respect to sections 5-3-106(2) and 212-14.3-104.3 of the Colorado Revised Statutes (as in effect on the date of enactment of the Fair and Accurate Credit Transactions Act of 2003); and

shall not be construed as limiting, annulling, affecting, or superseding any provision of the laws of any State regulating the use in an insurance activity, or regulating disclosures concerning such use, of a credit-based insurance score of a consumer by any person engaged in the business of insurance;

with respect to the frequency of any disclosure under section 612(a), except that this paragraph shall not apply –

with respect to section 12-14.3-105(1)(d) of the Colorado Revised Statutes (as in effect on the date of enactment of the Fair and Accurate Credit Transactions Act of 2003);

with respect to section 10-1-393(29)(C) of the Georgia Code (as in effect on the date of enactment of the Fair and Accurate Credit Transactions Act of 2003);

with respect to section 1316.2 of title 10 of the Maine Revised Statutes (as in effect on the date of enactment of the Fair and Accurate Credit Transactions Act of 2003);

with respect to sections 14-1209(a)(1) and 14-1209(b)(1)(i) of the Commercial Law Article of the Code of Maryland (as in effect on the date of enactment of the Fair and Accurate Credit Transactions Act of 2003);

with respect to section 59(d) and section 59(e) of chapter 93 of the General Laws of Massachusetts (as in effect on the date of enactment of the Fair and Accurate Credit Transactions Act of 2003);

with respect to section 56:11-37.10(a)(1) of the New Jersey Revised Statutes (as in effect on the date of enactment of the Fair and Accurate Credit Transactions Act of 2003); or

with respect to section 2480c(a)(1) of title 9 of the Vermont Statutes Annotated (as in effect on the date of enactment of the Fair and Accurate Credit Transactions Act of 2003); or

with respect to the conduct required by the specific provisions of –

section 605(g);

section 605A;

section 605B;

section 609(a)(1)(A);

section 612(a);

subsections (e), (f), and (g) of section 615;

section 621(f);

section 623(a)(6); or

section 628.

Definition of firm offer of credit or insurance. Notwithstanding any definition of the term "firm offer of credit or insurance" (or any equivalent term) under the laws of any State, the definition of that term contained in section 603(*l*) [§ 1681a] shall be construed to apply in the enforcement and interpretation of the laws of any State governing consumer reports.

Limitations. Subsections (b) and (c) do not affect any settlement, agreement, or consent judgment between any State Attorney General and any consumer reporting agency in effect on the date of enactment of the Consumer Credit Reporting Reform Act of 1996.

§ 626. Disclosures to FBI for counterintelligence purposes [15 U.S.C. § 1681u]

Identity of financial institutions. Notwithstanding section 604 [§ 1681b] or any other provision of this title, a consumer reporting agency shall furnish to the Federal Bureau of Investigation the names and addresses of all financial institutions (as that term is defined in section 1101 of the Right to Financial Privacy Act of 1978 [12 U.S.C. § 3401]) at which a consumer maintains or has maintained an account, to the extent that information is in the files of the agency, when presented with a written request for that information, signed by the Director of the Federal Bureau of Investigation, or the Director's designee in a position not lower than Deputy Assistant Director at Bureau headquarters or a Special Agent in Charge of a Bureau field office designated by the Director, which certifies compliance with this section. The Director or the Director's designee may make such a certification only if the Director or the Director's designee has determined in writing, that such information is sought for the conduct of an authorized investigation to protect against international terrorism or clandestine intelligence activities, provided that such an investigation of a United States person is not conducted solely upon the basis of activities protected by the first amendment to the Constitution of the United States.

Identifying information. Notwithstanding the provisions of section 604 [§ 1681b] or any other provision of this title, a consumer reporting agency shall furnish identifying information respecting a consumer, limited to name, address, former addresses, places of employment, or former places of employment, to the Federal Bureau of Investigation when presented with a written request, signed by the Director or the Director's designee, which certifies compliance with this subsection. The Director or the Director's designee in a position not lower than Deputy Assistant Director at Bureau headquarters or a Special Agent in Charge of a Bureau field office designated by the Director may make such a certification only if the Director or the Director's designee has determined in writing that such information is sought for the conduct of an authorized investigation to protect against international terrorism or clandestine intelligence activities, provided that such an investigation of a United States person is not conducted solely upon the basis of activities protected by the first amendment to the Constitution of the United States.

Court order for disclosure of consumer reports. Notwithstanding section 604 [§ 1681b] or any other provision of this title, if requested in writing by the Director of the Federal Bureau of Investigation, or a designee of the Director in a position not lower than Deputy Assistant Director at Bureau headquarters or a Special Agent in Charge of a Bureau field office designated by the Director, a court may issue an order ex parte directing a consumer reporting agency to furnish a consumer report to the Federal Bureau of Investigation, upon a showing in camera that the consumer report is sought for the conduct of an authorized investigation to protect against international terrorism or clandestine intelligence activities, provided that such an investigation of a United States person is not conducted solely upon the basis of activities protected by the first amendment to the Constitution of the United States. The terms of an order issued under this subsection shall not disclose that the order is issued for purposes of a counterintelligence investigation.

Confidentiality. No consumer reporting agency or officer, employee, or agent of a consumer reporting agency shall disclose to any person, other than those officers, employees, or agents of a consumer reporting agency necessary to fulfill the requirement to disclose information to the Federal Bureau of Investigation under this section, that the Federal Bureau of Investigation has sought or obtained the identity of financial institutions or a consumer report respecting any consumer under subsection (a), (b), or (c), and no consumer reporting agency or officer, employee, or agent of a consumer reporting agency shall include in any consumer report any information that would indicate that the Federal Bureau of Investigation has sought or obtained such information or a consumer report.

Payment of fees. The Federal Bureau of Investigation shall, subject to the availability of appropriations, pay to the consumer reporting agency assembling or providing report or information in accordance with procedures established under this section a fee for reimbursement for such costs as are reasonably necessary and which have been directly incurred in searching, reproducing, or transporting books, papers, records, or other data required or requested to be produced under this section.

Limit on dissemination. The Federal Bureau of Investigation may not disseminate information obtained pursuant to this section outside of the Federal Bureau of Investigation, except to other Federal agencies as may be necessary for the approval or conduct of a foreign counter intelligence investigation, or, where the information concerns a person subject to the Uniform Code of Military Justice, to appropriate investigative authorities within the military department concerned as may be necessary for the conduct of a joint foreign counter intelligence investigation.

Rules of construction. Nothing in this section shall be construed to prohibit information from being furnished by the Federal Bureau of Investigation pursuant to a subpoena or court order, in connection with a judicial or administrative proceeding to enforce the provisions of this Act. Nothing in this section shall be construed to authorize or permit the withholding of information from the Congress.

Reports to Congress. On a semiannual basis, the Attorney General shall fully inform the Permanent Select Committee on Intelligence and the Committee on Banking, Finance and Urban Affairs of the House of Representatives, and the Select Committee on Intelligence and the Committee on Banking, Housing, and Urban Affairs of the Senate concerning all requests made pursuant to subsections (a), (b), and (c).

Damages. Any agency or department of the United States obtaining or disclosing any consumer reports, records, or information contained therein in violation of this section is liable to the consumer to whom such consumer reports, records, or information relate in an amount equal to the sum of

$100, without regard to the volume of consumer reports, records, or information involved;

any actual damages sustained by the consumer as a result of the disclosure;

if the violation is found to have been willful or intentional, such punitive damages as a court may allow; and

in the case of any successful action to enforce liability under this subsection, the costs of the action, together with reasonable attorney fees, as determined by the court.

Disciplinary actions for violations. If a court determines that any agency or department of the United States has violated any provision of this section and the court finds that the circumstances surrounding the violation raise questions of whether or not an officer or employee of the agency or department acted willfully or intentionally with respect to the violation, the agency or department shall promptly initiate a proceeding to determine whether or not disciplinary action is warranted against the officer or employee who was responsible for the violation.

Good-faith exception. Notwithstanding any other provision of this title, any consumer reporting agency or agent or employee thereof making disclosure of consumer reports or identifying information pursuant to this subsection in good-faith reliance upon a certification of the Federal Bureau of Investigation pursuant to provisions of this section shall not be liable to any person for such disclosure under this title, the constitution of any State, or any law or regulation of any State or any political subdivision of any State.

Limitation of remedies. Notwithstanding any other provision of this title, the remedies and sanctions set forth in this section shall be the only judicial remedies and sanctions for violation of this section.

Injunctive relief. In addition to any other remedy contained in this section, injunctive relief shall be available to require compliance with the procedures of this section. In the event of any successful action under this subsection, costs together with reasonable attorney fees, as determined by the court, may be recovered.

§ 627. Disclosures to governmental agencies for counterterrorism purposes [15 U.S.C.§1681v]

Disclosure. Notwithstanding section 604 or any other provision of this title, a consumer reporting agency shall furnish a consumer report of a consumer and all other information in a consumer's file to a government agency authorized to conduct investigations of, or intelligence or counterintelligence activities or analysis related to, international terrorism when presented with a written certification by such government agency that such information is necessary for the agency's conduct or such investigation, activity or analysis.

Form of certification. The certification described in subsection (a) shall be signed by a supervisory official designated by the head of a Federal agency or an officer of a Federal agency whose appointment to office is required to be made by the President, by and with the advice and consent of the Senate.

Confidentiality. No consumer reporting agency, or officer, employee, or agent of such consumer reporting agency, shall disclose to any person, or specify in any consumer report, that a government agency has sought or obtained access to information under subsection (a).

Rule of construction. Nothing in section 626 shall be construed to limit the authority of the Director of the Federal Bureau of Investigation under this section.

Safe harbor. Notwithstanding any other provision of this title, any consumer reporting agency or agent or employee thereof making disclosure of consumer reports or other information pursuant to this section in good-faith reliance upon a certification of a governmental agency pursuant to the provisions of this section shall not be liable to any person for such disclosure under this subchapter, the constitution of any State, or any law or regulation of any State or any political subdivision of any State.

§ 628. Disposal of records [15 U.S.C. §1681w]
See also 16 CFR Part 682
69 Fed. Reg. 68690 (11/24/04)

Regulations
In general. The Federal Trade Commission, the Securities and Exchange Commission, the Commodity Futures Trading Commission, the Federal banking agencies, and the National Credit Union Administration, with respect to the entities that are subject to their respective enforcement authority under section 621, and in coordination as de- scribed in paragraph (2), shall issue final regulations requiring any person that maintains or otherwise possesses consumer information, or any compilation of consumer information, derived from consumer reports for a business purpose to properly dispose of any such information or compilation.
Coordination. Each agency required to prescribe regulations under paragraph (1) shall –

consult and coordinate with each other such agency so that, to the extent possible, the regulations prescribed by each such agency are consistent and comparable with the regulations by each such other agency; and

ensure that such regulations are consistent with the requirements and regulations issued pursuant to Public Law 106-102 and other provisions of Federal law.

Exemption authority. In issuing regulations under this section, the agencies identified in paragraph (1) may exempt any person or class of persons from application of those regulations, as such agency deems appropriate to carry out the purpose of this section.

Rule of construction. Nothing in this section shall be construed –

to require a person to maintain or destroy any record pertaining to a consumer that is not imposed under other law; or

to alter or affect any requirement imposed under any other provision of law to maintain or destroy such a record.

§629. Corporate and technological circumvention prohibited [15 U.S.C.§1681x]

The Bureau shall prescribe regulations, to become effective not later than 90 days after the date of enactment of this section, to prevent a consumer reporting agency from circumventing or evading treatment as a consumer reporting agency described in section 603(p) for purposes of this title, including--

by means of a corporate reorganization or restructuring, including a merger, acquisition, dissolution, divestiture, or asset sale of a consumer reporting agency; or

by maintaining or merging public record and credit account information in a manner that is substantially equivalent to that described in paragraphs (1) and (2) of section 603(p), in the manner described in section 603(p).

See also 16 CFR Part 611
69 Fed. Reg. 8531 (02/24/04)
69 Fed. Reg. 29061 (05/20/04)

IN THE CIRCUIT COURT
FOURTH JUDICIALCIRCUIT IN
AND FOR DUVAL COUNTY
FLORIDA

MY FIRST COMPLAINT

James Watson

Plaintiff

Equifax P.O. Box 105518 Atlanta, GA 30348
Experian P.O. Box 9701 Allen, TX 75013
Transunion PO Box 2000Chester, PA 19022

Defendants

FIRST COMPLAINT FILED

JURY TRIAL DEMANDED

1. On or about June of 2011 all three Credit reporting agencies Equifax, Experian, and Transunion created a duplicate of all Plaintiff credit accounts on files in Defendants digital computer system store on Plaintiff.

2. As results of Defendants inaccuracies duplications with regard to Plaintiff credit report, Defendants were in violation of FCRA rules.

3. This action by Defendants results in Cause of action of defamation, and negligence which cause injury to Plaintiff credit.

4. Plaintiff joinder on this same Complaint a negligent and defamation cause of action by Experian on or about Nov.2011 when Defendant (Experian) negligently failed to report an accurate credit report of Plaintiff to ____when Plaintiff applied for a personal loan.

   Wherefore, Plaintiff prays for Judgment against Defendants in the sum of $72,000 plus cost and interest on all three Defendants on cause of duplicating Plaintiff credit report and $50,000 for defamation and negligent cause of action by Experian pertained to the cause by Experian to Plaintiff.

If the Defendants would have settled my lawsuit when I filed the initial Complaint, I wouldn't be able to present to you all these Pleadings. because if I knew about all these Pleadings, it would have put me in a better demand position to litigate for a better settlement. So everyone that purchases this book is going to be better prepared to litigate in their case in Court especially under the FCRA Act.

IN THE CIRCUIT COURT, FOURTH
JUDICIAL CIRCUIT, IN AND FOR
DUVAL COUNTY, FLORIDA

CIVIL ACTION NO.:

DIVISION:

JIM FULLER
Clerk of the Circuit Court

                                    Plaintiff(s)

vs.

                                    Defendant(s)

SUMMONS

THE STATE OF FLORIDA:

To Each Sheriff of the State:

    YOU ARE COMMANDED to serve this summons and a copy of the complaint or petition in this action on defendant(s)

    Each defendant is required to serve written defenses to the complaint or petition on plaintiff's attorney, whose name and address is

within 20 days after service of this summons on that defendant, exclusive of the day of service, and to file the original of the defenses with the clerk of this court either before service on plaintiffs attorney or immediately thereafter. If a defendant fails to do so, a default will be entered against that defendant for the relief demanded 'in the complaint or petition.

                    WJTNESS my hand and the seat of this Court on

                                    JIM FULLER
                                    CLERK OF THE CIRCUIT COURT

                                    By_____
                                            Deputy Clerk_

A copy of the Summon along with a copy of the complaint must be served on each Defendant or Defendants in your case either by a private company that service Complaints or the local sheriff office in the area where Defendant is located, you as the Plaintiff will incur the cost of this process of servicing or serving the Defendant.

IN THE CIRCUIT COURT FOURTH
JUDICIAL CIRCUIT IN AND FOR
DUVAL COUNTY FLORIDA

JAMES L. WATSON

Plaintiff

VS

EQUIFAX: EXPERIAN: AND TRANSUNION

Defendants

COPY OF CERTIFICATE OF INDIGENCY

- I, JIM FULLER, Clerk of the Circuit and County Courts, Duval County, Florida, do
  hereby certify that_____ has filed an affidavit of indigence in this
  case in accordance with Section 57.081 (I), Florida Statutes, and it appears that said
  affidavit is sufficient and that the petitioner, is entitled to receive the services of the
  courts, sheriff, and clerks with respect to this proceeding.
  witness my hand and seal at Jacksonville, Florida, this <u>12</u> day of <u>APR. 2012</u>

If you can't afford to pay for filing the Complaint in Court you may be able
to qualify for indigency under the term, "IN FORMA PAUPERIS"
So get an application from Clerk of the Court and complete it before paying
for filing or file it during the filing process.

THE HISTORY OF CRAs

As one of the first federal law to regulate the use of personal information by private businesses.

Retail Credit Co. was first started in 1899 and grew by buying up smaller CRA's which allowed it to expand into selling reports to insurers and employers. Around the 1960 there where controversies because their reports were sometimes used to deny services and opportunities, where consumers weren't allowed to see their reports for various reasons.

The industry was becoming so abusive such as hiring investigators to obtain negative information on person they were investigating. Such information included lifestyle, sexual orientation, marital status, drinking habitats, etc. CRA's were also keeping outdated records, in some case providing Law enforcement with data records, as well as providing these records to unauthorized persons.

As I stated by 1960's Public exposure of CRA's wrong doing resulted in Representative Leonor Sullivan and Senator William Proxmire sponsoring and passage of a the FCRA of 1970. Over the next ten years Senator William Proxmire attempted to broaden FCRA. Before the FCRA could take effect CRA's lawsuits were being initiated against them for various violations of the FCRA Act.

In 1996 there were a comprehensive amendment to the FCRA in the Consumer Credit Reporting Reform Act (P.L. 104-208), the amendment contained many improvements to the FCRA but it also included provisions such as affiliate sharing of credit reports, prescreening of credit reports, and limited preemption of stronger state laws on credit.

The FCRA was also revisited by the 108th Congress in 2003, in which this congress enacted the Fair and Accurate Credit Transaction Act of 2003 known as (FACTA). National Specialty Credit Reporting Agencies such as—Insurance, Landlord-tenant, employment agencies are required to provide one free annual credit report upon your request.

Credit Headers came into importance when the FTC change the definition of a credit report when they settle a case with Experian. The FTC allows the CRA's to treat headers as "above the line" information and to sell it with no legal protection for the consumer individual.

The average cost for an attorney to represent your case in Court is roughly $23,000 this includes attorney fee and cost.

Remember, "Cash is King and credit is Queen and the marriage is good for commercial businesses as well as personal businesses" by James Watson.

Because credit reports can include sensitive personal information and because they are used to evaluate the ability to participate in so many different activities in modern day life, they are subject to regulations that follow a framework of Fair Information Practices.

MORE IMPORTANT INFORMATION TO PROTECT YOUR RIGHTS

The FCRA establishes rights and responsibilities for "consumers," "furnishers," and "users" of credit reports:

Consumers are individuals.

Furnishers are entities that send information to CRAs regarding creditworthiness in the normal course of business.

Users of credit reports are entities that request a report to evaluate a consumer for some purpose.

What qualifies as a Credit Reporting Agency (CRA)?

A consumer reporting agency (CRA) is an entity that assembles and sells credit information and financial information about individuals.

There are three national CRAs in the United States: Experian (formerly TRW), Trans Union, and Equifax (formerly Retail Credit Co.). There are also many smaller credit reporting agencies that usually concentrate on reporting on individuals living in certain regions of the country.

Inspection bureaus, companies that sell information to insurance companies and assist in performing background checks, often are considered CRAs as well. Tenant screening and check approval companies are also considered CRAs.

Depending on the nature of the operation, other companies can be considered CRAs. Courts have held that private investigators, detective agencies, collection agencies, and even college placement offices can be CRAs under the law.

Consumer Credit Reports and Investigative Consumer Reports (ICRs)

Consumer credit reports contain information on financial accounts, and include credit card balances and mortgage information. Credit reports are used for evaluating eligibility for credit, insurance, employment, and tenancy; the ability to pay child support; professional licensing (for instance, to become an attorney); or for any purpose that a consumer approves.

A consumer credit report will contain basic identifying information (name, address, previous address, Social Security Number, marital status, employment information, number of children) along with:

Financial information: Estimated income, employment, bank accounts, value of car and home.

Public records information: Such as arrests, bankruptcies, and tax liens.

Tradelines: Credit accounts and their status. This will also include the data subject's payment habits on credit accounts.

Collection Items: Whether the data subject has unpaid or disputed bills.

Current Employment and employment history.

Requests for the credit report: The number of requests for the data subject's report and the identity of the requestors.

Narrative information: A statement by the data subject or by the furnisher regarding disputed items on the credit report.

Health information.

Certain information about consumers are excluded from the definition of "credit report." This includes "transaction and experience" information, that is, records of purchases of goods and services by the consumer. Additionally, corporations may share credit report information among affiliates as long as

The FACTA provides further preemptions for disclosure of credit scores (subject to certain exceptions for existing California and Colorado statutes). Finally, free credit reports are also preemptively regulated by the FACTA (except for existing statutes in CO, GA, ME, MA, NJ, and VA).

The extent to which the FACTA preempts state identity theft laws remains unclear. The provisions appear to allow states to enact stronger laws to protect their citizens from identity theft. But certain areas of identity theft regulation are then specifically excepted, thus again providing preemption. These include areas such truncation of credit/debit card numbers on electronic receipts and requiring CRAs to block identity-theft related information.

Right to Correct Inaccurate Information

Individuals may dispute inaccurate information that appears in a credit report. CRAs are required to investigate disputes and provide a report back to the consumer. If the CRA cannot resolve the dispute, the individual can add a statement to the credit report. Inaccurate or unverifiable information must be removed within 30 days of notice of dispute. The Fair and Accurate Credit Transactions Act of 2003 (FACTA) -- amendments to the FCRA -- requires that investigation be "reasonable," although this standard is much lower than the requirements in creating the credit report which specify that there be "reasonable procedures to assure maximum possible accuracy."

Individuals may also dispute inaccurate information with the furnisher. If an individual disputes inaccurate information with a furnisher, that furnisher cannot report the information to a CRA without also including a notice of the dispute. If a furnisher determines that the information is inaccurate, it must block that information from being re-reported to CRAs -- a common and major problem in the credit reporting industry.

The FCRA limits the length of time some information can appear in a consumer report. For instance, bankruptcies must be removed from the report after 10 years. Civil suits, civil judgments, paid tax liens, accounts placed for collection, and records of arrest can only appear for 7 years. Records of criminal convictions can remain on the report indefinitely.

The FACTA provides consumers with additional rights to accurate credit information furnishing and reporting. The agencies that oversee FCRA enforcement will issue guidelines and regulations for credit information furnishers to ensure information accuracy and integrity.

Consumers may now directly dispute fraudulent transactions with the furnisher, the result of another FACTA amendment. Previously, a consumer was forced to pursue the dispute only with the CRA. The furnisher must investigate the disputed transactions and inform the consumer of the results. In exchange for this new right, the credit reporting industry successfully lobbied for a provision requiring that consumers be the party to initiate the dispute, disallowing "credit repair" agencies from disputing the transactions on behalf of the consumer. Additionally, the standard applied to furnishers in supplying credit information has been raised. Previously the FCRA required a furnisher to not report information that it "knows or consciously avoids knowing that the information is inaccurate." On the "other end," when a CRA determines that transaction information is fraudulent, it must notify the furnisher that the information has been modified or deleted.

Before the 2003 FACTA amendments, one of the consumers' only opportunities to discover the existence of negative information on their credit reports was when they were subjected to an adverse credit decision by a credit granting company. Now, when a furnisher reports negative information, it must notify the consumer within thirty days using a thirty-word maximum notice to be designed by the Federal Reserve Board. Unfortunately, it appears that furnishers will be able to avoid meaningful notices because they can insert the notice with the standard contract documentation.

Accountability

The FCRA affords individuals a private right of action that can be pursued in federal or state court against CRAs, users of credit reports, and furnishers. In certain circumstances, individuals can obtain attorney's fees, court costs, and punitive damages. Additionally, the FTC can enforce provisions of the act. Criminal penalties can be brought against those who knowingly and willfully obtain a consumer report under false pretenses.

The "qualified immunity provision" limits the situations in which a consumer can pursue legal action against a CRA. For the certain types of disclosures -- disclosures to consumers, condition and form of disclosure to consumers, requirements on users, and disclosure by user after taking adverse action against a consumer -- a consumer may only bring suit if the CRA acted with "malice or willful intent to injure." The Fair and Accurate Credit Transactions Act of 2003 (FACTA) amendments to the FCRA expanded the enumerated list of types of disclosure for which CRA liability is limited in this way. These new types of disclosures, which if violated are limited by the qualified immunity, include, among others: the requirement that agencies withhold the last five SSN digits when requested by a consumer; allowing identity theft victims to obtain business transaction information from businesses that have done business with the thief; and requiring mortgage lenders to disclose credit scores to loan applicants.

Furthermore, FACTA incorporated the new furnisher responsibilities into the qualified immunity provisions. These include, for example, requiring financial institutions to notify customers that they are furnishing negative information to the CRAs about that customer -- into the qualified immunity provision. Other liability provisions were also limited by FACTA with respect to other new responsibilities established by the amendments. One such limitation prevents consumers from forcing a CRA to issue red flag guidelines and regulations.

The ability of states to pursue legal action against a CRA was also limited by the FACTA amendments. Even for major violations -- failure to provide accurate information, failure to comply with guidelines to protect accuracy and integrity of consumer information, etc. -- states must first obtain an injunction against the CRA. Only then may it seek damages for violations of the FCRA.

Identity Theft

The FACTA added significant identity theft provisions to the FCRA, but most of these provisions are remedial and will not prevent identity theft.

These include the ability to issue one-call fraud alerts, extended fraud alerts and active military duty alerts. Additionally, new responsibilities are placed on users of credit reports (e.g. a lending company). These include red-flag guidelines, providing identity theft victims with business transaction information, and protecting certain consumer information.

All fraud alerts are now "one-call." If an agency receives a request for a fraud alert, it must notify the other CRAs also. The fraud alert is also communicated to users requesting the consumer's credit report. Additionally, the CRA must notify the consumer of her right to a free credit report which the FACTA requires to be delivered within three days of request. "Initial fraud alerts" last for ninety days.

A fraud alert indicates that consumer does authorize new credit, an additional card on an existing account, or increases in the credit limit of an existing account. A consumer may provide a telephone contact number in which case a credit user must verify the consumer's identity over the phone on that number. An exception to that rule allows a credit user to "take reasonable steps" instead of calling the consumer for an "initial fraud alert" or an "active military duty alert."

If the consumer has filed a report with a law enforcement agency, she may request an "extended fraud alert" that lasts for seven years. CRAs must also exclude the consumer from prescreening lists for five years. Finally, it must notify the consumer of her right to two free credit reports within twelve months of the fraud alert request. Deployed military personnel can request an "active military duty alert" that remains active for twelve months.

The FACTA requires the FTC, the National Credit Union Administration, and other certain banking agencies to jointly issue regulations requiring creditors to establish "reasonable policies and procedures" for implementing.

NOTICES TO FURNISHERS OF INFORMATION:
OBLIGATIONS OF FURNISHERS UNDER THE FCRA

The federal Fair Credit Reporting Act ("FCRA"), as amended, imposes responsibilities on all persons who furnish information to consumer reporting agencies ("CRAs"). These responsibilities are found in Section 623 of the FCRA. State law may impose additional requirements. All furnishers of information to CRAs should become familiar with the law and may want to consult with their counsel to ensure that they are in compliance. The FCRA, 15 U.S.C. §§ 1681-1681u, is set forth in full at the Federal Trade Commission's Internet web site *(http://www.ftc.gov)*. Section 623 imposes the following duties:

General Prohibition on Reporting Inaccurate Information:

The FCRA prohibits information furnishers from providing information to a consumer reporting agency ("CRA") that they know (or consciously avoid knowing) is inaccurate. However, the furnisher is not subject to this general prohibition if it clearly and conspicuously specifies an address to which consumers may write to notify the furnisher that certain information is inaccurate. *Sections 623(a)(1)(A) and (a)(1)(C)*

Duty to Correct and Update Information:

If at any time a person who regularly and in the ordinary course of business furnishes information to one or more CRAs determines that the information provided is not complete or accurate, the furnisher must provide complete and accurate information to the CRA. In addition, the furnisher must notify all CRAs that received the information of any corrections, and must thereafter report only the complete and accurate information. *Section 623(a)(2)*

Duties After Notice of Dispute from Consumer:

If a consumer notifies a furnisher, at an address specified by the furnisher for such notices, that specific information is inaccurate, and the information is in fact inaccurate, the furnisher must thereafter report the correct information to CRAs. *Section 623(a)(1)(B)*

If a consumer notifies a furnisher that the consumer disputes the completeness or accuracy of any information reported by the furnisher, the furnisher may not subsequently report that information to a CRA without providing notice of the dispute. *Section 623(a)(3)*

Duties After Notice of Dispute from Consumer Reporting Agency:

If a CRA notifies a furnisher that a consumer disputes the completeness or accuracy of information provided by the furnisher, the furnisher has a duty to follow certain procedures. The furnisher must:

• Conduct an investigation and review all relevant information provided by the CRA, including information given to the CRA by the consumer. *Sections 623(b) (1)(A) and (b)(1)(B)*

• Report the results to the CRA, and, if the investigation establishes that the information was, in fact, incomplete or inaccurate, report the results to all CRAs to which the furnisher provided the information that compile and maintain files on a nationwide basis. *Sections 623(b)(1)(C) and (b)(1)(D)*

• Complete the above within 30 days from the date the CRA receives the dispute (or 45 days, if the consumer later provides relevant additional information to the   CRA). *Section 623(b)(2)*

Duty to Report Voluntary Closing of Credit Accounts:

If a consumer voluntarily closes a credit account, any person who regularly and in the ordinary course of business furnishes information to one or more CRAs must report this fact when it provides information to CRAs for the time period in which the account was closed. *Section 623(a)(4)*

Duty to Report Dates of Delinquencies:

If a furnisher reports information concerning a delinquent account placed for collection, charged to profit or loss, or subject to any similar action, the furnisher must, within 90 days after reporting the information, provide the CRA with the month and the year of the commencement of the delinquency that immediately preceded the action, so that the agency will know how long to keep the information in the consumer's file. *Section 623(a)(5)*

NOTICE TO USERS OF CONSUMER REPORTS:
OBLIGATIONS OF USERS UNDER THE FCRA

The federal Fair Credit Reporting Act (FCRA) requires that this notice be provided to inform users of consumer reports of their legal obligations. State law may impose additional requirements. This first section of this summary sets forth the responsibilities imposed by the FCRA on all users of consumer reports. The subsequent sections discuss the duties of users of reports that contain specific types of information, or that are used for certain purposes, and the legal consequences of violations. The FCRA, 15 U.S.C. §§ 1681-1681u, is set forth in full at the Federal Trade Commission's Internet web site *(http://www.ftc.gov)*.

I.   OBLIGATIONS OF ALL USERS OF CONSUMER REPORTS
A.   Users Must Have a Permissible Purpose

Congress has limited the use of consumer reports to protect consumers' privacy. All users must have a permissible purpose under the FCRA to obtain a consumer report. Section 604 of the FCRA contains a list of the permissible purposes under the law. These are:

·   As ordered by a court or a federal grand jury subpoena. *Section 604(a)(1)* As instructed by the consumer in writing. *Section 604(a)(2)*

·   For the extension of credit as a result of an application from a consumer, or the review or collection of a consumer's account. *Section 604(a)(3)(A)* For employment purposes, including hiring and promotion decisions,
       where the consumer has given written permission. *Sections 604(a)*
       (3)(B) and 604(b)
For the underwriting of insurance as a result of an application from a
       consumer. *Section 604(a)(3)(C)*

·   When there is a legitimate business need, in connection with a business transaction that is initiated by the consumer. *Section 604(a)(3)(F)(i)*

·   To review a consumer's account to determine whether the consumer continues to meet the terms of the account. *Section 604(a)(3)(F)(ii)*

·   To determine a consumer's eligibility for a license or other benefit granted by a governmental instrumentality required by law to consider an applicant's financial responsibility or status. *Section 604(a)(3)(D)*

For use by a potential investor or servicer, or current insurer, in a valuation or assessment of the credit or repayment risks associated with an existing credit obligation. *Section 604(a)(3)(E)*

       · For use by state and local officials in connection with the determination of child support payments, or modifications and enforcement thereof. *Sections 604(a)(4) and 604(a)(5)*

In addition, creditors and insurers may obtain certain consumer report information for the purpose of making unsolicited offers of credit or insurance. The particular obligations of users of this "prescreened" information are described in Section V below.

B.   **Users Must Provide Certifications**

Section 604(f) of the FCRA prohibits any person from obtaining a consumer report from a consumer reporting agency (CRA) unless the person has certified to the CRA (by a general or specific certification, as appropriate) the permissible purpose(s) for which the report is being obtained and certifies that the report will not be used for any other purpose.

C.   **Users Must Notify Consumers When Adverse Actions Are Taken**

The term "adverse action" is defined very broadly by Section 603 of the FCRA. "Adverse actions" include all business, credit, and employment actions affecting consumers that can be considered to have a negative impact -- such as unfavorably changing credit or contract terms or conditions, denying or canceling credit or insurance, offering credit on less favorable terms than requested, or denying employment or promotion.

1.   **Adverse Actions Based on Information Obtained from a CRA**

If a user takes any type of adverse action that is based at least in part on information contained in a consumer report, the user is required by Section 615(a) of the FCRA to notify the consumer. The notification may be done in writing, orally, or by electronic means. It must include the following: The name, address, and telephone number of the CRA (including a toll-free telephone number, if it is a nationwide CRA) that provided the report. A statement that the CRA did not make the adverse decision and is not able to explain why the decision was made. A statement setting forth the consumer's right to obtain a free disclosure of the consumer's file from the CRA if the consumer requests the report within 60 days. A statement setting forth the consumer's right to dispute directly with the CRA the accuracy or completeness of any information provided by the CRA.

2.   **Adverse Actions Based on Information Obtained from Third Parties Who Are Not Consumer Reporting Agencies?**

If a person denies (or increases the charge for) credit for personal, family, or household purposes based either wholly or partly upon information from a person other than a CRA, and the information is the type of consumer information covered by the FCRA, Section 615(b)(1) of the FCRA requires that the user clearly and accurately disclose to the consumer his or her right to obtain disclosure of the nature of the information that was relied upon by making a written request within

60 days of notification. The user must provide the disclosure within a reasonable period of time following the consumer's written request.

3.   Adverse Actions Based on Information Obtained from Affiliates

If a person takes an adverse action involving insurance, employment, or a credit transaction initiated by the consumer, based on information of the type covered by the FCRA, and this information was obtained from an entity affiliated with the user of the information by common ownership or control, Section 615(b)(2) requires the user to notify the consumer of the adverse action. The notification must inform the consumer that he or she may obtain a disclosure of the nature of the information relied upon by making a written request within 60 days of receiving the adverse action notice. If the consumer makes such a request, the user must disclose the nature of the information not later than 30 days after receiving the request. (Information that is obtained directly from an affiliated entity relating solely to its transactions or experiences with the consumer, and information from a consumer report obtained from an affiliate are not covered by Section 615(b)(2).)

II.   OBLIGATIONS OF USERS WHEN CONSUMER REPORTS ARE OBTAINED   FOR EMPLOYMENT PURPOSES

If information from a CRA is used for employment purposes, the user has specific duties, which are set forth in Section 604(b) of the FCRA. The user must:

·   Make a clear and conspicuous written disclosure to the consumer before the report is obtained, in a document that consists solely of the disclosure, that a consumer report may be obtained.

·   Obtain prior written authorization from the consumer.

·   Certify to the CRA that the above steps have been followed, that the information being obtained will not be used in violation of any federal or state equal opportunity law or regulation, and that, if any adverse action is to be taken based on the consumer report, a copy of the report and a summary of the consumer's rights will be provided to the consumer.

·   Before taking an adverse action, provide a copy of the report to the consumer as well as the summary of the consumer's rights. (The user should receive this summary from the CRA, because Section 604(b)(1)(B) of the FCRA requires CRAs to provide a copy of the summary with each consumer report obtained for employment purposes.)

III. OBLIGATIONS OF USERS OF INVESTIGATIVE CONSUMER REPORTS

Investigative consumer reports are a special type of consumer report in which information about a consumer's character, general reputation, personal characteristics, and mode of living is obtained through personal interviews. Consumers who are the subjects of such reports are given special rights under the FCRA. If a user intends to obtain an investigative consumer report, Section 606 of the FCRA requires the following:

·   The user must disclose to the consumer that an investigative

consumer report may be obtained. This must be done in a written disclosure that is mailed, or otherwise delivered, to the consumer not later than three days after the date on which the report was first requested. The disclosure must include a statement informing the consumer of his or her right to request additional disclosures of the nature and scope of the investigation as described below, and must include the summary of consumer rights required by Section 609 of the

FCRA. (The user should be able to obtain a copy of the notice of consumer rights from the CRA that provided the consumer report.)

· The user must certify to the CRA that the disclosures set forth above have been made and that the user will make the disclosure described below.

· Upon the written request of a consumer made within a reasonable period of time after the disclosures required above, the user must make a complete disclosure of the nature and scope of the investigation that was requested. This must be made in a written statement that is mailed, or otherwise delivered, to the consumer no later than five days after the date on which the request was received from the consumer or the report was first requested, whichever is later in time.

IV.   OBLIGATIONS OF USERS OF CONSUMER REPORTS CONTAINING MEDICAL INFORMATION

Section 604(g) of the FCRA prohibits consumer reporting agencies from providing consumer reports that contain medical information for employment purposes, or in connection with credit or insurance transactions, without the specific prior consent of the consumer who is the subject of the report. In the case of medical information being sought for employment purposes, the consumer must explicitly consent to the release of the medical information in addition to authorizing the obtaining of a consumer report generally.

V.   OBLIGATIONS OF USERS OF "PRESCREENED" LISTS

The FCRA permits creditors and insurers to obtain limited consumer report information for use in connection with unsolicited offers of credit or insurance under certain circumstances. *Sections 603(l), 604(c), 604(e), and 615(d)* This practice is known as "prescreening" and typically involves obtaining a list of consumers from a CRA who meet certain pre-established criteria. If any person intends to use prescreened lists, that person must (1) before the offer is made, establish the criteria that will be relied upon to make the offer and to grant credit or insurance, and (2) maintain such criteria on file for a three-year period beginning on the date on which the offer is made to each consumer. In addition, any user must provide with each written solicitation a clear and conspicuous statement that:

· Information contained in the consumer's CRA file was used in connection with the transaction.

· The consumer received the offer because he or she satisfied the criteria for credit worthiness or insurability used to screen for the offer.

· Credit or insurance may not be extended if, after the consumer responds, it is determined that the consumer does not meet the criteria used for screening or any applicable criteria bearing on credit worthiness or insurability, or the consumer does not furnish required collateral.

· The consumer may prohibit the use of information in his or her file in connection with future prescreened offers of credit or insurance by contacting the notification system established by the CRA that provided the report. This statement must include the address and toll-free telephone number of the appropriate notification system.

VI.   OBLIGATIONS OF RESELLERS

Section 607(e) of the FCRA requires any person who obtains a consumer report for resale to take the following steps:

· Disclose the identity of the end-user to the source CRA.

Identify to the source CRA each permissible purpose for which the report will be furnished to the end-user. Establish and follow reasonable procedures to ensure that reports are resold only for permissible purposes, including procedures to obtain: (1) the identity of all end-users; (2) certifications from all users of each purpose for which reports will be used; and (3) certifications that reports will not be used for any purpose other than the purpose(s) specified to the reseller. Resellers must make reasonable efforts to verify this information before selling the report.

VII.   LIABILITY FOR VIOLATIONS OF THE FCRA

Failure to comply with the FCRA can result in state or federal enforcement actions, as well as private lawsuits. *Sections 616, 617, and 621* In addition, any person who knowingly and willfully obtains a consumer report under false pretenses may face criminal prosecution. *Section 619*

became effective in March 1978. was designed to eliminate abusive, deceptive. and unfair debt collection practices. It also protects reputable debt collectors from unfair competition and encourages consistent state action to protect consumers from abuses in debt collection.

The FDCPA applies only to the collection of debt incurred by a consumer primarily for personal, family, or household purposes. It does not apply to the collection of corporate debt or debt owed for business or agricultural purposes.

The FDCPA defines a *debt collector* as any person who regularly collects, or attempts to collect, consumer debts for another person or institution or uses some name other than its own when collecting its own consumer debts. The definition includes, for example. an institution that regularly collects debts for an unrelated institution, such as an institution that, under a reciprocal service arrangement, solicits the help of another in collecting a defaulted debt from a customer who has moved.

An institution is not considered a debt collector under the FDCPA when it collects Another institution's debts in isolated instances

Its own debts under its own name

Debts it originated and then sold but continues to service (for example, mortgage and student loans)

Debts that were not in default when they were obtained

Debts that were obtained as security for a commercial credit transaction (for example, accounts receivable financing)

Debts incidental to a bona fide fiduciary relation• ship or escrow arrangement (for example, a debt held in the institution's trust department or mortgage loan escrow for taxes and insurance)

Debts, regularly, for other institutions to which it is related by common ownership or corporate control

Other debt collectors that are not covered by the FDCPA include

Officers or employees of an institution who collect debts owed to the institution in the institution's name

Legal-process servers

For communications with a consumer or third party m connection with the collection of a debt, the term *consumer* is defined to include the borrower's spouse. parent (if the borrower is a minor). guardian, executor, or administrator.

A debt collector may not communicate with a consumer at any unusual time (generally before 8:00 a.m. or after 9:00 p.m. in the consumer's time zone) or at any place that is inconvenient to the consumer, unless the consumer or a court of competent jurisdiction has given permission for such contacts. A debt collector may not contact the consumer at his or her place of employment if the collector has reason to believe the employer prohibits such communications.
If the debt collector knows that the consumer has retained an attorney to handle the debt and can easily ascertain the attorney's name and address. all contacts must be with that attorney. unless the attorney is unresponsive or agrees to allow direct communication with the consumer.

Ceasing Communication with Consumers
When a consumer refuses, in writing, to pay a debt or requests that the debt collector cease further communication, the collector must cease all further communication, except to advise the consumer that
The collection effort is being stopped

Certain specified remedies ordinarily invoked may be pursued or, if appropriate. That a specific remedy will be pursued
Mailed notices from the consumer are official when they are received by the debt collector

Communicating with Third Parties
The only third parties that a debt collector may contact when trying to collect a debt are he consumer
The consumer's attorney
A consumer reporting agency (if permitted by local law)
The creditor
The creditor's attorney
The debt collector's attorney
The consumer or a court of competent jurisdiction may, however, give the debt collector specific permission to contact other third parties. In addition, a debt collector who is unable to locate a consumer may ask a third party *for* the consumer's home address, telephone number, and place of employment (location information). The debt collector must give his or her name and must state that he or she is confirming or correcting information about the consumer's location. Unless specifically asked, the debt collector may not name the collection firm or agency or reveal that the consumer owes any debt.
No third party may be contacted more than once unless the collector believes that the information from the first contact was wrong or incomplete and that the third party has since received better Information, or unless the third party specifically requests additional contact.

Contact with any third party by postcard. letter, or telegram is allowed only if the envelope or content of the communication does not indicate the nature of the collector's business.

A debt collector must provide the consumer with certain basic information. If that information was not in the initial communication and if the consumer has not paid the debt five days after the initial communication, all of the following information must be sent to the consumer in written form:

The amount of the debt

The name of the creditor to whom the debt is owed

Notice that the consumer has thirty days to dispute the debt before it is

assumed to be valid

Notice that upon such written dispute, the debt collector will send the consumer a verification of the debt or a copy of any Judgment

If the original creditor is different from the current creditor, notice that if the consumer makes a written request for the name and address of the original creditor within the thirty-day period, the debt collector will provide that information

If, within the thirty-day period. the consumer disputes in writing any portion of the debt or requests the name and address of the original creditor, the collector must stop all collection efforts until he or she mails the consumer a copy of a judgment or verification of the debt, or the name and address of the original creditor, as applicable.

A debt collector, in collecting a debt, may not harass, oppress. or abuse any person. Specifically, a debt collector may not

Use *or* threaten to use violence or other criminal means to harm the physical person. reputation, *or* property of any person

Use obscene, profane, or other language that abuses the hearer or *reader*

Publish a list of consumers who allegedly refuse to pay debts, except to a consumer reporting agency *or* to persons meeting the requirements of section 603(f) or 604(3) of the FDCPA

Advertise a debt for sale to coerce payment

Annoy, abuse, or harass persons by repeatedly calling their telephone number *or* allowing their telephone to ring continually

Make telephone calls without properly identifying himself or herself, except as allowed to obtain location information

A debt collector, in collecting a debt, may not use any false, deceptive, or misleading representation. Specifically, a debt collector may not

Falsely represent or imply that he or she is vouched for. bonded by, or affiliated with the United States or any state, including the use of any badge, uniform. or similar identification

Falsely represent the character. amount, or legal status of the debt. or of any services rendered. or information he or she may receive or collecting the debt

Falsely represent *or* imply that he *or* she an attorney or that communications are, from an attorney threaten to take any action that is not legal or intended

Falsely represent or imply that nonpayment of any debt will result in the arrest or imprisonment of any person or the seizure, garnishment. attachment, or sale of any property or wages of any person. unless such action is lawful and intended by the debt collector or creditor

Falsely represent or imply that the sale, referral, or other transfer of the debt will cause the consumer to lose a claim or a defense to payment, or become subject to any practice prohibited by the FDCPA

Falsely represent or imply that the consumer committed a crime or other conduct to disgrace the consumer Communicate, or threaten to communicate, false credit information or information that should be known to be false.

THE SUPREME COURT RULING ON TWOMBLY

One of the most important aspect of Twombly was the Court's decision to retire Conley v. Gibson no set of facts language. Under Conley, courts at the 12 (b) (6) stage merely took a quick look at the complaint to determine **if the plaintiff could prove some set of facts entitling him to relief.** But the Court viewed this standard as overly permissive, as it permitted a plaintiff to proceed to discovery on a frivolous claim so long as his pleading did not foreclose the possibility of establishing some set of undisclosed facts to support recovery.

The Supreme Court define "legal conclusions" as "formulaic recitations of the elements" of the plaintiff legal claim and urged district Courts to discard those allegations as conclusory. Iqbal like Twombly is fundamentally a Rule 8 decision that is now the most cited cases in the U.S. Court system.

Twombly introduced the concept of plausibility as the dividing line between complaints that do and do not state a claim, in an attempt to discern what level of factual specificity was needed to satisfy "plausibility." Iqbal was also decided on 12 (b)(6).

Remember each claim you plead in your complaint have elements for example a negligence claim has a duty, a breach the duty, proximate cause, and damages.
No matter what allegations you state in your complaint you must state the necessary elements in order to have a claim stated in the complaint.

You must adequately state a claim which looks more to the legal issues rather than the factual issues, but make no mistake about it factual issues are important.
Courts will view your complaint in a light most favorable to you and will resolve all ambiguities in your favor.

To state a claim which is proven as fact the law provides some remedy. I would recommend you read these two cases over and over several time over to get an understanding of their ruling by the Supreme Court.

A motion to dismiss for failure to state a claim under rule 12 (b) (6) Tests the legal sufficiency of a complaint. Navarro v. Block, 250 F.3d 729, 732 (9th Cir.2001). In considering whether the complaint is sufficient to state a claim, the Court must accept as true all of the factual allegations contained in the complaint Ashcroft v. Iqbal,129 S. CT. 1937, 1949 (2009).
READ AS MANY CASE LAWS THAT APPLIES TO YOUR CASE, AND THOSE RULINGS OR HOLDING WHICH DOES AND DOES NOT APPLY, WHICH WILL GIVE YOU A BETTER UNDERSTANDING OF THOSE JUDICIAL RULINGS TO ENABLE YOU TO WRITE A BETTER MORE SPECIIFC CLEARER BRIEF. SOME LAWYERS TAKE A NARROW POINT OF VIEW IN WRITING THEIR BRIEFS OTHERS TAKE A BROADER POINT OF VIEW.THAT DECISION SHOULD BE BASE ON THE FACTS OF YOUR CASE AND THE STATUE OR LAW THAT APPLY. I PERSONALLY THINK JUDGES RULE MORE IN FAVOR OF PRO SE's THAT PRESENT THEIR BRIEFS ON THE FACTS SPECIFICLY RELATED TO THE ISSUES WHEN YOU THEN APPLY THE LAW.

AMEND INITIAL COMPLAINT AND INFO ON ELEMENTS

Where my initial Complaint was so poorly drafted base on the Supreme Ruling in Conley v. Gibson which I thought was the precedent case to prevent a case from being dismiss in the Courts, I was wrong as you continue to read below.

To have my case accepted by the Court and not be dismissed by the Defendant's After the Defendants file their motion to dismiss I realized that Conley was not the precedent case but Twombly and Iqbal was. I must have read the Defendants brief motion to dismiss my case at least twenty times, then I precede to read the two cases Bell South Corp v. Twombly and Ashcroft v. Iqbal to get a better understand of what was needed to present by brief to the Court so that that it would not be dismiss.

The very first thing I knew I had to do was to Motion to the Court for leave to amend my Complaint(Pleading) base on the Fed. R.Civ.Proc. 15(a) which states: A party may amend the party's Pleading once as a matter of course at any time before a responsive pleading is served or, if the pleading is one to which no responsive pleading is permitted and the action has been place upon the trial calendar, the party may so amend it at any time within 20 days after it is served.

Once I got a better understanding of what was necessary to make sure my Pleading(Complaint) would not be dismiss such as each one of my cause of actions must have the Elements to support that cause of action. After doing extensive reading e.g. 4 hours per day, I felt like I had a good chance at winning my case in Court and defeating the Defendants which it turns out I was right.

I immediately without hesitation file a motion for leave from the Court to file an amended Complaint base F.R.CIV. Proc.15(a).

Any claim or cause of action must accompany separate Elements let's take e.g. you file a lawsuit on a claim of Negligence in order for you to win your case in Court at trial you must prove that the Defendant 1. Owed you a legal Duty of care 2. Defendant breach that duty of care, meaning they act careless or unreasonably. 3. Causation: The Defendant's carelessness directly caused you harm and 4. Damages; you suffered economic losses, property damages, personal injuries or psychological distress.

UNITEDSTATES DISTRICTCOURT

MIDDLE DISTRICT OF FLORIDA

JACKSONVILLE DIVISION

SERVICES, LLC,

Plaintiff,

vs. Case No

JAMES WATSON,

Defendant.

IMPORTANT INFORMATION ABOUT YOUR CASE PLEASE READ AND FOLLOW

TAKE NOTICE, that in accordance with Local Rule 3.05, this action is designated as a TRACK TWO CASE. The Court's goal is to try most Track Two cases within12-18 months of filing. The filing party that is, the party that instituted suit in this Court) is responsible for serving a copy of this Notice and its attachments upon all other parties. Pursuant to Local Rule3.05, the parties should conduct case management conference (either in person or by telephone [1] no later than 60 days after service or appearance of any defendant. The Case Management Report should be filed within 14 days of the case management conference. In preparing their Report, the parties shall consult the Federal Rules of Civil Procedure and the Local Rules (available from the Clerk or at http://www.flmd.uscourts.gov). Counsel for all parties share the obligation to timely comply with the requirements of Local Rule 3.5 and are reminded that they must do so despite the pendency of any undecided motions. All parties must send courtesy copies to chambers of all filings that exceed 25 pages, inclusive of exhibits, regardless of whether the filing is done electronically or in paper.

The parties are advised that if they fail to use the attached Case Management Report form, the Court will set a schedule and select a mediator as the Court deems appropriate.

SHERYL L. LOESCH. CLERK

Date: August 30, 2013

Deputy Clerk

Copies to:Counsel of
Record ProSe Parties

Attachments:Case Management Report form

AO 85 Consent to Magistrate Judge Jurisdiction form

Ifall parties agree to conduct the case management conference by telephone,they may do so without filing a motion with the Court.

JAMESLWATSON,

    Plaintiff,

                              Case No.

V

EQUIFAX. EXPERIAN, and
TRANS UNION,

Defendants.

DEFENDANT EQUIFAX INFORMATION SERVICES LLC

JOINER AND CONSENT TO REMOVAL

**Without waiving any other defenses, Defendant Equifax Information Services
LLC, here by joins and consents to the removal of this action from the Circuit
Court, Fourth Judicial Circuit, in and for Duval County, Florida, to this
Court.**

Dated May 7, 2012

UNITED STATES DICTRICT COURT
FOR THE MIDDLE DISTRICT OF FLORIDA

JAMES L. WATSON,

Plaintiff

v.

EQUIFAX, EXPERIAN, and

TRANSUNION,

Defendants.

DEFENDANT TRANS UNJON, LLC'S
JOINDER AND CONSENT TO REMOVAL

Without waiving any other defenses, Defendant Trans Union, LLC,

incorrectly named Trans Union, hereby joins in consents to the removal of this

action from the Circuit Court, Fourth Judicial Circuit, in and for Duval

County, Florida, to this Court. Removal is proper for the reasons stated in

Defendant Experian Information Solutions, Inc.'s Notice of removal. On May

1,2012, Trans Union was served with Plaintiff's Complaint, the initial pleading

setting forth the claim for relief upon which this action is based.

FILED

UNITED STATES DISTR ICT COURT

FOR THE MIDDLE DISTR ICT OF JACKSONVILLE, FL

JAMES L. WATSON,

    Plain tiff,

    vs.

EQUIFAX, EXPERIAN, a nd TRANSUNION,

    Defendants

NOTICE OF REMOV AL

Pursuant to 28 U.S.C. § 1441 Defendant Experian in formation Solutions, Inc. ("Experian"), hereby files its Notice of Removal of the above-captioned action to this Court and states as follows:

1. Experian, Equifax, more properly referred to as Equifax information Services LLC ("Equifax"), and Trans Union, more properly referred to as Trans Union, LLC ("Trans Union"), are named Defendants in Civil Action No. 16-2012-CA-004153, filed in the Circuit Court, Fourth Judicial Circuit, in and for Duval, County, Florida (the "State Court Action"). All Defendants have joined in and given their consent to this removal. True and correct copies of their Joiners and Consents to Removal are attached hereto as Exhibit A.

2. The Complaint in the State Court Action was filed with the Clerk of the

Circuit Court, Fourth Judicial Circuit, in and for Duval County, Florida,

on April 12, 2012. Defendant Experian was served with the

Complaint on April 17, 2012. Defendant Equifax was served with the

Complaint on April 20, 2012. Defendant Trans Union was served

with the Complaint on May 1, 2012.

3. This Notice is being filed with this Court within thirty (30) days after

Defendant Experian received a copy of Plaintiff's initial pleading setting forth the

claims for relief upon which Plaintiff action is based.

4. True and correct copies of all process, pleadings, and orders filed to date in the

State Court Action are attached hereto as Exhibit B. No other process, pleadings,

or orders have been served upon Defendants to date in this case. Trial has not

commenced in the State Court Action, and that Court has not issued any orders.

5. Experian is a corporation which, for monetary fees, regularly engages

6. in whole or in part in the practice of assembling consumer credit

information or other information on consumers for the purpose of furnishing

consumer reports to third parties. Experian uses means or facilities of interstate

commerce for the purpose of preparing or furnishing consumer reports, and

therefore is a "consumer reporting agency" within the meaning of 15 U.S.C. §

1681a(f).

of 19 Page ID 3 Equifax is a limited liability company which, for monetary fees, regularly engages in whole or in part in the practice of assembling consumer credit information or other information on consumers for the purpose of furnishing consumer reports to third parties. Equifax uses means or facilities of interstate commerce for the purpose of preparing or furnishing consumer reports, and therefore is a "consumer reporting agency, within the meaning of 15 U.S.C. § 168Ia(f).

7. Trans Union is a limited liability company which, for monetary fees, regularly engages in whole or in part in the practice of assembling consumer credit information or other information on consumers for the purpose of furnishing consumer reports to third parties. Trans Union uses mans or facilities of interstate commerce for the purpose of preparing or furnishing consumer reports, and therefore is a "consumer reporting agency, within the meaning of 15 U.S.C. § 168la(t).

8. The claims of relief against all defendants alleged in the State Court Action arise under the Fair Credit Reporting Act, 15 U.S.C. §§ 1681-168Iu ("FCRA Complaint, 2.

Thus, this Court has original subject matter jurisdiction over the above-captioned action pursuant to 28 U.S.C. § 1331 and 15 U.S.C.§ 1681p. The above-captioned action may properly be removed to this United States District Court pursuant to 28 U.S.C. § 144l(a) and (b).

9. Plaintiff also purports to assert claims for negligence and d e f a m a t i o n . Complaint 3-4. This Court has supplemental jurisdiction over Plaintiff's

state law claims. Those cl aims, like Plaintiffs federal question claims,

arise from the same set of operative facts relating to the alleged wrongful

conduct. *See id.* Accordingly, each of those claims is related to **Plaintiff**

federal claims, and form a part of the same case and controversy pursuant

to 28 U.S.C. *§* I 367(a)

10. Pursuant to 28 U.S.C. *§ 144* 1(a), venue of the removal action is proper

in the Middle District of Florida, Jacksonville Division because it is in the

district and division embracing the place where the state court action is

pending.

11. Promptly after the filing of this Notice of Removal Defendants shall provide

notice of the removal to Plaintiff in the State Coul 1Action and to the Clerk

of the Court in the State Court action, as required **by** 28 U.S.C. § 1446(d).

Dated: May 9, 2012 Respectfully submitted

JAMES L. WATSON, SR.,

       Plaintiff,

vs.   Case No. 3:12-cv-552-J-99MMH-JBT

EQUIFAX, EXPERIAN,
and TRANSUNION,

       Defendants.

<u>ORDER FROM THE COURT</u>

THIS CAUSE is before the Court on Defendants Equifax Information Services LLC, Experian Information Solutions, Inc., and Trans Union LLC's Joint Motion to Dismiss Plaintiff's Second Amended Complaint (0kt. No. 83), filed on November 2, 2012; the Memorandum in Support of Defendants Equifax Information Services LLC, Experian Information Solutions, Inc., and Trans Union LLC's Joint Motion to Dismiss Plaintiffs Second Amended Complaint (Dkt. No. 84), filed on November 2, 2012; Defendant Equifax Information Services LLC's Motion for Sanctions (0kt. No. 85), filed on November 9, 2012; and Defendant Equifax Information Services LLC's Memorandum in Support of Motion for Sanctions (0kt. No.86), filed on November 9, 2012. Pursuant to Local Rule 3.01(a), United States District Court, Middle District of Florida (Local Rule(s)), a motion shall include a concise statement of the relief requested, the basis for the request, and a memorandum of legal authority in support of the request, all of which shall be included in a single document not to exceed twenty-five (25) pages. In this case, Defendants have filed their motions and memoranda as separate documents. As these documents do not comply with the Local Rules of this Court, they are due to be stricken. In light of the foregoing, it is hereby

ORDERED:

1. Defendants Equifax Information Services LLC, Experian Information Solutions, Inc., and Trans Union LLC's Joint Motion to Dismiss Plaintiffs Second Amended Complaint (Dkt. No.83), the Memorandum in Support of Defendants Equifax Information Services LLC, Experian Information Solutions, Inc., and Trans Union LLC's Joint Motion to Dismiss Plaintiffs Second Amended Complaint (0kt. No.84), Defendant Equifax Information Services LLC's, Motion for Sanctions (Dkt. No.85), and Defendant Equifax Information Services LLC's, Memorandum in Support of Motion for Sanctions (0kt. No.86) are **STRICKEN.**

2. Defendants shall have up to and including **December 12, 2012,** to file amended motions that comply with the Local Rules of this Court.

3. Plaintiff shall have up to and including **January 11, 2013,** to file responses to the amended motions.

DONE AND ORDERED in Jacksonville, Florida, this 29th day of November, 2012.

UNITED STATESDISI'RICTCOURT
FOR THE MIDDLE DISTRICT OFFLORIDA

JAMESL.WATSON,   )

  Plaintiff   )

v.   )

  EQUIFAX, EXPERIAN, and   )
TRANSUNION,   )

Defendants.   )
_____)

ORDER

THIS CAUSE is before the Court on Plaintiff's Motion for access to ECF filing ("Motion") (Doc.

37). Upon due consideration, the Court will grant the Motion to the following extent. Plaintiff may

access CM/ECF at the Court's website, www.flmd.uscourts.gov, after obtaining a login and

password from the Clerk's Office. In addition to receiving a login and password, he will need

the following to fully access CM/ECF: Internet access, an e-mail account, PDF capabilities,

and a PACER account. For information about electronic filing and registration, he is directed

to visit the CM/ECF link on the Court's website. He is further advised that the document,

Administrative Procedures for Electronic Filing in Civil and Criminal Cases, is available under

the CM/ECF link on the Court's website.

Accordingly, it is**ORDERED:**
The Motion **(Doc. 37) is GRANTED** to the extent stated herein.

Fn. When I was litigating my case I learned that Pro se's aren't allowed to use to file their
pleading via Internet in the ECF system only lawyers.
some of the monies from the sale of this book will be used to get lobby legislation to
get approval so that Pro se's can use the ECF just like lawyers.

Strasburger

ATTORNEYS AT LAW

March 14, 2013

VIA CMRRR

James L. Watson, Sr.
5255 NW 29 Ave., #607
Miami, FL 33142

> RE: *Case No. 3:12-cv-00552-UAMH-TEM* (M.D. of Florida
> *James L. Watson, Sr. v. Equifax et al.*

Dear Mr. Watson:

Almost a year ago, at the start of this lawsuit, I provided you copies of your Trans Union credit reports dated on or about June 2011, the time period you allege Trans Union duplicated the reporting of your accounts. As we have discussed several times since this informal production, none of these reports showed any duplicated accounts. Further, you have not produced any documents showing these alleged duplications on any Trans Union credit report. As such, I hereby demand that you dismiss all claims against Trans Union at s time. If you do not, I will request the court award Trans Union its attorney's fees incurred in o defense of your frivolous claims. This is a risk you should take seriously. Trans Union h already incurred tens of thousands of dollars in attorney's fees responding to your lawsuit.

Should you have any questions regarding this letter please do   ot hesitate to call.

Sincerely,

AAR/jcs

cc: Frank Cosmen (via e-mail)

UNITED STATES DISTRICT COURT
MIDDLE DISTRICT OF FLORIDA
JACKSONVILLE DIVISION

JAMES WATSON,

    Plaintiff,

v.   CASE NO. 3:12-cv-552-J-99MM H-JBT

EQUIFAX, EXPERIAN, and
TRANS UNION,

    Defendants.

ORDER

THIS CAUSE is before the Court on Defendant Equifax Information Services LLC's Amended Motion for Sanctions (Doc. 93) ("Motion") and Plaintiffs Response (Doc. 99). Although the Court believes that Plaintiff should have withdrawn his Emergency Motion (Doc. 79) when Defendant Equifax Information Services, LLC, ("Equifax") provided Plaintiff with the relief he requested, the Court will not impose sanctions against Plaintiff at this time. The Motion is therefore **DENIED.**

Local Rule 3.01(e) allows litigating parties to designate a motion as an emergency. M.D. Fla. R. 3.01(e). When a party files an emergency motion, the Court often drops whatever it is doing and takes up the motion. In this case, the Court ordered and prepared for a hearing on Plaintiffs Emergency Motion on an expedited basis. Each defendant had to prepare for and attend this expedited hearing.

162

Plaintiff should know that it is not only the Court and the parties to this action who are inconvenienced when he files (or fails to withdraw) an improper emergency motion. Litigants in other cases have their matters delayed whenever an emergency motion is filed. The improper filing of an emergency motion "'unfairly disfavors other litigants who, despite expeditious prosecution of each case and scrupulous attention to each local and federal rule of procedure, must wait patiently while the court disposes of a feigned emergency.'" *Onward Healthcare, Inc., v. Runnels,* No. 6:12-cv-508, 2012 WL 1259074, at *2 (M.D. Fla. Apr. 13, 2012) (quoting *Bravado Int'l Grp. Merch. SE Servs., Inc., v. Smith,* No. 8:12-cv-613, 2012 WL 1155858, at *1 (M.D. Fla. Mar. 27, 2012)). Consequently, Local Rule 3.01(e) warns parties that "[t]he unwarranted designation of a motion as an emergency motion may result in the imposition of sanctions."

Nevertheless, the undersigned concludes that sanctions are not appropriate for several reasons. First, the "Court will proceed with particular caution when considering an award of attorney's fees against a *pro se* plaintiff." *Powell v. Accurate Inventory & Calculating Servs.,* 8:10-cv-1558, 2011 WL 1299514, at *2 (M.D. Fla. Apr. 4, 2011). Plaintiffs *pro se* status "renders [his] lack of familiarity with the nuances of federal civil procedure somewhat more understandable." *Id.* Additionally, IT is arguable that a prompt ruling on the Emergency Motion may have been desirable when IT was first filed. Finally, Plaintiff has not previously designated any of his motions as an emergency. For these reasons, sanctions will not be awarded.

Plaintiff is cautioned, however, not to file any additional emergency motions unless truly appropriate. It is particularly troubling that Plaintiff did not withdraw the Emergency Motion prior to the hearing, but apparently tried to use the hearing as leverage to obtain different relief from Equifax that was not a subject of the Emergency Motion. (See ooc. 113 at 18-20.) Therefore, Plaintiff is admonished that the Court will not be lenient in the future, should a similar action occur.

Accordingly, it is **ORDERED:**

The Motion **(Doc.** 93) is **DENIED.**

DONE AND ORDERED at Jacksonville, Florida on April 11, 2013.

Joel Toomey

United States Magistrate Judge

Copies to:

Counsel of Record
Pro Se Plaintiff

UNITED STATES DISTRICT COURT
MIDDLE DISTRICT OF FLORIDA
JACKSONVILLE DIVISION

JAMES WATSON,

Plaintiff,

v.   CASE NO. 3:12-cv-552-J-99MMH-JBT

EQUIFAX,
EXPERIAN, and
TRANSUNION,

Defendants.

ORDER ON CLARIFICATION REQUESTED BY PLAINIFF

THIS CAUSE is before the Court on Plaintiffs Affidavit requesting Disclosure of
Credit Accounts by Telephone ("Affidavit") (Doc. 18), Defendant Trans Union LLC's
Unopposed Motion to Quash Plaintiffs Request ("Motion to Quash") (Doc. 22), and Plaintiffs
unrelated Motion for Clarification From Court on Equifax['s] Motion to Dismiss ("Motion
for Clarification") (Doc. 26).

As to Plaintiffs Affidavit, to the extent that it constitutes discovery material, such
materials "must not be filed untilthey are used in the proceeding or the court orders filing."
Fed. R. Civ. P. 5(d)(1); see *also* M.D.Fla. R. 3.03(d). The Court has notordered Plaintiffto
file discovery materials and it does notappear that suchfiling isnecessary atthistime. To the
extent that the Affidavit constitutes a motion, itfails to comply with the Local Rules of this
Court, particularly Local Rule 3.01(g). This Rule provides inrelevant part
Beforefilingany motion ina civil case, except [motions not applicable

the moving party shall confer with counsel for the opposing party in a good faith effort to resolve the issues raised by the motion, and shall file with the motion a statement (1) certifying that the moving counsel has conferred with opposing counsel and (2) stating whether counsel agree on the resolution of the motion.

M.D. Fla. R. 3.01(g).

With respect to Local Rule 3.01(g), the Court has noted that "[t]he purpose of the rule is to require the parties to communicate and resolve certain types of disputes without court intervention." *Desai v. Tire Kingdom, Inc.*, 944 F. Supp. 876, 878 (M.D. Fla. 1996). At least one judge in the Middle District of Florida has construed Rule 3.01(g) to mean to "speak to each other in person or by telephone,

in a good faith attempt to resolve disputed issues." *Davis v. Apfel*, 2000 WL 1658575, *2 n.1 (M.D. Fla. 2000). Many disputes are more easily resolved when the parties actually speak with each other.

Regardless of whether the Affidavit is discovery material or a motion, it is due to be stricken as an improper filing. Moreover, as the Motion to Quash indicates, there was never any dispute to begin with, and thus no reason for this unnecessary filing. Thus, the Motion to Quash is due to be denied as moot.

Plaintiff's Motion for Clarification relates to the Court's Order dated June 11, 2012. (Doc. 20.) The Order explained that all three defendants had filed motions to dismiss. *(Id.* at 1.) The Court denied as moot "the pending motions to dismiss" but omitted in paragraph 4 of the Order the document number corresponding to Defendant Equifax's motion to dismiss. *(Id.* at 2.) Plaintiff now seeks to clarify whether the Court intended to deny that motion as well. Although the Order was clear on its face that the Court was denying as moot all of the pending motions to dismiss because the Court was granting Plaintiffs motion to amend the complaint, the omitted document number was an oversight. Thus, the Court grants clarification to the extent that the document number of Equifax's motion to dismiss (Doc. 11) should have been included in paragraph 4 of the Order.

The Court Cautions Plaintiff that his filings do not comply with the Federal Rules of Civil Procedure and the Local Rules of this Court. The Court will issue a separate Order informing Plaintiff of some of his responsibilities as a *pro se* litigant. A *pro se* litigant must adhere to the same law and rules of court as a litigant who is represented by counsel. Failure to do so may lead to sanctions.

Accordingly, it is **ORDERED:**

1.   Plaintiffs Affidavit **(Doc. 18) is STRICKEN.**

2.   .   The Motion to Quash **(Doc. 22) is DENIED** as moot.

3.   Plaintiff s Motion for Clarification **(Doc. 26) is GRANTED** to the extent stated herein.

DONE AND ENTERED at Jacksonville, Florida, on June 20, 2012.

Joel B. Toomey

United States Magistrate Judge

Copies to:
Counsel of Record
Pro Se Party

UNITED STATES DISTRICT COURT
MIDDLE DISTRICT OF FLORIDA
JACKSONVILLE DIVISION
CASE NO. 3:12-CV-00552-UAMH-JBT

JAMES WATSON,

        Plaintiff,

v.

EQUIFAX, EXPERIAN, TRANSUNION,
Defendants.

JOINT CASE MANAGEMENT REPORT

The Plaintiff Pro Se James Watson and Defendants Experian Information Solution Inc.

("Experian"), incorrectly identified in Plaintiff Amended Complaint as "Experian", Trans Union

LLC ("Trans Union"), incorrectly identified as "Trans Union", and Equifax Information Solution

LLC incorrectly identified as "Equifax" have agreed on the following dates and discovery plan

pursuant to Fed. R. Civ. P. 26(f) and Local Rule 3.05(c):

DEADLINE OR EVENT	AGREED DATE
Mandatory Initial Disclosures (pursuant to Fed. R. Civ. P. 26(a)(1)) [Court recommends 30 days after CMR meeting]	Aug 30, 2012
Certificate of Interested Persons and Corporate Disclosure Statement [all parties are directed to complete and file the attached]	Already filed by all Defendants.
Motions to Add Parties or to Amend Pleadings	Sept 28, 2012
Disclosure of Expert Reports Plaintiff: Defendant:	November 30, 2012 November 30, 2012
Discovery Deadline [Court recommends 5 months before trial to allow time for	Dec 14, 2012

DEADLINE OR EVENT	AGREED DATE
dispositive motions to be filed and decided; all discovery must be commenced in time to be completed before this date]	

Dispositive and <u>Daubert</u> Motions [Court requires 4 months or more before trial term begins]	Jan 14, 2013
Trial Term Begins [Local Rule 3.05 (c)(2)(E) sets goal of trial within 1 year of filing complaint in most Track Two cases, and within 2 years in all Track Two cases; trial term **must not** be less than 4 months after dispositive motions deadline (unless filing of such motions is waived). Trials before the District Judge will generally be set on a rolling trial term toward the beginning of each month, with a Final Pretrial Conference to be set by the Court the preceding month. If the parties consent to trial before the Magistrate Judge, they will be set for a date certain after consultation with the parties]	July 15, 2013
Estimated Length of Trial [trial days]	3-4 days
Jury / Non-Jury	Jury
Mediation Deadline: Mediator: Address: Telephone: [Mediation is <u>mandatory</u> in most Track Two cases; Court recommends either 2 - 3 months after CMR meeting, or just after discovery deadline; if the parties do not so designate, the Court will designate the mediator and the deadline for mediation. A list of certified mediators is available on the Court's website and from the Clerk's Office.]	Oct 15, 2012 Birchfield, W.O 1 Independent Dr. Ste. 3000 Jacksonville, FL 32202 (904) 354 2050
All Parties Consent to Proceed Before Magistrate Judge If yes, the parties shall complete and <u>all</u> counsel and/or unrepresented parties shall execute the attached Form AO-85. Defendants shall respond to the subpoena for Frozen Data Scan or whatever name designated by Trans Union or Experian to prove Multiple or Duplicated file exist in the month of June on Plaintiff credit file. When issue by Plaintiff appropriately as directed by the Court.	Yes_____ No <u>X</u>

I.   Meeting of Parties

Lead counsel shall meet in person or, upon agreement of all parties, by telephone. (If all parties agree to conduct the case management conference by telephone, they may do so without filing a motion with the Court.) Pursuant to Local Rule 3.05(c) (2) (B) or (c) (3) (A), a meeting was held on July 31, 2012 (date) at 11: AM (time) and was attended by:

Name	Counsel for (if applicable)
James Watson	Pro Se
Thomas W. Tierney Rossway Moore Taylor & Swan	Experian Information Solution Inc.
Allison Reddoch Strasburger &Price LLP	Trans Union LLC
Maureen Mcaneny Jones Day	Experian Information Solution Inc.
Brian Olson King & Spalding LLP	Equifax Information Solution LLC
Franklin G. Cosmen, Jr. Quintairos, Prieto, Wood &Boyer, P.A.	Trans Union LLC

II. Preliminary Pretrial Conference

Local Rule 3.05 (C) (3) (B) provides that preliminary pretrial conferences are **mandatory in**

Track three cases.

Track Two case: Parties (check one) [X]   Request   [ ] do not request a preliminary

Pretrial conference before entry of a Case Management and Schedule Order in this

Track Two cases. Unresolved issues to be address at such a conference include.

Yes, whether any information sent to Plaintiff by Trans Union, Equifax, and Experian CRAs is part of Plaintiff credit file. Specifically, documents sent by Trans Union on Jun, 4, 7, 9, 13, 17, 18, 24, 26, in 2011, on July 16, 30, 31, in 2011 and on Aug 2, 8, 17, in 2011. Whether or not duplicated or multiple credit accounts on Plaintiff credit accounts is considered by FCRA an inaccurate file, as well as are these documents part of Plaintiff credit file? Unless Defendants want to stipulate on this issue before the Court submit its Case Management and Scheduling Order.

III.   Pre-Discovery Initial Disclosures of Core Information

Fed.R.Civ.P. 26(a) (1) (A) - (D) Disclosures

The parties (check one) [   ] have exchanged [X] agree to exchange information described in Fed.R.Civ.P. 26(a)(1)(A) - (D) on or by Dec 14, 2012, especially Frozen   Data Scans belonging Equifax evidence during the month of June and July of 2011 on Plaintiff credit file.

IV.   Agreed Discovery Plan for Plaintiffs and Defendants

A.   Certificate of Interested Persons and Corporate Disclosure Statement

This Court makes an active effort to screen every case in order to identify parties and interested corporations in which the assigned judge may be a shareholder, as well as for other matters that might require consideration of recusal. Therefore, each party, governmental party, intervenor, non-party movant, and Rule 69 garnishee shall file and serve within **fourteen (14) days** from that party's first appearance a Certificate of Interested Persons and Corporate Disclosure Statement using the attached mandatory form. No party may seek discovery from any source before filing and serving a Certificate of Interested Persons and Corporate Disclosure Statement. All papers, including emergency motions, are subject to being denied or stricken unless the filing party has previously filed and served its Certificate of Interested Persons and Corporate

Disclosure Statement. <u>Any party who has not already filed and served the required certificate is</u>

<u>required to do so **immediately.**</u> Each party has a continuing obligation to file and serve an

amended Certificate of Interested Persons and Corporate Disclosure Statement within eleven

days of 1) discovering any ground for amendment, including notice of case reassignment to a

different judicial officer; or 2) discovering any ground for recusal or disqualification of a judicial

officer. A party should not routinely list an assigned district judge or magistrate judge

as an "interested person" absent some non-judicial interest.

B. Discovery Plan/Deadline

The parties shall not file discovery materials with the Clerk except as provided in Local Rule 3.03.

The Court encourages the exchange of discovery requests on diskette. <u>See</u> Local Rule 3.03 (e).

In propounding and responding to discovery, the parties are directed to consult and comply with

the Federal Rules of Civil Procedure, the Local Rules of the United States District Court for the

Middle District of Florida, and the Middle District of Florida's Discovery Handbook. Each party

shall timely serve discovery requests so that the rules allow for a response prior to the discovery

deadline. The Court may deny as untimely all motions to compel filed after the discovery deadline.

In addition, the parties agree as follows:

<u>CMR Applies to all Parties involved in this action.</u>

C.   Confidentiality Agreements/Motions to File Under Seal

Whether documents filed in a case may be filed under seal is a separate issue from whether the

parties may agree that produced documents are confidential. The Court is a public forum, and

disfavors motions to file under seal. The Court will permit the parties to file documents under seal only upon motion and order entered under Local Rule 1.09.

The parties may reach their own agreement (without Court endorsement) regarding the designation of materials as "confidential." The Court discourages unnecessary stipulated motions for a protective order. The Court will enforce appropriate stipulated and signed confidentiality agreements. See Local Rule 4.15. Each confidentiality agreement or order shall provide, or shall be deemed to provide, that "no party shall file a document under seal without first having obtained an order granting leave to file under seal on a showing of particularized need." With respect to confidentiality agreements, the parties agree as follows:

The parties do not anticipate entering into a confidentiality agreement, but any issues of confidentiality, that issue will be presented to the Court to resolve.

The evidence of the Frozen Data Scan was discussed shall not be confidential or privileged in this action.

D.   Disclosure or Discovery of Electronically Stored Information and Assertion of Claims of Privilege.

Pursuant to Fed.R.Civ.P. 26(f)(3), the parties have made the following agreements regarding the disclosure and discovery of electronically stored information as well as the assertion of claims of privilege or protection of trial preparation materials after production:

Any discoverable information that is electronically stored will be produced in hard-copy format (e.g., print-screen print-outs) or PDF. In any case in which the receiving party disagrees with the format in which the information is produced, the parties shall meet and confer at that time to attempt to resolve said dispute.

Inadvertent disclosure of information protected by the attorney-client and/or work-product privilege shall not constitute a waiver of an otherwise valid claim of privilege. A party that receives privileged information shall return it to the other party immediately upon discovery of the privileged information and but retaining a copy and consider the information as confidential between the Court, Pro Se, and the Party that owns that document.

V.   Mediation

All parties in good faith shall participate in mediation; the parties in every case will participate in Court-annexed mediation as detailed in Chapter Nine of the Court's Local Rules. The parties have agreed on a mediator from the Court's approved list of mediators as set forth in the table above, and have agreed to the date stated in the table above as the last date for mediation, but to hold their first mediation session on Sept 27, 2012 between all parties. The list of mediators is available from the Clerk, and is posted on the Court's web site at www.flmd.uscourts.gov. If the parties do not so designate, the Court will designate the mediator and the deadline for mediation.

VI.   Requests for Special Handling

Requests for special consideration or handling (requests may be joint or unilateral):

Plaintiff filed a Motion for Summary Judgment on June 19, 2012.   (Doc. 27). The Defendants jointly moved to extend the time to respond to Plaintiff's motion. (Doc. 31).   In granting Defendants' motion to extend the time to respond, the Court ordered that the response deadline would be set in the case management and scheduling order. (Doc. 38). Defendants have conferred regarding a reasonable response deadline as Feb. 2013 The Defendants respectfully request that they be permitted until 30 days after the close of discovery to respond to Plaintiff's summary judgment motion which is Jan14, 2013.

Plaintiff oppose but agree to give Defendants until Sept 14, 2012 to submit their opposition to

Plaintiff Summary Judgment. Defendants should not be given special privilege of having such a long period of time to respond to a Summary Judgment motion when the normal time as stated by FRCP is 14 Days, and Defendants already have had 90 days from the Jun 19, 2012 Plaintiff Summary Judgment date.

Plaintiff unilateral agrees to admit frozen   data scan into evidence on Plaintiff credit accounts in the months of June, July, and Aug 2011 on Oct 10, 2012 as discussed in CMC on July 31, 2012.

Respectfully submitted,
By: _____
James L. Watson Sr. Pro Se

Respectfully submitted this 27, date of Aug, 2012

UNITED STATES DISTRICT COURT FOR THE MIDDLE DISTRICT OF FLORIDA

JACKSONVILLE DIVISION

JAMES L. WATSON,	)	
	)	
Plaintiff,	)	
	)	
vs.	)	Case No. 3:12-cv-00552-UAMH-JBT
	)	
EQUIFAX, EXPERIAN, and	)	
TRANSUNION,	)	
	)	
Defendants	)	

DEFENDANTS' CASE MANAGEMENT REPORT

The Defendants in this action have agreed on the following dates and discovery plan pursuant to Fed. R. Civ. P. 26(f) and Local Rule 3.05(c):

DEADLINE OR EVENT	AGREED DATE
Mandatory Initial Disclosures (pursuant to Fed. R. Civ. P. 26(a)(l)) [Court recommends 30 days after CMR meeting]	July 30, 2012
Certificate of Interested Persons and Corporate Disclosure Statement [all parties are directed to complete and file the attached]	Already filed by all Defendants.
Motions to Add Parties or to Amend Pleadings	October 31, 2012
Disclosure of Expert Reports Plaintiff: Defendant:	November 30, 2012 December 31, 2012
Discovery Deadline [Court recommends 5 months before trial to allow time for dispositive motions to be filed and decided; all discovery must be commenced in time to be completed before this date]	January 13, 2013
Dispositive and Daubert Motions [Court requires 4 months or more before trial term begins]	March 1, 2013

[1] *See* Section I below regarding submission of Case Management Report by Defendants only.

DEADLINE OR EVENT	AGREED DATE
Trial Term Begins	October I, 2013
Estimated Length of Trial [trial days] _____ = -	3 days
Jury / Non-Jury	Jury
Mediation Deadline: Mediator: Address: Telephone: [Mediation is mandatory: in most Track Two **cases;** Court recommends either 2 - 3 months after CMR meeting, or just after discovery deadline; if the parties do not so designate, the Court will designate the mediator and the deadline for mediation. A list of certified mediators is available on the Court's website and from the Clerk's Office.]	February 15, 2013 Jay Cohen P.O. Box 2210 Winter Park, FL 32790-2210 (407) 6441181
All Parties Consent to Proceed Before Magistrate Judge If yes, the parties shall complete and all counsel and/or unrepresented parties shall execute the attached Form A0-85.	Yes_____ No _x_

Meeting of Parties Lead counsel shall meet in person or, upon agreement of all parties, by telephone. (If all parties agree to conduct the case management conference by telephone, they may do so without filing a motion with the Court.) Pursuant to Local Rule 3.05(c)(2)(B) or {c)(3){A}, a meeting was held on —   — —(date) at

—   (time) and was attended by:

Attorneys for the Defendants attempted in good-faith to conduct a case management

conference via telephone with Plaintiff on June 29, July 9, and July 11, 2012. Plaintiff was unable

or declined to participate in the conference on these dates and declined to propose subsequent

alternate dates for the conference. As such, Defendants' counsel conferred amongst themselves.

On July 18, 2012, Plaintiff was provided a copy of the proposed Report. *See* Exhibit! Defendants

solicited Plaintiff s input and requested his response by 12:00, July 20, 2012.

Plaintiff. however, never responded to Defendants' request.

Additionally, Counsel for Experian and Trans Union contacted Plaintiff on several

occasions, including immediately prior to filing the proposed Report on July 20, 2012, again

requesting his participation or comments in drafting this Report and   Defendants' intention of

complying with the Court's filing deadline.   Despite Defendants' good-faith efforts, Plaintiff

refused to participate in drafting the Report and indicated that he intended to file a separate

report. Defendants' counsel hereby submits this Case Management Report on behalf of the

Defendants only.

Counsel for the Defendants who participated in the preparation of this report are as

follows:

Counsel for (if applicable)

Preliminary Pretrial Conference

Local Rule 3.05(c)(3)(B) provides that preliminary pretrial conferences are mandatory in Track Three cases.

Track Two cases: Parties   (check one) [ ] request [ ] do not request a preliminary pretrial conference before entry of a Case Management and Scheduling Order in this Track Two case.   Unresolved issues to be addressed at such a conference include:

_____None_____   _____

Ill.   Pre-Discovery Initial Disclosures of Core Information

Fed.R.Civ.P. 26(a)(l)(A)-(D) Disclosures

The parties (check one) [ ] have exchanged [ ]agree to exchange   information described in Fed.R.Civ.P. 26(a)(l)(A) -(D) on or by July 30, 2012.

Agreed Discovery Plan for Plaintiffs and Defendants

Certificate of Interested Persons and Corporate Disclosure Statement

This Court makes an active effort to screen every case in order to identify parties and interested corporations in which the assigned judge may be a shareholder, as well as for other matters that might require consideration of recusal. Therefore, each party, governmental party, intervenor, non-party movant, and Rule 69 garnishee shall file and serve within fourteen (14) days from that party's first appearance a Certificate of Interested Persons and Corporate Disclosure Statement using the attached mandatory form. No party may seek discovery from any source before filing and serving a Certificate of Interested Persons and Corporate Disclosure Statement. All papers, including emergency motions, are subject to being denied or stricken unless the filing party has previously filed and served its Certificate of Interested Persons and

Corporate Disclosure Statement. <u>Any party who has not already filed and served the required certificate is required to do so immediately.</u>   Each party has a continuing obligation to file and serve an amended Certificate of interested Persons and Corporate Disclosure Statement within eleven days of 1) discovering any ground for amendment, including notice of case reassignment to a different judicial officer; or 2) discovering any ground for recusal or disqualification of a judicial officer. A party should not routinely list an assigned district judge or magistrate judge as an "interested person" absent some non-judicial interest.

B.   Discovery Plan/Deadline

The parties shall not file discovery materials with the Clerk except as provided in Local Rule 3.03. The Court encourages the exchange of discovery requests on diskette. <u>See</u>   Local

Rule 3.03 (e). In propounding and responding to discovery, the parties are directed to consult and comply with the Federal Rules of Civil Procedure, the Local Rules of the United States District Court for the Middle District of Florida, and the Middle District of Florida's Discovery Handbook. Each party shall timely serve discovery requests so that the rules allow for a response prior to the discovery deadline. The Court may deny as untimely all motions to compel filed after the discovery deadline.   In addition, the parties agree as follows:

N/A

Confidentiality Agreements/ Motions to File Under Seal

Whether documents filed in a case may be filed under seal is a separate issue from whether the parties may agree that produced documents are confidential. The Court is a public forum, and disfavors motions to file under seal. The Court will permit the parties to file documents under seal only upon motion and order entered under Local Rule 1.09.

The parties may reach their own agreement (without Court endorsement) regarding the designation of materials as "confidential." The Court discourages unnecessary stipulated motions for a protective order. The Court will enforce appropriate stipulated and signed confidentiality agreements. See Local Rule 4.15. Each confidentiality agreement or order

shall provide, or shall be deemed to provide, that "no party shall file a document under seal without first having obtained an order granting leave to file under seal on a showing of particularized need." With respect to confidentiality agreements, the parties agree as follows:

The parties anticipate entering into a confidentiality agreement, which will be presented to the Court only in the event a need for Court enforcement arises.

Disclosure or Discovery of Electronically Stored Information and Assertion of Claims of Privilege

Pursuant to Fed.R.Civ.P. 26(f)(3), Defendants have made the following agreements regarding the disclosure and discovery of electronically stored information as well as the assertion of claims of privilege or protection of trial preparation materials after production:

Any discoverable information that is electronically stored will be produced in hard-copy format (e.g., print-screen print-outs) or PDF. In any case in which the receiving party disagrees with the format in which the information is produced. the parties shall meet and confer at that time to attempt to resolve said dispute.

Inadvertent disclosure of information protected by the attorney-client and/or work-product privilege shall not constitute a waiver of an otherwise valid claim of privilege. A party that receives privileged information shall return it to the other party immediately upon discovery of the privileged information and without retaining a copy.

Mediation

Absent a Court order to the contrary, the parties in every case will participate in Court- annexed mediation as detailed in Chapter Nine of the Court's Local Rules. The parties have agreed on a mediator from the Court's approved list of mediators as set forth in the table above, and have agreed to the date stated in the table above as the last date for mediation. The list of mediators is available from the Clerk, and is posted on the Court's web site at www.flmd.uscourts.gov. If the parties do not so designate, the Court will designate the mediator and the deadline for mediation.

VI. Requests for Special Handling

Requests for special consideration or handling (requests may be joint or unilateral): <u>Plaintiff filed a Motion for Summary Judgment on June   19, 2012. Doc. 27). The Defendants jointly moved to extend the time to respond to Plaintiff s motion. (Doc. 31). In granting Defendants' motion to extend the time to respond, the Court ordered that the r e s p o n s e deadline would be set in the case management and scheduling order. {Doc. 38). Defendants have conferred regarding a reasonable response deadline. The Defendants respectfully request that they be permitted until sixty (60) days after the close of discovery to respond to Plaintiff's summary judgment motion.</u>

United States District Court
Middle District of Florida
Jacksonville, Division

James Watson

Plaintiff

Case No.3:12-cv-552-J-99MMH-TEH

Defendants

Equifax, Experian, Transunion

PLAINTIFF MOTION COURT TO FILE AMENDED COMPLAINT

Pursuant to Federal Rule of Civil Procedure S(a) Plaintiff move the Court to file the first Amended Complaint.

A Party may amend its Pleading once as a matter of course within: 21 days

after serving it or:

If the Pleading is one which a responsive Pleading is required, 21 days after service of a responsive Pleading or 21 days after service of a motion under Rule 12(b)(e) or (f) whichever's earlier.

Since Defendant has submitted to the Count a Motion to Dismiss Plaintiff motion to amend is within the rules of Law of the FRCP allowing **PLAINTIFF** to submit its Motion to amend its original Complaint.

Amendment of Complaint was freely granted in any event on rule 15(a)(2) for motion to amend in case not permitted under rule 5(a)(l) the, "Court should freely give leaved when justice so required.

Complaint need only be, "a short and plain statement of the claim showing that the Pleader is entitle to relief," FRCP 8(a)(2) Federal Rules "do not required a Claimant to set out in detail the facts upon which he based his claim. To the contrary, all that is required is a short and plain statement of the claim, that will give the Defendant fair notice of what the Plaintiff claim is and grounds upon which it rest," Conley V. Gibson.

Therein Plaintiff is giving notice to the Court and the Defendants that Plaintiff will amend its original Complaint and provide evidence documentation to prove the wrong and injury of (economic loss from loss of personal and business financial loss of income from injury of being denied personal credit and possible business revenue from the action of Defendants of Duplicating Plaintiff credit file and violated [15U.S.C.§1681](b) or section 602(b) of FRCA.

In the name of Justice Plaintiff Pray to the Court that after Plaintiff submit evidence of a front to back document Plaintiff received from Transunion, the Court will let the jury decide the Plaintiff case on its cause of action of Negligent, Defamation on the merits and facts of case.

In conclusion the defendant's Legal representative consented, acquiescence and waived their legal right to assert a legal claim of Dismissal on the issue that Plaintiff did not state a legal claim when he stated on exhibit (A), of:

Defendant Trans union LLC's Joiner and consent to Removal "On May 1, 2012, Trans union was served with Plaintiffs Complaint, the initial pleading setting forth the claim for relief upon which this action is base," "Franklin G. Cosmen, JR. This statement proved Attorney read complaint, and verified a claim exist in the body of Plaintiff Complaint.

CERTIFICATEOFSERVICE

I hereby verify that the statements above are true to the best of my knowledge and a copy was sent to all parties.

Brian. Olsen
King & Spalding LLP
1180 Peachtree St. N.E.
Atlanta, GA 30309-3521
404-215-5806
Fax 404-572-5100
bjolson@kslaw.com
Counsel for Equifax

Thomas W. Tierney
Rossway, Moore & Taylor
Suite 200
2101 Indian River Blvd
Vero Beach, FL 32960
772-321-4440
Fax 772-231-4430
ttierney@verobeachlawyers.com
Counsel for Experian

James Watson Pro Se

UNITED STATES DISTRICT COURT
MIDDLE DISTRICT OF FLORIDA
JACKSONVILLE DIVISION

James Watson
Plaintiff

V.

Equifax,
Experian and
Transunion
Defendants

Case No.3:12-cv-552-J-99MMH-JBT

JURY TRIAL DEMANDED

PLAINTIFF SECOND AMENDED COMPLAINT

This Court has Jurisdiction under the "Fair Credit Reporting act" of 15 U.S.C. § §1681-1681w to adjudicate the action between Plaintiff and all three CRAs Equifax information Services, LLC ("Equifax"), Experian information Solutions, Inc. ("Experian"), and Trans Union LLC ("TransUnion").

By order of the Court dated Sept. 18, 2012 due to Defendant's motions to dismiss under Rule 12(b) (6) of the Fed. Rules Civil Procedure, Plaintiff Complaint and first Amended Complaint, (Doc. # 1 and #16) respectful, Plaintiff was directed by Court to file this seconded Amended Complaint under FRCP (8) (a) (2), on or before Oct. 9, 2012.

Plaintiff brings this action under the following provisions of the Fair Credit Reporting Act (FCRA). More specifically Plaintiff allege violations of (i) [15 U.S.C. § 1681] (b), by all Defendant's, (ii) violations of [15 U.S.C. § 168la] (d) {l), by all Defendant's, {iii} violations of [15 U.S.C. § 1681a] {g}, by all Defendant's, (iv) violations of [15 U.S.C. § 168lb] (a), (3), (A), by Equifax and Experian, (v) violations of 604 (b)(3)(B) (1V) by all defendants, (vi) violations of [15 U.S.C. § 168le] (b) by all defendants, (vii) violation of [15 U.S.C. § 1681i](l)(A)(2)(A), by all defendants, and especially by Equifax Mr. Olson on Sept 14, 2012, (viii) violations of [15

U.S.C. § 168lp] By all Defendant's, (ix) violations of [l5 U.S.C. § 168la] (p), by all

defendants, violations of [15 U.S.C. § 16810] By all Defendant's, 168lh, and 1681n.

Pursuant to Federal Rules of Civil Procedure S(a)(2) Plaintiff file his second Amended

in accordance of directive of the Court, Plaintiff assert herein that Plaintiff Second

Amended Complaint does state a claim in which a claim for relief can be granted against

all three CRAs Defendants, and does satisfies all the requirements of specificity, and

Plausibility to state a claim for relief in this action.

Therefore, the Court should dismiss defendants Motion to dismiss (Doc. # 35 and #40) as moot

and grants Plaintiff Second Amended Complaint, and award actual, Statutory,

compensatory, and punitive liability damages in favor of Plaintiff.

The initial complaint, first amended complaint and second Amended Complaint are

referred to herein collectively as "Complaint."

BACK GROUND CASE INFORMATION

On April 122012, James Watson Pro Se brought an action in State Court Circuit, Fourth

Judicial Circuit in and Duval County, Florida against Defendants Equifax, Trans Union and

Experian for violation of have two accounts (duplicated accounts) for each of Plaintiff

creditor accounts on Plaintiff credit file. Plaintiff observed these inaccuracies of

Duplicated credit accounts (two accounts for each account on plaintiff file) on all three

CRAs websites while Plaintiff was trying to improve his credit standings. (Doc. # 2). On

May 9, 2012 Experian, Equifax, and Trans Union joiner and removed action from Duval

State Court to this Court, United States District Court Middle District of Florida

Jacksonville Division with Equifax, and Trans Union joining and consenting to the

removal. (Doc. #3& 4). On May 16, 2012 In response to Plaintiff Amended Complaint

with a stated legal claim, Equifax file motion to dismiss Plaintiff complaint and

Experian and Trans Union file their Rule 12(b)(6) Motion to Dismiss Plaintiff Complaint and Memorandum in Support for alleging Plaintiff did not state acclaim which Plaintiff considered meritless on all four comers on the face of the Complaint.

May 21, 2012, Plaintiff filed a Motion for leave to amend his Complaint (Doc. # 13). May 25, 2012, Plaintiff filed Propose Amend Complaint in this Court (Doc. # 16) as it pertains to Fed.R.Civ.P. 15(a)(1)(B) Plaintiff is allowed to Amend Is Complaint once as a matter of rule. On May 30, 2012 Plaintiff offered evidence attach to his Motion to Amend Plaintiff Complaint which was accepted by this Court. See exhibit(A)and(B). On June 11,2012 This Court Granted Plaintiff Motion to Amend Complaint (Doc.# 20) as filed, and dismissed all three Defendants Motions to Dismiss Plaintiff Complaint (Doc. # 9, 10, 11). On June 19,2012Plaintiff submitted his Summary Judgment Pursuant to Federal Rules of Civil Procedure (56) (Doc.#27), summary Judgment can be presented by the moving party if the case is more than 20 days.

Plaintiff Summary Judgment Affidavit accepted by the Court with Material evidence(Doc.#34). Plaintiff motion for Summary Judgment was denied without prejudice, (doc# 58).

Defendants file a motion for extension of time to respond to Plaintiff Summary Judgment oppose by Plaintiff but grant by Magistrate Judge Toomey with an issue order stating," The Court need not wait for Plaintiff response to this motion for extension of time."(Doc. # 38) COUNT I.

Negligence Cause of Action by Equifax On or about January 10,2011 Plaintiff signed up with all three CRA's for the sole purpose of Plaintiff becoming a member of all three CRA's (Equifax, Experian, and Trans Union) to find credit accounts in his credit file in which he could correct that were incomplete, inaccurate, an unverifiable creditor's accounts on his credit file.

Just before this wrongful action of all three CRA's placing duplicated accounts on Plaintiff credit file Plaintiff had successfully deleted, improve the status and settle in full several accounts on his file to improve his credit score from low 500's to about 620.

On or about the month of June, 2011 as recorded on Plaintiff Equifax credit file, Plaintiff login to Equifax credit monitoring website, Plaintiff notice that his credit file had credit accounts with two of the same accounts (duplicated accounts) with the same account numbers in his file. After viewing those same duplicated accounts Inaccurate accounts on Equifax credit monitoring service website, Plaintiff login to Experian and Trans Union and viewed that those same credit accounts where duplicated on their credit monitor services websites as well as, on Plaintiff credit file, i.e. two of the same accounts (duplication) of accounts on his credit file. Placing two of the same accounts with the same account numbers on Plaintiff credit file, e.g. two of the same accounts, two of the same ____ accounts, two of the same accounts, etc., Defendants failed to have reasonable procedure in place to prevent duplication of Plaintiff credit accounts on Plaintiff credit file, as stated by provisions of FCRA sections [15 U.S.C. § 1681e] (b), [15 U.S.C. § 1681] (b), and Trans Union [15 U.S.C. § 1681a] (g). 1681h and 1681n. Plaintiff use his cell telephone to dispute the inaccuracies by calling all three CRA's had several time during the month of June to dispute the duplication of Plaintiff credit accounts as reference above and finally in about the First of part of the month of August all three CRA's

correct the inaccuracy of having two of the same account with same the account number to just one account for each creditor on Plaintiff credit file.

As reference above Just before this wrongful action of all three Replacing duplicated accounts on Plaintiff credit file Plaintiff had successfully deleted, improve the status and settlement in full several accounts on his file to improve his credit score from low 500's to about 620. Plaintiff credit score of 620 alert Equifax computer program systems to sell Plaintiff credit account information to third party credit companies such as credit card company to solicit their credit product to consumers Equifax has in its computer data base.

After having a 620 credit score Plaintiff credit score of 620 meant the prequalification necessary to receive a preapprove application for a credit by several national credit card companies. Round about the same time when all three CRA's place the duplicated accounts on Plaintiff credit file Plaintiff applied for a credit card sent to him by credit card company with a preapprove application attach to their solicitation for Plaintiff to apply for their credit card.

It just so happened that while Equifax computer was in the process of either purging or correcting Plaintiff duplicated inaccurate accounts on his Equifax credit file, their quest for Plaintiff Equifax credit file information was read by computer indicated that Plaintiff Equifax credit file **had** no accounts on Plaintiff credit file therefore,__ computerproduce results which where that there were, "insufficient credit references" on Plaintiff credit file. All of this resulted from Equifax inaccurately Duplication of Plaintiff credit accounts on credit file resulting in a denial by ___credit card company when processing Plaintiff credit card application and a wrongful, **harmful** injury of Plaintiff not receiving **that** credit card which prevented Plaintiff from increasing his credit score and having the money from the approve credit card to improve his credit worthiness and improve the cash flow for business future business ventures projects, see exhibit (c).

A credit card results based on a decision by __of "insufficient credit references "base on Equifax's failure to maintain accurate credit account when Plaintiff applied for credit **in** addition to exclusion credit accounts information in Plaintiff credit file therefore Plaintiff is alleged a claim of negligence as it relates to injury to Plaintiff by Equifax FCRA [15 U.S.C. § 1681] (b), and [15 U.S.C. § 1681e] (b).
[15 U.S.C. § 168le] (b) Accuracy of report. "When a consumer reporting agency prepares a consumer report **it** shall follow reasonable procedures to assure maximum possible accuracy of the information concerning the individual about whom the report relates."

[15 U.S.C. § 1681] (b) Reasonable Procedures: It is the purpose of this title to require that consumers reporting agencies adopt Reasonable Procedures for meeting the needs of commerce for consumer credit, personnel insurance and other information in manner which is fair and equitable to the consumer, with regard to the confidentiality, accuracy, relevancy, and proper utilization of such information in accordance with the requirements of this title.

The inquiry application by __ credit inquiry of Plaintiff credit is considered by FCRA as a hard inquiry and should be place on Plaintiff credit file. As of this second Amended Comp. failure to include this inquiry on Plaintiff file is not only another example inaccuracy on Plaintiff credit file. But this act is an example of willful intent to injury Plaintiff by omission of this hard inquiry of Equifax failure to record this hard inquiry as hard inquiry on Plaintiff credit file after __denial Plaintiff a credit card.

A claim of a cause of action of defamation from willful intent to injured Plaintiff when Equifax did not record credit evaluating of Plaintiff as a hard inquiry as required by FCRA. *AB* of this date Equifax has not recorded any inquiry concerning that credit check about Plaintiff credit

File which Is defamation of the willful intent to injury Plaintiff. This omission on Plaintiff credit file produces a falsely print credit file on Plaintiff.
Therefore, damages are due to Plaintiff from this injury of Defamation, not only from loss of
money from not receiving money from a line of credit, but loss future business opportunity revenue, and loss of personal wages.

Also during this period in June 2011 Plaintiff not knowing how to download a file from a computer yet, was eventually by trial and error able to download a copy of Plaintiff June 8 Equifax credit file with the Duplicated credit accounts reference in this second Amended Complaint and sent to Equifax lead Counsel on record Mr. Brian Olson on Sept. 23, 2012 exhibit
(J) for purpose of discovery as reference (DOC.#73) submitted to the Court and recorded file on 9-12-2012 by Plaintiff.

COUNT II

Negligence Cause of Action by Experian

Reference all facts above as it relates to inaccuracy duplication of Plaintiff credit accounts by the three CRA's in the month of June 2011, except the facts relating to __ credit card. On or about Nov, 28 2011, while Plaintiff was making a deposit into his business checking account at _____, Plaintiff inquired about obtaining non-secured or secured credit card line of credit on a credit card to help boost his credit score.

Mr.___ ___ loan officer suggested that Plaintiff for a credit card since my credit score had reach 600 or higher, so on Nov. 28, 2011, Plaintiff went in to the branch office in and applied for a credit card line of credit on a credit card.

One of the requirements of ___ was that Plaintiff had to become a member of __third party credit agency, (Enhance Identity theft). The condition was that Plaintiff had to pay an upfront cost of one dollar to become a member but could cancel anytime within 30-day enrollment period.

Plaintiff agreed and paid the one dollar to become a member, after becoming a member Mr. __ pull Plaintiff credit file from all three CRA's. The format version of the account used by ___was vertical outline with the CRA's at the top with the accounts horizontal. Plaintiff Experian credit report was missing all of Plaintiff Experian credit report except two accounts.
While the other two CRA's were reporting correctly all Plaintiff credit account, ___ Loan officer ___stated that Plaintiff was denied credit due to
"insufficient credit," from exclusion of all or most Plaintiff credit accounts on Plaintiff Experian credit accounts file.

This inaccurate exclusion of Plaintiff accounts reported from Experian CRA of Plaintiff credit report as being the reason for the "insufficient credit, "denial. Excluded Plaintiff credit file accounts on the credit report requested by_____when he applied for a line of credit on a credit card.

A few days went by and on or about Dec. 5 20011, before Plaintiff remembered to file a dispute with Experian by cell phone the inaccurate of only2 accounts on Plaintiff credit report being reported on Plaintiff credit report file he received from __ from Experian while applying a credit card loan, exhibit (i), sent to Experian attorney Maureen Mcaneny. Plaintiff spoke to Mr. L about disputing the inaccurate exclusion of not having those accounts on Plaintiff credit report file and how Plaintiff was denied credit because of Experian in accurate reporting of Plaintiff credit account on Plaintiff file.
.

Plaintiff had disputed this same act of excluding Plaintiff credit account by cell phone in the prior month of Oct 2011 to Experian and he was told that the account would be corrected immediately but as the Court can see from Plaintiff Nov. 2011 credit report the inaccurate reporting by Experian remain in place. (See exhibit I of Summary Judgment) (Doc. #27) Statement from an Experian service rep. name Louis date Oct 5, 2011 stating Plaintiff had no Public record on his file but most important Louis said the same thing Mr. Tom Tierney said, "He has heard in that happen before. "When Plaintiff received a telephone conference call from him in the beginning or middle part of May, 2012, is proof there is no genuine issue of material facts from both Experian customer service rep. and Experian legal counsel. Paragraph 8(motion summary Judgment) (Doc.#27).

COUNT III.

Negligence Cause of Action by Trans Union

A claim of negligence cause of action from the injury of inaccurately Duplicating Plaintiff credit accounts while Plaintiff was a member of their credit monitoring service in the Month of June 2011, in which Plaintiff disputed this in accuracy with all three CRA (Equifax, Experian and Trans Union), by cell phone. All three CRA's committed this wrongful and harmful act of inaccurately placing two of the same accounts with the same account numbers on Plaintiff credit file, e.g. two of the same accounts, two of the same____accounts, two of the same ____account, etc. Defendants followed unreasonable procedure by placing duplicated accounts of Plaintiff credit accounts on Plaintiff credit file which violates FCRA sections [15 U.S.C. § 168le] {b), [15 U.S.C. § 168l] (b), and [15 U.S.C. § 168la] (g)..
The defendant's injury from theses wrongful acts of duplicating Plaintiff credit accounts at that moment in time in the month of June, 2011 negated Plaintiff progress of re-establishing his credit.

Reasonable Procedures: It is the purpose of this title to require that consumers reporting agencies adopt Reasonable Procedures for meeting the needs of commerce for consumer credit, personnel, insurance and other information in manner which is fair and equitable to the consumer, with regard to the confidentiality, accuracy, relevancy, and proper utilization of such information in accordance with the requirements of this title. [15 U.S.C. § 1681] {b).

[15 U.S.C. § 168la] (p), The term "consumer reporting agency compiles and maintains files on consumers on a nationwide basis" means a consumer reporting agency that regularly engages in practice of assembling or evaluating, and maintaining, for the purpose of furnishing consumer reports to third parties bearing on a consumer credit worthiness, credit standing, or credit capacity, each of the following regarding consumers residing nationwide.

604 (b)(3)(B) (1V), that the consumer may, upon providing proper identification, request a free copy of a report and may dispute and may dispute with the consumer reporting agency the accuracy or completeness of any information in a report.

[15 U.S.C. § 1681e] (b) Accuracy of report. "When consumer reporting agency prepares a consumer report it shall follow reasonable procedures to assure maximum possible accuracy of the information concerning the individual about whom the report relates."

[15 U.S.C. § 168lg] (a), Information on file; sources; report recipients. Every consumer reporting agency shall, upon request, and subject to 61O(a) (1) [§ 168lh], clearly and accuracy disclose to the consumer: (1) All information in the consumer's file at the time of the request except that. ... Provision 1681h(e):

No consumer may bring any action... in the nature of defamation ... with respect to

the reporting of information against any consumer reporting agency except as to

false information furnished with malice or willful intent to injure such consumer.

Trans Union Defamation

During a Telephone dispute of the duplication of Plaintiff credit accounts using Plaintiff cell phone in the month of June 2011, one Trans Union employee stated that although Plaintiff saw duplicated account there was only one account on his file this willful intent to injure Plaintiff by making a false statement of having one account per creditor on Plaintiff credit file when in fact there were two or duplicate accounts which causes a cause of action of Defamation by

Trans union on Plaintiff by false denying that there where one account for each account contrary to the accounts stated document received by Plaintiff from Trans Union on or about June 25, 2011, see doc # exhibit

Trans Union owe a duty to Plaintiff not to falsely make a statement that there was only one account for each account on Plaintiff credit file when there were in fact two account for each account with the same account number on Plaintiff credit file.

The publication of this false statement is evident by the Trans Union document Plaintiff received on June 19, dated on June 9th and 18th 2011 see exhibit (E & F), which showed several of the same accounts duplicated over and over again repeatedly front and back on each page.

Experian Defamation

When Plaintiff applied for a line credit on a credit card at bank on Nov. 28, 2011, Plaintiff was denied credit due to "insufficient credit, "as stated by Loan officer. Mr._____ This denial was due to Experian inaccurately excluding Plaintiff credit accounts on Plaintiff credit report requested by _____ while applying for a line credit on a credit card.

By Experian not reporting Plaintiff credit file accurately to, and Mr.___ making the statement, "insufficient credit," this statement is considered false information to a third party Mr.____, and since Experian owes a duty Plaintiff to report accurate credit account information when requested by Plaintiff. When Experian provided false from inaccurate account information which causes a cause of action of defamation injury to occur to Plaintiff, and therefore damages is duet Plaintiff from this injury of Defamation, not only from loss of money from not receiving money from a line of credit, but loss future business opportunity revenue, and loss of personal wages.

A willful acknowledgment of wrong and harmful injury occurred when Plaintiff made a cell phone called to Mr.___ one Experian employees about the inaccurate exclusion of accounts on Plaintiff credit accounts on his file. Mr. Louis stated that, "he has heard in that happen [sic] before" is a willful acknowledgment of willful wrong which causes a cause of action negligence by Experian. Experian owes Plaintiff a duty to provide accurate credit file report and information about Plaintiff credit file.

By Mr. __ stating that, "sometimes those things happen "appears to say to Plaintiff that this part of the risk of doing business as a CRA and if we because you harm so be it, but this was the same statement used by Mr. Tierney Experian attorney during our first conversation together.

This nonchalant and angry attitude of CRA's employees from Plaintiff frequent calling to correct inaccurate, incomplete, unverifiable accounts on his file give rise to a cause of action of defamation on the part of CRA's employees talking about what happen to Plaintiff when they go home to their spouses, family, friends, and release this information about Plaintiff credit account to release some of stress from working after a stressful day on the Job., as well as talking to coworkers which become third party confidants.

After about a month of calling all three credit bureaus the accounts where finally rectified or corrected and return to normal meaning Plaintiff could see only one account for each creditor on Plaintiff credit file with all three CRA's Plaintiff **had** with Defendants. By then the harm and wrong committed by Defendants to Plaintiff credit accounts could not be undone especially e.g. when Plaintiff applied for credit cards and was turn down during that same period of time when inaccuracies where happening to Plaintiff by Defendant Equifax.

l0. Meanwhile at the same time Plaintiff was applying for credit at various credit card companies being rejected and denied by credit card Division from the information in Plaintiff Equifax credit file. See exhibit (A) and (B) which will justify the following injuries below which flow from the June 2011 wrong and harm done by all three defendants of the duplication of Plaintiff credit file which is clearly in accuracies as stated by 15U.S.C. § 1681] (b) of the FRCA, 168ln, [15U.S.C 168le](b),

Loss of personal income and
wages Loss of Business income
Lack of Trust in others.

Denial Credit
Financial and relationship
Hardship Psychological Stress

Mr. ___ said that having an insufficient credit report was most likely the reason that Redacted Rejects Plaintiff loan application for a loan. This being said made Plaintiff credit file inaccurate," which cause the injury and **harm** of being denied credit from ___ Bank thru Enhance Identity Theft credit monitoring service the cause of action of negligence and defamation.

Enhance Identity Theft credit monitoring service used data provided by Experian a Credit reporting Agency to produce a negligence and defamation cause of action against Plaintiff hence the following injuries above flow from the cause of action of negligence and defamation caused by Experian.

The Plaintiff must prove that the publisher acted at least negligently in publishing the communication, Plaintiff can say for certain that most of the times the tone of voice of most of the reps. plaintiff called where hostile and argumentative a disgruntled employee could have done it to get back a tone of the three credit agencies or take their working conditions frustration out on Plaintiff for calling so frequent about the inaccuracies on his credit file.

This duplication of Plaintiff credit file could have led to malice or will intent to injure Plaintiff as a way of deterring Plaintiff to stop for calling so frequently to report incorrect, inaccurate and incomplete credit information on Plaintiff credit file.

Anger if acted on can be considered a form of malice, anger, hostility and argumentative behavior is a recipe for a willful intent toward others. Plaintiff has cited that the employees of the three CRA' s exhibit this form of behavior to Plaintiff while he **was** disputing the Duplication inaccuracy of Plaintiff credit accounts.

Pursuant to rule 1 of the F.R.C.P and Justice Plaintiff will submit to the Court partial copies of all exhibits document the court has already its possession, in this second Amended Complaint in an effort for the Court to make a speedy decision to file this Complaint and to dismiss Defendants Motions to dismiss as moot.

Experian negligence elements

The credit report contains in accurate information
Copies of Plaintiff October credit accounts from Experian shows where Experian excluded all Plaintiff credit accounts except two accounts sent to Plaintiff by Experian. As well Plaintiff Nov. 28, credit report received by Plaintiff from Redacted bank when applied from credit card line of credit excluded all Plaintiff credit accounts except two.

the inaccuracy resulted from the agency's
failure to follow reasonable procedures;
By Experian not providing Plaintiff with correct copy of Plaintiff credit accounts for the loan at well Fargo Bank as Plaintiff requested, Experian failure was an act of unreasonable procedure under FCRA which cause Plaintiff to be denied the loan. Reasonable procedure would have been to provide and place all of Plaintiff correct credit accounts on the report.

Plaintiff suffered damages and
Plaintiff suffered damages when __ rejected Plaintiff loan application from the cause of Experian providing Insufficient credit references on Plaintiff credit accounts to ____ Bank. This wrongful act as stated trigger money damages compensation as determined in undetermined amount.

The injury was cause by the inaccurate information The inaccurate exclusion of Experian not providing and place the correct accounts on Plaintiff pulled credit report for the loan request by Plaintiff was an injury to Plaintiff not receiving the Loan from Experian failure to place the correct account on plaintiff credit report.

Experian Defamation [15 U.S.C 1681h] (e)

(l) The defendants published a false statement
When Experian employee stated, "that although Plaintiff saw two of the same accounts there were actually one this was a false statement because the document prove that plaintiff was right in that Plaintiff viewed two accounts with the same account number making them two of the same accounts or duplicates accounts.

About the Plaintiff
The oral statement above in#1 was a false published statement about Plaintiff, as well as the statement made by Mr. ___, "insufficient credit reference" when Plaintiff was denied the Loan at _____Bank. This was a false statement triggered by Experian in accurately exclusion of Plaintiff credit accounts in the credit report pulled by_____Bank.

To a third party; and
This manifested statement o\f "insufficient credit reference" by the third party Mr.___ from the in accurate reporting and exclusion of credit accounts at_____

The falsity of the statement caused injury to the Plaintiff
The act of Experian not accurately providing the correct Plaintiff credit accounts was an injury of personal embarrassment.

Equifax Negligence

(1)the credit report contains inaccurate information

Exhibit (J) demonstrates from Plaintiff downloaded credit file with Duplicated accounts as stated in his stated of claim of negligence but most importantly exhibit(c) of Plaintiff motion for Summary Judgment where Plaintiff account are in two's front to back.

the inaccuracy resulted from the agency's
failure to follow reasonable procedures;
Equifax fail to follow reasonable procedure when it placed two of same accounts with the same account number on Plaintiff credit file at the same time a violation of FCRA.

Plaintiff suffered damage sand
Damage was cause when Plaintiff was denied a credit card from _____
Company which prevented Plaintiff from increase his credit score.

The injury was cause by inaccurate information
When Plaintiff or a consumer apply for credit and denied from the wrongful act of CRA such as Equifax duplicating the accounts of Plaintiff credit file this violation of Plaintiff's right under the FCRA "Act."

Equifax Defamation [15U.S.C 168lh]

(e) The defendants published a false

statement
When the credit card company ___ produce the statement of "insufficient credit references" from Plaintiff Equifax credit report this print words were falsely produce to the inaccurate accounts on Plaintiff credit file.

About the Plaintiff
This false statement of "insufficient credit references" about Plaintiff is cause for a cause of action of Defamation injury on Plaintiff.

To a third-party; and
Mr. __not only produce the statement above but became the third party to the statement of "insufficient credit references" produce by Experian inaccurate credit file on Plaintiff.

The falsity of the statement caused injury to the Plaintiff
The false statement directly related to Experian inaccurate reporting of Plaintiff credit account on Plaintiff credit file cause an injury of credit denial of not receiving a line of credit of monetary funds to use for personal and business purposes.

Trans Union Negligence

The credit report contains inaccurate information
Just as Plaintiff stated and claim on the other two CRA's about that June 2011 duplication of two credit accounts with the same account numbers in addition of Plaintiff receiving from Trans Union copies of this inaccurate duplication of Plaintiff was a document detail two of the same accounts front and back on a page denoting changes on Plaintiff credit file as evidence of this in accuracy occurring in the Month of June dated 9th and 18th 2011.

The in accuracy resulted from the agency's failure This inaccuracy resulted in Trans Union Placing two of the same account with the same account numbers on Plaintiff credit file in the month June 2011 as evidence from a document of Plaintiff credit file sent to him in the month of June dated June 9th and 18th. Plaintiff suffered damages and From this act of wrongful inaccurate duplication of Plaintiff credit accounts Plaintiff was not able to improve his credit score, and this action by Trans Union deter Plaintiff credit worthiness which is a violation of FCRA as stated above.

The injury was cause by the inaccurate information
Yes, this action of duplicated accounts on Plaintiff credit file cause an injury of preventing Plaintiff from procuring credit from creditors such as __ credit company, _____ Bank, and other financial institutions.

Trans Union Defamation [15 U.S.C

1681h](e) The defendants published a false statement
The Duplicated accounts place on Plaintiff credit file not only produced an inaccurate credit report on Plaintiff credit file but constituted a false publish report statement when printed and sent to Plaintiff via mail.

About the Plaintiff
Those false inaccurate printed duplicated accounts about Plaintiff were directly pertaining to Plaintiff credit accounts and to Plaintiff file only.

To a third party; and
The process of disputing the inaccurate duplicated accounts make the plaintiff and Trans Union employees a third party for defamation purpose.

The falsity of the statement caused injury to the Plaintiff
The moment Trans Union sent out the inaccurate report to Plaintiff those printed publishes Plaintiff inaccurate credit accounts became false and cause injury of inaccuracy preventing Plaintiff from applying for credit.

Wherefore, Plaintiff prays for Judgment against Defendants for damages in the amount of $125,000 each, plus cost and interest on all three Defendants as it relates to a cause of duplicating Plaintiff credit file which resulted to Plaintiff injuries and cause of action of defamation, negligent, cause by Equifax, Trans union and Experian. In addition to punitive damage if awarded by the Court.

I verify that the above statements are true to the best of my Knowledge on

     _____date 2012. This document is submitted to all
Parties involved.

                                      Plaintiff in Pro Se

Note: All documents and exhibits submitted to Court and Defendants attorneys in prior motions and submissions are to apply to this second Amended complaint in this claim.

UNITED STATES DISTRICT COURT
MIDDLE DISTRICT OF FLORIDA
JACKSONVILLE DIVISION

JAMES WATSON,

Plaintiff,

CASE NO. 3:12-cv-552-J-99MMH-JBT

EQUIFAX, EXPERIAN, and TRANSUNION,

Defendants.

REPORT AND RECOMMENDATION

—

THIS CAUSE is before the Court on the Joint Motion to Dismiss Plaintiffs Second

Amended Complaint by all three Defendants ("Motion") (Doc. 92) and Plaintiffs

Response (Doc. 100).[2] For the reasons that follow. the undersigned

RECOMMENDS that the Motion [1] "Within 14 days after being served with a copy of

[this Report and Recommendation], DENIED

party may serve and file specific written objections to the proposed findings and

recommendations. A party may respond to another party's objections within 14 days after
being served with a copy." Fed. R. Civ. P. 72(b)(2); *see also* 28 U.S.C. § 636(b)(1); M.D.
Fla. R. 6.02(a). "A judge of the court shall make a de novo determination of those portions of
the report or specified proposed findings or recommendations to which objection is made."
28 U.S.C. §636(b)(1).

[2] Plaintiff, proceeding *pro se*, has styled his response as follows: "Plaintiff Motion in Support
of Second Amended Complaint and Dismissing Defendants Amended Motion to Dismiss
Plaintiff Second Amended Complaint." Although styled a motion in its own right, this
document responds to the Motion and sets forth argument why Plaintiff's Second Amended
Complaint should not be dismissed. The undersigned therefore will treat it as a response
filed under Local Rule 3.01(b).

Summary of Recommendation

Pro se Plaintiff James Watson sues Defendants Equifax Information Services LLC ("Equifax"), Experian Information Solutions, Inc. ("Experian"), and Trans Union LLC ("Trans Union") for alleged inaccuracies in his credit report. Plaintiff brings claims against each Defendant for common law defamation and negligent non-compliance with the federal Fair Credit Reporting Act, 15 U.S.C. §§1681-81x ("FCRA"). *(See* Doc. 76.) Defendants jointly *move* to dismiss all claims against them. (*See* Doc. 92.) Although Plaintiff's Second Amended Complaint ("SAC") (Doc. 76) is far from a model of clarity, the undersigned recommends that, when construed liberally in Plaintiff's *favor,* the SAC barely states a claim against each Defendant for common law defamation and negligent non-compliance with the FCRA. Plaintiff minimally addresses all the necessary elements of these claims, and arguably includes sufficient factual material to plausibly support these allegations. Although many of Plaintiff's allegations would not suffice if filed by an attorney, under a liberal construction, the undersigned recommends that they barely pass muster.

Background

The Court previously took under advisement Defendants' joint motion to dismiss Plaintiff's first Amended Complaint (Doc. 16), and directed Plaintiff to file a second amended complaint. *(See* Doc. 63). In that Order, the Court set forth the elements of the claims Plaintiff were apparently attempting to allege. *(Id.* at 5-7.)

Plaintiff's allegations of wrongful conduct generally fall into three categories.[3] First, Plaintiff alleges that, in June 2011, duplicate entries began appearing on his credit reports. (Doc. 76 at 4.) Plaintiff alleges that he discovered these duplicate entries by monitoring his credit reports through Defendants' respective credit monitoring services. *(Id.)* The duplicated accounts allegedly included "__ accounts," "____ accounts, "and "___ Accounts." *(Id.)* Upon discovering these duplicate

entries, Plaintiff called each Defendant. *(Id.)* Defendants corrected the reports by August of the same year. *(Id.)* Nevertheless, Plaintiff alleges that these errors harmed him by "negat[ing] [his] progress of re- establishing his credit" *(id.* at 7) and by preventing him from obtaining credit to finance unspecified projects and business ventures *(id.* at 5).

Second, Plaintiff alleges that, as a result of attempting to correct the above error, Equifax improperly reported to ____ that Plaintiff had no credit history in connection with Plaintiff's credit card application. *(Id.)* redacted consequently denied the application. *(Id.)*

Third, Plaintiff alleges that in November 2011, Experian allegedly provided

---

3

  There are other questionable allegations of wrongful conduct, such as Equifax's alleged failure to record a credit inquiry as a "hard inquiry." (Doc. 76 at 5.) However, the undersigned has focused on the most coherent and well-pied allegations.

_____bank with an inaccurate credit report stating that Plaintiff had only two credit accounts. *(Id.* at 6.) Plaintiff alleges that as a result, _____denied Plaintiffs credit application due to "insufficient credit." (/d.) Plaintiff maintains that he in fact had a much more extensive credit history. (/d.)

Based primarily on the above allegations, Plaintiff sues Defendants for common law defamation, and for negligent violation of 15 U.S.C. § 1681e(b), which requires a consumer reporting agency to "follow reasonable procedures to assure maximum possible accuracy" of a consumer report, id*.; see also 1 5*

§ 16810 (creating a private right of action for negligent non-compliance with the FCRA).

III. Discussion

Rule 12(b)(6) Standard

To survive a motion to dismiss brought pursuant to Rule 12(b)(6) of the Federal Rules of Civil Procedure, "a complaint must contain sufficient factual matter, accepted as true, to state a claim to relief that is plausible on its face." *Ashcroft v. Iqbal,* 556 U.S. 662, 678 (2009) (internal quotation marks omitted). A claim is plausible on its face where "the plaintiff pleads factual content that allows the court to draw the reasonable inference that the defendant is liable for the misconduct alleged." *Id.* Plausibility means "more than a sheer possibility that a defendant has acted unlawfully." *Id.* "Where a complaint pleads facts that are merely consistent with a defendant's liability, it stops short of the line between possibility and plausibility of entitlement to relief." *Id.* (internal quotation marks omitted).

The determination of whether a complaint states a plausible claim for relief is "a context-specific task that requires the reviewing court to draw on its judicial experience and common sense." *Id.* at 679. The Court is "not bound to accept as true a legal conclusion couched as a factual allegation." *Id.* "[B]are assertions" that "amount to nothing more than a 'formulaic recitation of the elements'" of a claim "are conclusory and not entitled to be assumed true." *Id.* at 680.

However, it is well-established that the pleadings of *pro se* litigants, like Plaintiff, must be liberally construed and "are held to less stringent standards than formal pleadings drafted by lawyers." *Hughes v. Rowe,* 448 U.S. 5, 9 (1980) (per curium). Further, "[a] court must favor the plaintiff with all reasonable inferences from the allegations in the complaint." *Allmond v. Bank of America,* 3:07-cv-186- J-33JRK, 2008WL 205320, at *2 (M.D. Fla. Jan. 23, 2008).

In determining whether to grant or deny a motion to dismiss, the Court must evaluate the complaint "on two dimensions." *Id.,* at *3. First, the Court must assess whether all the necessary elements required for recovery are addressed in the complaint. *Id.* "Second, the Court must determine whether the complaint addresses these elements with factual material sufficient to raise a right to relief beyond mere speculation." *Id.* "This material can be either direct or inferential." .• *Id.,* at*5.

Analysis

Plaintiff's Claims for Negligent Violations of 15 U.S.C. §1681e(b)

The undersigned recommends that Plaintiff adequately states a claim against each Defendant for negligently violating 15 U.S.C. § 1681e(b). Section 1681e(b) provides-

Whenever a consumer reporting agency prepares a consumer report, it shall follow reasonable procedures to assure maximum possible accuracy of the information concerning the individual about whom the report relates.

15 U.S.C. § 1681e(b). Section 16810 of Title 15 creates a private right of action for a consumer reporting agency's negligent non-compliance with the FCRA, including this mandate.

As the Court observed in its prior Order taking under advisement Plaintiffs First Amended Complaint (see Doc. 63 at 5-6), a claim for negligent violation of § 1681e(b) has four elements: "(1) the credit report contained inaccurate information; (2) the inaccuracy resulted from the agency's failure to follow reasonable procedures; (3) [plaintiff] suffered damages; and (4) the injury was caused by the inaccurate information." *Jordan v. Equifax Info. Servs., LLC,* 410

F.Supp.2d 1349, 1357 (N.D. Ga. 2006). In that Order, the Court was most concerned with Plaintiff s failure to allege the second of these elements: that Defendants failed to follow reasonable procedures. (Doc. 63 at 6.)

In the SAC, Plaintiff has sufficiently alleged all of the above elements. Although Plaintiffs allegations regarding Defendants' failure to follow reasonable procedures are conclusory, courts have recognized that "in some cases, the nature of an inaccuracy itself can support an inference that the consumer reporting agency failed to follow reasonable procedures." *Allmond,* 2008 W L

205320, at *5. The undersigned concludes that this is such a case.

Plaintiff alleges that all three Defendants failed to follow sufficient reasonable procedures in allowing duplicate accounts to appear on Plaintiffs credit report. (Doc. 76 at 4 ("Defendants failed to have reasonable procedures in place to prevent duplication of Plaintiff['s] credit accounts on Plaintiff['s] credit file.").) Plaintiff also alleges that Equifax failed to follow reasonable procedures when it transmitted a credit report to __ showing that Plaintiff had no credit history. *(Id.* at 5.) And Plaintiff alleges that Experian failed to follow reasonable procedures when it transmitted a similarly inaccurate report to _____bank. *(Id.* at 11 ("Reasonable procedure[s] would have been to provide and place all of Plaintiff['s] credit accounts on the report.").)

It appears plausible that Defendants should have had reasonable procedures in place to prevent these types of errors, which involve merely avoiding erroneous duplications or omissions. It is further plausible that Defendants failed to follow such procedures. It would place an unreasonable burden on Plaintiff to have to plead this element with greater specificity at this point since presumably Plaintiff is not privy to Defendants' procedures. Plaintiff should be able to advance these negligent non-compliance claims beyond the pleading stage.

Defendants argue that the holding in *Allmond* supports their argument. But *Allmond,* in which a negligent non-compliance claim under the FCRA was dismissed without prejudice, is distinguishable. There, the aggrieved consumer's complaint contained no reference to the defendant reporting agency's purported procedures. Instead, the *Allmond* plaintiff alleged merely that the reporting agency prepared an inaccurate consumer report based on inaccurate information

. provided by a third party, *i.e.,* that plaintiff was "abus[ing] an automated teller machine by putting blank envelopes in the machine and receiving money." *Allmond,* 2008 WL 205320, at *4-7. Here, Plaintiff alleges that Defendants originated the inaccuracies, and the nature of the inaccuracies, which in this case involve erroneous duplications or omissions, is distinguishable as well.

For these reasons, the undersigned recommends that the Motion be denied with respect to Plaintiff's negligent non-compliance claims.

Plaintiff's Defamation Claims

Plaintiff also alleges common law defamation against all three Defendants. Under Florida law, "[d]defamation has the following five elements: (1)publication; (2) falsity; (3) actor must act with knowledge or reckless disregard as to falsity on matter concerning a public official, or at least negligently on a matter concerning a private person; (4) actual damages; and (5) statement must be defamatory." *Jews For Jesus, Inc. v. Rapp,* 997 So. 2d 1098, 1106 (Fla. 2008). However, the FCRA disallows defamation claims, even for private persons, "except as to false information furnished with malice or willful intent to injure such consumer." 15 U.S.C. § 1681h(e). "[M]alice is defined as a statement made 'with knowledge that it was false or with reckless disregard of whether it was false or not.'" *Hunt v. Liberty Lobby,* 720 F.2d 631, 642 (11th Cir. 1983)(citing *New York Times* Co. *v. Sullivan,* 376 U.S. 254, 279-80 (1964)).

In its prior Order, the Court took Plaintiff's defamation claims under advisement in part because Plaintiff did not sufficiently allege that Defendants acted willfully or with malice. The Order observed, "[a]lthough the Amended Complaint briefly references malice by stating that '[t]his duplication of Plaintiff['s] credit file could have led [sic] to malice or will [sic] intent to injure Plaintiff,' (Doc. 16 at 5), Plaintiff fails to state any plausible facts in support of malice or willful intent to injure him." (Doc. 63 at 7 (alterations in original).)

Although many of Plaintiff's factual allegations surrounding his conclusions that Defendants acted willfully appear questionable in the SAC (such as, for example, Experian's alleged "acknowledgment of willful wrong" by an employee indicating he has heard of such mistakes before (Doc. 76 at 9)), the undersigned recommends that Plaintiff's allegations of Defendants' mental states are sufficient. The sum of the allegations of the SAC, including those pertaining to the nature of the inaccuracies in the credit reports, gives rise to a reasonable plausible inference that Defendants acted with reckless disregard for the truth or perhaps less so, with willful intent to injure Plaintiff. The below authorities have been similarly lenient when allegations of mental state, particularly in a defamation context by a *pro se* litigant, are involved.

In *Allmond,* the court denied a credit reporting agency's motion to dismiss a defamation claim where the *pro se* plaintiff made only the following allegations of malice or willfulness: "Defendants violated the Privacy Act, 15 U.S.C. and the Anti-Fraud Exchange stat. and maliciously slander and libel the Plaintiff ..." *Allmond,* 2008 WL 205320, at *2. As the *Allmond* court stated in language applicable here: "[Plaintiff's] complaint is somewhat vague and confusing, but it is not so opaque that the Court cannot discern sufficient factual allegations addressed to each element of a defamation claim under Florida law." *Id.* at 7.

Similarly, in *Embrey v. First Franklin Financial Corporation,* 12-61233-Civ., 2013 WL 1289401 (S.D. Fla. Mar. 12, 2013), the Southern District of Florida held that a represented plaintiff sufficiently pleaded the FCRA's required mental state by alleging that "Defendants 'exhibited a knowing disregard for the truth.'" *Id.,* at

*5. The *Embrey* court concluded: "This is enough. Since the Plaintiffs have sufficiently alleged that the Defendants acted with malice, their defamation claim is not preempted by the Fair Credit Reporting Act." *Id.*

Moreover, many courts, including the Eleventh Circuit, have recognized that Rule 9(b), Fed. R. Civ. P., allows allegations regarding mental state to be alleged "generally." *United States ex rel. Matheny v. Medco Health Solutions, Inc.,* 671 F.3d 1217, 1224 (11th Cir. 2012); *see also Embrey,* 2013 WL 1289401,

*5; *Austin v. Auto Owners Ins.* Co., No. 12-0345, 2012 WL 3101693, at *4 (N.D Ala. Jul. 30, 2012) and cases cited therein. Given this rule, Plaintiff s *pro se* status, and the barely sufficient allegations of the SAC, the   undersigned

recommends that Plaintiff has adequately alleged malice or willful intent to injure pursuant to 15 U.S.C. § 1681h(e).

Similarly, the undersigned recommends that Plaintiff has barely sufficiently alleged the remaining elements of defamation against each Defendant. Plaintiff has alleged that Defendants published false statements about him, *i.e.,*   credit reports containing inaccuracies,[4] to third parties, *i.e.,* potential creditors,[5] which caused

him injuries, i.e., loss of credit.[6] Although these allegations at times are

"somewhat vague and confusing," they are "not so opaque that the Court cannot discern

sufficient factual allegations addressed to each element of a defamation claim under

Florida law." *Allmond,* 2008 WL 205320, at *7.

Conclusion

For the foregoing reasons, the undersigned respectfully **RECOMMENDS**

that:

It is also at least plausible that the inaccuracies were defamatory, although Plaintiff may face an uphill battle in proving how some inaccuracies in particular, such as missing credit entries, were defamatory. "[A] defamatory statement is one that tends to harm the reputation of another by lowering him or her in the estimation of the community or, more broadly stated, one that exposes a plaintiff to hatred, ridicule, or contempt or injures his business or reputation or occupation." *Jews For* Jesus, 997 So. 2d at 1108-09.

[5] The undersigned recognizes that Plaintiff's allegations regarding publication to third parties are particularly weak with respect to Defendant Trans Union. In enumerated paragraph 4 of page 13 of Plaintiff's SAC, however, Plaintiff alleges that "this action of duplicated accounts on Plaintiff['s] credit file caused an injury of preventing Plaintiff from procuring credit from creditors such as __ credit company, _____ Bank, and other financial institutions." (Doc. 76 at 13.) This allegation supports a reasonable inference that Trans Union published Plaintiff's credit report to third parties.

[6] Other alleged wrongs that Plaintiff characterizes as defamation clearly do not satisfy its elements. For example, Plaintiff's allegation that Trans Union employees constitute third parties for defamation purposes appears insufficient. Further, Plaintiff alleges that Experian committed defamation when its employees informed Plaintiff on the telephone that, "although Plaintiff saw two of the same accounts [on his credit report] there [was) only one." (Doc. 76 at 11.) This statement cannot be defamation as, among other issues, it was made to Plaintiff and not to a third party. *See Jews For Jesus,* 997 So. 2d at 1106. Similarly, Plaintiff's allegations that Defendants' employees discussed Plaintiff with "their spouses, family, [and] friends" appear unfounded and speculative. However, as previously noted, the undersigned has focused on Plaintiff's most coherent and plausible allegations.

Defendants' Motion (Doc. 92) be **DENIED;** and

Defendants be **DIRECTED** to answer the SAC within 10 days   of the

Court's Order on this Report and Recommendation.

DONE AND ENTERED at Jacksonville Florida, on April 24, 2013.

Joel Toomey

United States Magistrate Judge

Copies to:

The Honorable Marcia Morales Howard
United States District Judge

Counsel of Record

Pro Se Plaintiff

IN THE UNITED STATES DISTRICT COURT

MIDDLE DISTRICT OF FLORIDA

Jacksonville Division

James Watson

Plaintiff

Case No.3:12-cv-552-J-99MMH-JBT

Equifax, Experian, Transunion

Defendants

PLAINTIFF MOTION IN SUPPORT OF AMENDED COMPLAINT AND DISMISSING DEFENDANTS MOTION TO DISMISS PLAINTIFF AMENDED COMPLAINT

Pursuant to Federal Rules of Civil Procedure 8(a)(2) Plaintiff file this motion in

support of Plaintiff Amended Complaint and Dismissing all three Defendants

motion to dismiss Plaintiff Amended Complaint. Specifically, Plaintiff Amended

Complaint does state a claim against all three Defendants, and doe satisfies all

the requirements of specificity, Plausibility in Ashcroft v. Iqbal, and Bell Atlanta

Corp.v. Twombly.

Therefore the Court should dismiss defendants Motion as moot and grantPlaintiff

Amended Complaint, reliefshould begranted in favor ofPlaintiffin this action.

Under the FCRA Congress entrust allthree CRAs with the "Grave responsibility" to ensure that

information is accurate andtoproperly investigated disputes, [15U.S.C.§1681] (a)(4).

BACKGROUND CASE INFORMATION

On April 122012, James Watson Pro Se brought an action in State Court Circuit, Fourth Judicial

Circuit in and Duval County, Florida against Defendants Equifax, Trans Union and Experian for a

cause of action of Negligence and Defamation from violation of Duplicating or multiple creditor

accounts on Plaintiff credit file, Plaintiff observed these inaccuracies of Duplicated credit files

on all three CRAs websites while Plaintiff was trying to improve his credit standings. (Doc.# 2).

On May 9, 2012 Experian, Equifax, and Trans Union joiner and removed action from Duval State

Court to this Court, United States District Court Middle District of Florida Jacksonville Division

with Equifax, and Trans Union joining and consenting to the removal. (Doc. #3, 4). On May 16,

2012 In response to Plaintiff Amended Complaint with a stated legal claim, Equifax file motion to

dismiss Plaintiff complaint and Experian and Trans Union file their Rule 12(b) (6) Motion to

Dismiss Plaintiff Complaint and Memorandum in Support for alleging Plaintiff did not state a

claim which Plaintiff considered meritless on all four corners on the face of the Complaint.

Due to the fact their own attorney, Mr. Franklin G. Cosmen, JR PA stated "Defendant Trans

union LLC's Joiner and consent to Removal "On May 1,2012, Trans union was served with

Plaintiff's Complaint, the initial pleading setting forth the claim for relief upon which this

action is base."

May 21, 2012, Plaintiff filed a Motion for leave to amend his Complaint (Doc. # 13). May 25,

2012, Plaintiff filed Propose Amend Complaint in this Court (Doc. # 16) as It pertains to

Fed. R. Civ. P. 15(a) (1) (B). Plaintiff is allowed to Amend is Complaint once as a matter of rule.

On May 30,2012 Plaintiff offered evidence attach to his Motion to Amend Plaintiff Complaint which was accepted by this Court. See exhibit (A) and (B). On June 11,2012 This Court Granted Plaintiff Motion to Amend Complaint (Doc.# 20) as filed, and dismissed all three Defendants Motions to Dismiss Plaintiff Complaint (Doc.# 9, 10,11). On June 19,2012 Plaintiff submitted his Summary Judgment Pursuant to Federal Rules of Civil Procedure (56) (Doc.#28), summary Judgment can be presented by the moving party if the case is more than 20 days. Plaintiff Summary Judgment Affidavit accepted by the Court with Material evidence (Doc. #34).

Defendants file a motion for extension of time to respond to Plaintiff Summary Judgment oppose by Plaintiff but grant by Magistrate Judge Toomey with an issue order stating, "The Court need not wait for Plaintiff response to this motion for extension of time."(Doc.# 38)

II. MEMORANDUM IN SUPPORT OF PLAINTIFF CLAIM

It is axiomatic that in deciding a motion to dismiss pursuant to Rule 12(b)(6), the Court must accept all factual allegations as true and draw all inferences in favor of Plaintiff. Levy ex rel. Immunogen Inc. v. Southbrook Int'l Invs., Ltd. 263 F.3d 10,14(2d Cir.2001),cert. denied,535

U.S. 1054, 152L. Ed. 2d 821 (2002). "Dismissal is not appropriate unless it appears beyond doubt that the Plaintiff can prove no set of facts in support of his claim which would entitle him to relief. "Chance v. Armstrong,143 F.3d 698,701(2d Cir. 1998) (quoting

Conley v. Gibson,355

U.S.41,45-46,2L.Ed.2d80, 78S.Ct99(1957)."This rule applies with particular force...where the complaint is submitted Pro Se ...At the 12(b)(6) stage, 'the issue is not whether a Plaintiff is likely to prevail ultimately, but whether the Claimant is entitled to offer evidence to support the claims, see Summary Judgment Affidavit (Doc.# 34). Indeed, it may appear on the face of the pleading that a recovery is very remote and unlikely but that is not the test. " Id at 701 {citation omitted) As a result, where a Plaintiff is proceeding Pro Se, the Court Must construe the pleading liberally, and must "interpret them to raise the strongest arguments that they suggest. "Burgor v. Hopkins, 14F 3d 787,790 (2d Cir. 1994). Under Federal Rule of Civil Procedure 8{a} {2} a pleading must contain a "short and plain statement of the claim showing that the pleader is entitle to relief." As the Court held in Twombly, 550 U.S. 544, the pleading standard Rule 8 announces does not require "detail

factual allegations," ...(id) at 555{citing Papasan v. Allain 478 U.S. 265,286(1986). To survive a motion to dismiss, a complaint must contain sufficient factual matter accepted as true, to "state aa claim to relief that is plausible on its face," id., at 570. A claim has plausibility when the Plaintiff pleads factual content that allows the Court to draw the reasonable inferences that the Defendants is liable for Misconduct alleged, in the instance case negligent and defamation (id) at 556.Determining whether a complaint states a plausible claim for relief will, as the Court of Appeals observed, be context-specific task that requires the reviewing Court to draw on its judicial experience and common sense 490 F.3d at 157-158.

Moreover, based on *Maxcess, Inc. v. Techs., Inc.,* 433 F.3d 1377, 1340, n. 3 (11thCir.2005), the Court may consider relevant documents that are central to a Plaintiff claim, {again the Court

should examine Material document of Plaintiff exhibit {A (Band Affidavit submitted

with Summary Judgment.

Fai r Credit Reporting Act provides that: whenever a consumer reporting agency prepares a

consumer report it shall follow reasonable procedures to assure maximum possible accuracy of the

information concerning the individual about whom the report relates." 15U.S.C. 1681e(b.

In a reinvestigation of the accuracy of credit report, a credit bureau must bear some

responsibility for evaluating the accuracy of information obtain from subscriber" white v. trans

Union 462 F. Supp. 2d 1079(CD. Cal2006.

Whether a CRA has acted in "Willful noncompliance" with the FCRA under 1681nis and objective

assessment that encompasses action taken in reckless disregard of FCRA's obligations. Safeco,

551U.S. 47, 127 S. CT. at 2208-10, 2215.

15U.S.C. 1681nprovides that any "person who willfully fail to comply with any requirement under

this subchapter with respect to any consumer is liable to that consumer" for actual and punitive

damages. Hernandez v. Lamboy Furniture Inc., 2008 WL 4061344, at *8 (E.D. Pa Sept. 2, 2008).

"Congress bestowed on credit agencies special requirements for meeting the needs of commerce...

with regard to the confidentiality, accuracy, relevancy, and proper utilization of such information

in accordance with the requirements of this title Fair Credit Reporting Act 15U.S.C.§1681]

(b)."(Emphasis add on accuracy) 15U.S.C. § 168la](d) (1): In general, the term consumer report

means any written, oral, or other communication of any information by a consumer reporting

agency...

(Emphasis on "any information")

However, in the instance case where the Plaintiff has pleaded facts that in themselves adds up to a valid legal claim with the appropriate legal theories dismissal of Plaintiff Amended Complaint should not be granted to the Defendants.

Under section 15U.S.C. §1681a) (d) (3)(g) of the FCRA The term "file" when used in connection with information on any consumer, means all of the information on that consumer recorded and retained by a consumer reporting agency regardless of how the information is stored. (Emphasis on "all the information on that consumer" added)

Defendants argue the issue of "Insufficient credit Reference" as stated by __ bank credit card means that there is either "no credit" information available or not enough credit information to base another credit decision on. Base on Plaintiff credit profile dated on or around the month of June, that if all three CRA's especially Equifax had all Plaintiff Creditors on Plaintiff "file" during that time the Creditor was checking Plaintiff file for approval of his credit. The computer algorithm scan would have register Plaintiff credit file as not having "Insufficient credit Reference" when in fact Plaintiff had many credit references available to base their approval on by the credit card company.

Defendants position is that Plaintiff complaint is not Plausible, well the definition of Plausibility is "having an appearance of truth or reason: seemingly worthy of approval or acceptance credible believable." Plaintiff believes that this Court will know that the claims is not only believable, but the concrete justifiable truth.

Plaintiff satisfies the Plausibility principle of Ashcroft v. Iqbal with Plaintiff statement, "of seeing two __accounts on Plaintiff credit account on his file," as well as his statement of Defendants

Purging Plaintiff credit accounts when ____.was checking Plaintiff credit to approved Plaintiff for a credit card and was denied with the reason of "INSUFFICIENT CREDIT REFERENCES" (Doc. #16, Exhibit B), (Emphasis Added) pertaining to Iqbal specificity.

Specificity as it relates to ____Bank Loan representative _____ stated,"that Plaintiff was denied credit because Enhance Identity Theft provided Plaintiff with a report that contain only two or three credit accounts of Plaintiff credit file from Experian. An Experian Agent said that although Plaintiff sees two file it is only one (Emphasis Added).

Because all three Defendants computers programs were instructed to correct

the inaccuracies of the Plaintiff Duplicated accounts or Multiple credit accounts in Plaintiff

credit file, as in Angela Williams V. Equifax one of the claims of this case was the multiple files on her credit account that Equifax refuse to redact from her account. The heart of the litigation between the parties was the Frozen scans which would help show that Equifax violated 15

U.S.C. § 1681] (b)." by not following reasonable procedures to assure maximum possible accuracy.

As a precedent case similar to Plaintiff instance case with duplicated or multiple credit accounts between these three Defendants one of the main issues of the Angela Williams v. Equifax case was the Frozen scans. These frozen scans would prove that there was Multiple or Duplicated credit files on Plaintiff credit file even if accounts were purge by all three Defendants, Angela Williams V. Equifax 359 F. Supp. 2d. 1284(2005), (citation omitted)

Equifax refused to have Judge o have access to the Frozen scans because they are aware that this evidence would hurt Equifax case.

If materials extrinsic to the pleadings are submitted to the Court in support of or in opposition to a 12(b)(6) motion the Court does not have to consider them. Under FRCP 12(b), however, once the court does consider such matter the motion is automatically "converted to a motion for summary judgment pursuant to FRCP 56.

Material does not literally have to be bound into the Complaint to be considered "intrinsic" to it and a proper part consideration of a 12(b) (6) motion, without a "conversion" taking place.

It can fairly be said that any oral or written evidence not already "in the record" public or Court, physical or by reference is regarded as "extrinsic" and will spur a conversion.

Therefore, the Court has in its possession two Summary Judgments to decide because of the conversion of the Amended complaint and the Motion for Summary Judgment (doc. #28).

Plaintiff Amended Complaint on all four corners of the Complaint is stating claim, that claims all three Defendants created a duplicate or multiple credit accounts of Plaintiff's credit accounts in the month of June while Plaintiff was trying to improve his credit standing while visiting their website. Defendants was in violation of [15 U.S.C. § 1681] (b) and 15 U.S.C. 1681(e)(b) of the FCRA.
A definition of a claim as stated by Merriam's Webster's Dictionary of Law page 79 "3. A: A write to seek a judicial remedy rising from a wrong or injury suffered..." Plaintiff Amended Complaint satisfies all of F.R.C.P of Rule 8.
Plaintiff initiated this case on April 12, 2012 in the State Court of Duval, County (Doc. #1). On May 9, 2012 all three Defendants stipulated to Joiner to have the case moved to Federal District Court in Jacksonville (Doc. #2).

Plaintiff satisfies the claim requirement of the Amended Complaint when Plaintiff stated that

all three Defendants duplicated Plaintiff s credit accounts under F.C.R.A. 15U.S.C. 1681(b),

(Emphasis Added) on accuracy, that a cause of action of Negligence took place or occurred.

When Plaintiff stated that defendants made two__ accounts twice the specificity theory was

satisfied reference to Ashcroft v. Iqbal, 556 U.S. 662, 665(2009).

Plaintiff's Amended Complaint survives because it does state factual matters such as stating,

"__ accounts was reporting on Plaintiff's file twice..."

To survive a Motion to Dismiss a Complaint must contain factual matters accepted as truth to

state a claim to relief on its own face, Ashcroft v. Iqbal, 556 U.S. 662, 665(2009).

Another instance as stated by Defendants on Page 2, Second paragraph, "One day in the First of

June (specific month satisfied}. Plaintiff used his cell phone to dispute these inaccuracies by

calling each Defendant to notify Defendants of inaccuracies of the duplicated Plaintiff's credit

files. Furthermore, on Page 2, paragraph 8, Plaintiff's Complaint states, "An experienced agent

said that although Plaintiff sees two files it is only one", this statement in itself is a statement

satisfying specificity.

The fact that Defendants Duplicated Plaintiff credit file makes Defendants liable under a claim

of a cause of action of negligence as well as Malice when Defendants attorney Tom Tierney

Stated Those Things Happen when Plaintiff had his first telephone conference by Experian Lead

Attorney this appears to be the prevail attitude of all three credit bureaus Equifax, Experian and

Trans Union.

Under 15U.S.C. 1681(b)of the FCRA, in fact the act of duplicating any consumer credit files

of Plaintiff which are not accurate makes the file inaccurate and the Defendant's by definition

is liable for their injuries to the Plaintiff with the cause of action of negligence.

By Defendant's admitting the fact, the only provision that Plaintiff specifically cites to is the 15 U.S.C. 1681(sic) which should be S U.S.C. 1681 (b) this section of the FCRA stress the word accuracy when Plaintiff reported the dispute by cell phone to all three Defendants of the inaccuracies of not having one credit file only on Plaintiffs credit file. (Add material). By asserting a claim of all three violations of FCRA of the U.S.C. 1681(d) sic and 15U.S.C. 1681 (b) (Plaintiff satisfies a factual claim and identifies these sections in Plaintiff Amended Complaint. See Thrasher V. Armadillo Police Department, 346 Fed. Appx 991,992(Fifth Cir. 2009). Under the FRCA of 15 U.S.C. 1681 (b) (if any of Plaintiff's credit accounts which is the totality of . his entire file is inaccurate all three Defendants are subject to damages from their injuries and harm done to Plaintiff, Nelson v. Chase Manhattan Mortgage Corp. 282 F.3d 1057(2002)

Plaintiff states that after about a month of calling all three credit bureaus the accounts were finally rectified and returned to normal means Plaintiff sees only one account for each credit account Plaintiff had with Defendants. This statement by Plaintiff is explicit in nature that all three Defendants were put on notice of disputes by Plaintiff as required by FCRA 15U.S.C. §1681et seq. If the dispute was initiated in the first part of June, 2011 then after a month (would state that it was more than 30 days after the initial disputes) of calling all three Defendants had corrected the inaccuracies explicitly states that Defendants corrected Plaintiffs credit accounts but if only one of the accounts were not corrected a negligent liability exist with all three Defendants see when Plaintiff was denied a credit card from __.

Defendants mistakenly stated on page five second paragraph "While Plaintiff alleges that on a certain date her [sic] credit report was improperly assessed by each moving Defendants Plaintiff does provide factual support exhibit A and Exhibit B to address reasonable inference

UNITED STATES DISTRICT COURT
MIDDLE DISTRICT OF FLORIDA
JACKSONVILLE DIVISION

JAMES WATSON,

Plaintiff,

CASE NO. 3:12-cv-552-J-99MMH-JBT

EQUIFAX, EXPERIAN, and TRANSUNION,

Defendants.

COURT DENYING DISCOVERY MATERIAL FILED

THIS CAUSE is before the Court on Defendant Experian Information Solutions, Inc.'s

Notice of Service of Initial Disclosures ("Notice of Service") (Doc. 52), filed on July 30,

2012. Pursuant to Rule 5(d)(1) of the Federal Rules of   Civil

Procedure and Rule 3.03(d) of the Local Rules for the Middle District of Florida, discovery

materials are not to be routinely filed with the Court unless they are pertinent to a matter

before the Court or the Court orders that they be filed. Fed. R. Civ. P. 5(d)(1); M.D. Fla.

R. 3.03(d). Upon review of the Notice of Service, the Court considers it to constitute

discovery material not to be filed in the normal course. Moreover, the Notice of Service

does not appear relevant to any motion currently pending before the Court. In light of the

foregoing, it is

ORDERED:

Defendant Experian's Notice **(Doc. 52) is STRICKEN** without prejudice to filing at a later

time if necessary.

UNITED STATES DISTRICT COURT
FOR THE MIDDLE DISTRICT OF FLORIDA
JACKSONVILLE DIVISION

JAMES L. WATSON,	)	
	)	
Plaintiff,	)	
	)	
vs.	)	
	)	Case No. 3:12-cv-00552-UAMH-JBT
EQUIFAX, EXPERIAN, and	)	
TRANSUNION,	)	
	)	
Defendants.	)	

DEFENDANTS EQUIFAX INFORMATION SERVICES LLC, EXPERIAN INFORMATION SOLUTIONS, INC., AND TRANS UNION LLC'S AMENDED JOINT MOTION TO DISMISS PLAINTIFF'S SECOND AMENDED COMPLAINT AND MEMORANDUM IN SUPPORT

Pursuant to Federal Rule of Civil Procedure 12(b)(6), Defendants Equifax Information Services LLC ("Equifax"), incorrectly named in Plaintiff's Second Amended Complaint as "Equifax," Experian Information Solutions, Inc. ("Experian"), incorrectly named in Plaintiff's Second Amended Complaint as "Experian," and Trans Union LLC ("Trans Union"), incorrectly named in Plaintiff's Second Amended Complaint as "TransUnion" (collectively "Defendants"), file this Amended Motion to Dismiss Plaintiff's Second Amended Complaint.

I. STATEMENT OF RELIEF REQUESTED AND BASIS FOR REQUEST

Defendants respectfully request that this Honorable Court dismiss all claims asserted in Plaintiff's Second Amended Complaint against Defendants in their entirety, with prejudice, **and** to grant any further relief to which Defendants may be entitled. Defendants base this request on the failure of Plaintiff's Second Amended Complaint to state a claim against Defendants upon which relief may be granted.

II. MEMORANDUM OF LEGAL AUTHORITY

A. BACKGROUND

On April 12, 2012, *pro se* Plaintiff James Watson sued Defendants Equifax, Experian, and Trans Union. The case was removed from the Circuit Court, Fourth Judicial Circuit in and for Duval County, Florida on May 9, 2012. In response to Plaintiff's Complaint, on May 16, 2012, Equifax filed a Motion to Dismiss Plaintiff's Complaint (Doc. 11) and Experian and Trans Union filed their Joint Motion to Dismiss Plaintiff's Complaint (Doc. 9) for failure to state a claim upon which relief can be granted. On May 21, 2012, Plaintiff filed a Motion to Amend his Complaint (Doc. 13), and on May 25, 2012, he filed a Proposed Amended Complaint (Doc. 16). On June 11, 2012, this Court granted Plaintiff's Motion to Amend his Complaint (Doc. 20).

On June 25, 2012, Defendants Experian and Trans Union filed a Joint Motion to Dismiss Plaintiff's Amended Complaint (Doc. 35), and on June 28, 2012, Equifax filed its Motion to Dismiss Plaintiff's Amended Complaint (Doc. 40). By Order dated September 18, 2012, the Court took both motions to dismiss under advisement and permitted Plaintiff "one likely final opportunity to attempt to state a viable claim." (Doc. 63 at 2.) The Order directed Plaintiff to file a Second Amended Complaint, specifically noting, "Plaintiff is cautioned against making legal arguments and setting out legal standards in the complaint ... . In addition, the counts of a complaint should be clearly separated and all paragraphs should be numbered consecutively." (*Id.* at 7.)

Plaintiff filed his Second Amended Complaint on October 9, 2012. (Doc. 76.) The Court then accordingly denied Defendants' motions to dismiss the Amended Complaint as moot and set a deadline of November 2, 2012, for Defendants to respond to Plaintiff's Second Amended Complaint. (Doc. 77.) On November 2, 2012, Defendants filed a Joint Motion to Dismiss Plaintiff's Second Amended Complaint (Doc. 83) and a separate Memorandum in Support (Doc

84). The Court struck that Joint Motion and Memorandum because they were filed as separate documents, where Local Rule 3.01 requires that a motion be filed as a single document. (Doc. 89.) The Court permitted Defendants until December 12, 2012, to file an amended motion. (*Id.*)

Plaintiff's Second Amended Complaint (hereafter, "Complaint"), still fails to respond to or address the core pleading deficiencies contained within his Original and Amended Complaint, namely, Plaintiff fails to state a claim upon which relief can be granted. Further, Plaintiff has failed to heed the Court's cautionary comments regarding basic pleading standards in the Complaint. Plaintiff's Complaint purports to assert claims against the Defendants for violations of the Fair Credit Reporting Act ("FCRA"), 15 U.S.C. § 1681 *et seq.*, and for negligence and defamation, though it is by no means clear and is virtually impossible to follow given the numerous typos, grammatical errors, and incoherent narrative.

Moreover, while the Complaint does contain a laundry list of FCRA provisions allegedly violated by the Defendants, most are wholly inapplicable to the allegations asserted throughout the Complaint. Where Plaintiff does identify a provision of the FCRA that could in theory serve as the basis of a coherent claim against a consumer reporting agency such as the Defendants, he fails to address the necessary elements for recovery thereunder or assert plausible factual allegations against any Defendant sufficient to support any such claim. Further, as in his Original and first Amended Complaint, Plaintiff again makes general allegations of negligence and defamation yet, again, fails to allege sufficient facts that Defendants acted with the requisite malice or willful intent to injure Plaintiff. As discussed below, these indecipherable, vague, and conclusory statements fail to state a claim against Defendants. Therefore, Plaintiff's Second Amended Complaint should be dismissed.

B.   ARGUMENTS AND CITATIONS TO AUTHORITY

1.   *Pro Se* Litigants

As acknowledged in Defendants' previous motions to dismiss, Plaintiff is a *pro se* litigant. While the pleadings of a *pro se* plaintiff are to be held to less stringent standards than those drafted by an attorney, *see Haines v. Kerner*, 404 U.S. 519, 520 (1972), "a *pro se* litigant must still meet minimal pleading standards." *Roberts v. Choate Constr. Co.*, 2011 U.S. Dist. LEXIS 121551, at *5 (M.D. Fla. Oct. 20, 2011) (quoting *Eidson v. Arenas*, 910 F. Supp. 609, 612 (M.D. Fla. 1995) (citation omitted)); *see also Braggs v. Keith Realty Midtown/Corp. Overseer*, 2010 WL 2985591, at *3 (S.D. Ala. 2001) ("A pro se litigant 'is subject to the relevant law and rules of court, including the Federal Rules of Civil Procedure.'") (quoting *Moon v. Newsome*, 863 F.2d 835, 837 (11th Cir. 1989)); and *Price v. Porter*, 351 Fed. Appx 925, 926 (5th Cir. 2009) ("[P]ro se litigants are not exempt from compliance with the relevant rules of procedure and substantive law"). This Court reminded Plaintiff of these obligations in its order dated June 20, 2012 (Doc. 30).

While courts should show leniency to *pro se* litigants, "leniency does not give a court license to serve as *de facto* counsel for a party ... or to rewrite an otherwise deficient pleading in order to sustain an action ..." *Roberts*, 2011 U.S. Dist. LEXIS 121551, at *4-5 (quoting *GSR Invs., Inc. v. County of Escambia, Fla.*, 132 F.3d 1359, 1369 (11th Cir. 1998)). The Eleventh Circuit has held that a court's "duty to construe a plaintiff's complaint liberally is not equivalent to a duty to rewrite it." *Dunson v. McKinney*, 412 Fed. Appx. 196, 198 (11th Cir. 2011) (citing *Peterson v. Atlanta Housing Auth.,*, 998 F.2d 904, 912 (11th Cir. 1993)). Additionally, "even a *pro se* litigant must allege the essential elements of a claim for relief, and vague and conclusory allegations are insufficient to state a claim." *Michaels v. Satish*, 2011 U.S. Dist. LEXIS 86568, at *5 (S.D. Fla. July 18, 2011). Courts have repeatedly refused to supply essential elements of a claim for a *pro se* plaintiff if those facts are not initially plead in the complaint. *Id.* (citing *Harris v. Evans*, 20 F.3d 1118 (11th Cir. 1994)).

2.   Standard of Review

A court has authority to dismiss a suit for failure to state a claim upon which relief can be granted if the allegations, taken as true, show that the plaintiff is not entitled to relief. *See Jones v. Bock*, 549 U.S. 199, 215, 127 S. Ct. 910, 920, 166 L. Ed. 2d 798 (2007); *Kirwin v. Price Commc'n Corp.*, 391 F.3d 1323, 1325 (11th Cir. 2005). To survive a motion to dismiss, "a complaint must contain sufficient factual matter, accepted as true, to 'state a claim to relief that is plausible on its face.'" *Ashcroft v. Iqbal*, 556 U.S. 662, 129 S. Ct. 1937, 1949 (2009) (quoting *Bell Atlantic Corp. v. Twombly*, 550 U.S. 544, 570 (2007)). "A claim has facial plausibility when the plaintiff pleads factual content that allows the court to draw the reasonable inference that the defendant is liable for the misconduct alleged.... Where a complaint pleads facts that are merely consistent with a defendant's liability, it stops short of the line between possibility and plausibility of entitlement to relief." *Iqbal*, 129 S. Ct. at 1949 (citations and internal quotation marks omitted).

Although detailed factual allegations are not required, "a plaintiff's obligation to provide the grounds of his entitlement to relief requires more than labels and conclusions, and a formulaic recitation of the elements of a cause of action will not do." *Twombly*, 550 U.S. at 555 (citations omitted). *See also Eidson*, 910 F.Supp. at 612 ("Conclusory allegations and unwarranted deductions of fact are not accepted as true."). Plaintiff must provide "more than an unadorned, the-defendant-unlawfully-harmed-me accusation." *Iqbal*, 129 S. Ct. at 1949. Additionally, "[t]hreadbare recitals of the elements of a cause of action, supported by mere conclusory statements, do not suffice." *Id.* "[C]onclusory allegations or legal conclusions masquerading as factual conclusions" will not prevent a motion to dismiss. *Oxford Asset Mgmt. v. Jaharis*, 297 F.3d 1182, 1188 (11th Cir. 2002) (citing *Fernandez-Montes v. Allied Pilots Ass'n*, 987 F.2d 278, 284 (5th Cir.1993)).

This Court has followed these settled principles and has dismissed cases that, like Plaintiff's Second Amended Complaint, completely fail to satisfy minimum pleading standards. *See, e.g., Durham v. Dept. of Agriculture and Consumer Serv.*, 2012 WL 760859, *1 (M.D. Fla. Feb. 9, 2012) (dismissing case where "the Complaint fails to meet the minimum pleading requirements even for *pro se* litigants"); *Peavey v. Black*, 2011 WL 2457901, *1 (M.D. Fla. June 20, 2011) (dismissing complaint: "It cannot be determined from the complaint which facts support which claim, and which claims are being brought against which defendants. Many of the facts and claims are incomprehensible, and the complaint is laced with unfounded legal conclusions.").

Likewise, courts in this Circuit routinely dismiss FCRA claims where the plaintiff fails to supply any factual basis for the claims, identify specific provisions of the FCRA that the defendant allegedly violated, and generally does not provide any basis for the defendants to be able to defend the claim. *See, e.g., Edwards v. Auto Showcase Motor Cars of Palm Beach, LLC*, 2010 WL 1524289, *2 (S.D. Fla. Apr. 14, 2010) ("[T]he Complaint fails to allege or provide reasonably specific facts or occurrences sufficient to support a claim under the FCRA. While plaintiff alleges that on a certain date her credit report was improperly accessed by each Moving Defendant, plaintiff fails to provide any factual support that [would] draw the reasonable inference that the Moving Defendants are liable for the misconduct alleged.").

As the Court explained in its Order taking under advisement Defendants' Motions to Dismiss

Plaintiff's Amended Complaint, when deciding to grant or deny a motion a dismiss, the

Court must evaluate the complaint under a two-prong test: first, whether all of the necessary elements required for recovery are addressed in the complaint, and second, "whether the complaint addresses these elements with factual material sufficient to raise a right to relief beyond mere speculation." (Doc. 63 at p.4) (citing *Allmond v. Bank of America*, No. 3:07-cv-186-J-33JRK, 2008 U.S. Dist. LEXIS 4788, at *8-9 (M.D. Fla. June 16, 2008)). Plaintiff fails both prongs here.

3.   The Complaint Ignores This Court's Direction Regarding Pleading Standards.

As a threshold matter, Plaintiff has ignored the Court's direction to clearly separate the counts of a complaint, to number all paragraphs consecutively, and to avoid making legal arguments and setting out legal standards in the complaint. (Doc. 63 at 7.) After three pages of unnumbered paragraphs, the Complaint contains three labeled counts: Count I, "Negligence Cause of Action by Equifax;" Count II, "Negligence Cause of Action by Experian;" and Count III, "Negligence Cause of Action by Trans Union." The contents of these Counts, however, are muddled, sporadically touching upon negligence, defamation, and in some of the Counts, Plaintiff has included random FCRA provisions.

For example, in Count III, "Negligence Cause of Action by Trans Union," where the consecutive numbering of paragraphs abruptly ends, various sections of the FCRA are quoted, and then several claims against individual Defendants are asserted in a nonsensical order: "Trans Union Defamation" (p.8); "Experian Defamation" (p.9); "Experian negligence elements" (p.11); "Experian Defamation" (p.11); "Equifax Negligence" (p.12); "Equifax Defamation" (p.12); "Trans Union Negligence" (p.13); and "Trans Union Defamation" (p.13). In addition, legal arguments and purported legal standards are sprinkled throughout the Complaint, though it is unclear what Plaintiff is alleging.[1] Further, the Complaint repeatedly refers to exhibits that are not attached to the Complaint. (Doc. 76 at 3 (referring to "exhibit (A) and (B)"), 6 ("exhibit (J)"), 7 ("exhibit (i)"), 9 (exhibits "E,&F"), and 10 ("exhibit (A) and (B)"). Such a confusing collection of assertions hardly constitutes a short and plain statement of the claim showing that Plaintiff is entitled to relief, as required by Federal Rule of Civil Procedure 8(a). Moreover, it ignores this Court's express directions regarding the proper content of a complaint.

4.   Plaintiff Fails to State Any Claim Upon Which Relief May Be Granted.

Plaintiff's Complaint begins with a random, nonsensical list of 12 FCRA sections Defendants allegedly violated. (Doc. 76 at 1-2). Plaintiff then asserts three counts of negligence against the Defendants, into which he incorporates claims of defamation. (*Id.* at 3-14). The Complaint is subject to dismissal under Rule 12(b)(6) because it fails to "contain either direct or inferential allegations respecting all the material elements necessary to sustain recovery under some viable legal theory." *Meeks v. Murphy Auto Grp., Inc.*, 2009 U.S. Dist. LEXIS 101063, at *10 (M.D. Fla. Oct. 30, 2009) (quoting *Twombly*, 550 U.S. at 562)). Below, Defendants first address Plaintiff's failure to state a claim for negligence or defamation against any Defendant, and then turn to Plaintiff's FCRA claims.

(a) Failure of Claims for Defamation or Negligence

As discussed in the Defendants' motions to dismiss Plaintiff's first Amended Complaint, the FCRA makes clear that no consumer may bring any action for negligence or defamation against a consumer reporting agency, with respect to the agency's disclosure of information pursuant to provisions of the FCRA, "except as to false information furnished with malice or

---

[1] *See, e.g.*, Complaint at p.2 ("Plaintiff assert herein that Plaintiff second Amended Complaint does state a claim in which a claim for relief can be granted..." [*sic*]), p.3 ("[S]ummary Judgment can be presented by the moving party if the case is more than 20 days."), and p.11 ("Anger if acted on can be considered a form of malice, anger, hostility and argumentative behavior is a recipe for a willful intent toward others.").

willful intent to injure such consumer." 15 U.S.C. § 1681h(e). Here, Plaintiff's purported claims for negligence or defamation against the Defendants arise out of Defendants' alleged disclosure of information pursuant to the provisions of the FCRA. The discernible factual allegations contained in the Complaint underlying those purported claims appear to be: all Defendants duplicated credit accounts in Plaintiff's credit file (Doc. 76 at 3-4, 7); Equifax did not display a credit inquiry by __ on Plaintiff's Equifax credit report (*id.* at 5-6); and Experian excluded credit accounts from a credit report provided to Wells Fargo (*id.* at 6-7).

The Court has made clear that it follows the plain language of 15 U.S.C. § 1681h(e), which states that without a showing of willful intent to injure or publication of a report with malice, any state or common law claim for defamation or negligence are preempted. As such, absent any evidence of malice or willfulness, Plaintiff's state law claims are preempted by the FCRA. "Recovery for common law defamation is precluded by the FCRA where the information that gives rise to the cause of action is disclosed pursuant to FCRA provisions, unless the consumer pleads and proves malice or willful intent to injure." *Lee v. Security Check, LLC*, 2010 WL 3075673, at *5 (M.D. Fla. Aug. 5, 2010). The Court further explained that the applicable malice or willfulness standard requires that the credit reporting agencies acted "with knowledge that the information was false or reckless disregard of whether it was false or not." 2010 WL 3075673 at *5 (citing *Thornton v. Equifax, Inc.*, 619 F.2d 700, 703 (8th Cir. 1980)).

Plaintiff fails to state any plausible facts in support of malice or willful intent to injure on the part of Defendants. With respect to Plaintiff's claim of defamation based on Defendants' alleged duplication of credit accounts in his credit file, Plaintiff essentially repeats the allegations in his first Amended Complaint. Plaintiff again references the "tone of voice" of Defendants' employees as being "hostile and argumentative," and asserts that "duplication of Plaintiff credit file could have led to malice or will intent to injure Plaintiff … .[*sic*]" (Doc. 76 at 10.) The

Court has already found that these allegations fail to meet the malice or willfulness standard.

(Doc. 63 at 7.)

In another attempt to assert a defamation claim, Plaintiff alleges that "__credit card

company" denied Plaintiff credit based on information reported by Equifax, and:

> (11) The inquiry application by__credit inquiry of Plaintiff credit is
> considered by FCRA as a hard inquiry and should be place on Plaintiff
> credit file. As of this second Amended Comp. failure to include this
> inquiry on Plaintiff file is not only another example inaccuracy on Plaintiff
> credit file. But this act is an example of willful intent to injury Plaintiff by
> omission of this hard inquiry of Equifax failure to record this hard inquiry
> as hard inquiry on Plaintiff credit file after ___ denial Plaintiff a credit
> card. [*sic*]
>
> A claim of a cause of action of defamation from willful intent to injured
> Plaintiff when Equifax did not record___credit evaluating of Plaintiff as a
> hard inquiry as required by FCRA. As of this date Equifax has not
> recorded any inquiry concerning that credit check about Plaintiff credit file
> which is defamation of the willful intent to injury Plaintiff. This omission
> on Plaintiff credit file produces a falsely print credit file on Plaintiff. [*sic*]
>
> Therefore damages are due to Plaintiff from this injury of Defamation, not
> only from loss of money from not receiving money from a line of credit,
> but loss future business opportunity revenue, and loss of personal wages.
> [*sic*]

(Doc. 76 at 5-6.) These facts do not even hint at malice or willful intent to injure on Equifax's

part. Plaintiff does not indicate how the alleged omission of an inquiry by a potential creditor

could injure him, or what injury Equifax could possibly have intended to cause by such an

omission. Plaintiff simply concludes that the alleged inaccuracy of omitting a creditor inquiry

from his credit report is an example of willful intent. Rather, this assertion by Plaintiff is an

example of a conclusory allegation and unwarranted deduction of fact insufficient to state a

plausible fact in support of malice or willful intent to injure.

Further, regarding Plaintiff's allegation that Experian reported inaccurate information to Wells Fargo, the Complaint does not contain any plausible facts indicating malice or willful intent by Experian. Rather, Plaintiff relies on unsubstantiated and conclusory assertions such as:

- When Experian provided false from inaccurate account information which causes a cause of action of defamation injury to occur to Plaintiff, and therefore damages is due to Plaintiff from this injury of Defamation... [*sic*]

- A willful acknowledgement of wrong and harmful injury occurred when Plaintiff made a call phone called to Mr. Louis one Experian employees about the inaccurate exclusion of accounts on Plaintiff credit accounts in his file. Mr. Louis stated that, "he has heard in that happen [sic (*in original*)] before" is a willful acknowledgement of willful wrong which causes a cause of action negligence by Experian.... [*sic*]

- This nonchalant and angry attitude of CRAs employees from Plaintiff frequent calling to correct inaccurate, incomplete, unverifiable accounts on his file give rise to a cause of action of defamation on the part of CRAs employees talking about what happen to Plaintiff when they go home to their spouses, family, friends, and release this information about Plaintiff credit account to release some of stress from working after a stressful day on the Job, as well as talking to coworkers which become third party confidants. [*sic*]

(Doc. 6 at 9). With regard to Trans Union, Plaintiff merely claims that a statement by a Trans Union employee that "there was only one account on his file" evidences a "willful intent to injure Plaintiff by making a false statement..." Plaintiff's conclusory allegations, however, are factually unsupported and fail to state any plausible facts in support of malice or willful intent to injure him. Under the standards set by the FCRA and acknowledged by this Court, Plaintiff has therefore failed to state a valid claim for negligence or defamation against any Defendant, and his claims should be dismissed.

(b) Failure of FCRA Claims

To properly state a claim under the FCRA, Plaintiff must, at the very minimum, state the section of the FCRA he alleges Defendants violated and aver factual statements in support of the material elements of his claim. *See Thrasher v. Amarillo Police Dep't*, 346 Fed. Appx. 991, 992 (5th Cir. 2009) (*Iqbal*'s holding requiring more than "threadbare recitals" "holds true even for *pro se* litigants"). In the introductory portion of the Complaint, Plaintiff states that he brings this action under the FCRA and lists 12 sections of the FCRA allegedly violated by the Defendants. (Doc. 76 at 1-2.)[2]   Each of these FCRA provisions is discussed below.

(1) Alleged Violation of "[15 U.S.C. § 1681] (b)" by All Defendants (Doc. 76 at 1)

This Court, in its Order on Defendants' previous motions to dismiss, explained:

> [T]he [first] Amended Complaint erroneously cites to 15 U.S.C. § 1681b of the Act. (Doc. 16 at 2.)   This provision concerns the permissible purposes of consumer reports. The Amended Complaint fails to allege any facts showing that any Defendant used consumer reports for an impermissible purpose.   Therefore, reference to this section appears erroneous.

(Doc. 63 at 5). In addition to his broad assertion in the Complaint's introductory section that all Defendants violated this FCRA provision, Plaintiff mentions this section in at least six other places in the Complaint, despite the Court's previous finding that this was in error. (*See* Doc. 76 at 4 (¶4), 5 (¶¶9-10), 7 (¶20 and following paragraph), and 10 (¶10).) Not only does the Complaint fail to address the necessary elements required for recovery under this FCRA provision, it - like its inadequate predecessor complaint - fails to allege any facts showing that any Defendant used consumer reports for an impermissible purpose. Even so, Plaintiff persists in asserting that this specific section of the FCRA was violated by Defendants. Any claims brought under §1681b are clearly erroneous and should be dismissed as Plaintiff has failed to plead any facts sufficient to state a claim against any Defendant under § 1681b upon which relief may be granted.

(2) Alleged Violation of "[15 U.S.C. § 1681a] (d) (1)" by All Defendants (Doc. 76 at 1)

---

[2] Plaintiff also cites "[15 U.S.C. § 1681g](a)" (Doc. 76 at 8), but he does not allege anywhere in the Complaint that any Defendant violated this provision. Plaintiff merely quotes the language of that provision, among a list of quotes from other FCRA provisions.

Section 1681a is the "Definitions; rules of construction" provision of the FCRA, and 15 U.S.C. § 1681a(d)(1) defines "consumer report." While it is difficult to surmise how a violation of a definition could occur, Plaintiff repeatedly makes such bold, unsubstantiated, and nonsensical claims, though makes no attempt to address the elements of such a claim or to explain how Defendants violated this definition. Further, aside from its inclusion among numerous FCRA sections listed in the introductory section of the Complaint as allegedly violated by Defendants, neither this provision nor its subject matter is ever mentioned again in the Complaint. While the Court must, for the purposes of this motion, take every allegation contained in the Complaint as true, the Complaint states no valid claim for relief under this FCRA section.

(3) Alleged Violation of "[15 U.S.C. § 1681a] (g)" by All Defendants (Doc. 76 at 1)

Section 1681a(g) defines "file." Aside from the Complaint's introductory section, "[15 U.S.C. § 1681a] (g)" is cited in the Complaint in two places. (Doc. 76 at 4 (¶4) and 7 (¶20)). Both times, the cite follows allegations concerning alleged duplication of Plaintiff's credit accounts, and the presumptive conclusion that Defendants therefore failed to maintain reasonable procedures to prevent such duplication. There is no plausible allegation that would support a claim that the Defendants violated the definition of "file," and Plaintiff does not attempt to allege how such a violation occurred. As with 15 U.S.C. § 1681a(d)(1), the Complaint fails to state a claim under 15 U.S.C. § 1681a(g) upon which relief may be granted.

(4) Alleged Violation of "[15 U.S.C. § 1681b] (a), (3), (A)" by Equifax and Experian (Doc. 76 at 1)

Again, 15 U.S.C. § 1681b concerns the permissible purposes of consumer reports. As discussed above, the Complaint fails to address the necessary elements required for recovery under this provision or to allege any facts showing that any Defendant used consumer reports for an impermissible purpose. Again, any reference to 15 U.S.C. § 1681b appears erroneous, and the Complaint fails to state a claim, there under, upon which relief may be granted.

(5) Alleged Violation of "604(b)(3)(B) (1V)" by All Defendants (Doc. 76 at 1)

Section 604 of the FCRA is codified at 15 U.S.C. § 1681b – once again, the provision concerning permissible purposes of consumer reports. Meanwhile, 15 U.S.C. § 1681b(b) specifically concerns conditions for furnishing and using consumer reports *for employment purposes*. While "604(b)(3)(B)(1V)" [*sic*] is mentioned in one other place in the Complaint (Doc. 76 at 8), aside from the introduction, Plaintiff merely sets out the language of 15 U.S.C. § 1681b(b)(3)(B)(i)(IV). There is no allegation in the Complaint that relates to the furnishing or use of Plaintiff's consumer report for any purpose, let alone employment purposes. For the reasons discussed in Sections II.B.4(b)(1) and (4) above regarding other claims purportedly asserted under the "permissible purposes" provisions of the FCRA, the reference to "604(b)(3)(B)(1V)" appears erroneous and the Complaint fails to state a claim there under, upon which relief may be granted.

(6) Alleged Violation of "[15 U.S.C. 1681e] (b) by All Defendants (Doc. 76 at 1)

"Section 1681e(b) does not impose strict liability upon consumer reporting agencies for inaccuracies." *Cahlin v. General Motors Acceptance Corp.*, 936 F.2d 1151, 1156 (11th Cir. 1991)). Rather, consumer reporting agencies are liable only if they have failed to follow reasonable procedures in preparing consumer reports. *Id.* Failure to follow reasonable procedures is a material element necessary to sustain recovery under § 1681e(b) and it is Plaintiff's burden to plead facts sufficient to allege Defendants failed to use reasonable procedures to assure maximum accuracy. *See Allmond v. Bank of America*, 2008 U.S. Dist. LEXIS 4788, at *14-15 (M.D. Fla. Jan. 23, 2008) (citing *Stewart v. Credit Bur., Inc.*, 734 F.2d

47, 51 (D.C. Cir. 1984) ("[A] plaintiff cannot rest on a showing of mere inaccuracy, shifting to the defendant the burden of proof on the reasonableness of procedures for ensuring accuracy: there is no indication that Congress meant to so shift the nominal plaintiff's burden of proof as to requisite components of a claim...")).

This Court clarified in its Order on Defendants' motion to dismiss Plaintiff's first Amended Complaint that a plaintiff must allege the following elements to state a claim under Section 1681e(b):

(1) the credit report contained inaccurate information;
(2) the inaccuracy resulted from the agency's failure to follow reasonable procedures;
(3) [plaintiff] suffered damages; and
(4) the injury was caused by the inaccurate information.

(Doc. 63 at 6.) Plaintiff alleges that he logged onto Defendants' "credit monitor service websites" and that his credit accounts were duplicated on each website. (Doc. 76 at 4 (¶4).) While Plaintiff's Second Amended Complaint provides more factual allegations than his Original and First Amended Complaint, they are still insufficient to establish a claim under the FCRA as the allegations concern notifications sent to Plaintiff as a result of his subscriptions to credit monitoring services. Plaintiff has not alleged with particularity any inaccuracies contained in his consumer report. Further, the exhibits Plaintiff failed to attach to his Second Amended Complaint are likely the notifications sent to Plaintiff as a result of his subscription to Defendants' credit monitoring services. Plaintiff's proof, as well as his unsupported conclusion that "Defendants failed to have reasonable procedure in place to prevent duplication of credit accounts on Plaintiff credit file, as stated by provisions of FCRA sections...," *Id.*, are insufficient to establish a cause of action under the FCRA.

Further, Plaintiff's allegation that after viewing the alleged duplication, he disputed the inaccuracies by telephone with each Defendant, and the Defendants corrected the duplication,

Doc. 76 at 4 (¶5)[3], fails to bolster his claims. Alleging that a credit file contained an inaccuracy is not equivalent to alleging that a consumer reporting agency failed to follow reasonable procedures. At best, Plaintiff has alleged that he notified Defendants of an alleged inaccuracy and they corrected it, admittedly within the 30-day time frame allowed by the FCRA. *See Mamani v. Berzain*, 654 F.3d 1148, 1154 (11th Cir. 2011) ("[W]ithout adequate factual support of more specific acts by *these* defendants, [plaintiff's] 'bare assertions' are 'not entitled to be assumed true.'") (emphasis in original) (citing *Iqbal*, 129 S. Ct. at 1951). Such allegations, taken as true, do not support a claim that Defendants failed to follow reasonable procedures.

Similarly, Plaintiff alleges that Experian provided a credit report to Wells Fargo that did not show all of his credit accounts, and concludes without more that Experian therefore failed to follow reasonable procedures. (Doc. 76 at 11.) As noted above, failure to follow reasonable procedures is a material element necessary for a Section 1681e(b) claim, and it is Plaintiff's burden to plead plausible facts sufficient to allege Defendants failed to use those procedures. Conclusory allegations and unwarranted deductions of fact will not suffice. While a Court must accept well-pled facts as true in evaluating a motion to dismiss, these allegations do not plausibly support a claim under Section 1681e(b).

(7) Alleged Violation of "[15 U.S.C. § 1681i] (1)(A)(2)(A)" by All Defendants (Doc. 76 at 1)

While 15 U.S.C. § 1681i(1)(A)(2)(A) does not exist in the FCRA, 15 U.S.C. § 1681i(a)(2)(A) does exist and concerns "prompt notice of dispute to furnisher of information." Specifically, that section provides that when a consumer disputes information in his consumer file with a consumer reporting agency, the agency has five business days to notify the furnisher

---

[3] In one part of the Complaint, Plaintiff alleges that he called Defendants in June to dispute the alleged duplication and the corrections were made "in about the First of part of the month of August..." (Doc. 76 at 4(¶5)). In another part, Plaintiff states that the corrections were made "[a]fter about a month of calling all three credit bureaus..." (*Id.* at 10 (¶9)).

of that information about the dispute. The Complaint fails to address any elements of a claim under this section or to allege any facts showing that any Defendant failed to timely notify a furnisher of consumer information about a dispute.

Further, aside from the one cite to "[15 U.S.C. § 1681i] (1)(A)(2)(A)" in the introductory section of the Complaint, Plaintiff does not elsewhere even mention the broader subsection, 15 U.S.C. § 1681i, "Procedure in case of disputed accuracy." The Complaint does not address any elements of a claim under § 1681i or raise sufficient factual matter to state a claim to relief under this section.

(8) Alleged Violation of "[15 U.S.C. § 1681p]" by All Defendants (Doc. 76 at 1-2)

Section 1681p concerns jurisdiction of courts and limitation of actions under the FCRA. Aside from a statement that "[t]his Court has Jurisdiction under the 'Fair Credit Reporting act' [*sic*] …," nothing in the Complaint touches upon either jurisdiction or time limitations on the filing of actions under the FCRA. Consequently, like the other FCRA sections included in the laundry list in the Complaint's introductory section, Plaintiff's sole cite to this provision appears misplaced. As such, the Complaint utterly fails to state a claim under 15 U.S.C. § 1681p upon which relief may be granted.

(9) Alleged Violation of "[15 U.S.C. § 1681a] (p)" by All Defendants (Doc. 76 at 2)

Section 1681a(p) is yet another definition, as it defines "consumer reporting agency that compiles and maintains files on consumers on a nationwide basis." Again, it is inconceivable that Defendants could have violated a definition, and nothing in the Complaint supports such an illogical proposition. No elements required for recovery under this FCRA provision are addressed in the Complaint, and there is no factual material indicating such a claim would be plausible. Plaintiff has accordingly failed to state a claim under 15 U.S.C. § 1681a(p) upon which relief may be granted.

(10) Alleged Violation of "[15 U.S.C. § 1681•]" by All Defendants (Doc. 76 at 2)

Section 1681o governs civil liability for negligent noncompliance with the requirements imposed under the FCRA. Plaintiff mentions this provision only once, in the introductory section of the Complaint. (Doc. 76 at 2.) In order for the liability provisions of 15 U.S.C. § 1681o to apply, there necessarily must be a failure to comply with FCRA requirements. As the instant memorandum shows, Plaintiff has failed to state a valid claim for violation of any FCRA provision by any Defendant. Accordingly, Plaintiff has failed to state a claim under 15 U.S.C. § 1681o upon which relief may be granted.

(11) Alleged Violation of 15 U.S.C. § 1681h by All Defendants (Doc. 76 at 2)

Section 1681h concerns "conditions and form of disclosures to consumers." Aside from the mention of 15 U.S.C. § 1681h in the introductory section of the Complaint, "1681h" is mentioned in one other place – following statements regarding the alleged duplication of Plaintiff's credit accounts in his credit file. (Doc. 76 at 4 (¶4).) The citation is included among citations to four other FCRA provisions. Again, Plaintiff does not address the elements of a claim under 15 U.S.C. § 1681h, nor does he attempt to relate the allegations regarding duplication to such a claim.

The Complaint does subsequently cite to 15 U.S.C. § 1681h(e), in connection with Plaintiff's claims of defamation against Defendants. (Doc. 76 at 8, 11, 12.) Defendants have already addressed the Complaint's failure to meet the standard of 15 U.S.C. § 1681h(e) in Section II.B.4(a), *supra*, regarding Plaintiff's failure to state a valid claim for defamation or negligence.

(12) Alleged Violation of 15 U.S.C. § 1681n by All Defendants (Doc. 76 at 2)

Section 1681n governs civil liability for willful noncompliance with the FCRA. Aside from its inclusion in the introductory section of the Complaint, it is also mentioned in connection with Plaintiff's allegations of duplication of credit accounts in his consumer file. (Doc. 76 at 4 (¶4), at 10 (¶10).) The Complaint does not, however, address any necessary elements required for recovery under 15 U.S.C. § 1681n.

The Middle District of Florida has addressed the willfulness standard applicable to 15 U.S.C. § 1681n. In *Lee v. Security Check*, discussed in Section II.D.1 above, the Court noted that the Eighth Circuit "has distinguished between the malice or evil motive required to establish a cause of action for common law defamation as different from the willfulness needed to establish entitlement to punitive damages under the FCRA (15 U.S.C. § 1681n)." 2010 WL 3075673, at *5, n.3 (citing *Thornton v. Equifax, Inc.*, 619 F.2d 700, 705-06 (8th Cir. 1980)). The Court then clarified that it disagrees with that approach and is instead "of the opinion that the definitions of willfulness under both sections overlap..." *Id.* Defendants have explained why Plaintiff's Complaint fails to meet the willfulness standard with regard to Plaintiff's defamation and negligence claims. *See* Section II.B.4(a), *supra*. Any claim asserted by Plaintiff under 15 U.S.C. § 1681n fails for the same reason his claims under § 1681h(e) fail, namely Plaintiff's failure to plead facts sufficient to establish Defendants acted willfully.

In sum, Plaintiff claims Defendants have violated a lengthy laundry list of apparently randomly selected provisions of the FCRA, yet he fails to plead sufficient facts to support his claims. Generally, Plaintiff merely includes haphazard sections of the FCRA and then fails to ever mention, address, or allege facts to support his claim that Defendants violated these provisions. Even where Plaintiff attempts to allege facts sufficient to assert a claim under the

FCRA, Plaintiff attempt largely fails.   He does not address the elements required for recovery under those provisions nor support any elements with plausible factual allegations.   In total, Plaintiff's claims asserted under the FCRA cannot survive dismissal.

C.   CONCLUSION

For the foregoing reasons, Plaintiff's Second Amended Complaint fails to state any claim upon which relief may be granted against Defendants for any alleged FCRA violations, negligence, defamation or any other cause of action.   As such, pursuant to Federal Rule of Civil Procedure 12(b)(6), Plaintiff's Second Amended Complaint against Defendants Experian, Equifax, and Trans Union should be dismissed.

UNITED STATES DISTRICT COURT MIDDLE DISTRICT OF
FLORIDA JACKSONVILLE DIVISION

James Watson
                    Plaintiff

Case No.3:12-cv-552-J-99MMH-JBT

JURY TRIAL DEMANDED
Equifax, Experian and
Trans union
Defendants

PLAINTIFF MOTION IN SUPPORT OF SECOND AMENDED COMPLAINT
AND DISMISSING DEFENDANTS AMENDED MOTION TO DISMISS

PLAINTIFF SECOND AMENDED COMPLAINT

This Court has Jurisdiction under the "Fair Credit Reporting act" of 15 U.S.C. § §1681- 1681w to

adjudicate the action between Plaintiff and all three CRA's Equifax information Services, LLC

("Equifax"), Experian information Solutions, Inc. ("Experian"), and Trans Union LLC ("Trans

Union").

PLAINTIFF CLAIM THAT ALL PLAINTIFF CUMULATNE COMPLAINTS COMBINED

INCLUDING SECOND AMENDED COMPLAINT CONTAIN A STATEMENT OF A CLAIM

FOR RELIEF AND DEFENDANTS AMENDED MOTION TO DISMISS PLAINTIFF

COMPLAINTS SHOULD BE DISMISS

Pursuant to Federal Rules of Civil Procedure 8(a)(2) Plaintiff file this motion in support of all of

Plaintiff Amended Complaints and Dismissing all three Defendants motion to dismiss Plaintiff

Second Amended Complaint. Specifically, Plaintiff Complaint, Amended Complaint, and

Second Amended Complaint does state a claim against all three Defendants, and doe satisfies

all the

requirements of specificity, and Plausibility in Ashcroft v. Iqbal, and Bell Atlanta Corp. v. Twombly.

Therefore, the Court should dismiss defendants Motion as moot and grant Plaintiff Second Amended Complaint, of which all relief should be granted in favor of Plaintiff in this action. Under the FCRA Congress entrust all three CRAs with the "Grave responsibility" to ensure that information is accurate and to properly investigated disputes, [15 U.S.C. § 1681] (a)(4).

The gist of three Defendants argument in their motion to dismiss Plaintiff Second Amended Complaint is on page nine in second paragraph, "The Court has made clear that it follows the plain language of 15 U.S.C. § 1681h(e), which states that as how in go willful intent to injure or publication of a report with malice, anystateorcommonlawclaim for defamation or negligence are preempted. As such, absent any evidence of malice or willfulness, Plaintiff state law claim are preempted by FCRA. "Recovery for common law defamation is precluded by the FCRA where the information that give rise to the cause of action is disclosed pursuant to FCRA provisions unless the consumer pleads and proves malice orwillfulness intent to injures." Lee v. Security Check, LLC, 2010 WL 3075673, *S (M.D. Fla. Aug 5, 2010).

This case does not apply to the case at hand because Plaintiff pleaded malice and willfulness in his Complaint, and the Precedent holding and rule by the U.S. Supreme Court on the issue of malice and willfulness has not been overturned. The U.S. Supreme Court has held in Safeco Ins. Co v. Burr, that defendant willfully violated the FCRA where the defendant knowingly or recklessly violated the act. The Court rejected the argument of the petitioner insurance companies that liability under section 1681n occurs only when there is a knowing violation, holding that in the context of civil liability it has generally construed willfulness to include not only knowing violations but also reckless violation of statute.

BACKGROUND CASE INFORMATION

On April 12 2012, James Watson Pro Se brought an action in State Court Circuit, Fourth Judicial Circuit in and Duval County, Florida against Defendants Equifax, Trans Union and Experian for violation of have two accounts (duplicated accounts) for each of Plaintiff creditor accounts on Plaintiff credit file. Plaintiff observed these inaccuracies of Duplicated credit accounts (two accounts for each account on plaintiff file) on all three CRAs websites while Plaintiff was trying to improve his credit standings. (Doc.# 2). On May 9, 2012 Experian, Equifax, and Trans Union joiner and removed action from Duval State Court to this Court, United States District Court Middle District of Florida Jacksonville Division with Equifax, and Trans Union joining and consenting to the removal. (Doc. #3& 4). On May 16, 2012 In response to Plaintiff Amended Complaint with a stated legal claim, Equifax file motion to dismiss Plaintiff complaint and Experian and Trans Union file their Rule 12(b)(6) Motion to Dismiss Plaintiff Complaint and Memorandum in Support for alleging Plaintiff did not state acclaim which Plaintiff considered meritless on all four corners on the face of the Complaint.

May 21, 2012, Plaintiff filed a Motion for leave to amend his Complaint (Doc. # 13). May 25, 2012, Plaintiff filed Propose Amend Complaint in this Court (Doc.# 16) as it pertains to Fed. R. Civ. P. 15(a)(1)(B). Plaintiff is allowed to Amend is Complaint once as matter of rule. On May 30, 2012 Plaintiff offered evidence attach to his Motion to Amend Plaintiff Complaint which was accepted by this Court. See exhibit (A) and (B). On June 11, 2012 This Court Granted Plaintiff Motion to Amend Complaint (Doc. #20) as filed, and dismissed all three Defendants Motions to Dismiss Plaintiff Complaint (Doc.# 9, 10, 11). On June 19, 2012 Plaintiff submitted his Summary Judgment Pursuant to Federal Rules of Civil Procedure (56) (Doc.#27), summary Judgment can be presented by the moving party if the case is more than 20 days. Plaintiff Summary Judgment Affidavit accepted by the Court "with Material evidence (Doc.#34). Plaintiff motion for Summary Judgment was denied without prejudice, (doc# 58).

Defendants file a motion for extension of time to respond to Plaintiff Summary Judgment oppose by Plaintiff but grant by Magistrate Judge Toomey with an issue order stating, "The Court need not wait for Plaintiff response to this motion for extension of time."(Doc. # 38)

Plaintiff considers Defendant's motion to dismiss Plaintiff Second Amended Complaint meritless on all fourcomers on the face of their Pleading.

Due to the fact their own attorney, Mr. Franklin G. Cosmen, JR PA stated "Defendant Transunion LLC's Joiner and consent to Removal "On May 1, 2012, Transunion was served with Plaintiffs Complaint, the initial pleading setting forth the claim for relief upon which this action is base."

II. MEMORANDUM IN SUPPORT OF PLAINTIFF CLAIM

It is axiomatic that in deciding a motion to dismiss pursuant to Rule 12(b)(6), the Court must accept all factual allegations as true and draw all inferences in favor of Plaintiff. Levy ex rel. Immunogen Inc. v. Southbrook Int'l Invs., Ltd., 263 F.3d 10, 14 (2d Cir. 2001), cert. denied, 535 U.S. 1054, 152 L. Ed. 2d 821 (2002). "Dismissal is not appropriate unless it appears beyond doubt that the Plaintiff can prove no set of facts in support of his claim which would entitle him to relief." Chancev. Armstrong, 143F.3d 698,701 (2d Cir. 1998) (quoting Conley. Gibson, 355 U.S. 41, 45-46, 2 L.Ed. 2d 80,78 S. Ct 99 (1957). "This rule applies with particular force... where the complaint is submitted Pro Se ... At the 12(b)(6) stage, 'the issue is not whether a Plaintiff is likely to prevail ultimately, but whether the Claimant is entitled to offer evidence to support the claims, see Summary Judgment Affidavit (Doc. # 34). Indeed, it may appear on the face of the pleading that a recovery is very remote and unlikely but that is not the test. "Id at 701 (citation omitted) As a result, where a Plaintiff is proceeding Pro Se, the Court Must construe the pleading liberally, and must "interpret them to raise the strongest arguments that they suggest. "Burgorv. Hopkins, 14 F 3d 787,790 (2d Cir. 1994).

Under Federal Rule of Civil Procedure 8(a)(2) a pleading must contain a "short and plain statement of the claim showing that the pleader is entitle to relief." As the Court held in Twombly, 550 U.S.544, the pleading standard Rule 8 announces does not require "detail factual allegations,"...id at 555(citing Papasan v. Allain 478 U.S. 265, 286(1986).

To survive motion to dismiss, a complaint must contain sufficient factual matter accepted as true, to "state a claim to relief that is plausible on its face," id., at 570.

A claim has plausibility when the Plaintiff pleads factual content that allows the Court to draw the reasonable inferences that the Defendants is liable for Misconduct alleged, in the instance case negligent and defamation id at 556.

Determining whether a complaint states a plausible claim for relief will, as the Court of Appeals observed, be context-specific task that requires the reviewing Court to draw on its judicial experience and common sense 490 F.3d at 157-158.

Moreover, based on *Maxcess, Inc.* v. *Techs., Inc.,* 433 F.3d 1377, 1340, n.3 (IIth Cir.2005), the Court may consider relevant documents that are central to a plaintiff's claim, (again the Court should examine Material document of Plaintiff exhibit(A)(B) and Affidavit submitted with Summary Judgment).

Note1: The reason Plaintiff did not submit an opposing motion to Defendant's motion to dismiss Plaintiff Second Amended Complaint is Plaintiff thought he could do it electronic via the internet but found out Pro se are not permitted only lawyers with a bar number

Fair Credit Reporting Act provides that: whenever a consumer reporting agency prepares a consumer report it shall follow reasonable procedures to assure maximum possible accuracy of the information concerning the individual about whom the report relates.

"15 U.S.C. 168le(b). In are investigation of the accuracy of credit report, a credit bureau must bear some responsibility for evaluating the accuracy of information obtain from subscriber") white v. trans Union 462 F. Supp. 2d 1079 (CD. Cal 2006).

Whether a CRA has acted in "Willful noncompliance" with the FCRA under 1681n is and active assessment that encompasses action taken in reckless disregard of FCRA's obligations. Safeco, 551 U.S. 47, 127 S.CT. at 2208-10, 2215.

15 U.S.C. 168ln provides that any "person who willfully fail to comply with any requirement under this subchapter with respect to any consumer is liable to that consumer" for actual and punitive damages. Hernandez v. Lamboy Furniture Inc., 2008 WL 4061344, at *8 (E.D. Pa Sept. 2, 2008).

"Congress bestowed on credit agencies special requirements for meeting the needs of commerce... with regard to the confidentiality, accuracy, relevancy, and proper utilization of such information in accordance with the requirements of this title Fair Credit Reporting Act 15U.S.C. § 1681) (b)."(Emphasis add on accuracy)

15U.S.C. § 168la] (d)(l): In general, the term consumer report means any written, oral, or other communication of any information by a consumer reporting agency ... (Emphasis on "any information")

However, in the instance case where the Plaintiff has pleaded facts that in themselves adds up to a valid legal claim with the appropriate legal theories dismissal of Plaintiff Amended Complaint should not be granted to the Defendants.

Under section 15U.S.C.§ 1681a] (g)of the FCRA **The** term "file" when used in connection

with information on any consumer, means all of the information on **that** consumer

recorded and retained by a consume reporting agency regardless of how the information

is stored. (Emphasis on" all the information on that consumer" added)

Defendants argue the issue of "Insufficient credit Reference" as stated by __bank credit card

means that there is either "no credit" information available or not enough credit information to

base another credit decision on. Base on Plaintiff credit profile date donor around the month of

June, that if all three CRAs especially Equifax had all Plaintiff Creditors on Plaintiff

"file"during that time the Creditor redacted was checking Plaintiff file for approval of his

credit. The computer algorithm scan would have register Plaintiff credit file as not having

"Insufficient credit Reference" when in fact Plaintiff had many credit references available to

base their approval on by the credit card c o m p a n y redacted.

Defendants position is that Plaintiff complaint is not Plausible, well the

definition of Plausibility is "having an appearance of truth or reason: seemingly worthy of

approval or acceptance credible believable. "Plaintiff believes that this Court will know

that the Plaintiff has stated a claim is not only Plausible, but believable, and is truthful.

Plaintiff satisfies the Plausibility principle of Ashcroft v. Iqbal with Plaintiff statement, "of

seeing two __ accounts on Plaintiff credit account on his file, "as well as his statement of

Defendants Purging Plaintiff credit accounts when __was checking Plaintiff credit to

approved Plaintiff for accredit card and was denied with the reason of " INSUFFICIENT

CREDIT REFERENCES" (Doc. #16, Exhibit B), (Emphasis Added) pertaining to Iqbal

specificity. Specificity as it relates to ____Bank Loan representative _____stated, "that

Plaintiff was denied credit because Enhance Identity Theft provided Plaintiff with a report

that

contain only two or three credit accounts of Plaintiff credit file from Experian. An Experian

Agent said that although Plaintiff sees two file it is only one (Emphasis Added).

Because all three Defendants computers programs were instructed to correct

The in accuracies of the Plaintiff Duplicated accounts or Multiple credit accounts in

Plaintiff credit file, as in Angela Williams V.Equifax one of the claims of this case was

the multiple files on her credit account that Equifax refuse to redact from her account.

The heart of the litigation between the parties was the Frozen scans which would help

show that Equifax violated 15 U.S.C. § 1681] (b)."by not following reasonable procedures to

assure maximum possible accuracy.

As a precedent holding case similar to Plaintiff instance case with duplicated or multiple credit

accounts between these three Defendants one of the main issues of the Angela Williams v.

Equifax Case was the Frozen scans. These frozen scans would prove that there was

Multiple or Duplicated credit files on Plaintiff credit file even

if accounts were was purge by all three Defendants, Angela Williams V. Equifax 359F.

Supp.2d. 1284(2005), (citation omitted) Equifax refused to have Judge Sprinkel Court to

have access to the Frozen scans because they are aware that this evidence would hurt Equifax

case.

If materials extrinsic to the pleadings are submitted to the Court in support of or in

opposition to a 12(b)(6) motion, the Court does not have to consider them. Under FRCP

12(b), however, once the court does consider such matter the motion is automatically

"converted to a motion for summary judgment pursuant to FRCP56. Material does not

literally have to be bound into the Complaint to be considered "intrinsic" to it and a proper part

consideration of a 12(b)(6) motion, without a "conversion" taking place.

It can fairly be said that any oral or written evidence not already "in the record" public or

Court, physical or by reference is regarded as "extrinsic "and will spur a conversion.

Plaintiff Amended Complaint on all four corners of the Complaint is stating a claim, that claim

is all three Defendants created a duplicate or multiple credit accounts of Plaintiff's credit file

in the month of June while Plaintiff was trying to improve his credit standing while visiting

their website. Defendants was in violation of [15 U.S.C.§ 1681] (b) as stated below and

15 U.S.C. 1681 (e)(b) of the FCRA.

602 (b) *Reasonable procedures.* It is the purpose of this title to require that consumer reporting agencies adopt reasonable procedures for meeting the needs of commerce for consumer credit, personnel, insurance, and other information in a manner which is fair and equitable to the consumer, with regard to the confidentiality, accuracy, relevancy, and Proper utilization of such information in accordance with the requirements of this title. A definition of a claim as stated by Merriam's Webster's Dictionary of Law page 79 "3. A:

A right to seek a judicial remedy rising from a wrong or injury suffered..."Plaintiff

Amended Complaint satisfies all of FRCP of Rule 8.

Plaintiff initiated this case on April 12, 2012 in the State Court of Duval County (Doc.#1). On

May 9, 2012, all three Defendants stipulated to Joiner to have the case moved to Federal

District Court in Jacksonville(Doc.#2).

Plaintiff satisfies the claim requirement of the Amended Complaint when Plaintiff stated that

all three Defendants duplicated Plaintiff's credit accounts under F.C.R.A. 15 U.S.C. 1681 (b),

(Emphasis Added) on accuracy, that cause of action of Negligence took place or occurred.

When Plaintiff stated that defendants made two __ accounts twice the specificity theory

was satisfied reference to Ashcroft v. Iqbal, 556 U.S. 662, 665 (2009).

Plaintiff's Amended Complaint survives because it does state factual matters such as

stating, "__ accounts was reporting on Plaintiff's file twice..."

To survive motion to Dismiss a Complaint must contain factual matters accepted as truth to state a claim to relief on its own face, Ashcroft v. Iqbal, 556 U.S. 662, 665 (2009).

Another instance as stated by Defendants on Page 2, Second paragraph, "One day in the First of June (specific month satisfied). Plaintiff used his cell phone to dispute these inaccuracies by calling each Defendant to notify Defendants of inaccuracies of the duplicated Plaintiff's credit files. Furthermore, on Page 2, paragraph 8, Plaintiff's Complaint states, "An Experian agent said that although Plaintiff sees two files it is only one", this statement in itself is a statement satisfying specificity.

The fact that Defendants Duplicated Plaintiff credit file makes Defendants liable under a claim of a cause of action of negligence as well as Malice when Defendants attorney Tom Tierney Stated Those Things Happen when Plaintiff had his first telephone conference by Experian Lead Attorney this appears to be the prevail attitude of all three credit bureaus Equifax, Experian and Trans Union.

Under 15 U.S.C. 1681(b) of the FCRA, in fact the act of duplicating any consumer credit files of Plaintiff which are not accurate makes the file inaccurate and the Defendant's by definition is liable for their injuries to the Plaintiff with a cause of action of negligence.

By Defendant's admitting the fact, the only provision that Plaintiff specifically cites to is the 15 U.S.C. 1681 (sic) which should be 15 U.S.C. 1681 (b) this section of the FCRA stress the word accuracy when Plaintiff reported the dispute by cell phone to all three Defendants of the inaccuracies of not having one credit file only on Plaintiff's credit file. (Add material). By asserting a claim of all three violations of FCRA of the U.S.C. 1681 (d) sic and 15 U.S.C.1681 (b) (Plaintiff satisfies a factual claim and identifies these sections in Plaintiff Amended Complaint. See Thrasher v. Amadillo Police Department, 346 Fed. Appx 991, 992 (Fifth Cir. 2009).

Under the FRCA of 15 U.S.C. 1681 (b) (If any of Plaintiff's credit accounts which is the totality

of his entire file is inaccurate all three Defendants are subject to damages from their injuries and

harm done to Plaintiff, Nelson v. Chase Manhattan Mortgage Corp. 282 F.3d 1057 (2002)

Plaintiff states that after about a month of calling all three credit bureaus the accounts were

finally rectified and returned to normal means Plaintiff sees only one account for each credit

account Plaintiff had with Defendants. This statement by Plaintiff is explicit in nature that all

three Defendants were put on notice of disputes by Plaintiff as required by FCRA 15 U.S.C.

§1681 et seq. If the dispute was initiated in the first part of June, 2011 then after a month (would

state that it was more than 30 days after the initial disputes or the first of August 2011) of calling

all three Defendants had corrected the inaccuracies explicitly states that Defendants corrected

Plaintiff's credit accounts but if only one of the accounts were not corrected a negligent liability

exist with all three Defendants see when Plaintiff was denied a credit card from ___.

Defendants mistakenly stated on page five second paragraph "While Plaintiff alleges that on a

certain date her [sic]credit report was improperly assessed by each moving Defendants Plaintiff

does provide factual support exhibit A and Exhibit B to address reasonable inference that the

moving Defendants are liable for damages of injury and negligence and defamation. See Nelson

Chase Manhattan Corp., 282 F. 3d 1057 (2002), also the Court said that, "it is not for the Court

to remake the balance struck by congress"... Nelson v. Chase Manhattan Corp., 282 F. 3d

1057,1060(9thCir.2002).

Clearly Defendants Equifax admits to Plaintiff's Amended Complaint contained specificity with

regard to Equifax, page 5 paragraph (3) Exhibit B, __. The mere fact that Equifax deleted or the

computer purge this inquiry on Plaintiff's credit file (Exhibit is in direct violation of FCRA

because Equifax by law is supposed to have this inquiry recorded on Plaintiff's credit file because it is Hard inquiry and the FCRA states all hard inquires must be recorded on the

consumer credit file, Equifax is subject to the FCRA violation, not only for actual damages but

for punitive damages and willful malice recklessness, Supreme Court held in Safeco Ins. Co

v. Burr, that defendant willfully violated the FCRA where the defendant knowingly or

recklessly violated the act. The Court rejected the argument of the petitioner insurance

companies that liability under section 168ln occurs only when there is a knowing violation,

holding that in the context of civil liability it has generally construed willfulness to include

not only knowing violations but also reckless violation of statue.

The Supreme Court recognized that reckless conduct maybe sufficient to establish a

willful violation of the FCRA Act.

Wherefore, Plaintiff prays for Judgment against Defendants for damages in the amount of
$125,000 each, plus cost and interest on all three Defendants as it relates to a cause of
duplicating Plaintiff credit file which resulted to Plaintiff injuries and cause of action of
defamation, negligent, cause by Equifax, Transunion and Experian. In addition to punitive
damage if awarded by the Court.

I verify that the above statements are true to the best of my Knowledge on_____

date   2013. This document is submitted to all Parties involved via email.

Plaintiff in Pro Se

Note2: All documents and exhibits submitted to Court and Defendants attorneys in prior
motions and admission to apply to this second Amended complaint in this claim, Plaintiff
believes the legal term is "carried forward.

IN THE UNITED STATES DISTRICT COURT
MIDDLE DISTRICT OF FLORIDA

James Watson

Plaintiff

v.   Case No. 3:12-cv-SS2-J-99MMH-TEM

Defendants Equifax, Experian,

Transunion

PLAINTIFF'S MOTION FOR SUMMARY JUDGMENT

Plaintiff, James Watson, by and through undersigned Pro Se and pursuant to Rule 56, Federal Rules of Civil Procedure, moves for the entry of an Order granting summary judgment in his favor and against Defendants, Equifax, Transunion, and Experian on grounds as states:

I. Plaintiff filed this action on April 12, 2012 against Equifax Information Systems, LLC ("Equifax"), Experian Information Service, Inc. ("Experian") and Trans union LLC ("Transunion"). Plaintiff initial complaint contain the following cause of actions, Negligent and defamation under the Fair Credit Reporting Act of section (15U.S.C. §1681) of the FCRA against all three Credit Reporting Agencies.

Plaintiff while monitoring all three credit   Bureaus one day in the first part June Plaintiff   notice that all three credit bureaus Equifax, Experian, and Trans union where reporting duplicating accounts of Plaintiff entire credit file, e.g. Plaintiff __ account was reporting a Plaintiff file twice this action by Defendants is a cause of action of negligent by credit bureaus Equifax, Experian, and Trans union, (15 U.S.C. § 1681) (b) and [15 U.S.C. § 1681e] b of the FCRA states,"

Meanwhile at the same time Plaintiff was applying for credit at various credit card companies being rejected and denied by __Bank credit card Division from the information in Plaintiff Equifax credit file. See exhibit (A) and (BJ which will justify the following injuries below which flow from the June 7, AND 24,2011wrong and harm done by Equifax of the duplication of Plaintiff credit file which is clearly inaccuracies as stated by15U.S.C. §1681](b)of the FCRA.

Note: Outline, 1. Summary Judgment 2. Plaintiff affidavit& Doc. Admitted into Evidence
3. Exhibit (C) 4. Notice before legal action exhibit (D) 5. Duplicate Trans union acct of Plaintiff Exhibit (E)
6. Duplicate Trans union acct of Plaintiff Exhibit (F) date 118117. Disputed letter sent to all three CRA's
Exhibit(G) 8. Admission statement of Experian Rep. & Confirmation of acct not Plaintiff Credit file.

Furthermore, a letter from __ Bank rejecting a credit card application by Plaintiff on June

24, 2011 from information provided by Equifax, Plaintiff admits into evidence as exhibit (c).

4. Plaintiff sent a letter to Tran sunion on 123·2011 title "NOTICE BEFORE LEGAL ACTION" if Trans union do not respond to some type settlement agreement within 7 days of receipt of letter; Plaintiff got no response from Trans union exhibit (D)

Exhibit (E) consist of five pages' front to back from Defendant Trans union dated June 9, 2011.

Exhibit (F) consist of five pages' front to back from Defendant Trans union dated June 18, 2011.

Exhibit (G) a one-page letter address to Experian with an attach copy account of Home Loan Services which was sent to Trans union as well as Equifax. Trans union Attorney Allison acknowledge she had the letter in her possession on Tuesday or Wednesday when Plaintiff spoke to her concerning the Trans union documents she wanted me to send her either by mail or email.

Exhibit (H) consist of one-page front to back from Defendant Experian dated Oct 4, 2011 sent to Plaintiff with his Credit score and a statement from an Experian service rep. name Louis date Oct 5, 2011 stating Plaintiff had no Public record on his file but most important Louis said the same thing Mr. Tom said, "He has heard in that happen before." When Plaintiff received a telephone conference call from him in the beginning or middle part of May, 2012.

All three CRA received a letter dated 6-6·2011 informing Defendant that Plaintiff was not aware of the changes made to _____ on Plaintiff credit file, evidence as exhibit (d).

A. Loss of personal income B. Loss of Business income C. Lack of Trust in others D. Denied Credit
E. Financial Hardship F. Psychological Stress

all three CRA (Defendants) in their membership agreement states that in order to become a member Plaintiff had to agree that Defendants were allow to share Plaintiff credit file with the other CRA's before Plaintiff could becoming a member of any of the CRA.

The sharing of Plaintiff credit file is what the computers analog pick upon and cause the Multiple or duplication of Plaintiff credit file by all three Defendants computer systems.

Summary Judgment is proper in any case where there is no genuine issue of material
Fact S. Fed. R. Civ. P., Rule 56 (c). A Plaintiff moving for summary judgment may satisfy its
burden by submitting summary judgment proof that establishes all elements of its cause of action as
a matter of law. San Pedro v. U.S., 79 F.3d 1065, 1068 (lllh Cir. 1996). Plaintiff must show that no
reasonable trier of fact can find other than for Plaintiff. Calderone v. U.S., 799 F.2d 254, 259 (fu
Cir.1986).

Summary Judgment should be granted to Plaintiff in this case because there are no genuine Issue
of material facts that all 3 defendants did duplicate Plaintiff credit files from the documents sent to
Plaintiff by the defendants as submitted to the Court by Plaintiff, as well as:

Statement from a Experian service rep. name Louis date Oct 5, 2011stating Plaintiff had no
Public record on his file but most important Louis said the same thing Mr. Tom Tierney said,
"He has heard in that happen before. "When Plaintiff received a telephone conference call
from him in the beginning or middle part of May,2012, is proof there is no genuine issue of
material facts from both Experian customer service rep. and Transunion and Experian legal
counsel.

Summary Judgment should be granted to Plaintiff in this case because there is no genuine
issue of material facts that Experian did not provided Enhance Identity Theft with an accurate
credit file on Plaintiff on Nov 28, 2012 while Plaintiff was applying for a credit loan at

When defendants motion for dismissal of Plaintiff Complaint in lieu of answering with a defense
strategy defendants Acquiescence that their defense of genuine issue of material facts
and Plaintiff is permitted to file a Summary Judgment under Fed. R. Civ. Rule 56 (c).

Since defendants are in possession of all digital files in a computer age there is no dispute that
defendants possess all the documents Plaintiff have in his possession unless allegation of
Defendant Purging the files then they are in violation of the FTC.

Memorandum of Law

Ina prior holding case between Plaintiff Angela, Williams v. Equifax solution LLC Circuit Ct 9
Judicial Circuit Orange County, FL NO. 48-2003-CA-903-5-0 Nov.172007 verdict Nov 302007,
Defendant Equifax created multiple files of Plaintiff by merge a file of another debtor with almost
the same name with the last two digits of the social security number being different and the
computer did not pick it up or distinguish it from the name Angela's Williams.
The cases are similar in that there were multiple or duplicate files created by the Defendant Equifax
on the Plaintiff Angela Williams, and in the instant case James Watson Plaintiff.

Motion, Memorandum and its attachments Affidavits establishes there is no genuine issue of Material fact Defendants possess of all evidence unless allegation of purging by defendants occurs.

WHEREFORE, Plaintiff, James Watson Pro Se, respectfully requests this Court to grant this motion and enter an Order granting Summary Judgment in favor of Plaintiff in the amount of $125,000 dollars against Defendant Equifax, $75,000 against Trans union and $125,000 against Experian and for such further relief as this Court deems just and proper.

—

CERTIFICATE OF SERVICE

WE HEREBY CERTIFY that a true and correct copy of the foregoing was either email, facsimile, or mailed this day of June, 2012.

Note: Defendants have the financial resources to postpone this case for several years, if they do not act like good corporate citizens, and display goodwill toward their customers and Members.

James Watson
                    Plaintiff

V.   Case No. 3:12-cv-552-J-99MMH-JBT

                                            JURY TRIAL DEMANDED

Equifax, Experian and
Transunion
                    Defendants

PLAINTIFF SUMMARY JUDGMENT MOTION

Watson, and pursuant to Rule 56 summary judgment, Federal Rules of Civil Procedure, Plaintiff

moves for the entry of an Order granting summary judgment in his favor and against Defendants,

Equifax information Services, LLC ("Equifax"), Experian information Solutions, Inc.

("Experian"), and Trans Union LLC ("Trans Union") and bring claims of negligent non-

compliance and common law defamation as stated by this Court under federal Fair Credit

Reporting Act , 15 U.S.C. §§ 1681x (See Doc.76.) Defendants move jointly to dismiss all claims

against Plaintiff(See Doc.92.).

This Court has Jurisdiction under the "Fair Credit Reporting act" of 15 U.S.C. § §1681-

1681P to adjudicate the action between Plaintiff and all three CRAs Equifax information

Services, LLC ("Equifax"), Experian information Solutions, Inc. ("Experian"), and Trans Union

LLC ("Trans Union").

This Court ruled, affirmed and granted Plaintiff SAC, (See Doc.63.), indeed had two claims (See

Doc.130.), of negligent non-compliance and common law defamation as stated by the facts

1

Plaintiff SAC and the facts as it relates back to all Plaintiff Complaints (See Doc.2 and.16.), filed

with this Court.

PLAINTIFF IS FILING HIS SECOND SUMMARY JUDGMENT MOTION AS INSTRUCTED BY THE COURT

FROM COURT RULING ON PLAINTIFF FIRST SUMMARY JUDGMENT MOTION WITHOUT PREJUDICE

(See Doc. 58.).

Plaintiff prays from persuasive arguments on claims of negligent non-compliance and common

law defamation as stated by this Court, that the wisdom of this Court will grant plaintiff second

Summary Judgment motion on all claims name herein against all three Defendants in this law

suit.

STATEMENT OF FACTS

This case arise as a results bring this action against Equifax information Services, LLC

("Equifax"), Experian information Solutions, Inc. ("Experian"), and Trans Union LLC ("Trans

Union") inaccurate duplicating his credit account on his consumer credit file while monitoring

his credit report in the month of June 2011 (Doc.76 at 4), in which the Court rule in Plaintiff

favor under FCRA 1681(b) and 1681(e) (b) which this Court held the Defendants committed

non-negligence and defamation claims as stated by the facts in Plaintiff SAC.

As the Court has stated and ruled these claims of wrongful injuries fell in three categories. First

the inaccurate duplications begin appearing on Plaintiff credit report in June 2011, while Plaintiff

was monitor his consumer credit report through all three credit monitoring service. (id.)

The duplicated accounts alleged and claim by the Court were "__ accounts," "Home Loan

Services accounts," "____ accounts," etc. (id) When Plaintiff discovered these duplicated

accounts on his consumer report Plaintiff called all three and reported the duplicated accounts to

all three CRAs (Equifax information Services, LLC ("Equifax"), Experian information Solutions,

Inc. ("Experian"), and Trans Union LLC ("Trans Union") (id). Within a month or so in 2011, all three Defendants had corrected Plaintiff consumer credit report and there were only one account for each of Plaintiff creditor on his consumer credit file. (id). These inaccurate accounts errors on Plaintiff consumer credit file during the month of June 2011 has negated Plaintiff from reestablishing his credit (id at 7) which prevented Plaintiff from obtaining personal credit which ultimately he was not able to raise his credit worthiness for personal consumer buying and financing business projects and ventures. (id at 5.)

Second, Plaintiff claims and the Court agreed that as a result of the inaccurate duplicated accounts when the credit card Company ___ pulled Plaintiff Equifax credit file. Which Plaintiff believed Equifax was at that time either in the process of purging or correcting the accounts back to a normal consumer credit file of one account for each creditor on Plaintiff consumer credit file, notwithstanding HBSC reported that plaintiff had "insufficient credit references" which indicated no accounts on Plaintiff consumer credit file, therefore denying Plaintiff the credit card application which was much needed at that time.

Third, Plaintiff claims and the Court agreed that as a result of the inaccurate accounts omission by Experian on Plaintiff credit file on Nov. 28, 2011 while applying for line of credit at Wells Fargo Bank, Experian which resulted in under reporting of only two accounts of Plaintiff many numerous creditors or "a much more extensive credit history as stated by the Court" on Plaintiff file Plaintiff was denied credit from the "insufficient credit references" history being reported and provided by Experian to Wells Fargo Bank (3rd party) on Plaintiff on Nov. 28, 2011. In addition Experian committed the same act of omission in the prior Month of Oct 2, 2011 as

stated in Prior Plaintiff Complaints SAC (Doc # 124 page7).

Base on claims and facts above Plaintiff brought suit on claims of negligent non-compliance and common law defamation as stated by this Court, against all three CRAs Equifax information

Services, LLC ("Equifax"), Experian information Solutions, Inc. ("Experian"), and Trans Union LLC ("Trans Union") under FCRA 15 U.S.C. § 1681e (b), which requires these three credit reporting agencies stated above to follow reasonable procedures to assure maximum possible accuracy of a consumer report id.; which in the instant case violated Plaintiff rights under FCRA and therefore Plaintiff has a right to bring a private action under 15 U.S.C. § 1681o(creating a private right for negligent non-compliance with the FCRA).

Trans Union LLC ("Trans Union") under FCRA 15 U.S.C. § 1681e (b), wrongful act herein are the same as the other two CRAs in the Month of June which was alleged in his SAC and relate back to Plaintiff prior complaints and adjudicate as a claims of negligent non-compliance and common law defamation.

(Emphasis) on the words "Your credit file" "Your credit Report" Duplication is not conclusory when Plaintiff submits Prima Facie Evidence such as stated by Plaintiff credit monitor file sent to Plaintiff in the Month of June by Trans Union and reported by Equifax, "Here is what is stated on account information" "Here are the details" An account information has appeared on your credit report" "As a benefit of your Trans Union credit Monitoring Membership." You are being notified that on June 4, 2011 the following change(s) appeared in your credit file."

These statements on these documents are concrete proffer that these documents are part of Plaintiff credit report or file.

Base on claims and facts above Plaintiff brought suit on claims of negligent non-compliance and common law defamation as stated and Rule as claims by this Court in Doc # 124.

The first admission to Plaintiff having a claim on his Complaint, Mr. Franklin G. Cosmen, JR PA stated "Defendant Transunion LLC's Joiner and consent to Removal "On May 1, 2012,

Transunion was served with Plaintiff's Complaint, the initial pleading setting forth the claim for relief upon which this action is base." (Emphasis added)

Due to Plaintiff first complaint being accepted by this Court by Magistrate Judge Thomas E.

Morris with attach affidavit evidence of su bmitted alone with it converted the Amended

Complaint to Summary Judgment. See Doc #

When Facts as it pertain to common law defamation action is disclosed pursuant to FCRA provisions (unless the consumer pleads and proves malice or willfulness intent to injuries.

For example Plaintiff used his cell phone to dispute these inaccuracies by calling each Defendant to notify Defendants of inaccuracies of the duplicated Plaintiff's credit files. Furthermore on Page 2, paragraph 8, Plaintiff's Complaint states, "An Trans Union agent said that although Plaintiff sees two files it is only one", this Rep knowing that this statement in and of itself is a false statement of willfulness by Trans Union.

"Malice is defined as a statement made with knowledge that it was false or with reckless disregard of whether it was false or not."

Another example of willfulness and malice as stated by Plaintiff." Plaintiff can say for certain that most of the times the tone of voice of most of the reps plaintiff called where hostile and argumentative, a disgruntled employee could have done it to get back at one of the three credit agencies or take their working conditions frustration out on Plaintiff for calling so frequently about the inaccuracies in his credit file.

This duplication of Plaintiff credit file could have led to malice or will intent to injure Plaintiff as a way of deterring Plaintiff to stop calling so frequently to report incorrect, inaccurate and incomplete credit information on Plaintiff credit file.

Anger if acted on can be considered a form of malice; anger, hostility and argumentative behavior are a recipe for a willful intent toward others. Plaintiff has cited that the employees of the three CRA's exhibit this form of behavior to Plaintiff while he was disputing the Duplication inaccuracy of Plaintiff credit accounts.

Plaintiff used the cell phone to Dispute these inaccuracies by calling each defendant to notify defendants of inaccuracies. none of service reps where pleasant and one was very upset with Plaintiff from calling and said, "These things happen some times, which is admission of knowing violation which results in a claims for Plaintiff against Defendants by default on the part of defendants and characterized this injury on Plaintiff as just another mishap in the industry of Big Three credit reporting Agencies.

The credit Agencies Reps has become desensitized to Debtors needs. The exact same Quote use by attorney Mr. Tierney P.A in conference with Plaintiff on May 2, 2012 while talking to Mr. Tierney Experian legal attorney on the telephone, this in and of itself is a cause of action of defamation.

In the same instance employees go home and discuss what happen at work to their family, friends, wives, and significant others when this happen defamation occurs.

Malice is define as a statement made with knowledge that it was false or with reckless disregard of whether it was false or not Hunt v. Liberty Lobby 720 F. 2d 631,642 (11th Cir. 1983) (citing New York Times Co v. Sullivan, 376 U.S. 254, 279-80 (1964).

Summary Judgment Standard

A party shall be entitle to Summary Judgment "if the pleadings, depositions, answers to interrogatories, and admissions on file, together with affidavits, if any show that is no genuine issue as to any, show that there is no genuine issue as to any material facts and that the moving party is entitled to a Judgment as a matter of law." Fed. R. Civ. P. 56(c). When the Court is deciding a motion for Summary Judgment, the Court must review the evidence in light most favorable to the nonmoving party and draw all reasonable inference in the nonmoving party's favor. Cadle Co. v. Hayes, 116 F. 3d. 957, 959 (1st Cir. 1997).

Summary Judgment involves shifting burdens between the moving and the nonmoving parties in the instant case would be these three CRAs Equifax, Experian and Trans Union.

Initially the burden requires the moving party to aver "an absence of evidence to support the nonmoving party's case Garside v. Osco Drug, Inc., 895 F. 2d. 46, 48 (1st Cir. 1990) (quoting Celotex Corp. v. Catrett, 477 U.S. 317, 325, 106 S. Ct. 2548, 2554, 91 L. Ed 2d. 265 (1986). Once the moving party meets this burden, the burden falls upon the nonmoving party, who must oppose the motion by presenting facts that show a genuine "trial worthy issue remains" Cadle 116 F. 3d at 960 (citing Nat'l Amusement, Inc. V. Town of Dedham, 43 F.3d. 731, 735 (1st Cir. 1995); Maldonado-Denis v. Castillo-Rodriquez, 23 F. 3d 576, 581 (1st Cir 1994). An issue of fact is "genuine" if it "may reasonably be resolved in favor of either party." Id. (citing Maldonado-Denis, 23 F. 3d. at 581).

To oppose the motion successfully, the nonmoving party must present affirmative evidence to rebut the motion. See Anderson v. liberty lobby, Inc., 477 U.S. 242, 256-57, 106 S. Ct. 2505, 2514-2515, 91 L. Ed. 2d 202, (1986). "even in cases where elusive concepts such as motive or intent are at issue, summary Judgment may be appropriate if the nonmoving party rests merely upon conclusory allegations, improbable inferences [or] unsupported speculation." Medina-Munoz v. R.J. Reynolds Tobacco Co., 896 F. 2d 5, 8 (1st Cir 1990). Moreover, the evidence illustrating the factual controversy cannot be conjectural or problematic; it must have substance in the sense that it limns differing versions of the truth which a fact finder must resolve...." Id. (quoting Mack v. Great Atl. & Pac. Tea Co., 871 f. 2D 179, 181 (1st Cir. 1989).

Therefore, to defeat a properly supported motion for Summary Judgment, the nonmoving party must establish a trial worthy issue by presenting "enough competent evidence to enable a finding favorable to the nonmoving party." Goldman v. First Nat'l Bank of Boston, 985 F. 2d 1113, (1st Anderson, 477 U.S. at 249).

MEMORANDUM OF LAW

First Plaintiff would like to begin by stating that Equifax is possible misleading the Court when Equifax stated in their Answers and Defenses bottom of page 2 #5 "Reponding to allegations contained in paragraph 5, Equifax states that it did not received any disputes communication from Plaintiff in June 2011." "Equifax is without knowledge or information sufficient to form a belief as to the truth of the remaining allegations contained in paragraph 5," see exhibit (P)
As the Court can note from exhibit (G) submitted by Plaintiff to Experian June 6, 2011 and the two other Defendants, Equifax and Trans Union during the same time period in month of June 6, 2011 this far from the truth.

(Emphasis) on the words "Your credit file" "Your credit Report" Duplication is not conclusory when Plaintiff submits Prima Facie Evidence such as stated by Plaintiff credit monitor file sent to Plaintiff in the Month of June by Trans Union and reported by Equifax, "Here is what is stated on account information" "Here are the details" An account information has appeared on your credit report" "As a benefit of your Trans Union credit Monitoring Membership." You are being notified that on June 4, 2011 the following change(s) appeared in your credit file."
These statements and words on these documents is concrete proof that these documents are part of Plaintiff credit file.

This act of providing a Membership Monitor credit report that was not requested by Plaintif instead of sending Plaintiff his normal regular report as requested by Plaintiff is a wrongful act of false reckless, ___ on the Plaintiff by these Defendants.

Under the FCRA Congress entrust all three CRAs with the "Grave responsibility" to ensure that information is accurate and to properly investigated disputes [15 U.S.C. § 1681] (a) (4).

"The Court has made clear that it follows the plain language of 15 U.S.C. § 1681h (e), which states that a showing of willful intent to injure or publication of a report with malice, any state or common law claim for defamation or negligence is preempted. As such, absent any evidence of malice or willfulness, Plaintiff state law claims are preempted by FCRA. "Recovery for common law defamation is precluded by the FCRA where the information that gives rise to the cause of action is disclosed pursuant to FCRA provisions unless the consumer pleads and proves malice or willfulness intent to injuries." Lee v. Security Check, LLC, 2010 WL 3075673, *5(M.D. Fla. Aug 5, 2010).

DEFEND ANTS STATE OF MIND

Many courts including the Eleventh Circuit, has recognizes that Rule 9(b) Fed. R. Civ. P., allows allegations regarding mental state to be alleged in "general" United States ex rel. Matheny v. Medco Health Solutions, Inc., 672 F. 3d 1217 (11th Cir. 2012); see also Embrey, 2013 WL 1289401, *5 Austin v. Auto owners Ins. Co. 12-0345, 2012 WL 3101693, at *4 (N.D. Ala. Jul. 30, 2012) and other parallel cases.

PLAINTIFF DEFAMATION CLAIM

This Court has rule and held that although the amended Complaint briefly reference malice by stating that this duplication of Plaintiff credit file could have led to malice or willful intent to injure Plaintiff (Doc. 16 at 5). This Court has ruled facts stated from the SAC alludes to the state of mind of Defendants as being enough for defamation claim as in the almond Court and

similarly in Embrey v. First Franklin Financial Corporation, 12-61233-civ., 2013 WL 1289401

(S.D. Fla. Mar. 12, 2013) "The Southern District of Florida Held that a represented Plaintiff

sufficiently pleaded the FCRA's required mental state by alleging that "Defendants exhibited a

knowing disregard for the truth Id., at *5. The Embrey Court concluded: "This is enough.

"Since Plaintiffs has sufficiently alleged that the Defendants acted with malice, their defamation

The Ruling Held

claim is not preempted by the Fair Credit Reporting Act" id. These case law ruling are in these

Courts are applicable to the facts of malice to bring about a claim of defamation against these

Defendants,

The perfect example of hostile emotions getting the best of a person is when Mr. Olson cursing

Plaintiff during his Deposition on March 19, 2013 excluded from page 74 lines 14 and 15.

In relation to the actions of Mr. Brian is the derogatory remark by Mrs. Reddoch on or about Mar

24, of this year stating, "She was tired of Plaintiff submitting gibberish disputes to her and

Plaintiff should not submit any more to her." This is the reason I never called her back to dispute

the wells Fargo Dealer account, Plaintiff has since forgiven her for her statement, but never the

less emotionally, you forgive but never forget.

Plaintiff has pleaded malice and willfulness in his Complaints, and the Precedent holding and

rule by the U.S. Supreme Court on the issue of malice and willfulness has not been over turned.

The U.S. Supreme Court has held in Safeco Ins. Co v. Burr, that defendant willfully violated the

FCRA where the defendant knowingly or recklessly violated the act. The Court rejected the

argument of the petitioner insurance companies that liability under section 1681n occurs only

when there is a knowing violation, holding that in the context of civil liability it has generally construed willfulness to include not only knowing violations but also reckless violation of a statue.

Safeco, 551 U.S. 47, 127 S. CT. at 2208-10, 2215, 15 U.S.C. 1681n provides that any "person who willfully fail to comply with any requirement under this subchapter with respect to any consumer is liable to that consumer" for actual and punitive damages. Hernandez v. Lamboy Furniture Inc., 2008 WL 4061344, at *8 (E.D. Pa Sept. 2, 2008).

Fair Credit Reporting Act provides that: whenever a consumer reporting agency prepares a consumer report it shall follow reasonable procedures to assure maximum possible accuracy of the information concerning the individual about whom the report relates."15 U.S.C. 1681e (b). In a reinvestigation of the accuracy of credit report, a credit bureau must bear some responsibility for evaluating the accuracy of information obtain from subscriber") white v. Trans Union 462 F. Supp. 2d 1079 (CD. Cal 2006).

Whether a CRA has acted in "Willful noncompliance" with the FCRA under 1681n is and objective assessment that encompasses action taken in reckless disregard of FCRA's obligations. Safeco, 551 U.S. 47, 127 S. CT. at 2208-10, 2215.

15 U.S.C. 1681n provides that any "person who willfully fail to comply with any requirement under this subchapter with respect to any consumer is liable to that consumer" for actual and punitive damages. Hernandez v. Lamboy Furniture Inc., 2008 WL 4061344, at *8 (E.D. Pa Sept. 2, 2008).

"Congress bestowed on credit agencies special requirements for meeting the needs of commerce... with regard to the confidentiality, accuracy, relevancy, and proper utilization of such information in accordance with the requirements of this title Fair Credit Reporting Act 15 U.S.C. § 1681] (b)." (Emphasis add on accuracy)

15 U.S.C. § 1681a] (d) (1) : In general, the term consumer report means any written, oral, or other communication of any information by a consumer reporting agency ...

(Emphasis on "any information")

However, in the instance case where the Plaintiff has pleaded facts that in themselves adds up to a valid legal claim with the appropriate legal theories for Summary Judgment for Plaintiff should be granted.

Under section 15 U.S.C. § 1681a](g) of the FCRA The term "file" when used in connection with information on any consumer, means all of the information on that consumer recorded and retained by a consumer reporting agency regardless of how the information is stored. (Emphasis on "all the information on that consumer" added)

Plaintiff argues the issue of "Insufficient credit Reference" as stated by ___ bank credit card means that there is either "no credit" information available or not enough credit information to base their credit decision on. Base on Plaintiff credit profile dated on or around the month of June, that if all three CRAs especially Equifax had all Plaintiff Creditors on Plaintiff "file" during that time the Creditor was checking Plaintiff file for approval of his credit. The compute Algorithm scan would not have registered Plaintiff credit file as not having

"Insufficient credit Reference," when in fact Plaintiff had many credit references available to base their approval on by the credit card company .

EXTRINSIC AND INTRINSIC EVIDENCE

The Court is not limited to the facts alleged in the Second Amended Complaint, all accepted as true. *See Fleischfresser v. Directors of Sch. Dist. 200*, 15 F.3d 680, 684 (7th Cir. 1994). If, on a motion under Rule 12(b)(6) or 12(c), "matters outside the pleadings [are] presented to and not excluded by the court, ... the motion must be treated as one for summary judgment." *Miller v. Heman*

600 F.3d 726, 733 (7th Cir. 2010); *see also* Fed. R. Civ. P. 12(d). See Plaintiff amended

Complaint with attached affidavit, see exhibit (A) (B).

If materials extrinsic to the pleadings are submitted to the Court in support of or in opposition to

a 12(b) (6) motion, the Court does not have to consider them. Under FRCP 12(b), however, once

the court does consider such matter the motion is automatically "converted to a motion for

summary judgment pursuant to FRCP 56, this is the legal situation with the instant case against

these defendants.

Material does not literally have to be bound into the Complaint to be considered "intrinsic" to it

and a proper part consideration of a 12(b) (6) motion, without a "conversion" taking place.

It can fairly be said that any oral or written evidence not already "in the record" public or Court,

physical or by reference is regarded as "extrinsic" and will spur a conversion.

Plaintiff Amended Complaint on all four corners of the Complaint is stating claims of non-

compliance negligence and Defamation.

All three Defendants created a duplicate or multiple credit accounts on Plaintiff's credit file in

the month of June 2011 while Plaintiff was trying to improve his credit standing while visiting

their Website. Defendants was in violation of [15 U.S.C. § 1681] (b) as stated below and 15

U.S.C. 1681 (e) (b) of the FCRA.

(Emphasis Added) on accuracy, that a cause of action of Negligence took place or occurred.

When Plaintiff stated that defendants made two _ accounts twice the specificity theory was

satisfied reference to Ashcroft v. Iqbal, 556 U.S. 662, 665 (2009).

The fact that Defendants Duplicated Plaintiff credit file makes Defendants liable under a claim

of a cause of action of negligence as well as Malice when Defendants attorney Tom Tierney

Stated "those things Happen sometimes" when Plaintiff had his first telephone conference by Experian Lead Attorney this appears to be the prevail attitude of all three credit bureaus Equifax, Experian and Trans Union.

Under 15 U.S.C. 1681 (b) of the FCRA, in fact the act of duplicating any consumer credit files of which are not accurate makes the file inaccurate and the Defendant's by definition is liable for their injuries to the Plaintiff with a cause of action of negligence.

By Defendant's admitting the fact, the only provision that Plaintiff specifically cites to is the 15 U.S.C. 1681 (sic) which should be 15 U.S.C. 1681 (b) this section of the FCRA stress the word accuracy when Plaintiff reported the dispute by cell phone to all three Defendants of the inaccuracies of not having one credit file only on Plaintiff's credit file. (Add material). By asserting a claim of all three violations of FCRA of the U.S.C. 1681 (d) sic and 15 U.S.C. 1681 (b) (Plaintiff satisfies a factual claim and identifies these sections in Plaintiff' Amended Complaint. See Thrasher v. Amadillo Police Department, 346 Fed. Appx 991, 992 (Fifth Cir. 2009).

Under the FRCA of 15 U.S.C. 1681 (b) (If any of Plaintiff's credit accounts which is the totality of his entire file is inaccurate all three Defendants are subject to damages from their injuries and harm done to Plaintiff, Nelson v. Chase Manhattan Mortgage Corp. 282 F.3d 1057 (2002) Plaintiff states that after about a month of calling all three credit bureaus the accounts were finally rectified and returned to normal means Plaintiff sees only one account for each credit account Plaintiff had with Defendants. This statement by Plaintiff is explicit in nature that all three Defendants were put on notice of disputes by Plaintiff as required by FCRA 15 U.S.C. §1681 et seq. Defendants mistakenly stated on page five second paragraph "While Plaintiff alleges that on a certain date her[sic] credit report was improperly assessed by each moving

Defendants Plaintiff does provide factual support exhibit A and Exhibit B to address reasonable inference that the moving Defendants are liable for damages of injury and negligence and defamation. See Nelson v. Chase Manhattan Corp., 282 F. 3d 1057 (2002), also the Court said that,"it is not for the Court to remake the balance struck by congress"... Nelson v. Chase Manhattan Corp., 282 F. 3d 1057, 1060 (9th Cir. 2002).

Clearly Defendants Equifax admits to Plaintiff's Amended Complaint contained specificity with regard to Equifax, page 5 paragraph (3) Exhibit B, ____. The mere fact that Equifax deleted or the computer purge this inquiry on Plaintiff's credit file (Exhibit (B) is in direct violation of FCRA because Equifax by law is supposed to have this inquiry recorded on Plaintiff's credit file because it is Hard inquiry and the FCRA states all hard inquires must be recorded on the consumer credit file, Equifax is subject to the FCRA violation, not only for actual damages but for punitive damages ~~and~~ from willful malice recklessness, And Supreme Court held in Safeco Ins. Co v. Burr, that defendant willfully violated the FCRA where the defendant knowingly or recklessly violated the act. The Court rejected the argument of the petitioner insurance companies that liability under section 1681n occurs only when there is a knowing violation, holding that in the context of civil liability it has generally construed willfulness to include not only knowing violations but also reckless violation of a statue.

The Supreme Court recognized that reckless conduct may be sufficient to establish a Willfulness violation of the FCRA Act.

All documents and exhibits submitted to Court and Defendants attorneys in prior motions and

Furthermore, a letter from ___ Bank rejecting a credit card application by Plaintiff on June admission to apply to this second Amended complaint in this claim, Plaintiff believes the legal 24, 2011 from information provided by Equifax, Plaintiff admits into evidence as exhibit (c).

Plaintiff sent a letter to Transunion on 12-3-2011 title "NOTICE BEFORE LEGAL ACTION" if

Transunion do not respond to some type settlement agreement within 7 days of receipt of letter;

Plaintiff got no response from Trans union exhibit (D) Exhibit (E) consist of five pages front to

back from Defendant Trans union dated June 9, 2011.

Exhibit (F) consist of five pages front to back from Defendant Transunion dated June 18, 2011.

Exhibit (G) a one page letter address to Experian with an attach copy account of Services which

was sent to Trans union as well as Equifax. Trans union Attorney Allison acknowledge she

had the letter in her possession on Tuesday or Wednesday when Plaintiff spoke

to her concerning the Trans union documents she want me to send her either by mail or email.

Exhibit (H) consist of one page front to back.

Experian dated Oct 4, 2011 sent to Plaintiff with his Credit score and a statement from a

Experian service rep name Louis date Oct 5, 2011 stating Plaintiff had no Public record on his

file but most important Louis said the same thing Mr. Tom Tierney said, "He has heard in that happen

before." When Plaintiff received a telephone conference call from him in the beginning

or middle part of May, 2012.

All three CRA received a letter dated 6-6-2011 informing Defendant that Plaintiff was not aware

of the changes made to Home Loan Services on Plaintiff credit file, evidence as exhibit(d).

Plaintiff claiming injuries of A. Loss of personal income B. Loss of Business income C. Lack of

Trust in others D .Denied Credit E. Financial Hardship F. Psychological Stress from the wrong

of negligent and Defamation by these Defendants.

All three CRA (Defendants) in their membership agreement states that in order to become a

member Plaintiff had to agree that Defendants were allow to share Plaintiff credit file with the

other CRAs before Plaintiff could becoming a member of any of the CRA.

Plaintiff believed the sharing of Plaintiff credit file is what the computers analog pick up on and cause the Multiple or duplication of Plaintiff credit file by all three Defendants computer systems.

Summary Judgment is proper in any case where there is no genuine issue of material facts. Fed. R. Civ. P., Rule 56 (c). A Plaintiff moving for summary judgment may satisfy its burden by submitting summary judgment proof that establishes all elements of its cause of action as a matter of law. San Pedro v. U.S., 79 F.3d 1065, 1068 (11th Cir. 1996). Plaintiff must show that no reasonable trier of fact can find other than for Plaintiff. Calderone v. U.S., 799 F.2d 254, 259 (6th Cir.1986).

Since defendants are in possession of all digital files in a computer age there is no dispute that defendants possess all the documents Plaintiff have in his possession unless Defendant (Equifax) Purged Plaintiff credit the file which makes Equifax in violation of the FTC.

Motion, Memorandum and its attachments Affidavits establish there is no genuine issue of disputed material facts Defendants then Summary Judgment should be granted to Plaintiff.

Plaintiff brings this action under the following provisions of the Fair Credit Reporting Act (FCRA). More specifically Plaintiff allege violations of (i) [15 U.S.C. § 1681] (b), by all Defendant's,(ii) violations of [15 U.S.C. § 1681a] (d) (1), by all Defendant's, (iii) violations of [15 U.S.C. § 1681a] (g), by all Defendant's, (iv) violations of [15 U.S.C. § 1681b] (a), (3), (A), by Equifax and Experian, (v) violations of 604 (b)(3)(B) (1V) by all defendants, (vi) violations of [15 U.S.C. § 1681e] (b) by all defendants,(vii) violation of [15 U.S.C. § 1681i] (1)(A)(2)(A), by all defendants, and especially by Equifax Mr. Olson on Sept 14, 2012, (viii) violations of [15 U.S.C. § 1681p] By all Defendant's, (ix) violations of [15 U.S.C. § 1681a] (p), by all defendants, x) violations of [15 U.S.C. § 1681o] By all Defendant's, 1681h, and 1681n.

Plaintiff's credit accounts but if only one of the accounts was not corrected a negligent liability

exists with all three Defendants see when Plaintiff was denied a credit card from _____.

Defendants mistakenly stated on page five second paragraph "While Plaintiff alleges that on a

certain date her[sic] credit report was improperly assessed by each moving Defendants Plaintiff

does provide factual support exhibit A and Exhibit B to address reasonable inference that the

moving Defendants are liable for damages of injury and negligence and defamation. See Nelson

v. Chase Manhattan Corp., 282 F. 3d 1057 (2002), also the Court said that, "it is not for the Court

to remake the balance struck by congress"… Nelson v. Chase Manhattan Corp., 282 F. 3d 1057,

1060 (9th Cir. 2002).

All three CRA received a letter dated 6-6-2011 informing Defendant that Plaintiff was not aware

of the changes made to Home Loan Services on Plaintiff credit file, evidence as exhibit(d)

all three CRA (Defendants) in their membership agreement states that in order to become a

member Plaintiff had to agree that Defendants were allow to share Plaintiff credit file with the

other CRAs before Plaintiff could becoming a member of any of the CRA.

Summary Judgment is proper in any case where there is no genuine issue of material

facts. Fed. R. Civ. P., Rule 56 (c). A Plaintiff moving for summary judgment may satisfy its

burden by submitting summary judgment proof that establishes all elements of its cause of action

as a matter of law. San Pedro v. U.S., 79 F.3d 1065, 1068 (11th Cir. 1996). Plaintiff must show

that no reasonable trier of fact can find other than for Plaintiff. Calderone v. U.S., 799 F.2d 254,

259 (6th Cir.1986).

CERTIFICATE OF SERVICE

WHEREFORE, Plaintiff, James Watson Pro Se, respectfully requests this Court to grant this motion and enter an Order granting Summary Judgment in favor of Plaintiff in the amount of $125,000 each against all three CRAs and for such other and further relief as this Court deems just and proper.

Respectfully submitted,

By: _____

James Leon Watson Sr.
2357 Stardust Ct #9
Jacksonville, FL 32211
904-226-0536

Brian J. Olsen
King & Spalding LLP
1180 Peachtree St. N.E.
Atlanta, GA 30309-3521
404-215-5806
Fax 404-572-5100
bjolson@kslaw.com
Counsel for Equifax

Thomas W. Tierney
Rossway, Moore & Taylor
Suite 200
2101 Indian River Blvd
Vero Beach, FL 32960
772-321-4440
Fax 772-231-4430
ttierney@verobeachlawyers.com
Counsel for Experian

Mrs. Allison Reddoch PA
9300 South Dadeland Blvd 4th Floor
Miami, FL 33156
305-670-1101
Facsimile: 305-670-1161
Counsel for Transunion

FN1: FRE 201 (b) Federal Rules of evidence permit Judges to take notice of two categories of facts Permissive, Mandatory must take judicial notice of facts proffer.

FN2. Rule 9 (1) and (2) which limit judicial notice of facts to those "so universally known that they cannot reasonably be the subject of dispute of "those so generally known of such common notified within the territorial jurisdiction of the Court that they cannot reasonably be the subject of the dispute.

FN3: All documents and exhibits submitted to Court and Defendants attorneys in prior motions and admission apply to this second Summary Judgment and "relate back." to first MSJ as stated in Plaintiff SAC.

UNITED STATES DISTRICT COURT MIDDLE DISTRICT OF
FLORIDA JACKSONVILLE DIVISION

JAMES L. WATSON,

Plaintiff,

    -vs-   Case No.   3:12-cv-552-J-99MMH-TEM

EQUIFAX, et al.,

Defendants.

SUMMARY JUDGMENT NOTICE

Motion(s) for summary judgment pursuant to Rule 56, Federal Rules of Civil Procedure,

have been filed in this case. Unless the Court notifies the parties otherwise, there will not be

a hearing on these motion(s); instead, the Court will decide the motion(s) on the basis of the

motion(s), responses, briefs or legal memoranda, and evidentiary materials filed by the

parties. Unless otherwise specifically ordered by the Court, any response to these

motion(s), as well as all supporting evidentiary materials (counter- affidavits, depositions,

exhibits, etc.) must be filed with the Clerk of this Court in accordance with the Federal

Rules of Civil Procedure. The Court will consider these motion(s) ripe for review <u>twenty-one</u>

<u>21) days</u> from the date of the filing of the motion(s).'

<u>The following explanatory admonitions are included here for the benefit of pro se</u>

<u>parties (i.e.• parties not represented by an attorney) who oppose the summary judgment</u>

<u>motion(s).</u> In addition to the above paragraph, you are also advised that if the Court

grants the motion(s) for summary judgment, such would be a final decision of the Court

If the motion is served electronically or by mail, the parties have an additional three consecutive mailing
days to file a response.   Fed.R.Civ.P. 6(e).

in favor of the party filing the motion(s) ("the movant"). As a result of such final decision, there would be no trial or other proceedings in this case, and you would likely be precluded from later litigating this matter or any related matters. Therefore, **you are hereby further advised:** (1) failing to respond to these motion(s) will indicate that the motion(s) are not opposed; (2) all material facts asserted by the movant in the motion(s) will be considered to be admitted by you unless controverted by proper evidentiary materials (counter• affidavits, depositions, exhibits, etc.) filed by you; and (3) you may not rely solely on the allegations of the issue pleadings (e.g., complaint, answer, etc.) in opposing these motion(s). See Griffith v. Wainwright, 772 F.2d 822,825 (11th Cir. 1985).

FOR THE COURT

Date: August 20, 2013
By:

                                   Patricia Morawski,
                                   Deputy Clerk

Copies to: Counsel
of Record
Pro Se Party(s), if any

JAMESL.WATSON,   )
)
    Plaintiff,   )
)
vs)   Case   No.3:12-cv-00552-UAMH-
JBT
)
EQUIFAX, EXPERIAN, and   )
TRANSUNION,   )
)
    Defendants.   )

DEFENDANTS EXPERIAN INFORMATION SOLUTIONS, INC.'SAND EQUIFAX INFORMATION SERVICES LLC'S JOINT MOTION FOR SUMMARY JUDGMENT AND BRIEF IN SUPPORT THEREOF

TABLE OF CONTENTS

Pursuant to Federal Rule of Civil Procedure 56, Defendants Experian Information Solutions, Inc. ("Experian"), incorrectly named in Plaintiff's Second Amended Complaint as "Experian," and Equifax Information Services LLC ("Equifax"), incorrectly named in Plaintiff's Second Amended Complaint as "Equifax," move the Court to enter summary judgment in their favor on all claims asserted by Plaintiff, James L. Watson. There is no genuine issue as to   any material fact and Experian and Equifax are entitled to judgment in their favor as a matter of law.

I. INTRODUCTION

Plaintiff's Second Amended Complaint (Doc. 76) purports to assert claims against Experian, Equifax, and a third Defendant, Trans Union LLC ("Trans Union"), for violations of the Fair Credit Reporting Act ("FCRA"), 15 U.S.C. §§ 1681-1681x, and for defamation. Plaintiff's claims stem from three sets of alleged facts: (I) the alleged reporting by all Defendants of Plaintiff's consumer file accounts in duplicate in or around June 2011; (2) the alleged reporting by Equifax to ___ in 2011 that Plaintiff had no credit accounts in connection with Plaintiff s credit card application, resulting in a denial by ___; and (3) the alleged reporting by Experian in November 2011 to __ of only a few of Plaintiff's consumer file accounts in connection with a loan application, resulting in a denial by_____. (Doc. 76 at 4-6.)

Experian's and Equifax's motion should be granted because Plaintiff cannot furnish any evidence to support. the basic elements of the FCRA claim or the defamation claim. First, Plaintiff has failed to proffer any evidence that either Experian or Equifax reported inaccurate information resulting from an alleged failure to follow reasonable procedures; likewise, he has not proffered any evidence of damages caused by either Defendant. For either reason, Experian and Equifax are entitled to summary judgment on Plaintiff's FCRA claim. Second, summary judgment should be granted on Plaintiff's defamation claims because they are preempted by the

FCRA. Plaintiff cannot demonstrate that Experian or Equifax acted with malice, which is required for Plaintiff to avoid the FCRA's strong preemption bar. Accordingly, the FCRA and defamation claims fail, and Experian and Equifax respectfully request that this Court grant their Motion for Summary Judgment.

II.

STATEMENT OF MATERIAL FACTS AS TO WHICH NO GENUINE ISSUE EXISTS

l. Experian and Equifax are "consumer reporting agency[ies]" within the meaning of the FCRA. (Ex. A, Affidavit of Kimberly Hughes ("Hughes Aff.") 'If 4; Ex. B, Declaration of Mackenzie Cole ("Cole Deel.") 'If 5.) As such, Experian and Equifax act as conduits of credit information pertinent to credit granting and related decisions. (Hughes Aff. 'If 4; *see* Cole Deel.'If'If 7-9.) Each gathers credit information originated by others and makes that information available to customers engaged in credit related transactions. (Hughes Aff. 'If 4; Cole Deel. 'Il'If7- 8.) Experian and Equifax do not originate or create any credit information, and they do not make loans or decide who should receive credit. (Hughes Aff. 'If 4; Cole Deel. 'If 9.) Those functions are handled entirely by the credit granting industry. (Hughes Aff. 'I! 4.),

> Experian and Equifax essentially act as storehouses of credit information by assembling, storing, and furnishing data as allowed by the FCRA and similar state laws. (Hughes Aff.'If 5; *see* ColeDeel.'If 7-9.) After credit data is received by Experian or Equifax and before it is added to a consumer's credit file, the information is subjected to rigorous quality control and statutory compliance procedures to ensure that only accurate information is reported. (Hughes Aff. 'If 6; *see* Cole Deel. 'If 15-17.) Automated procedures are designed to ensure no information that

would violate the prescriptions of the FCRA or similar state statutes will be reported on any consumer's credit report. *(Id.)*

Experian and Equifax each have extensive procedures for assuring the maximum possible

accuracy of reported credit information, which include: (l) working with credit grantors to ensure

that they supply the most complete and accurate data possible; (2) subjecting all incoming data

to numerous systems and checks designed to prevent errors; (3) continually reviewing and

refining their computer systems in an ongoing effort to assure maximum possible

accuracy of information in their reports; and (4) working with consumers to proactively prevent errors

in consumer credit reports. (Hughes Aff. ‚ Г 7; *see* Cole Deel. ‚ Г‚ Г 11-21.) To proactively prevent errors

in consumer credit reports, Experian and Equifax each provide consumers with access to their credit

files and means to request reinvestigations if consumers disagree with items appearing in their credit

reports.   (Hughes Aff. ‚ Г 8; Cole Deel.‚ Г 20.) The agencies have also implemented procedures

designed to involve consumers in the overall process that assures the maximum possible accuracy of

their consumer reports. (Hughes Aff.‚ Г 8; *see* Cole De_cl.‚ Г 21.)

A consumer who disagrees with the accuracy or completeness of any item of credit information

reported by Experian or Equifax in a consumer file disclosure (or in consumer credit

report provided to a credit grantor) may submit a dispute of that item to the reporting agency. (Hughes

Aff. ‚ Г 9; Cole Deel. ‚ Г 20.) Experian and Equifax actively encourage consumers to request file

disclosures, review them, and submit disputes of any items believed to be inaccurate

or incomplete in order to assure that the information reported by the agency is as accurate as possible.

(Hughes Aff. ‚ Г 9; Cole Deel. ‚ Г 21.)

If the information submitted to Experian or Equifax by a consumer for a dispute does not allow the

agency to use the information to update the consumer's file internally, the agency does an external

reinvestigation.   (Hughes Aff. ‚ Г I O; Cole Deel. ‚ Г‚ Г 23-24.) Experian and

283

Equifax generally conduct external reinvestigations by contacting the source of the disputed

information, explaining the consumer's dispute, and asking for a response concerning the accuracy of

the disputed item. (Hughes Aff., ¶ 10; Cole Deel., ¶ 24.)

Typically, Experian and Equifax contact the creditor by sending (either manually or electronically)

to the creditor a "Consumer Dispute Verification" form or an "Automated

Consumer Dispute Verification" form (collectively referred to as "ACDV"). (Hughes Aff., ¶ 10;

Cole Deel., ¶ 26.) That form identifies the consumer and the basis for the consumer's dispute, and

asks the creditor to verify or amend the information reported. *(Id.)*

The creditor then returns the completed verification form to the reporting agency, Experian or

Equifax, providing the consumer's identifying information contained in the

creditor's account records, instructing the agency either to leave the item as it is, delete the item, or

change it in some specified manner. (Hughes Aff., ¶ 11; Cole Deel., ¶ 28.) The agency then

compares the creditor's response to what is contained in its own records.   If the creditor's

response is logical, the agency makes any appropriate updates to or deletions from the consumer's file

based on the creditor's information. (Hughes Aff., ¶ 11; Cole Deel., ¶ 28.)

At the conclusion of the reinvestigation, the agency advises the consumer of the reinvestigation results,

typically by sending the consumer a summary reflecting the status of the disputed item following there

investigation. (Hughes Aff., ¶ 12; Cole Deel., ¶ 30.) The summary also contains a statement regarding

procedures the consumer may follow if the consumer disagrees with the results, including directly

contacting the furnisher of the disputed information and adding a statement to the consumer's credit file

disputing the accuracy or completeness of

the disputed account. (Hughes Aff., ¶ 12.) Experian has criteria for determining whether two accounts in

a consumer file are

duplicates and for removing one of the accounts in question without contacting the data furnisher. (Hughes Aff., ⌐ 13.) Experian's criteria include evaluation of the following data elements: same or similar account number; same account type; same credit limit, original

amount, or charge-off amount; and same open date. *(Id)* If evaluation of this criteria does not allow for

removal pursuant to policy, Experian will initiate a reinvestigation with the reporting source. *(Id.)*

Plaintiff alleges that, in or around June 2011, he viewed duplicates of at least four credit accounts on

each Defendant's "credit monitoring website," which he cannot identify by website address or name.

(Doc. 76 at 4; Ex. C, Declaration of Maureen P. McAneny ("McAneny Decl.") and Ex. 1 thereto,

Deposition of Plaintiff excerpts ("Plf. Dep.") 12:24-13:23, 248:3- 249: 15; and McAneny Deel.

Ex.2 (Plf. Response to Int. No. 14)). Plaintiff alleges that he contacted Experian and Equifax by

telephone and that the alleged duplication was resolved by each Defendant within about a month.

(Doc. 76 at 4, 10; Plf. Dep. 251: 13-253:17.)

Plaintiff does not have any documentation showing the alleged duplication that he claims he viewed on Experian's credit monitoring website. (Plf. Dep. 249: 16-250:5.) Plaintiff can specify only four accounts that were allegedly duplicated by each Defendant -, _____ and___ PP. *(Id.* 14:25-15:13, 248:3-249:2.) He claims as a possibility that some or all of the other accounts in his consumer file were duplicated by Experian and Equifax, but he does not know and he cannot identify any other allegedly duplicated account. *(Id.)*

In early July 2011, Plaintiff disputed with Experian an _____account (also known as Springleaf

Financial Services) on the basis of his assertion that the

creditor was required to attend a meeting of creditors in ·connection with a bankruptcy proceeding but

did riot attend and therefore, according to Plaintiff, Experian should delete the account from his credit

file. (Ex. D, Affidavit of Teresa Iwanski ("Iwanski Aff.") 'l) 4 and Ex. 1 thereto (July 1, 2011 letter

from Plaintiff to Experian)). In investigating Plaintiff's dispute, Experian noticed that there were two

__Finance/Springleaf Financial Services accounts reporting with very similar account information on

Plaintiff's consumer file, and Experian deleted one of those account appearances from his file on that

basis. *(Id.* 'l) 5.) Plaintiff was notified of the deletion in a "Dispute Results" notice sent to Plaintiff on

August 5, 2011. *(Id.* 'l) 5 & Ex. 2.) Experian does not have a record of any other account that appeared

in duplicate in Plaintiff's consumer file. *(Id.* 'l)6.)

> Plaintiff has no evidence of Defendants' procedures for assuring the maximum possible accuracy of
> the credit information they report. (Plf. Dep. 18:1-20:15; McAneny Deel. Ex. 2 (Plf. Resp. to Int.
> No. 16 (referring to allegations of complaint in response to request to state basis for §168le(b)
> claim)). Discovery has closed, and Plaintiff has failed to request information relevant to this
> issue from Experian or Equifax.

> Plaintiff does not know what procedures of Experian or Equifax are unreasonable, and provided no
> expert testimony on the matter; he simply offers his personal opinion that their procedures are
> unreasonable because the alleged duplication occurred. (Plf. Dep. 18:1-20:15.)

Plaintiff claims the alleged duplication harmed him by negating his progress in reestablishing his

credit and by preventing him from obtaining credit to finance a business venture. (Doc. 76 at 2, 4, 5,

7.) Plaintiff's attempts to reestablish his credit consisted of applying for credit accounts

withredacted and submitting account disputes to the CRAs. (Plf.   Dep.

129:4-23.)

Plaintiff has not produced evidence of any denial of a credit application based on the alleged duplication of accounts by Experian or Equifax. (McAneny Deel. Ex. 2 (Resp. to Int. No. 8); Plf. Dep. 26:2-37:20 & Exs. 2-3,5-7.)

The business venture that Plaintiff claims he was unable to finance as a result of the duplication was the advertisement and on-line placement of two poetry books written by Plaintiff, which Plaintiff intended to finance through approximately $2500 to $5000 from credit cards. (Plf. Dep. 38:2-39:20.)

Plaintiff does not believe Experian acted willfully in allegedly duplicating his credit accounts. *(Id.* 255:1-16.) It is Plaintiff s opinion that an employee's denial of the existence of duplicate accounts in his consumer file when he believed there were duplicate accounts, coupled with the general belief that "people can be very rude ... and very cruel in their everyday working environment," could indicate willful intent *(Id.* 238: 15-239:13.) Plaintiff does not contend Experian made a false statement by allegedly denying the existence of duplicate accounts in his Experian consumer file. *(Id.* 266:14-267:3.)

Plaintiff believes that, although he perceived Equifax's representatives to be rude at times, they listened to his concerns, helped open up disputes, and did not intentionally try to harm him personally. *(Id.* 44:12-45:7.)

In June 2011, __ Card Services denied two credit card applications submitted by Plaintiff. *(Id.* 21:24-24:10; 27:7-30:18 & Exs. 2-3.) The notification of each of those credit card denials provides that the reason for the denial was "insufficient credit references," and that the decision was based in whole in or in part on information provided by Equifax. *(Id.)* Plaintiff has provided no further documentation regarding the __ denials, or the credit reporting provided by Equifax to___ but speculates that "in sufficient credit references" implies Equifax was in the process of correcting the alleged account duplication at the time of___inquiries and Equifax therefore reported to___ that Plaintiff's credit file contained no credit accounts. *(Id.* 21:24-23:2.) Plaintiff has no evidence to show the meaning of "insufficient credit references." *(Id.*22:24-23:2.)

Plaintiff claims that, on November 28, 2011, he applied for a loan with _____that was denied because Experian reported only two of his credit accounts in response to ____credit inquiry. (Doc. 76 at 6.) According to Plaintiff, a ____representative told him such was the basis for the denial, and Plaintiff produced a copy of a tri-bureau report apparently generated by an entity named ___. *(Id.;* Plf. Dep. 30:19-32:20, 259:4-261: 15 & Exs. 58-60.)

Plaintiff does not know whether ____provided a copy of the ____tri• bureau report to him or whether he directly retrieved it from ____. (Plf. Dep. 259:25- 260:7.) Plaintiff has no documentation linking the ____ report to ____alleged November 2011 loan denial, nor does he have any adverse-action letter or other documentation from ____regarding the alleged denial. *(Id.* 259:23-261:15; McAneny Deel.,Γ3.)

Plaintiff has no evidence that any credit application he submitted to any entity was denied on the basis of an Experian consumer report. (Plf. Dep. 267:4-269:12.)

Plaintiff admits he has at times missed payments on some of his accounts, possibly all of his accounts, around the time his work load slowed in 2007-2008. *(Id.* 86: 11-87:18.) Plaintiff filed for bankruptcy in 2009. *(Id.* 46:20-47:25,87:19-88:1.)

Plaintiff cannot differentiate the portion of his alleged damages he claims is attributable to each Defendant. *(Id.*98:9-23.)

III. ARGUMENTS AND AUTHORITIES

Summary judgment is appropriate where "the pleadings, depositions, answers to interrogatories and admissions on file, together with the affidavits, if any, show that there is no genuine issue as to any material fact and that the moving party is entitled to judgment as a matter of law." Fed. R. Civ. P. 56(c). Once a moving party has properly supported its summary judgment motion, the burden shifts to the non-moving party, who "may not rest on mere allegations or denials of his pleading, but must set forth specific facts showing there is a genuine issue for trial" and "present affirmative evidence" to defeat the motion. *Anderson* v. *Liberty Lobby, Inc.,* 477 U.S: 242, 256-257 (1986).

A.   Plaintiff's FCRA § 1681e(b) Claim Fails as a Matter of Law.

When preparing *"consumer reports,"* the FCRA requires consumer reporting agencies to "follow reasonable procedures to assure maximum possible accuracy of the information concerning the individual about whom the report relates." 15 U.S.C. § 168le(b) (emphasis added). As the Court in this action noted, "a claim for negligent violation of § 1681e(b) has four elements: '(I) the credit report contained inaccurate information; (2) the inaccuracy resulted from the agency's failure to follow reasonable procedures; (3) [plaintiff] suffered damages; and

the injury was caused by the inaccurate information." (Doc. 124 at 6) (citing *Jordan* v.

Equifax Info. Servs. LLC, 410 F. Supp. 2d 1349, 1357 (N.D. Ga. 2006)). Plaintiff alleges that: Defendants failed to follow reasonable procedures in allowing duplicate accounts to appear on his credit report; Equifax failed to follow reasonable procedures when it transmitted a credit report to __ showing no credit history for Plaintiff; and Experian failed to follow reasonable procedures when it transmitted a credit report to _____ displaying only a few of his credit accounts. (Doc. 76 at 4, 5,11; *see also* Doc. 124 at 7). There is simply no evidence to satisfy the elements of a § 1681e(b) claim against Experian or Equifax.

Plaintiff's § 168le(b) Claim Based on the Alleged Duplication of Accounts Fails as a Matter of Law.

Plaintiff's Second Amended Complaint alleges that, in June 2011, each Defendant displayed "two accounts (duplicated accounts) for each of Plaintiff creditor accounts on Plaintiff credit file" and that he "observed these inaccuracies of Duplicated credit accounts (two accounts for each account on plaintiff file) on all three CRAs websites." (Doc. 76 at 2, 4.) Plaintiff also alleges that, about a month later, this alleged duplication of accounts was resolved. (Statement of Material Fact("SMF") (13.)

. No Evidence of A "Consumer Report"

Plaintiff cannot satisfy the first element of a § 1681e(b) claim based on the alleged duplications for two reasons. First, Plaintiff does not claim that Equifax or Experian issued a "consumer report" displaying a duplication, and there is no evidence of the issuance of any such report. While the FCRA does not define "credit report, "it defines "consumer report" as:

> [A]nywritten, oral, or other communication of any information by a consumer reporting agency bearing on a consumer's credit worthiness, credit standing, credit capacity, character, general reputation, personal characteristics, or mode of Jiving *which is used or expected to be used or collected in whole or in part for the purpose of serving as a factor in establishing the consumer's eligibility for* (A) credit or insurance ...; (B) employment purposes; or (C) any other purpose authorized under [the Act].

15 U.S.C. § 1681a(d)(I) (emphasis added). Thus, "[a] 'consumer report' is a report prepared for third parties while a 'consumer disclosure' is the consumer reporting agency's file it reveals to the consumer, not a third party. Reports prepared solely for the consumer do not constitute 'consumer reports' under the FCRA." *Johnson v. Equifax, Inc.,* 510 F. Supp. 2d 638, 645 (S.D. Ala. 2007) (citations omitted).

Plaintiff claims only that he viewed the duplication on the CRAs' credit monitoring websites, which, as discussed below, he cannot specifically identify. (SMF 12.) Information _____accounts did appear in Plaintiff's file in July2011, Plaintiff did not dispute the accounts on that basis, but rather, Experian itself determined that the two accounts should be treated as duplicates, deleted one of the accounts in accordance with policy, and promptly notified Plaintiff of the deletion. (SMF 11, 16.) Experian's records do not show any other potentially duplicate account in Plaintiff's consumer file. (SMF 16.)

Plaintiff s testimony regarding the alleged duplication of multiple accounts by all defendants is ambiguous and hardly probative. Plaintiff cannot even specify whether only four, or all, of the accounts in his consumer files were allegedly duplicated, or, if not all, which accounts were allegedly duplicated. (SMF 15.) The Second Amended Complaint provides examples of the allegedly duplicated accounts to be "__ accounts, ... ___accounts, ... ___ accounts, etc." (Doc. 76 at 4.) In his deposition, when asked by counsel for Equifax if those were all of the duplicated accounts, Plaintiff noted that a _____account was also duplicated but stated that he "can't recall" if there were others. (SMF 15.) Plaintiff later confirmed to counsel for Experian that his claim was only in regard to those four accounts, but the in stated:

It could have been all the accounts, but specifically I know that those accounts, I saw those accounts. I don't know what took place at that particular time. When I pull up the screen, look at the screen, I saw accounts being duplicated.

At that time, I didn't say, well, maybe this account....

(Plf. Dep. 248:10-24.) Plaintiff has not otherwise provided any evidence to identify the allegedly

duplicated accounts or the extent of any such duplication. For example, Plaintiff testified with respect

to Experian's alleged duplication:

Q.   [D]o you recall the exact name of the website that you used?

A. It was, from my recollection, it was Experian membership website. That's all I know. That's when I clicked in, it says Experian.

disclosed to Plaintiff through a website, however, does not constitute a "consumer report" as there is no allegation or proof that such information was provided to any third party for credit, insurance, employment, or other purposes.   "Section 168le(b) does not allow a consumer to sue the [CRA] for creating, possess[ing], or revealing to a consumer credit files containing adverse information." *Johnson,* 510 F. Supp. 2d at 645.[1] Because there is no allegation or proof of the issuance of a consumer report by Equifax or Experian displaying the allegedly duplicated accounts, Plaintiff cannot satisfy, as a matter of law, the first element of a § 1681e(b) for purposes of his duplication claim.   *See id.* ("Because a prerequisite to a cause of action under § 1681e(b) is evidence showing that a consumer report was furnished to a third party, all of Johnson's FCRA claims fail as a matter of law."); *Thomas v. Gulf Coast Credit Services, Inc.,* 214 F. Supp. 2d 1228, 1233-34 (M.D. Ala. 2002) ("the volumes of credit information Defendants relayed to Plaintiff do not constitute 'consumer reports' under the FCRA"; thus, claims   under § 168le(b) "fail as a matter of law."); *Heupel v. Trans Union LLC,* 193 F. Supp. 2d 1234, 1239 (N.D. Ala. 2002) ("Because there is no evidence that Trans Union reported the Sears account to a third party,

... it provides no basis for a prima facie case" under § !681e(b)); *see also Wantz v. Experian Info. Solutions,* 386 F.3d 829, 834 (7th Cir. 2004) (no liability under § 1681e(b) "without disclosure [of the consumer's information] to a third party."); *Zotta v. NationsCredit Fin. Servs. Corp.,* 297 F. Supp. 2d 1!96, 1205 (E.D. Mo. 2003) (granting summary judgment where plaintiffs produced "no evidence that an Experian report...was seemly third party").

Second, Plaintiff cannot meet the first element because he has no evidence that the alleged duplication actually occurred. While Experian acknowledges that two very similar

The document enclosed with Plaintiff's June 1 1, 201 1 letter to Experian, which displays the two _____ [1] Finance/Springleaf accounts, is an excerpt from a consumer file disclosure prepared by Experian and sent directly to Plaintiff, and was not a part of a report to a third party. (Iwanski Aff. '![3.)

Q. Okay. But it was, as you refer to it, I think a credit monitoring website that would be specific to Experian?

A.   Right.

Q. Okay. Did you print out a copy of what you saw on that Experian website?

A. No, I didn't. What happened is at the time I did not know how to save and print out the account. The only one I went back, I think the following day and tried it with Equifax. And
that show I got Equifax's....

Q.   So no printed copy, no saved copy on a computer, no saved copy in e-mail?

A. No.

Q.   Did you otherwise receive a copy of what you saw there through any method?

A. No.

(Id. 249:6-250:5.) Consequently, not only has Plaintiff failed to produce any Experian or Equifax consumer report that hints at such duplication of his credit accounts, he cannot specifically identify the accounts duplicated or the source on which he observed the duplication. There is simply no evidence of the alleged duplication by Experian or Equifax in a consumer report, and Plaintiff's uncertain testimony is not sufficiently probative to establish that his Experian or Equifax consumer report contained inaccurate information in the form of the alleged duplicated accounts. Accordingly, Plaintiff cannot establish the first element of a § 1681e(b) claim arising out of his duplication allegations and those claims against Experian and Equifax should be dismissed.

No Evidence of Duplication Resulting from Failure to Follow Reasonable Procedures

Even where a plaintiff can prove a consumer reporting agency prepared a report containing inaccurate information, the "agency can escape liability if it establishes that an inaccurate report was generated despite the agency's following reasonable procedures. *"Guimond v. Trans Union Credit Information Co.,* 45 F.3d 1329, 1333 (9th Cir. 1995) *(citing)*

UNITED STATES DISTRICT COURT FOR THE MIDDLE
DISTRICT OF FLORIDA
JACKSONVILLE DMSION

JAMES L. WATSON,   )
)
Plaintiff,   )
)   Case No. 3:12-cv-00552-UAMH-JBT
vs.   )
)
)
EQUIFAX, EXPERIAN, and   )
TRANSUNION,   )
)
Defendants.   )
)

AMENDED DECLARATION OF MAUREEN P. MCANENY IN SUPPORT OF
DEFENDANTS EXPERIAN INFORMATION SOLUTIONS, INC.'S AND EQUIFAX
INFORMATION SERVICES LLC'S JOINT MOTION FOR SUMMARY

JUDGMENT

I, Maureen P. McAneny, hereby amend my Declaration (Doc. 143-3) filed in support of

Defendants Experian Information Solutions, Inc.'s and Equifax Information Services LLC's

Joint Motion for Summary Judgment (Doc. 143), with regard to Paragraph 4 and declare as

follows:

Also during the March 19, 2013 deposition of Plaintiff, Plaintiff stated that he would

"specify and write [the damages], the amount and everything else, "and specifically link

damages to each of his claims against Experian. (Plf Dep., 270: 1-13.) At the time of the filing

of my initial Declaration (Doc. 143-3) in support of Experian and Equifax's Joint Motion for

Summary Judgment, I was not aware of any writing I received from Plaintiff after his

deposition regarding the amount of damages claimed against Experian. Upon further review, I

note that attached to a confidential settlement communication sent to me by Plaintiff via email

on May 29, 2013, was a one-page list of estimated amounts of damages that Plaintiff

designated as

confidential. Without divulging the confidential contents of the estimate list, it did not differentiate damages among the defendants or contain detail as to the broad categories of damages and estimated amounts listed.

I declare under penalty of perjury under the laws of the United States of America and the State of Georgia that the foregoing is true and correct.

This day of August, 2013.

INTHE UNITED STATES DISTRICT COURT
MIDDLE DISTRICT OF
JACKSONVILLE FLORIDA

James Watson

Plaintiff

Case No. 3:12-cv-552-J-99MM H-JBT

Defendants
Equifax, Experian, Transunion

PLAINTIFF AFFIDAVIT AS IT RELATES TO PLAINTIFF RESPONSE'

MOTION FOR SUMMARY JUDGMENT AGAINST DEFENDANTS

For Good cause and in Good Faith Plaintiff hereby affirm that all statements and documents attached to this Summary Judgment are true to best of his knowledge.

This information herein is within my personal knowledge base upon receiving documents as a consumer from credit monitoring services, financial institutions, monitoring my credit report online from June of 2011 to the present in an attempt to dispute and improve Plaintiff credit worthiness, applying for credit as consumer, and litigating this case as a Pro Se.

This Supplementary Motion for Summary Judgment relates back to all documents attach to this case including Plaintiff First Motion for Summary Judgment. And Affidavit and all documents attached herein to this Affidavit to prove his claims of non-compliance negligence and Defamation, based on the facts, the laws, and evidence A-Z documents and exhibits submitted in this case.

Plaintiff affirms that all of the following statements that were said by the following persons identified by name or title.

Attorney Tom Tierney Stated "those things Happen sometimes" when Plaintiff had his first telephone conference with Experian Lead Attorney. This rebut Experian answer and Defense page 8 paragraph 19, Doc.# 131

2. The perfect example of hostile emotions getting the best of a person is when Mr. Olson loudly hollering cursing Plaintiff stating, "Shut your damn mouth" during Plaintiff Deposition on March 19,2013 excluded from page 74 lines 14 and 15.

3. Mrs. Reddoch on or about Mar 24, 2013, of this year stating, "She was tired of Plaintiff submitting gibberish disputes to her and Plaintiff should not submit any more to her." See doc. #

Mr. Lewis Stated, "those things Happen sometimes" when Plaintiff spoke to him On the phone on 12/5/11 see exhibit (H).

Trans Union Rep. stated," he saw only one account when Plaintiff explain to him that Plaintiff saw two of the same accounts" on Plaintiff consumer credit file in the Month of June 2011.

From the Document produce from Trans Union by Plaintiff Trans made an error on Plaintiff Birth date instead of 8/5/1950 it was stated 8/1/1950this is an example as shown by the T.V special60 minutes Show "40 million Mistakes." as Aired this year in Feb. 2013.

Plaintiff affirmed that Experian CRA provided third party _____ Bank credit service Identity Theft a report from their data base on Plaintiff date 11/28/11while Plaintiff was applying for a secured credit card to improve his credit see Doc. #131 page7 Paragraph 16and Plaintiff exhibit (i). Exhibit (i) is admitted by virtue of being attach to Plaintiff Summary Judgment acceptance by this Courtland Rule without prejudice. This rebut Experian answer and Defense page 7 paragraph 16,18, and page 8, paragraph 19 Doc. #131

Exhibits are attached by Plaintiff footnote statement page his SAC document #124.

Plaintiff affirmed that all three CRA's received completed copy of exhibit (J) as submitted on Summary Judgment Affidavit Doc. #58.

Plaintiff affirmed that the main reason he was applying for redacted and Household credit cards in the Month of June 2011 was to improve his credit see Exhibit (B) and (C).

Exhibit (R) demonstrates that on May 27, 2011Trans Union sent Plaintiff a credit report as requested by Plaintiff through Trans Union monitoring membership, this prima facie evidence disproves lead attorney's Allison Reddoch claim that the prima facie evidence sent to Plaintiff which are duplicated Plaintiff accounts is not part of Plaintiff consumer credit file, see exhibits (C) and (D) Doc.#58.

The redacted that was duplicated on Plaintiff June 2011 consumer credit file remain on Plaintiff credit file by Equifax and Trans Union see Plaintiff exhibit # 7 Doc. # 106, in addition to Spring Leaf or AKA _____ Finance that was duplicated on Plaintiff June 2011 consumer credit file remain on Plaintiff credit file by Experian.

Trans Union has fail and continue to not comply with FCRA by not deleting all disputed accounts by Plaintiff as stated in Trans Union Answer and Defense #8 page 12

Trans Union has acted with Negligence as claim by the Court in Doc #124 page #8, Date 4/24/13.

As Plaintiff explained and counted out all the accounts that were duplicated or multiple files to

Attorney Allison Reddoch PA Transunion Attorney on Tuesday or Wednesday June 2012.

Plaintiff sent a letter to Transunion on 6-6-2011 stating that Plaintiff did not see changes on an

account, "redacted with either of C R A s .

Shortly after Plaintiff sent the letter Plaintiff received credit account information from Trans

union date 6-9-2011 and 6-18-2011 because Plaintiff stated in the letter, "I think the

Situation is that your online service did not alert me to these changes and these changes was

not updated on these accounts on your website at any time while I was looking at my credit

report either on Equifax, Transunion, and Experian credit monitoring memberships."

At this time Plaintiffs admitting into evidence a letter in title "NOTICE BEFORE LEGAL

ACTION" sent to Transunion on 12-3-2011 with the FCRA section 15 U.S.C. section 1681(d)

in which Plaintiff is basing his claim and legal right to damages in addition to the same cause of

action of defamation and change from Gross negligence to Negligence, Plaintiff admission

into evidence as exhibit(d).

Furthermore, a letter from ___ Bank rejecting a credit card application by Plaintiff on June 2011 from

information provided by Equifax, Plaintiff admits into evidence as exhibit(c).

Exhibit (E) consist of five pages' front to back from Defendant Trans union dated June 9, 2011.

Exhibit (F) consist of five pages' front to back from Defendant Trans union dated June 18, 2011.

Exhibit (G) a one-page letter address to Experian with an attach copy account of ____ which

was sent to Trans union as well as Equifax. Trans union Attorney Allison acknowledge she

had the lettering her possession on Tuesday or Wednesday when Plaintiff spoke to her concerning the Transunion documents she wants me to send her either by mail or email.

Exhibit(H) consist of one-page front to back from Defendant Experian dated Oct 4, 2011 sent to Plaintiff with his Credit score and a statement from an Experian service rep name Louis date Oct 5, 2011 stating Plaintiff had no Public record on his file but most important Louis said the same thing Mr. Tom Tierney said, "He has heard in that happen before." When Plaintiff received a telephone conference call from him in the beginning or middle part of May, 2012.

Plaintiff is submitting Exhibits (AA) Trans Union inaccuracy of Plaintiff Birthdate

Plaintiff is submitting (BB) Plaintiff Experian Oct. 25, 2011 which Experian denied issuing to Plaintiff.

Plaintiff is submitting (CC) proposal for settlement of general damages.

Plaintiff is submitting (DD) Watches and Jewelry actual damages as referencing

to watches and jewelry in Trans Union Summary Judgment Brief.

Deposition Page # 74 Mr. Olson Requesting to exclude his cursing Plaintiff during

deposition March 19, 2013 see exhibit (EE). Medical diagnosis of Anxiety in 1999 from a doctor at

that particular time which is known to flare up under extreme stress, see exhibit(FF).

Credit card application from credit companies when Plaintiff credit score reaches a certain FICO

score, see exhibit(GO). Interrogatories answered by Plaintiff from Trans Union, See exhibit (HH).

Proof of Denial of credit card application of Mr.____ name attached, See exhibit (ii). Disproving a

statement of fact with envelopes with the zip code of two with Trans Union with the zip # 48068

and 48150 date June 10, 2011, June 21, 2011 respectfully. Label exhibit (JJ)

Asset acceptance LLC.A third party which inquired into Plaintiff credit file during the Month of June 15,2011 while Plaintiff credit file account where Duplicated by defendants Trans Union, see exhibit(JJ).

Denial of credit application from _____Bank initiated from a simple request by Mr._____loan Rep. Included with Plaintiff Response Summary Judgment is two Affidavits from Ms. Patricia Smith Plaintiff Girlfriend. —

These documents are Prima Facie evidence to prove his Summary Judgment should be granted by this Court. Plaintiff prays that this Court grant Plaintiff Summary Judgment in his favor on all claims in this lawsuit.

Plaintiff prays that this Court will use Rule one of Fed. R. Civ.Proc.to expedite the grant of This Summary Judgment in Plaintiff favor to alleviate the financial hardship Plaintiff is experiencing daily from bring the truth of this case for justice to be rendered.

CERTIFICATE OFSERVICE

Plaintiff hereby certify that a true and correct under penalty perjury a copy of the foregoing was either email, facsimile, mailed this day of September 2013.

James Watson
Pro Se

I always provided the Court with an Affidavit when I wanted it known that something I submitted was the truth.

UNITED STATES DISTRICT COURT FOR THE MIDDLE DISTRICT
OF FLORIDA

JAMES L. WATSON,	)	
	)	
Plaintiff,	)	
	)	Case No. 3:12-cv-552-99MMH-JBT
vs.	)	
	)	
EQUIFAX, EXPERIAN, and	)	
TRANSUNION,	)	
	)	
Defendants.	)	

_____)

BRIEF IN SUPPORT OF DEFENDANTS EQUIFAX INFORMATION SERVICES LLC, EXPERIAN INFORMATION SOLUTIONS, INC. AND TRANS UNION LLC'S JOINT MOTION FOR EXTENSION OF TIME TO RESPOND TO PLAINTIFF' S MOTION FOR SUMMARY JUDGMENT

Pursuant to Local Rule 3.01, Defendants Equifax Information Services LLC, incorrectly identified in Plaintiff s Amended Complaint as "Equifax" ("Equifax"), Experian Information Solutions, Inc., incorrectly identified in Plaintiff s Amended Complaint as "Experian" ("Experian"), and Trans Union LLC, incorrectly identified in Plaintiff s Amended Complaint as "TransUnion" ("Trans Union"), file this their brief in support of their Joint Motion for Extension of Time to Respond to Plaintiff s Motion for Summary Judgment. The Defendants respectfully show the Court as follows:

BACKGROUND

On April 12, 2012, pro se Plaintiff James Watson sued Defendants Equifax, Experian and Trans Union, in the Circuit Court, Fourth Judicial Circuit in and for Duval County Florida. (Doc. 2). On May 9, the case was removed from that state court to this Court. (Doc 1). On May 16, Equifax filed a Motion to Dismiss Plaintiff s Complaint (Doc. 11), and Experian and Trans

Union filed a Joint Motion to Dismiss Plaintiff's Complaint (Doc. 12). On May 21, Plaintiff filed a

Motion for Leave to File Amended Complaint (Doc. 13), and on May 25, Plaintiff filed a Proposed

Amended Complaint (Doc. 16). On June 11, this Court granted Plaintiff's Motion for Leave to File

Amended Complaint, permitting the proposed Amended Complaint to stand as filed, and denied the

Defendants' motion to dismiss as moot. (Doc. 20). Defendants' responses to Plaintiff's Amended

Complaint are due June 25, 2012. *See* F.R.C.P. 15(a)(3).

On June 19, 2012, Plaintiff filed his Motion for Summary Judgment (Doc. 27). Pursuant to federal

and local rules, the Defendants' responses to Plaintiff's summary judgment motion are due July 6. *See*

Local Rule 3.01 and F.R.C.P. 6(d). Plaintiff and counsel for Experian have conferred regarding

Defendants' request for an extension of this deadline. Plaintiff opposes this request, saying he believes

that five days would be a sufficient discovery period in this case.

The deadline for the parties' case management conference is July 6, 2012. *See* Local Rule 3.05; and

"Important Information About Your Case" issued in this action (Doc. 7). The parties' Case

Management Report is to be filed within 14 days of the case management conference. *See id.* The

parties have not yet held the case management conference, and no Case Management Order is in place.

Discovery may not be commenced until the case management conference. *See* Local Rule

3.05(c)(2)(B).

ARGUMENT

Any response to Plaintiff's summary judgment motion filed by Defendants on or before July 6, 2012,

would be premature. At this early stage of the litigation, the parties have not even responded to the

Amended Complaint, and they have until June 25 to do so. Further, the case

management conference has not yet been held, and may possibly not be held until July 6 -the

same date as the deadline for responses to Plaintiff's motion. The Defendants need to conduct discovery in order to properly respond to Plaintiff's summary judgment motion, but service of discovery is not even permitted until the case management conference is held. As a result, the Defendants cannot properly and fully respond to Plaintiff's motion by July 6, or further, until such time as sufficient discovery is conducted.

The Defendants therefore respectfully request that the July 6 deadline for their responses to Plaintiff's summary judgment motion be set aside. At the parties' case management conference, the deadline for responses to Plaintiff's motion will be discussed, in light of the setting of this action as a Track Two case and Defendants' need to conduct discovery, and it will be addressed in the parties' Case Management Report. Accordingly, the Defendants further request that the response deadline be postponed until the date set in the Case Management Order by the Court.

A proposed Order granting this Motion is attached as Exhibit A.

WHEREFORE, the Defendants respectfully request that the Court extend the time period for Defendants' responses to Plaintiff's Motion for Summary Judgment to the date to be set in the Case Management Order.

IN UNITED STATES DISTRICT COURT
FOR THE MIDDLE DISTRICT OF FLORIDA
JACKSONVILLE DIVISION

JAMES L. WATSON,

Plaintiff, vs.
EQUIFAX, EXPERIAN, and TRANSUNION,

Defendants.

ORDER GRANTING DEFENDANTS' MOTION FOR EXTENSION OF TIME TO RESPOND TO PLAINTIFF'S MOTION FOR SUMMARY JUDGMENT

This matter, having come before the Court on Defendants Equifax Information Services LLC, Experian Information Solutions, Inc., and Trans Union LLC's Joint Motion for Extension of Time to Respond to Plaintiff's Motion for Summary Judgment, and having reviewed the records in this matter and being otherwise fully advised, it is hereby:

ORDERED AND ADJUDGED:

1. The Joint Motion for Extension of Time to Respond to Plaintiff's Motion for Summary Judgment is GRANTED; and

2. The Defendants shall have through the date to be set in the Case Management Order to respond to Plaintiff's Motion for Summary Judgment.

DONE AND ORDERED this_____ day of_____2012.

_____
JUDGE, UNITED STATES DISTRICT COURT

cc: All Counsel of Record
James L. Watson,
pro se

IN THE UNITED STATES DISTRICT COURT FOR THE MIDDLE
DISTRICT OF FLORIDA JACKSONVILLE DMSION

JAMES L. WATSON,   )
)

Plaintiff,   )
)

V.   )   CASE NO. 3:12-CV-00552-UAMH-JBT
)

EQUIFAX, EXPERIAN, and   )
TRANSUNION,   )
)

Defendants.   )
)

**DEFENDANTS EXPERIAN INFORMATION SOLUTIONS, INC.'S AND EQUIFAX
INFORMATION SERVICES LLC'S JOINT MOTION FOR LEAVE TO FILE COMBINED
REPLY IN SUPPORT OF JOINT MOTION FOR SUMMARY JUDGMENT AND
<u>OPPOSITION TO PLAINTIFF' S MOTION FOR SUMMARY JUDGMENT</u>**

COMES NOW Defendants Experian Information Solutions, Inc. ("Experian"), incorrectly named in

Plaintiff's Second Amended Complaint as "Experian," and Equifax Information Services LLC

("Equifax"), incorrectly named in Plaintiff's Second Amended Complaint as "Equifax" (collectively

"Defendants"), by and through their undersigned counsel, and respectfully request leave to file a Joint

Reply in Support of their Joint Motion for Summary Judgment, combined in one document with a

Joint Opposition to Plaintiff's Motion for Summary Judgment. As the basis for this request, the

Defendants respectfully show the Court as follows:

Experian and Equifax filed their Joint Motion for Summary Judgment on August 2, 2013. (Doc. 143.)[1]

On July 31, 2013, Plaintiff filed a Motion to File More than Twenty-Five Pages (Doc. 134), and a

purported "supplementary motion for summary judgment" (Doc. 137). By Order dated August 2, 2013,

the Court terminated Plaintiff's Motion   to File More than Twenty-

---

[1] The Court granted Experian's and Equifax's joint motion for a one-day extension of the dispositive motion period, thereby extending the deadline to August 2, 2013. (Doc. 151.)

Five Pages and directed Plaintiff to file his motion for summary judgment containing a memorandum of

legal authority by August 19, 2013. (Doc. 144.)

On August 19, 2013, Plaintiff filed his "Response Brief Against Defendants Trans Union, Equifax,

and Experian Motion for Summary Judgment" (Doc. 152), and "Plaintiff Refiling Supplementary

Motion for Summary Judgment as Order by This Court to Be Filed On or Before Aug 19, 2013

During Dispositive and Daubert" ("Plaintiff's Motion for Summary Judgment") (Doc. 154.) Pursuant

to Local Rule 3.0l(b) and the Court's Summary Judgment Notice dated August 20, 2013 (Doc. 155),

Experian and Equifax should have until September 3, 2013 to file an opposition to Plaintiff's Motion

for Summary Judgment.2

After reviewing Plaintiff's Response to their Joint Motion for Summary Judgment, Experian and

Equifax believe there is good cause to file a Reply in Support of their motion. Accordingly, pursuant

to Local Rule 3.0l(c), the Defendants are seeking leave herein to file a Joint Reply in Support of their

Joint Summary Judgment Motion.

In the interest of efficiency and to avoid duplicative arguments in a reply in support of the

Defendants' Joint Motion for Summary Judgment, and in an opposition to Plaintiff's Motion for

Summary Judgment, Experian and Equifax request that they be permitted to file a combined reply

in support of their Joint Motion for Summary Judgment and a joint response to Plaintiff's Motion for

Summary Judgment.

WHEREFORE, Experian and Equifax respectfully request that the Court permit the Defendants until

September 3, 2013, to file a combined reply in support of their Joint Motion for Summary Judgment

and a joint response in opposition to Plaintiff's Motion for Summary Judgment.

---

2 September 2, 2013 is fourteen days after the filing of Plaintiff Motion for Summary Judgment, but Labor Day falls on

that date. In light of the holiday. the Defendants understand that the deadline becomes September 3, 2013.

IN THE UNITED STATES DISTRICT COURT FOR THE MIDDLE
DISTRICT OF FLORIDA JACKSONVILLE DIVISION

JAMES L. WATSON,	)	
	)	
Plaintiff,	)	
	)	
V.	)	CASE NO. 3:12-CV-00552-UAMH-JBT
	)	
EQUIFAX, EXPERIAN, and	)	
TRANSUNION,	)	
	)	
Defendants.	)	
	)	

DEFENDANTS EXPERIAN INFORMATION SOLUTIONS, INC.'S AND EQUIFAX
INFORMATION SERVICES LLC'S RESPONSE
IN OPPOSITION TO PLAINTIFF'S MOTION FOR SUMMARY JUDGMENT

Defendants Experian Information Solutions, Inc. ("Experian"), incorrectly named in Plaintiff's Second Amended Complaint as "Experian," and Equifax Information Services LLC ("Equifax"), incorrectly named as "Equifax" (collectively "Defendants"), submit the following memorandum of law in opposition to Plaintiff's Motion for Summary Judgment (Doc. 154) and in further support of Defendants' Joint Motion for Summary Judgment (Doc. 143). For the reasons discussed below and in the brief accompanying Defendants' joint motion, [1] the Court should deny Plaintiff's Motion for Summary Judgment, grant Defendants' Joint Motion for

Summary Judgment, and dismiss all of Plaintiff's claims against Experian and Equifax.

I.   SUMMARY OF THE ARGUMENT

Plaintiff, proceeding *pro se,* has completely failed to marshal the evidence required for a grant of summary judgment in his favor, or even to overcome the motion for summary judgment filed by Experian and Equifax. Plaintiff has a long history of negative credit as the result of not

---

[1] In the interest of efficiency, Experian and Equifax incorporate herein the supporting affidavits and exhibits attached to their Joint Motion for Summary Judgment. (Doc. 143.)

paying his debts in a timely manner and has filed for bankruptcy. His assertion that the appearance of

"duplicate accounts" on his credit file caused him to be denied credit is simply not supported by any

evidence whatsoever. \'Indeed, Plaintiff failed to take the depositions of

Experian, Equifax, and/or any third party, and such failure is fatal to his attempts to overcome

Defendants' Joint Motion for Summary Judgment'

Plaintiff brings three claims against Defendants under § !68le(b) of the Fair Credit

Reporting Act ("FCRA"), 15 U.S.C. §§ 1681-1681x. Section 168le(b) is not a strict liability

Plaintiff would suggest, but instead requires consumer reporting agencies to "follow   -

reasonable procedures to assure maximum possible accuracy" of the consumer reports

(commonly known as "credit reports") they issue. "As discussed above, Plaintiff has not taken any

depositions in this case and has no evidence that any of the procedures followed by Experian

or Equifax were unreasonable or that he has been damaged by any consumer reports issued to any

third parties. To the contrary, Experian and Equifax have provided their own declarations

reflecting their proper handling of Plaintiff's credit files. Plaintiff has wholly failed to carry his burden

of proof. He certainly is not entitled to summary judgment and, indeed, has so little evidence in support

of his claims that summary judgment should be granted in favor of Defendants instead.

Plaintiff's "Refiling [sic] Supplementary Motion for Summary Judgment as Order [sic] By This Court

to Be Filed On or Before Aug 19, 2013 During Dispositive and Daubert [sic]" (Doc. 154) (Plaintiff's

"Motion for Summary Judgment") and his "Response Brief Against Defendants Trans Union, Equifax,

and Experian [sic] Motion for Summary Judgment" (Doc.

152) (the "Response Brief ') are largely the same. In both, Plaintiff attempts to satisfy the standard to

survive a motion *to dismiss, rather* than a motion for summary judgment, and misinterprets the Court's Order on the Defendants' Joint Motion to Dismiss (Doc. 130), which adopted the Report and Recommendation of Magistrate Judge Toomey (R&R") (Doc. 124. Continuing his reliance upon the allegations of his Second Amended Complaint ("SAC"), Plaintiff fails to present proper evidence either to controvert the material facts asserted in the Defendants' Joint Motion for Summary Judgment or to support his own Motion for Summary Judgment. As pointed out by Defendants in their own motion, Plaintiff has no evidence that: (I) Defendants issued a consumer report containing allegedly inaccurate information; (2) he incurred damages caused by Defendants' alleged FCRA violations; or (3) the alleged inaccuracies resulted from use of unreasonable procedures, all of which are required for a successful claim under § 168le(b). *See* Doc. 143 at 9-24.

Plaintiff also brings a frivolous defamation claim against Defendants under state law. That claim fails for multiple reasons. First and foremost, the claim is preempted by the FCRA. It also fails under state law because Plaintiff cannot demonstrate that Defendants published any defamatory information about him, or that Defendants acted with "express malice."

In short, Plaintiff s claims have no basis in fact or law and should be summarily dismissed. Defendants respectfully ask the Court to deny Plaintiff s Motion for Summary Judgment (Doc. 154) and to grant Experian's and Equifax's Joint Motion for Summary Judgment (Doc. 143) instead.

STATEMENT OF MATERIAL FACTS

Defendants' Joint Motion for Summary Judgment lists 31 statements of material facts   as
to which no genuine issue exists and those facts are incorporated herein. (Doc. 143 at 2-8.) **
Plaintiff s Response Brief does not specifically address any of them, and they should therefore be
deemed admitted by Plaintiff.   *See* Summary Judgment Notice (Doc. 146 at 2) ("all material

facts asserted by the movant in the motion(s) will be considered to be admitted by you unless

controverted by proper evidentiary materials ...").

Plaintiff's Response Brief and his Motion for Summary Judgment appear to contain identical purported

"Statement of Facts" sections. (Doc. 152 at 2-6; Doc. 154 at 2-7.) Plaintiff s "Statement of Facts" is

riddled with hearsay, conclusory allegations, and impermissible legal arguments. ————

Plaintiff does not include references to any evidence within his "Statement of Facts," but rather merely

refers to the SAC and Judge Toomey's R&R, which Plaintiff misinterprets and is inappropriate at this

stage in any event. The bulk of Plaintiff's "Statement of Facts" is a repetition of the allegations from

the SAC. The first sentence of the statement includes a cite to "Doc. 76 at 4," which is the SAC, and the

only other citations in the statement, aside from references to the R&R, are to "id." *(See Doc.* 152 at

2-3; Doc. 154 at 2-4). Although Plaintiff filed an affidavit purportedly "relate[d] to" Plaintiff's Motion

for Summary Judgment (Doc. 154-1), with over 25 exhibits (Docs. 154-2 to), neither the affidavit nor

any of the exhibits are mentioned in Plaintiff's "Statement of Facts."[2]

Plaintiff's misinterpretation of the R&R and the Court's Order adopting it is evidenced by the following

excerpts from Plaintiff's Response Brief and Motion for Summary Judgment:

---

[2] Although about half of the exhibits to Plaintiff's affidavit are mentioned elsewhere within Plaintiff s Motion for Summary Judgment, the other half are not mentioned. As a result, the purpose of at least half of the exhibits is not explained or otherwise apparent. Of the half of the exhibits that are mentioned in the motion: five, Exhibits A, D, E, F, and R (Docs. 154-2, -5, -6, -7, -20), relate to Defendant Trans Union LLC; Exhibits B, C, and J (Docs. 154-3, -4, -11) are discussed in Sec. III.C.l(a) herein; and Exhibits H and I (Docs. 154-9, -10) are addressed in Sec. lll.C. l(b). Exhibits G and P (Docs. 154-8, -18) import to be June 2011 letters to Experian and Equifax, respectively. While it is not clear, Plaintiff appears to include Exhibits G and P to show that he submitted disputes to the Defendants in June 2011. *(See* Doc. 154 at 9.) From the face of the documents, the letters appear wholly unrelated to the claims in this action because their content has nothing to do with alleged account duplication or under• reporting of accounts, but rather address the reporting of a balance on one specific account. Those exhibits therefore appear irrelevant to the claims at issue here.

"... in which the Court rule in Plaintiff favor under FCRA 1681(b) and 1681e(b) which this Court held the Defendants committed non-compliance negligence and defamation claims as stated by the facts in Plaintiff SAC." (Doc. 152 at 2, Doc. 154 at 2.)

"Second, Plaintiff claims and the Court agreed that as a result of the inaccurate duplicated accounts when the credit card Company __pulled Plaintiff Equifax credit file." (Doc. 152 at 3; Doc. 154 at 3.)

"Third, Plaintiff claims and the Court agreed that as a result of the inaccurate accounts omission by Experian on Plaintiff credit file on Nov. 28, 2011 while applying for a line of credit at ___Bank, Experian which resulted in under reporting of only two accounts..." (Doc. 152 at 3; Doc. 154 at 4.)

"In addition Experian committed the same act of omission in the prior Month of Oct 2, 2011 but from looking evidence it was as well Sept 2, 2011 but not stated in Plaintiff Prior Complaints SAC (Doc # 124 [R&R] page 7)." *(Id.)*

"the Court Rule these three credit reporting agencies stated above fail to follow reasonable procedures to assure maximum possible accuracy of a consumer report...." (Doc. 152 at 4; Doc. 154 at 4).

It is evident Plaintiff does not appreciate that the Court's ruling on Defendants' motion to dismiss found only that Plaintiff had sufficiently -albeit barely -*stated claims* for negligent violation of Section !68le(b) and for common law defamation, and did not rule that Plaintiff had proven those claims. *See* Doc. 124 at 2.

Further, as noted above, Plaintiff repeatedly relies upon inadmissible hearsay in his "Statement of Facts." *See, e.g.,* Doc. 154 at 6 (alleging that an unidentified Experian representative said in a telephone call, "These things happen sometimes [sic]"); *id.* at 6-7 ("The credit Agencies ['] Reps has [sic] become desensitized to Debtor ['] s needs. The exact same Quote [was] use[d] by attorney Mr. Tierney P.A. in conference with Plaintiff. .."). In addition, Plaintiff s continued reliance upon unsubstantiated conclusions of fact and law is readily apparent throughout his "Statement of Facts." The final paragraph of Plaintiff s statement is a prime example:

In the same instance employees go home and discuss what happen [sic] at work to their family, friends, wives, and significant others when this happen [sic] 3rd party defamation occurs. Malice is defining [sic] as a statement made with knowledge that it was false or with reckless disregard of whether it was false or not [Cit.omitted].

(Doc. 152 at 5; Doc. 154 at 7.)

In sum, not only has Plaintiff failed to controvert Experian's and Equifax's Statement of Material

Facts, he has completely failed to provide a valid statement of material facts to support his own

motion. For this reason, his motion should be denied.

ARGUMENT

Summary Judgment Standard

Summary judgment should be denied unless "the movant shows that there is no genuine dispute as to

any material fact and the movant is entitled to judgment as a matter of law." Fed. R. Civ. P. 56(a).

"When the *moving* party has the burden of proof at trial, that party must show *affirmatively* the absence

of a genuine issue of material fact: it must support its motion with credible evidence that would entitle

it to a directed verdict if not controverted at trial." *US.*

v. Four Parcels of Real Prop. in Greene & Tuscaloosa Cntys. in State of Ala., 941 F.2d 1428, 1438

(IIth Cir.1991) (en ban) (quotation marks and alterations omitted, emphasis original); *accord Rich v.*

Secretary, Florida Dept. of Corrections, 716 F.3d 525, 530 (I Ith Cir. 2013); *see also* Fed. R. Civ. P.

56(c) (l)(A). "In other words, the moving party must show that, on all t h e

essential elements of its case on which it bears the burden of proof at trial, no reasonable jury could

find for the nonmoving party." *Rich,* 716 F.3d at 530 (quoting *Four Parcels of Real Prop.,* 941 F.2d

at 1438 (citation, quotation marks, and alterationsomitted)).

Plaintiff Mistakenly Applies the Standard for a Fed. R. Civ. P. 12(b)(6) Motion to Dismiss.

Although Plaintiff s Motion for Summary Judgment Quotes Fed. R. Civ.P. 56(c) and cites case law pertaining to that rule *(see* Doc. 154 at 7-8), his arguments throughout his motion are that he has sufficiently pleaded his claims, even directly referencing Rule 12(b)(6) *(see id.* at 13). For example, Plaintiff states:

"Many courts including the Eleventh Circuit, has [sic] recognizes [sic] that Rule 9(b) Fed. R. Civ. P. allows allegations regarding mental state to be alleged in 'general' ..." (Doc. 154 at   10.)

"This Court has ruled [that the] facts stated in Plaintiff{'s] SAC alludes [sic] to the state of mind of Defendants as being enough for [a] defamation claim ..." *(Id.)*

"Plaintiff has pleaded malice and willfulness in his Complaints, and the Precedent holding and rule [sic] by the U.S. Supreme Court on the issue of malice and willfulness has not been overturned." *(Id.* at 11)

"[I]n the instant case where the Plaintiff has pleaded facts that in themselves adds [sic] up to a valid legal claim with the appropriate legal theories Summary Judgment for Plaintiff should be granted." *(Id.* at 12.)

"If materials extrinsic to the pleadings are submitted to the Court in support of or in opposition to a 12(b)(6) motion, the court does not have to consider them." *(Id.* at 13.)

"It is axiomatic that in deciding a motion to dismiss pursuant to Rule 12(b)(6), the Court must accept all factual allegations as true and draw all inferences in favor of Plaintiff." *(Id.* at 17.)

Plaintiff therefore does not appear to be attempting to carry his burden as either a movant or non-movant in the summary judgment context. Further, as shown below, Plaintiff has failed to satisfy his duty in either role to present affirmative evidence rather than rest on mere allegations of his pleading.

All of Plaintiff's Claims Fail as a Matter of Law for Lack of Evidence.

The R&R on Defendants' Joint Motion to Dismiss noted that Plaintiff's SAC was "far from a model of clarity," but found that "when construed liberally in Plaintiff's favor, the SAC barely states a claim against each Defendant for common law defamation and negligent non- compliance with the FCRA." (Doc. 124 at 2) (further clarifying that the FCRA provision at issue is 15 U.S.C. § 1681e(b) *(id.* at 6)). Plaintiff s claims stem from three sets of alleged facts: (!) the alleged reporting by all Defendants of several of Plaintiff's consumer file accounts in duplicate in or around June 2011 *(id.* at 4); (2) Plaintiff's receipt of a letter from ___ in June, 2011 stating that his credit card application was denied due to "insufficient credit history," *(id.* at 5); and (3) the alleged reporting by Experian in November 2011 to ___ of only a few of Plaintiff's consumer file accounts in connection with a loan application, resulting in a denial by___. *(Id.* at 5-6.)

Plaintiff Cannot Establish the Elements of a Claim Under FCRA Section 1681e(b).

As the Court in this action has noted, "a claim for negligent violation of § 1681e(b) has four elements: "(]) the credit report contained inaccurate information; (2) the inaccuracy resulted from the agency's failure to follow reasonable procedures; (3) [plaintiff] suffered damages; and (4) the injury was caused by the inaccurate information." (Doc. 124 at 6) (citing *Jordan* v. *Equifax Info. Serves.,* LLC, 410 F. Supp. 2d 1349, 1357 (N.D. Ga. 2006)). Experian's and Equifax's Joint Motion for Summary Judgment addressed each element of a § 1681e(b) claim and demonstrated Plaintiff's lack of evidence as to those elements under each of the three sets of alleged facts described above. *(See* Doc. 143 at 9-24.) Neither Plaintiff's Response nor

his Motion for Summary Judgment offers admissible evidence to establish those elements.

Failure of Section 1681e(b) Claim Based on Alleged Account Duplication

As explained in Defendants' summary judgment motion, Plaintiff s § 1681e(b) claims based on the alleged duplication of his accounts fail because Plaintiff has no evidence that: (I) Experian or Equifax issued a consumer report to any third party containing the alleged duplication *(see* Doc. 143 at 10-13); (3) the alleged duplication resulted from a failure to follow reasonable procedures on the part of either Defendant *(see id.* at e13-16); or (3) he incurred damages or injury caused by the alleged FCRA violation *(see id.* at 16-20). Plaintiff has not come

forward, in either his Response Brief or his Motion for Summary Judgment, with any documentation

displaying duplicated accounts by Experian. With regard to Equifax, although Exhibit J to Plaintiff's

Affidavit appears to contain some account duplication, Exhibit J is not a "consumer report," as that term

is defined by the FCRA. *See Johnson v. Equifax, Inc., 5 1 0*

F. Supp. 2d 638, 645 (S.D. Ala. 2007) ("Reports prepared solely for the consumer do not constitute

'consumer reports' under the FCRA."); 15 U.S.C. § 1681a(d)(l).[3] Plaintiff has no evidence that Exhibit

J, which Plaintiff downloaded from Equifax's website (Doc. 72 at I), w as

transmitted to any third party, including , for credit, insurance, employment or other purposes, which

bars Plaintiff from relying upon Exhibit J to establish the first element of a § 1681e(b) claim

against Equifax. *See Johnson.,* 510 F. Supp. 2d at 645 (; *see also* Doc. 143 at 10-

"Section 1681e(b) does not allow a consumer to sue the consumer reporting agency for creating,

possessi[ng], or revealing to a consumer credit files containing adverse information." *Id.*

Moreover, Plaintiff still has not furnished any proof that any alleged duplication, by

either Experian or Equifax, resulted from a failure to follow reasonable procedures, or caused any

damages or injury to Plaintiff rather than such damages being caused by his own poor credit history.

Beyond the inarticulate and incorrect conclusion that "the Court Rule[d] these three credit reporting

agencies stated above fail[ed] to follow reasonable procedures to assure

---

[3] Plaintiff's Motion for Summary Judgment makes wholly unsubstantiated assertions regarding Exhibit J and Brian Olson, counsel for Equifax. *(See Doc.* 154 at 19.) Plaintiff asserts that, during the Defendants' *deposition of Plaintiff,* Mr. Olson's declining to answer question posed by Plaintiff, the deponent, regarding the exhibit means that Equifax has waived a right to object to this "evidence" at trial. *(Id.)* Plaintiff provides no support for this illogical theory. Plaintiff also accuses Mr. Olson of yelling at him during the deposition and instructing him to shut his "damn mouth." (Doc. 153 at.) As the transcript page cited by Plaintiff demonstrates, this allegation is utterly false. *(See* Doc. 153-5 (Ex. EE to Plaintiff's Response Brief)).

maximum accuracy of a consumer report" (Doc. 154 at 4), Plaintiff's motion does not address Experian's or Equifax's procedures.

Plaintiff s argument that the alleged duplication caused him harm appears to amount to his assertion that his "credit file contained duplicated accounts which is in itself an inaccuracy which harm[ed] Plaintiff by denial of credit by __card Company and ___Bank from reestablishing his credit, *see* SAC page 6 Doc. 124 paragraph 17." (Doc. 154 at 20.) First, Plaintiff again impermissible relies on allegations in the SAC. Second, Plaintiff does not have any evidence or declarations from ____ and/or ___demonstrating why they apparently denied him credit. His reliance on unauthenticated, hearsay adverse-action letters should be rejected. As neither Plaintiff s Motion for Summary Judgment nor his Response Brief provides any proper evidence to establish any element of his § 1681e(b) claim based on alleged account duplications, his request for summary judgment on that claim should be denied, and Defendants' motion for summary judgment should be granted.

Failure of Section 1681e(b) Claims Based on Alleged Under-Reporting of Accounts

Plaintiff also alleges that he was denied credit by _____based upon his receipt of adverse action letters from these companies. As discussed in Defendants' Joint Motion for Summary Judgment, the two credit-denial letters that Plaintiff allegedly received from ___do not establish any connection between those denials and the alleged account duplication. [4] Indeed, the letters state that Plaintiff was denied credit based on *insufficient credit* references. *See Doc.* 154-4. The letters are also inadmissible because they have not been! authenticated and, therefore, constitute inadmissible hearsay. *See* Doc. 143 at 20-2 l. Further,

_____

[4] The letters that Plaintiff allegedly received from __ are attached as Exhibits B and C to Plaintiff's Affidavit related to his Motion for Summary Judgment, and they were also attached as Exhibits 1(2) and 1(3) to the Declaration of Maureen P. McAneny in support of the Defendants' Joint Motion for Summary Judgment. (Doc. 143-3.)

even if the letters were admissible, they do not provide any evidence of the specific content of the alleged consumer reports received and relied upon by __ Without such evidence, Plaintiff cannot demonstrate that the reports contained inaccurate information, or that he was denied credit as a result of the alleged FCRA violation. *See id.* at 21. In light of the evidential inadequacies of the ___letters, Plaintiff's allegations of under-reporting of accounts by Equifax to ___are not supported by any evidence.

Plaintiff s claim against Experian based on its alleged under-reporting of accounts to ___similarly fails. For that claim, Plaintiff relies upon alleged verbal statements of representatives of ___and Experian, and a tri-bureau report apparently issued by an entity named ____, which shows more accounts reported by Equifax and Trans Union

than by Experian. [5] *See* Doc. 154 at 20 (devoting two sentences to the alleged statements of "Mr. Lewis"); Doc. 154-9 (Ex. H to Plaintiff s Affidavit (page displaying Plaintiff's credit score with handwritten notes referring to alleged statements by "Louis" including "he said he has heard of that happened before")); and Doc. 154-10 (Ex. I to Plaintiff s Affidavit (copy of apparent __ report, also attached to the Defendants' Motion for Summary Judgment)). As explained in the Defendant's motion, Plaintiff simply has no credible proof to show that any reporting by Experian was utilized by___ in its loan determination, or that any such reporting, if utilized by ___, was inaccurate. *See* Doc. 143 at 22-24.

In addition, even if Experian or Equifax did not include all of Plaintiff's credit accounts in the consumer reports allegedly provided to, respectively, no FCRA violation occurred. *See, e.g., A-1 Credit and Assur. Co., Inc. v. Trans Union Credit Info. Co.,(*

---

[5] Plaintiffs Response Brief attaches as an exhibit a credit card application to __dated 11/28/2011. (Doc. 153-9.) Although Plaintiff wrote on the document, "proof of denial application initiated by __employee, "there is no indication whatsoever on the document of ___decision on the loan request. *(Id.)*

678 F. Supp. 1147, 1151 (E.D. Pa. 1988) ("[I]t is quite clear that Congress did not intend 15 U.S.C. § 168lb to impose any duty upon a consumer reporting agency to disclose information, but merely to permit disclosure under specified limited circumstances."); *see also* Doc. 143 at 21-23 (Defendants' further discussion of this issue).

In sum, Plaintiff's lack of evidence as to any alleged violation of § 168le(b) of the FCRA by either Experian and Equifax requires denial of Plaintiff's Motion for Summary Judgment and warrants summary judgment in Defendants' favor on all such claims.

Plaintiff's Defamation Claims Have No Merit. Plaintiff's Defamation Claims Are Preempted by the FCRA Because He Cannot Show the Requisite Malice. "The FCRA is a comprehensive statutory scheme designed to regulate the consumer reporting industry." *Spencer* v. *Nat'! City Mort.,* 831 F. Supp. 2d 1353, 1357 (N.D. Ga. 2011) (quoting *Ross v. F.D.I.C.,* 625 F.3d 808, 812 (4th Cir. 2010)); *see also Thornton v. Equifax, Inc.,* 619 F.2d 700, 703 (8th Cir. 1980).

The trade-off for these federally mandated obligations and remedies is that consumers alleging wrongdoing by consumer reporting agencies must bring their claims pursuant to the FCRA. *See Ross,* 625 F.3d at 814; *Thornton,* 619 F.2d at 703. The FCRA specifically prohibits consumers from "bring[ing] any action or proceeding in the nature of defamation, invasion of privacy, or negligence with respect to the reporting of information against any consumer reporting agency . . . except as to false information furnished with malice or willful intent to injure such consumer." 15 U.S.C. § *168*lh(e). "The only exception to this bar is a narrow one, requiring proof of 'malice or willful intent to injure [the] consumer.'" *Ross, 625* F.3d at 814; *see also Lofton-Taylor v. Verizon Wireless,* 262 Fed. Appx. 999, 1002 (I Ith Cir. 2008); *Lee v. Security Check, LLC,* 2010 WL 3075673, at *5 (M.D. Fla. Aug. 5, 2010). To overcome preemption, Plaintiff must prove that Defendants acted "with knowledge that the information was false or reckless disregard of whether it was false or not." *Lee,* 2010 WL 3075673 at *5 (citing *Thornton v. Equifax, Inc.,* 619 F.2d 700, 703 (8th Cir. 1980)).

Plaintiff spends a good deal of his Motion for Summary Judgment attempting to address the malice standard and to explain how Defendants' actions allegedly met that standard. *(See* Dkt. 152 at 9-18.) He does not provide any *evidence* that Experian or Equifax acted with malicious intent. Plaintiff s Response Brief further demonstrates his continued reliance on the "barely sufficient allegations of the SAC" (Doc. 124 at 11). He speculates that Defendants' employees acted maliciously based on his assertions that a Trans Union agent told Plaintiff that he did not see any account duplication in Plaintiff s credit file and that "the tone of voice of most of the rep's plaintiff called where hostile and argumentative." (Doc. 152 at 5.) According to Plaintiff, "a disgruntled employee could have done it to get back at one of the three credit agencies or take their working conditions frustration out on Plaintiff for calling so frequently about the inaccuracies in his credit file." *Id.* Presumably, the "it" to which Plaintiff refers is the duplication of accounts in his credit file.

Plaintiff explained:

This duplication of Plaintiff's] credit file could have led to malice or willful intent to injure Plaintiff as a way of deterring Plaintiff to stop calling so frequently to report incorrect, inaccurate and incomplete credit information on Plaintiff: I's] credit file.

The service Reps. Had an Anger tone, and if acted on can be considered a form of malice; anger, hostility and argumentative behavior are a recipe for a willful intent toward others. Plaintiff has cited that the employees of the three CRA's exhibit this form of behavior to Plaintiff while he was disputing the Duplication inaccuracy of Plaintiff credit accounts.

(Doc. 152 at 5.) Plaintiff s imaginative speculation regarding the state of mind of Defendants' employees does not constitute evidence of malicious intent on the part of Experian or Equifax.

In *Morris v. Equifax Itifo. Servs.,* 457 F.3d 460 (5th Cir. 2006), for example, the Fifth Circuit held that a consumer defamation claim was preempted by the FCRA under circumstances similar to those present here. Although the consumer reporting agency knew that the consumer had disputed certain information in the consumer's credit file, that fact alone did was not sufficient to show that the agency "knew these statements were false." *Morris,* 457 F.3d at 471. Allegations of malice "based on pure speculation" are "insufficient to establish a genuine issue of material fact for purposes of summary judgment." *Joiner v. Revco Discount Dmg Centers, Inc.,* 467 F. Supp. 2d 508, 515 (W.D.N.C. 2006).

While Plaintiff may have sufficiently plead, under the standard of Fed. R. Civ. P. 12(b)(6), willfulness or malice required to avoid the FCRA's preemption of his defamation claims, he has completely failed to proffer evidence from which willfulness or malice could be inferred. Accordingly, even if Plaintiff could prove a violation of the FCRA by Experian or Equifax, which he cannot, his defamation claims are preempted by the FCRA. Consequently, his Motion for Summary Judgment should be denied. Summary judgment should be granted in Defendants' favor instead.

Plaintiff's Defamation Claims Also Fail Under State Law.

Even if Plaintiff could overcome the hurdle of FCRA preemption, which he cannot, his defamation claims fail for at least two reasons under state law. First, as discussed above with respect to Plaintiff's FCRA claims, Plaintiff has no evidence that Defendants reported false information about him to a third party. "Because the publication of a statement is a necessary element in a defamation action, only one who publishes can be subject to this form of tort liability." *Doe v. America Online, Inc.,* 783 So. 2d 1010, 1017 (Fla. 2001) (quotation marks omitted).

Second, Plaintiff cannot demonstrate that Defendants acted with "express malice," which

is required to overcome a conditional privilege applicable to Defendants. Under Florida law,

statements "made by one having an interest or duty in the subject matter thereof, to

another

person having a corresponding interest or duty therein" are "conditionally privileged," and therefore exempt from defamation claims, "even though the statement may be false and otherwise actionable." *Jarzynka v. St. Thomas Univ. Sch. of Law,* 310 F. Supp. 2d 1256, 1267 (S.D. Fla. 2004) (citing *Nodar v. Galbreath,* 462 So. 2d 803, 809 (Fla. 1984)). "The determination that defendant's statements are qualifiedly privileged eliminates the presumption of malice attaching to defamatory statements bylaw. The privilege instead raises a presumption of good faith and places upon the plaintiff the burden of proving express malice -that is, malice in fact as defined by the common-law doctrine of qualified privilege." *Nodar,* 462 So._2d at 8IO (overturning jury verdict in favor of plaintiff in a defamation case). Only when express malice is proven is the privilege waived. *See id.* at 806.

Florida "embraces a broad range" of privileged communications. *Nodar,* 462 So. 2d at 809. The privilege applies whenever there is "mutuality of interest of speaker and listener." *Id.* at 806. Reports made by consumer reporting agencies to creditors plainly fall within the "broad range "of privileged communications recognized in Florida. Consumer reporting agencies are in the business of "assembling or evaluating consumer credit information . . . for the purpose of furnishing consumer reports to third parties." 15 U.S.C. § 1681a(f). Both the agency and the creditor have a mutual interest in determining the consumer's creditworthiness. This Court and other courts in Florida have held, as a matter of law, that the privilege applies under similar circumstances. *See, e.g., Gunder's Auto Center V. State Farm Ins.,* 699 F. Supp. 2d 1339 (M.D. Fla. 2010) (remarks made by an insurance company to customers in need of insured auto repairs regarding the plaintiff auto-repair business), *aff'd,* 422 Fed. Appx. 819 (IIth Cir. 2011); *Jarzynka,* 310 F. Supp. 2d at 1267-68 (remarks made by a university counselor to other university officials regarding the plaintiff-student's mental stability and possible threat to other students); *Thomas v. Tampa Bay Downs, Inc.,* 761 So. 2d 401, 404 (Fla. 2d DCA 2000) (report made by racetrack director regarding a former employee to other members of a racing-industry organization). Given that Defendants' alleged consumer reports were privileged; Plaintiff must prove express malice for a successful claim. *See Jarzynka,* 310 F. Supp. 2d at 1268. Express <u>malice</u>, under F l o r i d a law, is "ill will, hostility *and* an evil intention to defame and injure." *Id.* (quotations omitted, emphasis original); *see also Nodar,* 462 So. 2d at 806. The alleged facts must be capable of "showing that the speaker used his privileged position 'to gratify his malevolence.'" *Nodar,* 462 So. 2d at 811 (quoting...*ll{yers v. Hodges,* 44 So. 2d 357, 362 (1907)). "If the statements were made without express malice - that is, if they were made for a proper purpose in light of the interests sought to be protected by legal recognition of the privilege -then there can be no recovery." *Id.* at 810.

Plaintiff has no evidence that Defendants were "motivated more by a desire to harm [him]" than by a desire to fulfill their function as consumer reporting agencies. *See Nodar,* 462 So. 2d at 811. Even if Plaintiff could prove, which he certainly cannot, that Defendants acted recklessly, this would not be sufficient to establish express malice under Florida law. *See, e.g., Jarzynka,* 310 F. Supp. 2d at 1268 (granting motion to dismiss because complaint alleged only that counselor had "acted 'recklessly' and without any clinical evidence to support her opinion" when reporting information about the student to university officials); Gunder's Auto *Ctr.,* 699

F. Supp-.2d at 1341-43 (no evidence of express malice, even if statements were false, where each statement concerned "the quality, timeliness, or value of the plaintiff's automobile repairs - subjects about which the insured and State Farm share a 'corresponding interest'"). Plaintiff's inability to prove express malice provides an additional basis for denying his Motion for Summary Judgment and for granting Equifax's motion.

IV.   CONCLUSION

For the foregoing reasons, as well as those set forth in Experian's and Equifax's Joint Motion for Summary Judgment, Defendants respectfully ask the Court to deny Plaintiff's Motion for Summary Judgment (Doc. 154) and to grant their Joint Motion for Summary Judgment (Doc. 143).

Respectfully submitted this 3rd day of September, 2013.

Isl Maureen P. McAneny

Thomas W. Tierney Florida
Bar No. 0390150
Rossway Moore Swan, P.L.
210l Indian River Blvd., Suite 200 Vero Beach, Florida 32960 Telephone: (772) 231-4440
Facsimile: (772) 231-4430
ttiemey@verobeachlawyers.com

and

Maureen P. McAneny
Admitted Pro Hae Vice Jones Day
1420 Peachtree Street, N.E., Suite 800
Atlanta, Georgia 30309
mmcaneny@jonesday.com
Telephone: (404) 581-8327
Facsimile: (404) 581-8330

Attorneys for Defendant Experian Information Solutions, Inc.

Isl Brian J. Olson

Brian J. Olson _Admitted_
Pro Hae Vice King & Spalding LLP
1180 Peachtree Street, N.E.
Atlanta, Georgia 30309
bjolson@kslaw. com
Telephone: (404) 215-5806
Facsimile: (404) 572-5100

and

James B. Thompson, Jr.
Florida Bar No. 0872938
Thompson Goodis Thompson Groseclose Richardson & Miller, PA
700 Central Avenue, Suite 500 St Petersburg, Florida 33701
jthompson@thompsongoodis.com
Telephone: (727) 823-0540
Facsimile: (727) 823-0230

Attorneys for Defendant Equifax: Information Services LLC

Strasburger
ATTORNEYS AT LAW

September 3, 2013

CHRISTIAN BROWN

<u>VIA CM, RRR # 7179 1000 1649 1931 2113</u>

James Watson,
Sr. 2790 Tall
Pine Lane, #8
Jacksonville, FL 32277

     RE: James L. Watson, Sr. v. Equifax *et al.*
United States District Court - Middle District of Florida
Case No. 3:12-cv-00552-UAMH-TEM

Dear Mr. Watson:

Enclosed please find a copy of *Trans Union LLC's Objections to Plaintiff's Summary Judgment Evidence and Response in Opposition to Plaintiff's Motion for Summary Judgment.*

Should you have any questions, please do not hesitate to contact me.

Sincerely,

Christian T. Brown

INTHEUNITEDSTATES DISTRICTCOURT

FOR THE MIDDLE DISTRICT OF FLORIDA

JACKSONVILLE DIVISION

James Watson

     Plaintiff

V.

Equifax, Experian, Trans

    Union Defendants

TRANS UNION LLC'S OBJECTIONS TO PLAINTIFF'S SUMMARY JUDGMENT EVIDENCE AND RESPONSE IN OPPOSITIONTO PLAINTIFF'S MOTION FOR SUMMARY JUDGMENT

COMES NOW, Trans Union LLC ("Trans Union"), one of the Defendants in the above-styled and numbered cause, and files its Objections to Plaintiffs Summary Judgment Evidence and memorandum of law in Opposition to Plaintiff's Motion for Summary Judgment ("Response"), and would respectfully show the Court as follows:

OBJECTIONS TO PLAINTIFF'S SUMMARY JUDGMENT EVIDENCE

On August 19, 2013, Plaintiff filed his "Response Brief Against Defendants Trans Union, Equifax, and Experian Motion for Summary Judgment" ("Plaintiffs Response") (Doc. 152) and "Plaintiff Affidavit as it Relates to Plaintiff Response' Motion for Summary Judgment Against Defendants" ("Plaintiff's Response Affidavit") (Doc. 153) with exhibits attached.

On August 19, 2013, Plaintiff also filed his "Plaintiff Refiling Supplementary Motion for Summary Judgment as Order by This Court to Be Filed On or Before Aug 19, 2013 During Dispositive and Daubert" ("Plaintiff's Motion for Summary Judgment") (Doc. 154) which included "Plaintiff Affidavit as it Relates to Plaintiff Supplementary Motion for Summary Judgment Against Defendants" ("Plaintiff's Summary Judgment Affidavit") with exhibits attached.

Trans Union objects to the summary judgment evidence submitted by Plaintiff as follows:

EVIDENCE OBJECTED TO	DESCRIPTION	OBJECTIONS
Plaintiff Affidavit as it Relates to Plaintiff Supplementary Motion for Summary Judgment Against Defendants	Plaintiff's Summary Judgment Affidavit	Unsworn and not made under penalty of perjury, and contains portions of documents that are not part of the summary judgment record.
Exhibit R	Trans Union Interactive Letter and attached documents.	Unauthenticated, irrelevant, and contains hearsay statement by Plaintiff. In addition, Trans Union objects to this exhibit because it was not produced by Plaintiff during discovery.
Exhibit Z	Incomplete Third Party Consumer	Unauthenticated, incomplete and
Plaintiff Affidavit as it Relates to Plaintiff Response' Motion for Summary Judgment Against Defendants	Plaintiff's Response Affidavit	Unsworn and not made under penalty of perjury, lack of foundation, contains hearsay statements by Plaintiff, irrelevant, speculative, conclusory
	unsubstantiated assertions, unsupported	
		by facts set forth in

		affidavit or evidence in the summary judgment record, contains portions of documents that are not part of the summary judgment record, and self-serving in that it cannot be readily controverted.
Plaintiff Affidavit as it Relates to Plaintiff Response' Motion for Summary Judgment Against Defendants	Numbered Paragraph 3	Irrelevant, contains hearsay statement by Plaintiff, and unsubstantiated assertions.
Plaintiff Affidavit as it Relates to Plaintiff Response' Motion for Summary Judgment Against Defendants	Numbered Paragraph 5	Irrelevant, contains hearsay statement by Plaintiff, and unsubstantiated assertions.
Plaintiff Affidavit as it Relates to Plaintiff Response' Motion for Summary Judgment Against Defendants	Numbered Paragraph 6	Irrelevant and unsubstantiated assertions.
Plaintiff Affidavit as it Relates to Plaintiff Response' Motion for Summary Judgment Against Defendants	Numbered Paragraph 11	Irrelevant, contains hearsay statement by Plaintiff, conclusory and unsupported by facts set forth in affidavit or evidence in the summary judgment record.
Plaintiff Affidavit as it Relates to Plaintiff Response' Motion for Summary Judgment Against Defendants	Numbered Paragraph 12	Irrelevant, conclusory and unsupported by facts set forth in affidavit or evidence in the summary judgment record.
Plaintiff Affidavit as it Relates to Plaintiff Response' Motion for Summary Judgment Against Defendants	Numbered Paragraph 13	Irrelevant, conclusory and unsupported by facts set forth in affidavit or evidence in the summary judgment record.
Plaintiff Affidavit as it Relates to Plaintiff Response' Motion for Summary Judgment	Numbered Paragraph 14	Conclusory and unsupported by facts set forth in the affidavit or evidence in the summary

327

Against Defendants		judgment record.
Exhibit DD	Pawnbroker Contract	Unauthenticated and irrelevant. In addition, Trans Union objects to this exhibit because it was not produced by Plaintiff during discovery.
Exhibit FF	Medical Correspondence	Unauthenticated and irrelevant.
Exhibit GG	Credit Solicitations	Unauthenticated and irrelevant. In addition, Trans Union objects to this exhibit because it was not produced by Plaintiff during discovery.
Exhibit JJ	Scans of Envelopes	Unauthenticated and irrelevant. In addition, Trans Union objects to this exhibit because it was not produced by Plaintiff during discovery.
Exhibit KK	Incomplete Consumer Report	Unauthenticated, irrelevant, conclusory and contains portions of documents that are not part of the summary judgment record. In addition, Trans Union objects to this exhibit because it was not produced by Plaintiff during discovery.

For the foregoing reasons, Trans Union moves the Court to sustain its objections to the above identified summary judgment evidence.

INTRODUCTION

Plaintiffs Response and Motion for Summary Judgment are examples of the underlying problem with Plaintiffs allegations and arguments since the filing of the

Original Complaint-a complete lack of understanding of the law, both substantively

and procedurally. Plaintiffs Response is a confusing collection of unsupported and

conclusory allegations that fail to raise any discernible or supportable material fact issues.[1]

Plaintiff failed to respond to most of the facts and grounds upon which Trans Union seeks

summary judgment. Similarly, Plaintiffs Motion for Summary Judgment

is riddled with irrelevant and unsubstantiated allegations which lack citation to any

arguably supportive summary judgment evidence in the record. Plaintiff continually

confuses the meaning of the Court's prior rulings and demonstrates a complete lack of

understanding of the burden of proof at summary judgment. Plaintiff has completely

failed to produce the evidence required to prevail at summary judgment, or even to

overcome Tran Union's Motion for Summary Judgment. As such, Trans Union respectfully

moves the Court to deny Plaintiffs Motion for Summary Judgment and grant summary

judgment to Trans Union on all claims asserted by the Plaintiff.

III. STATEMENT OF FACTS

Plaintiffs Response and Motion for Summary Judgment appear to contain identical

"Statement of Facts" sections.[2] Plaintiff fails to address most of the asserted facts in Trans

Union's Motion for Summary Judgment.[3] Plaintiff s "Statement of Facts "consists

of hearsay statements, unfounded legal arguments, and conclusory

Plaintiff did not assert in his Original or Amended Complaint, and the Court did not recognize in its Order

[1]
and Recommendations, any potential FCRA claims related to an alleged failure by Trans Union to provide Plaintiff with a copy of his credit file or an alleged failure by Trans Union to conduct a reasonable reinvestigation. In his filings, Plaintiff makes vague arguments that could be construed as
Relating to such claims. However, since these claims were never asserted, the Court should disregard any such arguments.
[2]

[3]
Dkt. 152, 2-6; Dkt. 154, 2-7.
dkt. 141, Section IA-E. These facts are incorporated herein.

allegations, none of which contain any references to evidence in the summary judgment record. The majority of Plaintiff's "Statement of Facts" is regurgitation of the allegations within his Second Amended Complaint.

Plaintiff Failed to Respond to Most of Trans Union's Statement of Facts

Rule 56(e) requires "the non-moving party to go beyond the pleadings and by [his] own affidavits, or by the 'depositions, answers to interrogatories, and admissions on file,' designate 'specific facts showing that there is a genuine issue for trial."[4] If party fails to properly address another party's assertion of fact as required, the Court may consider the fact undisputed for purposes of the motion and grant summary judgment if the motion and supporting materials, including the facts considered undisputed, show that the movant is entitled to it.[5] Plaintiff's Response and Motion for Summary Judgment contain identical "Statement of Facts" sections which consist of nothing more than a series of false and conclusory statements, lacking citation to any evidence in the summary judgment record. While it is difficult to ascertain Plaintiff's specific factual assertions, Plaintiff appears to make three assertions relating to Trans Union, which are simply false, in his Response and Motion for Summary Judgment.

First, Plaintiff claims that "Trans Union acknowledged that Plaintiff['s] membership monitoring service is part of Plaintiff['s] consumer credit file" and then

---

[4] *Celotex Corp. v. Catrett,* 477 U.S. 317, 324 (1986); see also Fed. R. Civ. P. 56(e).
[5] Fed. R. Civ. P. 56(e)(2), (3).

cites to "1681a(g).'. s Even assuming that Plaintiff is citing to § 1681a(g), that section does not support Plaintiff's conclusory statement that Trans Union "acknowledged" that "Plaintiff membership monitoring service" is part of his credit file. Infect, Trans Union produced affirmative evidence that conclusively establishes that the TUI notifications Plaintiff produced were only sent to Plaintiff as a benefit of his TUI membership.7 Those notifications were never made part of the Plaintiffscredit file and were never published to any third parties.[8]

Plaintiff further misinterprets the FCRA and the TUI notifications by stating "These statements on these documents are concrete proof that these documents are part of Plaintiff credit report or file."[9] Plaintiff simply misinterprets the following sentence contained in the TUI notifications -"As a benefit of your TransUnion Credit Monitoring membership, you are being notified that on June 4, 2011 the following change(s) appeared in your credit file." Plaintiff fails to explain how this statement leads to his conclusion and has not cited to any additional evidence or case law that supports his assertion.

Second, Plaintiff claims Trans Union acted willfully when "'An Trans Union agent said that although Plaintiff sees two files it is only one,' this Rep knowing that this statement in and of itself is a false statement."[10] Plaintiff has not cited any supporting evidence nor explained how the alleged statement was proven false or how the statement amounts to willfulness.

Plaintiff's Motion for Summary Judgment 4113
Dkt. 142, Section IIA.1.a; TU App. 34-35.
8
Dk!. 142, Section IIA 1.a; TU App. 34-35.
Plaintiff's Motion for Summary Judgment 4111-2.

Plaintiff's Response at 51!4.

Finally, Plaintiff mistakenly believes that the Defendants share credit file information. Plaintiff claims that in order to become a member of a credit monitoring service, he had to agree that the Defendants were allowed to share his credit information.[11] Yet, Plaintiff cannot, and has not, identified any evidence to support these unfounded assertions. Trans Union produced affirmative evidence that conclusively establishes that all the information on Plaintiffs Trans Union credit file was reported to Trans Union by creditors or furnishers of credit data.[12]

Plaintiff has failed to specifically address the remaining portions of Trans Union's Statement of Facts; accordingly, those facts should be considered undisputed by the Court.[13] Thus, Plaintiff has failed to controvert Trans Union's Statement of Facts and has failed to provide a proper statement of facts in support of his motion for summary judgment. Therefore, Plaintiffs motion for summary judgment should be denied.

Plaintiff Has Not Provided Any Summary Judgment Evidence to Support His Claims.

To support a motion for summary judgment, "the moving party [has] the burden of showing the absence of genuine issues as to any material fact...•.[14] A party seeking summary judgment always bears the initial responsibility of informing the district court of the basis for its motion, and identifying those portions of the

---

[11] Plaintiffs Response, 8'!13.

[12] Dkt. 142, Section IIA.3. b; TUApp. 50-51; Ex. C (Romanowski Deel.)'!18.

[13] See Summary Judgment Notice (Dkt. 146 at 2) ("all material facts asserted by the movant in the motion(s) will be considered to be admitted by you unless controverted by proper evidentiary materials...").

[14] *Adickes v.* S.H. *Kress* & Co., 398 U.S. 144, 157 (1970).

pleading, depositions, answers to interrogatories, and admissions on file, together

with the affidavits, if any, which it believes will demonstrate the absence of any

genuine issue of material fact.[15] Federal Rule of Civil Procedure 56{c) requires a party

moving for summary judgment to support his assertion that a fact cannot be genuinely

disputed by citing to particular parts of materials in the record.[16] Plaintiff's

Motion for Summary Judgment fails to identify, much less demonstrate, the absence of any

genuine issues of material facts. Plaintiff's Motion for Summary Judgment consists of

numerous nonsensical, conclusory assertions with citations which fail to correspond with

any part of the record that supports Plaintiff's vague assertions.

Accordingly, Trans Union respectfully requests the Court to deny Plaintiff's Motion for

Summary Judgment.

Plaintiffs Conclusory Statements Regarding the Relationship Between Credit Reporting Agencies Are Not Evidence of Inaccuracy

As previously demonstrated, Plaintiff mistakenly claims in his Motion for Summary

Judgment that the Defendants share credit file information which resulted in the alleged

duplication of accounts. Plaintiff still has not identified or attached any evidence to support

these unfounded allegations. Trans Union produced affirmative evidence that conclusively

establishes that all the information on Plaintiff's Trans Union credit file was reported to

Trans Union by creditors or furnishers of credit

---

[15] *Celotex Corp.,* 477 U.S. at 323.
[16] Fed. R. Civ. P. 56(c)(1).

data.[17] Plaintiff does not identify or cite to any other evidence showing the alleged duplication in Trans Union's credit file. Accordingly, Plaintiff s Motion for Summary Judgment should be denied.

b. *Plaintiff's Unfounded Allegations and Conclusory Statements Are Not Evidence of Malice or Willful Intent*

Plaintiff attempts to support his defamation arguments with speculative and unsupported allegations regarding Trans Union employees, assertions that this Court has already recognized as insufficient to satisfy the elements of Plaintiff s common law defamation claim.[18]

In support of his defamation claim, Plaintiff also attempts to argue "the act of providing Membership Monitor credit report that was not requested by Plaintiff...is

a knowing act of false recklessness willful and malice, wrongful act on the Plaintiff...".[19] It is unclear how Plaintiff links this argument to his defamation claim, but even if these allegations were true, which they are not, they would not amount to

summary judgment evidence that Trans Union acted with malice or willful intent.

Finally, Plaintiff attempts to argue that this Court has ruled that the questionable and conclusory allegations regarding the Defendants' mental state amount to conclusive evidence the Defendants acted with malice or willful intent.[20]

Again, Plaintiff misunderstands the burden of proof at summary judgment. This Court recognized Plaintiff's questionable allegations regarding the Defendants'

---

[17] Dkt 142, Section IIA.3. b; TUApp. 50-51; Ex.C(Romanowski Deel.), ls.
[18] Plaintiffs Motion for Summary Judgment 5, I4-5.6-7; Dkt.124,fn.6.
[19] Plaintiffs Motion for Summary Judgment 9 1!4.
[20] Plaintiffs Motion for Summary Judgment 10-11.

mental state as sufficient to survive a Motion to Dismiss;[21] however, without further substantiating evidence, Plaintiffs assertions fail to rise to the required evidentiary level for the court's consideration at summary judgment.

Plaintiff does not identify or cite to any other evidence of malice or willful intent. Accordingly, Plaintiff has not produced any evidence of malice or willfulness on the part of Trans Union. Thus, Plaintiffs claims for common law defamation are preempted by the FCRA and Plaintiff's Motion for Summary Judgment should be denied.

Trans Union Did Not *Publish* a *Consumer Report* to *Any Third Party*

PlaintiffarguesthatTransUnionpublishedaconsumerreporttoathirdparty, "___"and "____," and cites Exhibit Z.[22] Exhibit Z consists of one page of what appears to be a multi-page consumer disclosure in November 2011 from _____. While Exhibit Z is incomplete, it is clearly not a consumer report that was published by Trans Union. This exhibit is not evidence that Trans Union published a consumer report to a third party. Plaintiff does not identify or cite to *any* other evidence of publication of a Trans Union consumer report, an essential element of Plaintiff's § 1681(e)(b) claim. Accordingly, Plaintiff's Motion for Summary Judgment should be denied.

Trans Union Followed Reasonable Procedures

---

[21] Dkt. 124,10'ff1.
[22] Plaintiffs Response, 7'1]4.

Plaintiff states that Trans Union did not maintain and follow reasonable procedures because Trans Union failed to have Plaintiff's birthdate correct at some point and cites to Exhibit AA.[23] Exhibit AA is a copy of a July 2011 Trans Union internal document, not a consumer report. Plaintiff fails to explain how Exhibit AA amounts to any evidence that Trans Union failed to follow reasonable procedures to ensure the maximum possible accuracy of a published Trans Union consumer report. Plaintiff does not identify or cite to any other evidence showing Trans Union failed to follow reasonable procedures, an essential element of Plaintiffs § 1681(e)(b) claim. Accordingly, Plaintiff's Motion for Summary Judgment should be denied.

Plaintiff Failed to Respond to Several of Trans Union's Summary Judgment Arguments

The summary judgment procedure is designed to isolate and dispose of factually unsupported claims.[24] The plain language of Fed. R. Civ. P. 56(c) mandates the entry of summary judgment against a party who fails to make a showing sufficient to establish the existence of an element essential to the party's case, and on which that party will bear the burden of proof at trial.[25] A complete failure of proof concerning an essential element of the nonmoving party's case renders all other facts immaterial.[26]

[23] Plaintiffs Response, 81J1.
[24] Celotex *Corp.,* 477 U.S. at 323-24; see also Fed. R. Civ. P. 56(a), (c).
[25] *Celotex Corp.,* 477 U.S. at 322.
[26] Id. at 323.

Plaintiff's Motion for Summary Judgment and Response fails to address the following

Trans Union summary judgment arguments regarding essential elements to Plaintiff's

claims:

In regards to Plaintiff's 1681(e)(b) claims, Plaintiff did not address the fact that

Plaintiff's damages are not recoverable and were not caused by Trans Union.[27]

In regards to Plaintiff's common law defamations claims, Plaintiff did not address the fact

Plaintiff's damages are not recoverable and were not

caused by Trans Union and did not provide any evidence of a defamatory statement

made by Trans Union.[28]

Each of these grounds are essential elements of Plaintiff's claims which Plaintiff will bear

the burden of proof at trial, as recognized by this Court.[29] Plaintiff

has failed to show that any of his alleged damages are recoverable under the FCRA

or under a common law defamation action. Further, the affirmative evidence

establishes that Trans Union did not cause any of the alleged damages. As Plaintiff

has failed to respond to the above-referenced arguments, Trans Union respectfully

moves the Court to grant summary judgment on all such grounds.

VI. **CONCLUSION**

For the reasons outlined above, Trans Union LLC respectfully requests that this Court

sustain Trans Union's Objections to Plaintiff's Summary Judgment

Evidence, deny Plaintiff's Motion for Summary Judgment, and grant Trans Union's

Motion for Summary Judgment.

Respectfully submitted this 3rt1 day of September, 2013.

[27] Dkt. 142, Section IIA.1-4.
[20] Dkl 142, Section 118.2.
[29] Dkt. 124, 6, 9.

IN THE UNITED STATES DISTRICT COURT
FOR THE MIDDLE DISTRICT OF FLORIDA
JACKSONVILLE DIVISION

JAMES L. WATSON,	)	
	)	
Plaintiff,	)	
	)	
V.	)	CASE NO. 3:12-CV-00552-UAMH-JBT
	)	
EQUIFAX, EXPERIAN, and	)	
TRANSUNION,	)	
	)	
Defendants.	)	
	)	

DEFENDANTS EQUIFAX INFORMATION SERVICES LLC AND EXPERIAN INFORMATION SOLUTIONS, INC.'S UNOPPOSED JOINT MOTION FOR LEAVE FOR CLIENT REPRESENTATIVES TO ATTEND MEDIATION VIA TELEPHONE

COME NOW Defendants Equifax Information Services LLC ("Equifax"), incorrectly named in Plaintiffs Second Amended Complaint as "Equifax," and Experian information Solutions, Inc. ("Experian"), incorrectly named in Plaintiff s Second Amended Complaint as "Experian," (collectively "Defendants"), by and through their undersigned counsel, and seek leave of Court for their client representatives to attend the mediation set for April 10, 2013 via telephone, as necessary. In support of this motion the Defendants respectfully show the Court as follows:

l. Mediation is scheduled for April 10, 20 13, at 9:00 am with Michael Coulson in Jacksonville, Florida.

2.   Experian's national counsel, Maureen P. McAneny of the law firm of Jones Day in Atlanta, Georgia, will attend the mediation i n person in Jacksonville, Florida. Experian requests that its client representative, Abril Turner, be allowed to participate in the mediation of this matter by telephone from her office location in Costa Mesa, California.

3.   Equifax's national counsel, Brian J. Olson of the law firm of King & Spald ing in Atlanta, Georgia, will attend the mediation in person in Jacksonville, Florida. Equifax requests its client representative, Mackenzie Cole, be allowed to participate in the mediation of this matter by telephone, from his office location in Atlanta, Georgia.

4.   Experian and Equifax' s client representatives will have full authority to settle this matter and have done so in numerous prior mediations.

5.   Experian and Equifax will incur significant travel expenses if their client representatives are required to travel to Jacksonville, Florida, to participate in the mediation in person. The parties' goal of conserving costs and expenses associated with this litigation would be furthered by allowing Experian and Equifax's client representatives to participate in the mediation by telephone.

6.   Experian and Equifax's client representatives have participated in numerous mediations and settlement conferences by telephone. Therefore, Experian and Equifax do not believe that the parties' ability to seek a resolution of this matter at mediation would be negatively impacted should Experian and Equifax's client representatives be permitted to participate by telephone.

7.   Plaintiff does not oppose Experian and Equifax 's Joint Motion for Leave for Client Representatives to Attend Mediation via Telephone.

For the reasons set forth above, Experian and Equifax request that their client representatives be allowed to participate in the upcoming mediation by telephone, as needed.

UNITED STATES DISTRICT COURT

DISTRICT OF OREGON

PORTLAND DIVISION

JULIE MILLER,

      Plaintiff,

v.

EQUIFAX INFORMATION SERVICES
LLC, a foreign limited liability company,
      Defendant.

COMPLAINT

Fair Credit Reporting
Act (15 U.S.C
§ 1681 et seq.)

Demand for Jury Trial

Plaintiff alleges that at all times material:

1.

This is a civil action brought under the Fair Credit Reporting Act ("FCRA"), 15 U.S.C. § 1681et.seq. The Court has jurisdiction pursuant to 15 U.S.C. § 1681p.

2.

Plaintiff Julie Miller ("plaintiff) is a natural person residing in the State of Oregon, as defined by the Fair Credit Reporting Act ("FCRA"), 15 U.S.C. § 1681a(c).

3.

Defendant Equifax Information Services, LLC, ("Equifax" or "Defendant") is a consumer reporting agency as defined by the FCRA, 15 U.S.C. § 1681a(f).

4.

Plaintiff was denied credit from Bank due to her Equifax credit report. On or about December 8, 2009, plaintiff requested her credit report from Equifax. On or about January 5, 2010, Equifax sent plaintiff a form letter requesting she provide additional identifying information.

5.

On or about January 11, 2010, plaintiff again requested a copy of her Equifax credit report, enclosing the additional identifying information Equifax requested in its January 5, 2011 letter. On January 21, 2011, Equifax sent plaintiff a copy of her January 18, 2010 Equifax credit report. The report contained false identification information, an incorrect Social Security number, a false birthday and false derogatory collection accounts attributed to her.

6.

On or about January 22, 2010, plaintiff disputed the false information appearing in her January 21, 2010 Equifax credit report via facsimile. On or about January 26,2010 plaintiff disputed her credit report for a second time. Plaintiff enclosed a copy of her Equifax credit report with the false information highlighted. Equifax did not conduct an investigation of her dispute. On or about February 5, 2010, Equifax sent plaintiff a third form letter indicating it needed additional identifying information to process her dispute.

7.

On or about February 8, 2011 plaintiff requested a new copy of her Equifax credit report. Equifax did not respond to her request for her credit report.

8.

On or about February 16,2010, plaintiff disputed to Equifax a third time the false, derogatory information displaying in her January 21,2010 credit report. She again included the identifying information requested by Equifax.

9.

On or about February 26,2010, plaintiff received her Equifax investigation results. Equifax had not changed anything on her credit report. It contained the same false information that was in her January 21,2010 Equifax credit report.

10.

On or about March 2,2010 plaintiff disputed a fourth time her Equifax credit report. She included with her dispute all the identifying information Equifax required to process a dispute.

11.

On or about March 4,2010, plaintiff received a denial of credit from Key Bank based upon information appearing in her Equifax credit report

12.

On or about March 21, 2011, plaintiff again requested a copy of her Equifax credit report. On or about April 4, 2011, plaintiff received the same form letter, for a fifth time, requesting additional identifying information. The next day she again requested her Equifax credit report, using the identifying information Equifax requested she use to obtain her credit report.

13.

On or about April 21, 2011, plaintiff received a sixth form letter, requesting she provide the identical identifying information she had already provided on numerous occasions. On or about April 27, 2011, plaintiff sent a new request for a copy of her credit report, again containing the identical information that Equifax had previously requested she provide. Equifax received her request on April 30, 2011. Equifax did not respond to plaintiffs request for a credit report.

14.

On June 28, 2011, plaintiff called Equifax to dispute any false information appearing in her credit report and to find out why she could not get Equifax to provide her a copy of her Equifax credit report. Plaintiff provided the Equifax consumer representative her name, Social Security number and address. She also provided account information regarding her creditors. The Equifax representative told her that she was mixed with another person and she needed to dispute the false information directly to the creditors before they would release her credit report. Plaintiff complained that she did not know what was on her credit report and needed a copy to determine what was necessary to dispute. Equifax agreed to send her a copy of her credit report. On or about July 5, 2011, plaintiff received a copy of her Equifax credit report. The report contained a wrong Social Security number and numerous false, derogatory accounts.

15.

On or about July 19, 2011, plaintiff disputed to Equifax for a sixth time her Equifax credit report. Equifax received her dispute on July 23, 2011. In her dispute she informed Equifax of the false identifying information and that she had never defaulted on a single account in her life. She also detailed all the false accounts and identifying information Equifax was reporting about her.

16.

On or about August 1, 2011, Equifax sent plaintiff the same form letter, for a seventh time, requesting that she provide the same identifying information she had previously provided on numerous occasions. There were no results of any investigations regarding any of her previous disputes of the false information being reported about her. On or about August 2, 2011 plaintiff disputed a seventh time, again providing the identical identifying information Equifax requested.

17.

On or about August 15, 2011, plaintiff received Equifax's August 8,2011 credit report. She did not receive any results of investigation from her many disputes. There was no change in her credit report.

18.

On or about August 25, 2011, plaintiff disputed an eighth time to Equifax. Plaintiff enclosed the same identifying information she had previously provided. In her dispute she pleaded with Equifax to investigate her credit report and detailed the same false information she had been disputing for a year and a half. Equifax received her dispute on August 29, 2011.

19.

On or about September 2, 2011, Equifax sent plaintiff Equifax's form letter requesting she provide additional identifying information. There were no results of investigation for any of her numerous disputes.

20.

On or about September 13, 2011, plaintiff sent Equifax the identical information Equifax requested in their form letter so that it could process her dispute. On or about September 28, 2011, Equifax sent plaintiff the same form letter requesting she submit the identical identifying information which it claimed was necessary prior to processing this ninth request to dispute. Equifax would not investigate her disputes. After approximately two years of disputing, plaintiff gave up and filed this lawsuit.

FIRST CLAIM FOR RELIEF

(FCRA-15 U.S.C. §1681n)

21.

Plaintiff realleges paragraphs 1- 20 as if fully set forth herein.

22.

Equifax willfully failed to comply with the requirements imposed under the FCRA, 15 U.S.C. §1681 et seq., including but not limited to:

a) failing to follow reasonable procedures to assure maximum possible accuracy of the information in consumer reports, as required by 15 U.S.C. §1681e(b);

b) failing to comply with the reinvestigation requirements in 15 U.S.C. §1681i;

c) providing plaintiffs credit file to companies without determining that these

companies had a permissible purpose to obtain plaintiffs credit file pursuant to U.S.C. §1681b

and

d) failing to provide plaintiff her credit file pursuant to 15 U.S.C. §1681g.
23.
As a result of Equifax's violations of the FCRA, Plaintiff has suffered, continues to suffer, and will suffer future damages, including denial of credit, lost opportunity to receive credit, damage to reputation, worry, distress, frustration, embarrassment, and humiliation, all to her damages, in an amount to be determined by the jury.

24.

Plaintiff's entitled to punitive damages in an amount to be determined by the jury.

25.

Plaintiff's entitled to actual damages in an amount to be determined by the jury in addition to any statutory damages in an amount to be determined by the Court.

26.

Plaintiff's entitled to her attorney fees, pursuant to 15 U.S.C. § 1681n(a).

SECOND CLAIM FOR

RELIEF (FCRA-15

U.S.C. §1681o)

27.

Plaintiff realleges paragraphs 1 - 20 as if fully set forth herein.

28.

Equifax negligently failed to comply with the requirements imposed under the FCRA, including but not limited to:

a) failing to follow reasonable procedures to assure maximum possible accuracy of the information in consumer reports, as required by 15 U.S.C. §1681e(b);

b) failing to comply with the reinvestigation requirements in 15 U.S.C. §1681i;

c) providing plaintiffs credit file to companies without determining that these

companies had a permissible purpose to obtain plaintiffs credit file pursuant to U.S.C.

§168 lb and d) failing to provide plaintiff her credit file pursuant to 15 U.S.C. §1681g.

29.

As a result of Equifax's violations of the FCRA, plaintiff has suffered, continues to suffer and will suffer future damages, including denial of credit, lost opportunity to receive credit, damage to reputation, worry, distress, frustration, embarrassment, and humiliation, all to her damages, in an amount to be determined by the jury.

30.

Plaintiff's entitled to actual damages in an amount to be determined by the jury.

31.

Plaintiff's entitled to her attorney fees, pursuant to 15 U.S.C. § 1681o(a).

PRAYER

Plaintiff demands a jury trial on all claims. Wherefore plaintiff Julie Miller prays for a judgment as follows

1. On Plaintiffs First Claim for Relief for willful violations of the FCRA against Defendant Equifax:

        a. Actual damages in an amount to be determined by the jury;

        b. Punitive damages in an amount to be determined by the jury; and,

        c. Statutory damages as determined by the court; and

        d. Attorney fees and costs.

2. On Plaintiffs Second Claim for Relief for negligent violations of the FCRA against Defendant Equifax:

        a. Actual damages in an amount to be determined by the jury;

        b. Attorney fees and costs.

3. On All Claims for Relief, costs and expenses incurred in this action.

SETTLEMENT AGREEMENTS AWARDS BY CRA's

"credit bureaus — Experian, Equifax and TransUnion — have long been criticized for the convoluted process that consumers must endure to get their credit reports fixed, among other things. Under the agreement, they will improve their dispute resolution process, which is largely automated, and instead use specially trained employees.

The three companies will also establish a six-month waiting period before reporting medical debts on consumers' credit reports, providing more time for consumers to resolve issues that might amount only to a delayed insurance payment or another dispute. The credit agencies will also remove medical debts from an individual's report after the debt is paid by insurance.

Additionally, the credit reporting bureaus will take steps to make consumers aware that their credit reports are available free at least once a year from each of the credit agencies through the website annualcreditreport.com. The agencies will now have to include links to that website on their home pages, as well as provide another free report to consumers who experience a change in their credit reports after initiating a dispute.

The settlement requires the agencies to introduce the changes, which the bureaus said would be instituted nationwide, over three years. But most changes will be carried out over the next six to 18 months, according to the Consumer Data Industry Association, a trade group that represents the credit bureaus."

There is a proposed settlement with TransUnion LLC, Experian Information Solutions, Inc., and Equifax Information Services LLC ("Defendants") in a class action lawsuit about whether they violated the Fair Credit Reporting Act ("FCRA") and state laws when reporting debts that had been discharged in bankruptcy as not discharged, whether Defendants conducted proper investigations of consumer disputes regarding such debts, and whether consumers were damaged as a result. The Settlement will provide payments of damage awards from a $45 million settlement fund.

The lawsuit alleges that the Defendants violated the FCRA and related state laws by incorrectly reporting debts discharged in bankruptcy on credit reports. The Court did not decide which side was right. But both sides agreed to the Settlement to resolve the case and get benefits to customers.

Before any money is paid, the United States District Court for the Central District of California ("the Court") must approve the Settlement.

A jury awarded an Oregon woman $18.6 million **after she spent two years unsuccessfully trying to get Equifax Information Services to fix** major mistakes on her credit report.

The judgement, likely to be appealed, appears to be one of the largest awarded to a consumer in a case against one of the nation's major credit bureaus.

Julie Miller of Marion County, who was awarded $18.4 million in punitive and $180,000 in compensatory damages, contacted **Equifax** eight times between 2009 and 2011 in an effort to correct inaccuracies, including erroneous accounts and collection attempts, as well as a wrong Social Security number and birthday. Yet over and over, the lawsuit alleged, the Atlanta-based company failed to correct its mistakes.

"There was damage to her reputation, a breach of her privacy and the lost opportunity to seek credit," said **Justin Baxter, the Portland attorney who teamed on the case with his father and law partner, Michael Baxter.** "She has a brother who is disabled and who can't get credit on his own and she wasn't able to help him."

Tim Klein, an Equifax spokesman, said Friday that he didn't have any details about the decision from the **Oregon Federal District** Court.

FTC STUDY

A Federal Trade Commission study of the U.S. credit reporting industry found that five percent of consumers had errors on one of their three major credit reports that could lead to them paying more for products such as auto loans and insurance.

Overall, the congressionally mandated study on credit report accuracy found that one in five consumers had an error on at least one of their three credit reports.

"These are eye-opening numbers for American consumers," said Howard Shelanski, Director of the FTC's Bureau of Economics. "The results of this first-of-its-kind study make it clear that consumers should check their credit reports regularly. If they don't, they are potentially putting their pocketbooks at risk."

The study, in which participants were encouraged to use the Fair Credit Reporting Act (FCRA) process to resolve any potential credit report errors, also found that:

One in four consumers identified errors on their credit reports that might affect their credit scores;

One in five consumers had an error that was corrected by a credit reporting agency (CRA) after

it was disputed, on at least one of their three credit reports;

Four out of five consumers who filed disputes experienced some modification to their credit report;

Slightly more than one in 10 consumers saw a change in their credit score after the CRAs

modified errors on their credit report; and

Approximately one in 20 consumers had a maximum score change of more than 25 points

and only one in 250 consumers had a maximum score change of more than 100 points.

Other study results can be found in the executive summary of the report.

"Your credit report has information about your finances and your bill-paying history, so it's important to make sure it's accurate," said Charles Harwood, Acting Director of the FTC's Bureau of Consumer Protection. "The good news for consumers is that credit reports are free through annualcreditreport.com, and if you find an error, you can work with the credit reporting company to fix it."

About the Study

The FTC report is the first major study that looks at all the primary groups that participate in the credit reporting and scoring process: consumers; lenders/data furnishers (which include creditors, lenders, debt collection agencies, and the court system); the Fair Isaac Corporation, which develops FICO credit scores; and the national credit reporting agencies (CRAs). It is based on work with 1,001 participants who reviewed 2,968 credit reports with a study associate who helped them identify and correct possible errors on their credit reports.

Consumers in the study were selected to match the demographic and credit score information of the general public, and participants were encouraged to dispute errors that could affect their credit standing. Credit reports with potential errors identified by study participants were sent to Fair Isaac (FICO) for rescoring.

After completing the FCRA dispute process, study participants were provided with new credit reports and credit scores. The original reports were then compared with the new reports. If any modifications were made as a result of the disputes, the impact of errors on the consumer's credit score was determined.

Congress directed the FTC to conduct a study of credit report accuracy and provide interim reports every two years, starting in 2004 and continuing through 2012, with a final report in 2014. The reports are being produced under Section 319 of the Fair and Accurate Credit Transactions Act, or FACT Act.

Information for Consumers

The FTC has a wide range of general information for consumers on credit reporting issues, including Free Credit Reports, Disputing Errors on Credit Reports, and Your Source for a Truly Free Credit Report? AnnualCreditReport.com, as well as a new consumer blog posted titled It Pays to Check Your Credit Report.

It also has information available on how credit scores affect the price of credit and insurance and what consumers need to know about their credit reports when looking for a job. Finally, the FTC has a video for consumers on how to get a free credit report.

The Commission vote authorizing the staff to issue the report to Congress was 5-0, with former Commissioner J. Thomas Rosch participating. It is the fifth interim report to Congress describing the progress the agency has made on a national study examining the accuracy of credit reports.

We know that often times our readers like to read about actual lawsuits that are filed so we will be posting more of these in the future. This lawsuit is a FCRA (Fair Credit Reporting Act) against the following companies:

Discover Bank

Equifax

Experian

TransUnion

All of this arises out of a collection lawsuit filed by Discover against our client that he won. After he won the case he smartly disputed the credit reporting showing he owed money when a judge had ruled he owed no money.

You can see how the credit reporting agencies don't care what judges say — they will always (it seems) go with their paying customer — in this situation Discover Bank.

We are hopeful that our client standing up for his rights and taking action will bring about a change in the industry.

SAMPLE COMPLAINT NUMBER TWO

COMPLAINT

COMES NOW the Plaintiff, by and through counsel, and for Plaintiff's Complaint against the Defendants states as follows:

This action arises out of Defendants' violations of the Fair Credit Reporting Act [1] (15 U.S.C. § 1681 et seq. [hereinafter "FCRA"]), out of state law violations and out of the invasion of Plaintiff's personal and financial privacy by the Defendants.

The Plaintiff was sued by _____ for a debt ___ claimed Plaintiff owed.

Defendant _____ never had any intention of offering any proof at trial.

Instead, the lawsuit against Plaintiff was filed by Defendant ___ Bank with the hope of obtaining a default judgment or coercing Plaintiff into paying on a debt ___ refused to prove.

This is the pattern of collection activity by Defendant ___ in its collection lawsuits in Alabama. Defendant

Discover Bank offered no proof even after being told to do so by the Circuit Court judge.

The Plaintiff won the lawsuit.

All Defendants refused to remove the ___ entry from Plaintiff's credit reports as the credit reporting agencies refused to follow the court Order but instead only care about their paying customer Bank which still wants to be paid even though it lost the collection lawsuit.

JURISDICTION

Personal jurisdiction exists over Defendants as they had the necessary minimum contacts with the State of Alabama and this suit arises out of their specific conduct with Plaintiff in Alabama. All the actions described in this suit occurred in Alabama.

Subject matter jurisdiction exists under federal question jurisdiction (28 U.S.C. Section 1331) and through diversity jurisdiction (28 U.S.C. Section 1332) as the amount claimed exceeds $75,000.00 between these diverse parties.

VENUE

Venue is proper as Plaintiff lives in Alabama and the Defendants do business in this judicial district.

350

PARTIES

Plaintiff Charles J. Rogers (hereinafter "Plaintiff") is a natural person who is a resident of Alabama.

Defendant Bank, ("Defendant" or ") is a foreign company that engages in the business of suing consumers and/or reporting consumer credit information to credit reporting agencies. It conducts business in this Judicial District. Its principal place of business is the State of Delaware and it is incorporated in Delaware.

Defendant Equifax Information Services, LLC, ("Defendant" or "Equifax") is a foreign company that engages in the business of maintaining and reporting consumer credit information and does business in this Judicial District. Its principal place of business is the State of Georgia and it is incorporated in Georgia.

Defendant Experian Information Solutions, Inc., ("Defendant" or "Experian") is a foreign company that engages in the business of maintaining and reporting consumer credit information and does business in this Judicial District. Its principal place of business is the State of California and it is incorporated in Ohio.

Defendant Trans Union, LLC, ("Defendant" or "Trans Union") is a foreign company that engages in the business of maintaining and reporting consumer credit information and does business in this Judicial District. Its principal place of business is the State of Illinois and it is incorporated in Delaware.

FACTUAL ALLEGATIONS

On December 28, 2011, Defendant Discover sued Plaintiff Rogers in the Circuit Court of Barbour County, Alabama, with a case number of CV-2011-000016.

This suit was filed by the Couch, Conville & Blitt, LLC collection law firm.

The state court set the case for trial. Notice was sent to Defendant Discover and Plaintiff Rogers.

At all times Plaintiff was prepared for trial.

The case resulted in a judgment in favor of Plaintiff Rogers on March 22, 2013, dismissing the case with prejudice.

The Order stated "This case being set for Final Hearing on March 19, 2013, Plaintiff failed to provide testimony pursuant to this Courts instructions on previous court date. This being Final Hearing the Court finds in favor of the Defendant, Mr. Charles J. Rogers. The case is hereby dismissed with prejudice."

Defendant Discover knew it had lost the case.

Defendant Discover knows losing the case means Plaintiff Rogers does not owe the debt to Defendant Discover.

Defendant Discover reported and has continued to report (even after losing the case) to the credit reporting agencies that Plaintiff Rogers owed this money and was in default.

Plaintiff Rogers does not owe this money to Defendant Discover.

After Plaintiff Rogers won the case, he called and sent one or more letters to Defendants Equifax, Experian, and Trans Union requesting an investigation of the Defendant Discover's account that still appeared on Plaintiff Rogers' credit reports.

Plaintiff Rogers requested that the Defendant Discover's account be deleted.

Defendants Discover Bank, Equifax, Experian, and Trans Union were not concerned and did not care about what the state court did in the case as Defendants Discover Bank, Equifax, Experian, and Trans Union did not intend to perform a reasonable investigation.

Defendants Discover Bank, Equifax, Experian, and Trans Union did not perform any type of reasonable investigation.

Defendants Equifax, Experian, and Trans Union notified Defendant Discover in accordance with the FCRA of the dispute by Plaintiff Rogers.

Alternatively, Defendants Equifax, Experian, and Trans Union did not properly notify Defendant Discover and, as part of this failure, did not include all relevant information provided by Plaintiff Rogers in its notification of Defendant Discover. This includes notification that the state court entered an Order in favor of Plaintiff Rogers.

Defendants failed to properly investigate this dispute as if Defendants had properly investigated, the Discover account would have been deleted.

Several examples of the lack of investigation are listed below.

On April 16, 2013, Defendant Equifax issued its results of investigation, which shows the Defendant Discover's account with a balance due and that it is a charged off account.

On May 3, 2013, Defendant Experian issued its results of investigation, which shows the Defendant Discover's account with a balance due and that it is a charged off account.

On May 7, 2013, Defendant Experian sent a letter to Plaintiff Rogers which stated "We are responding to your request to verify item(s) on your personal credit report. We have already investigated this information and the credit grantor has verified its accuracy."

The letter goes on to state "…we will not be investigating your dispute again at this time. If you still believe the item is inaccurate, then we can add a statement of continued dispute to your personal credit report at your request, or you may wish to contact the credit grantor directly to resolve your issue." (Emphasis added).

On May 21, 2013, Defendant Trans Union issued it results of investigation, which shows the Defendant Discover's account with a balance due and that it is a charged off account.

All Defendants were provided with more than sufficient information in the dispute and in their own internal sources of information (which includes the knowledge of Defendant Discover through its state court trial counsel that the case was a defeat for Defendant Discover) to conduct an investigation and to conclude that the account complained of was being reported incorrectly.

Defendants Equifax, Experian, and Trans Union have previously proclaimed that they are obligated to rely upon whatever the public records state about a consumer.

For example, had Plaintiff Rogers lost the suit and a judgment was entered in favor of Defendant Discover, and Plaintiff Rogers disputed with Equifax, Experian, and Trans Union, Plaintiff Rogers would have been told by Defendants Equifax, Experian, and Trans Union that they were bound by the state court judgment which says Plaintiff Rogers owes the money.

These same Defendants Equifax, Experian, and Trans Union, however, refused to rely upon what the state court judge actually said – – an Order for Plaintiff Rogers.

These Defendants refused to read the Order or they read the Order and then chose to ignore it.

The Order in favor of Plaintiff Rogers means Plaintiff Rogers does not owe the money claimed by Defendant Discover.

The state court ruling was a final judgment.

This final judgment was not appealed.

There is no avenue for appeal for Defendant Discover of this judgment as the time to appeal has passed.

Despite this knowledge, Defendants Equifax, Experian, and Trans Union have completely abdicated their obligations under federal and state law and have instead chosen to merely "parrot" whatever their customer, Defendant Discover, has told them to say.

Defendants Equifax, Experian, and Trans Union have a policy to favor the paying customer, in this situation Defendant Discover, rather than what the consumer or the state court says about a debt.

As one example, on or about May 16, 2013, Plaintiff Rogers spoke with Defendant Experian and Defendant Experian stated it would ignore the court Order as it would instead accept whatever Defendant Discover Bank told it regardless of the court Order.

The primary reason for this wrongful policy is that furnishers (such as Defendant Discover) provide enormous financial rewards to Defendants Equifax, Experian, and Trans Union.

The importance of keeping balances on credit reports is that all the Defendants understand that one of the most powerful methods furnishers such as Defendant Discover have to wrench payments from a consumer is by placing accounts with balances on the consumer's credit reports.

Defendants have a policy and procedure to refuse to properly update credit reports of consumers, like Plaintiff Rogers, who do not owe the alleged debt. That reason is to keep false information on the credit report. The false information consists of a balance shown as owed or charged off when Defendants know no money is owed.

Defendant Discover has promised through its subscriber agreements or contracts with the credit reporting agencies to accurately update accounts but Defendant Discover has willfully, maliciously, recklessly, wantonly, and/or negligently failed to follow this requirement as well as the requirements set forth under the FCRA and state law, which has resulted in the intended consequences of this information remaining on Plaintiff Rogers' credit reports.

Defendant Discover assumed a duty, through the subscriber agreement and other actions, to accurately report the balances and this duty was breached in a negligent, wanton, reckless, willful, intentional, and/or malicious manner.

Defendants have a policy to "park" false information on at least one of the consumer's credit reports. This is a term in the industry for keeping a false balance (or false account) on the credit report so that the consumer will be forced to pay off the balance in order to obtain a refinancing or to qualify for a loan or to increase the consumer's credit score from the artificially lowered score which directly resulted from the Defendants' intentional and malicious conduct.

In parking or allowing the parking of an account, all Defendants know they are violating their obligations and duties under federal and state law to accurately report the account and the balance.

All Defendants know that parking a balance will lead to false and defamatory information being published every time the Plaintiff Rogers' credit report is accessed and this is the malicious and intentional design behind Defendants' actions with the goal to force Plaintiff Rogers to pay on an account Plaintiff Rogers does not owe.

All Defendants maliciously, willfully, intentionally, recklessly, and/or negligently failed to review the information provided in the disputes and that was already in their files and to conduct a reasonable investigation on Plaintiff Rogers' disputes, which led as a direct result and consequence to all of the Defendants either failing to delete information found to be inaccurate, failing to replace the inaccurate information with accurate information, and/or reinserting the information without following the dictates of the FCRA.

At all relevant times the Defendants Equifax, Experian, and Trans Union failed to maintain and failed to follow reasonable procedures to assure maximum possible accuracy of Plaintiff Rogers' credit reports, concerning the account in question, violating 15 U.S.C. § 1681e(b) and state law.

Defendant Discover failed to properly maintain and failed to follow reasonable procedures to assure maximum possible accuracy of Plaintiff Rogers' credit information and Plaintiff Rogers' credit report, concerning the account in question, thus violating state law as set forth in this Complaint. These violations occurred before, during, and after the dispute process began with the consumer reporting agencies.

Defendant Discover has taken illegal aggressive actions in a continued effort to collect the alleged debt against Plaintiff Rogers. This includes the continued reporting of the debt to third parties (even after losing the state court trial), including consumer reporting agencies such as Defendants Equifax, Experian, and Trans Union, and stating that Plaintiff Rogers owes the debt.

Defendants Equifax, Experian, and Trans Union have failed to maintain Plaintiff Rogers' account with maximum accuracy and these Defendants and Defendant Discover have failed to properly investigate the account in response to the disputes made by Plaintiff Rogers.

The conduct of the Defendants has proximately cause Plaintiff Rogers past and future monetary loss, past and future damage to Plaintiff Rogers' credit worthiness, past and future mental distress and emotional anguish, and other damages that will be presented to the trier of fact.

It is a practice of all of the Defendants to maliciously, willfully, recklessly, wantonly and/or negligently ignore and refuse to follow the requirements of the FCRA and state law.

All Defendants are sophisticated businesses and they know their conduct is wrong.

For example, Defendants have been sued for this identical misconduct in Alabama.

All actions taken by the Defendants were done with malice, were done willfully, and were done with either the desire to harm Plaintiff Rogers and/or with the knowledge that their actions would very likely harm Plaintiff Rogers and/or that their actions were taken in violation of the FCRA and/or state law and/or that they knew or should have known that their actions were in reckless disregard of the FCRA and/or state law.

All Defendants have engaged in a pattern and practice of wrongful and unlawful behavior with respect to accounts and consumer reports and as such all Defendants are subject to punitive damages and statutory damages and all other appropriate measures to punish and deter similar future conduct by these Defendants and similar companies.

Defendants are liable to Plaintiff Rogers through the doctrine of Respondeat Superior for the wrongful, intentional and negligent acts, errors, and omissions done in violation of state and federal law by its employees and agents.

Plaintiff has suffered actual damages as a result of these illegal actions by Defendants in the form of anger, anxiety, emotional distress, fear, frustration, upset, humiliation, embarrassment, amongst other negative emotions, as well as suffering from unjustified and abusive invasions of personal privacy.

CAUSES OF ACTION

COUNT I.

VIOLATIONS OF THE FAIR CREDIT REPORTING ACT

15 U.S.C. § 1681 et seq.

Plaintiff incorporates by reference all of the above paragraphs of this Complaint as though fully stated herein.

Defendants Equifax, Experian and Trans Union are "consumer reporting agencies," as codified at 15 U.S.C. § 1681a(e).

Defendant Discover is an entity who, regularly and in the course of business, furnishes information to one or more consumer reporting agencies about its transactions or experiences with any consumer and therefore constitutes a "furnisher," as codified at 15 U.S.C. § 1681s-2.

Plaintiff Rogers notified Defendants Equifax, Experian and Trans Union directly of a dispute on the Defendant Discover account's completeness and/or accuracy, as reported.

Defendants Equifax, Experian and Trans Union properly notified Defendant Discover of Plaintiff's dispute in accordance with the FCRA requirements.

Alternatively, Defendants Equifax, Experian and Trans Union failed to notify Defendant Discover of Plaintiff's dispute in accordance with the FCRA requirements.

Defendants failed to delete information found to be inaccurate, reinserted the information without following the FCRA, or failed to properly investigate Plaintiff Rogers' disputes.

Plaintiff Rogers alleges that at all relevant times Defendants Equifax, Experian and Trans Union failed to maintain and failed to follow reasonable procedures to assure maximum possible accuracy of Plaintiff Rogers' credit reports, concerning the account in question, violating 15 U.S.C. § 1681e(b).

Plaintiff Rogers alleges that all Defendants failed to conduct a proper and lawful reinvestigation. For example, Defendants were given notice that the suit resulted in a victory for Plaintiff Rogers, but Defendants apparently failed to review the Order, the court file or contact the court or contact counsel for Defendant Discover. Other examples will become apparent once discovery is commenced.

All actions taken by the Defendants were done with malice, were done willfully, and were done with either the desire to harm Plaintiff Rogers and/or with the knowledge that their actions would very likely harm Plaintiff Rogers and/or that their actions were taken in violation of the FCRA and state law and/or that knew or should have known that their actions were in reckless disregard of the FCRA and state law.

All of the violations of the FCRA proximately caused the injuries and damages set forth in this Complaint.

COUNT II.

INVASION OF PRIVACY

Plaintiff incorporates by reference all of the paragraphs of this Complaint as though fully stated herein.

Alabama law recognizes Plaintiff's right to be free from invasions of privacy and Defendants violated Alabama state law as described in this Complaint.

Congress explicitly recognized a consumer's inherent right to privacy in collection matters in passing the Fair Debt Collection Practices Act, when it stated as part of its findings:

Abusive debt collection practices contribute to the number of personal bankruptcies, to marital instability, to the loss of jobs, and **to invasions of individual privacy.**

15 U.S.C. § 1692(a) (emphasis added).

Congress further recognized a consumer's right to privacy in financial data in passing the Gramm Leech Bliley Act, which regulates the privacy of consumer financial data for a broad range of "financial institutions" including debt collectors (albeit without a private right of action), when it stated as part of its purposes:

It is the policy of the Congress that **each financial institution has an affirmative and continuing obligation to respect the privacy of its customers** and to protect the security and confidentiality of those customers' nonpublic personal information.

15 U.S.C. § 6801(a) (emphasis added).

Defendants intentionally, recklessly, and/or negligently interfered, physically or otherwise, with the solitude, seclusion and or private concerns or affairs of the Plaintiff.

Defendants intentionally, recklessly, and/or negligently caused emotional harm to Plaintiff by engaging in highly offensive conduct in the course of collecting or credit reporting this debt thereby invading and intruding upon Plaintiff's right to privacy.

Plaintiff had a reasonable expectation of privacy in Plaintiff's solitude, seclusion, private concerns or affairs, and private financial information.

The conduct of Defendants, in engaging in the above-described illegal conduct against Plaintiff, resulted in multiple intrusions and invasions of privacy by Defendants which occurred in a way that would be highly offensive to a reasonable person in that position.

As a result of such intrusions and invasions of privacy, Plaintiff is entitled to actual damages in an amount to be determined at trial from Defendants.

All acts of Defendants were committed with malice, intent, wantonness, and/or recklessness and as such Defendants are subject to punitive damages.

COUNT III.

NEGLIGENT, WANTON, AND/OR INTENTIONAL HIRING AND

SUPERVISION OF INCOMPETENT EMPLOYEES OR AGENTS

Plaintiff incorporates by reference all of the paragraphs of this Complaint as though fully stated herein.

Defendants' agents or employees are allowed and encouraged to break the law.

Defendants are aware of the wrongful conduct of its employees or agents.

Defendants negligently, wantonly, and/or intentionally hired, retained, or supervised incompetent employees or agents, who were allowed or encouraged to violate the law as was done to Plaintiff, and Defendants are thereby responsible to the Plaintiff for the wrongs committed against Plaintiff and the damages suffered by Plaintiff.

COUNT IV.

STATE LAW CLAIMS

Plaintiff incorporates by reference all of the paragraphs of this Complaint as though fully stated herein.

Defendants intentionally published false and defamatory information related to the Defendant Discover account.

Defendants acted with negligence, malice, wantonness, recklessness, and/or intentional conduct in their dealings with and about Plaintiff Rogers as set forth in this Complaint. This includes the initial reporting of Defendant Discover account; the handling of any investigations on the accounts; and all other aspects as set forth in this Complaint, including the collection suit by Defendant Discover.

Defendants assumed a duty, through the subscriber agreement and other actions, to accurately report the balances and account.

Defendants violated all of the duties the Defendants had and such violations were made intentionally, willfully, recklessly, maliciously, wantonly, and negligently.

It was foreseeable, and Defendants did in fact foresee it, that refusing to properly update and investigate would cause the exact type of harm suffered by the Plaintiff Rogers.

Defendants invaded the privacy of Plaintiff Rogers as set forth in Alabama law, including publishing false information about Plaintiff Rogers' personal financial obligations.

The Defendants acted with intentional, reckless, or wanton conduct in attempting to collect this debt (Defendant Discover) and reporting this false information (all Defendants).

Such negligence, malice, wantonness, recklessness, willfulness, and/or intentional conduct proximately caused the damages set forth in this complaint and such conduct occurred before, during and after the disputes to Defendants Equifax, Experian and Trans Union.

As a result of this conduct, action, and inaction of all Defendants, Plaintiff Rogers has suffered damages as set forth in this Complaint.

COUNT V

MALICIOUS PROSECUTION AND ABUSE OF PROCESS AGAINST

DEFENDANT DISCOVER

All paragraphs of this Complaint are expressly adopted and incorporated herein as if fully set forth herein. Defendant Discover instituted and continued prosecuting the lawsuit against Plaintiff with no reasonable basis to do so.

Defendant Discover filed the lawsuit with no intention of ever proving its case.

Defendant Discover continued to prosecute the case with no intention of ever proving its case.

Defendant Discover filed and used this case as a means of attempting to extort money out of Plaintiff or obtaining a default judgment against Plaintiff if Plaintiff did not answer the suit.

Defendant Discover instituted and continued prosecuting the lawsuit against Plaintiff with malice and with the design and plan that the lawsuit would result in an illegal judgment against the Plaintiff or would cause Plaintiff to pay Defendant Discover money on a non-existent debt.

The malicious plan of Defendant Discover included the knowledge that the fraudulent judgment would be devastating to Plaintiff's credit report and credit scores and would lead to garnishments and the Defendant Discover tried to accomplish this by the Defendant Discover's malicious and abusive actions.

Throughout the entire illegal lawsuit against Plaintiff, Defendant Discover knew at all times that there was no basis for the lawsuit and the intent and design of filing the lawsuit and continuing to prosecute the lawsuit was to extort money from the Plaintiff Which Defendant Discover knew it was not entitled to receive.

The litigation against Plaintiff filed by Defendant Discover eventually resulted in adjudication in favor of Plaintiff.

The illegal and improper actions of the Defendant Discover constitute malicious prosecution and abuse of process.

This is the pattern and practice of Defendant Discover – to file suits with no basis and no intention of ever proving the case in an attempt to obtain default judgments against Alabama consumers or to obtain settlements from Alabama consumers who do not realize the bogus nature of the suit filed by Defendant Discover.

The Plaintiff suffered past and future emotional distress and monetary loss as a direct and proximate result of Defendant Discover's abuse of process and malicious prosecution.

PRAYER FOR RELIEF

WHEREFORE, PREMISES CONSIDERED, Plaintiff prays that judgment be entered against Defendants for all damages allowable (including statutory, actual, compensatory, nominal and punitive the total of which Plaintiff claims more than $75,000.00), costs, expenses, fees, injunctive relief to prevent further violations, and for such other and further relief as may be just and proper.

Respectfully Submitted,
John G. Watts (ASB-5819-t82j)
M. Stan Herring (ASB-1074-n72m)
The Kress Building
301 19th Street North
Birmingham, Alabama 35203
(205) 879-2447
john@wattsherring.com

Key things you must keep in mind when litigating

1. Read and follow the FCRA Act.

2. Know the local rules of your Court, especially how many days you have to answer any motion, pleading, etc. Rule of thumb of days 10, 14, 21, 30 days, you must know, also with electronic filing you have three extra days.

3. In my case I practice filing my case 3 days before they were due or immediately 3 days after my adversary filed any papers in Court.

4. Memorize all of the Defenses available to you and try to come up with counter claims if you can.

5. If you believe you are right keep in mind of those Pro se, who have laid the pathway by believing in their cases enough to stay the course to win, and just maybe you will become of them just as I have joined them.

6. In my research it was said that Plaintiff only win 42 percent of the case and Defendants win 58 percent of the time, keep in mind no Lawyer win all their cases, all the time.

7. Read each and every case law you can get your hands on, because you may find one or several cases with issues similar to yours or ruling you can insert into your case as a good argument to give you the upper hand.

8. The cost involved in you copying all of my case's docket would run into mid hundred or almost a thousand dollars by itself, no litigation is not cheap whether or not you are rich or poor, but especially if you are poor. There is a sense of self-satisfaction not to mention rewarding when you win a monetary award or a stipulation of Dismissal with prejudice in a lawsuit filed against you.

9. Read the applicable Federal Rules of Civil Procedure as it pertains to your case, several times so you understand them clearly.

Author's testimony

A collector filed a lawsuit against me in state Court, and because the CRA's filed Answers and Defenses during our Summary Judgment stage in a prior case, I was able to learn from that experience to file an answer and defense with a <u>counterclaim</u>. This counterclaim gave me the upper hand from filing a counterclaim in my A&D in my pleading, which persuaded the collector to agree to dismiss the Complaint with prejudice, if I would agree to dismiss my counterclaim with prejudice which I did or stipulated to resolve the case in my favor.

Had I not learned from my first case experienced on how the defendant's submits Answers and Defenses in a pleading I would not have known what to do and the Plaintiff would have had the upper hand and possibly won a Judgment against me.

STATUTES OF LIMITATION FOR CREDIT CARD DEBT

Creditors and Collectors have a limited time to sue you over unpaid credit card debts due to the Statute of limitation of your state Law and the written contract or open accounts terms.

State laws are concerned with contracts and agreements, and how long they may be in enforced.

Creditors and Collectors have a limited time frame in which to sue debtors for nonpayment of credit card debts, this time frame is set by your states statute of limitation.

Usually the statute of limitation on most debts is three to ten years, check your state SOL for credit cards debts.

The SOL does not prevent a Collector or Creditor from collecting debt, they just can't successfully sue or obtain a Judgement, unless you do not show up in Court to defend your right of SOL has run out.

Although a debt is a promise to pay if the SOL expire is in force and the collector or creditor attempts to collect the debt you have the right not to fulfill that promise due the SOL.

A debt is time-barred if the debt has lingered longer than the statutes allowed. If the debt is time-barred, you can have the lawsuit dismissed.

The FDCPA is the Federal law that governs how and when a debt collector can contact you the consumer and collect on unpaid debts and where legal action on those debts can be filed, therefore some credit card agreements may stipulate where the laws governing whether it's the home state of the issuer or the home state of the debtor and can be determine by the terms and provisions of the contract.

The various types of Debt Agreements

1. Oral contract

2. Written Contract

3. Promise Note- a mortgage is an example of a promissory note

4. Open-ended Accounts i.e. a credit card account

Most consumer's everyday pay off collection accounts that does not belongs to them because the accounts are on their credit report. When all they have to say to the Collector is, "I have an absolute defense since the SOL has expired.

The SOL (statute of limitation) doesn't make the cause debt to go away after it expires.

The SOL Starts when you fail to make payment on the account or the credit card company sends you a demand letter for the full amount; what is called an acceleration clause which must be invoke before a creditor has a cause of action.

If a creditor failed to bring sue in the time allowed by the applicable SOL, you as a debtor has an affirmative defense of SOL against the creditor's claim which can serve as a bar to Creditor's recovery of the debt.

UNITED STATES DISTRICT COURT
MIDDLE DISTRICT OF FLORIDA
JACKSONVILLE DIVISION

James Watson

Plaintiff

V.   Case No. 3:12-cv-552-J-99MMH-JBT
          JURY TRIAL DEMANDED

Equifax, Experian and Transunion

Defendants

PLAINTIFF OPPOSE SANCTION TO BE AWARDED TO DEFENDANT EQUIFAX

Equifax fail to have Plaintiff credit file online at the financial institution as required by FCRA Act when Plaintiff applied for a loan at those commercial financial institutions, after repeatedly being tolded over two-week period by Plaintiff that the financial institutions could not retrieved his credit report for a loan he was applying for.

Plaintiff is not stating he is a perfect person, Mr. Olson reminded Plaintiff that his English is not the best well we all have our weaknesses and strengths nevertheless Plaintiff has written and self-published two books, as I have said we all have our weakness and we all have good traits and bad traits. Pastor Trey Brunson of First Baptist of Jacksonville once said, "Bitterness is a choice to respond negatively to a negative wounded situation in your life." My God is a God of love and teaches us to love not to hate. Someone once said, "what a person does for himself he takes to his grave, but what he does for others becomes immortal forever."

The first time Mr. Brian and Plaintiff got into a verbal altercation is when Mr. Brian called me and started casual talking about the case and then mention to me that the Judge is going to dismiss this case so I should go ahead and accept his offer of deleting all the Negative accounts from my file, if I would send him a dismissal letter. I told him I would consider it but never did.

REFLECTION

As the author of this book let me remind you as well as emphasize that the moment you received something from any Court do not ignore it, but start right away how you are going to defend it as well as if you receive a summons you are already under their jurisdiction and therefore have to follow their rules or else lose your case or forfeit your rights. For the most part all Lawsuit have similarity such as noticing a defendant to try to resolve the matter before a complaint is filed.

Once you file a complaint in the Courts, you must serve a summons with the complaint on the defendant within 14-20 days in most cases except maybe the Government, if I am not mistaken you have 30 days, follow Your local rules of the Court, and your Federal rule of Civil Procedure, Under the F. Rules Civ. Proc. If I am not mistaken Defendants have twenty days to answer a complaint or have just cause why they were not able to answer or be in default, and received a judgement on them. In my book I tried to provide to you a comprehensive outline of filing Pleadings by both parties, this is not all the Pleadings by both parties but it represents at least some of the Pleadings that took place in the Lawsuit between the parties, there were about 164 dockets in my case as recorded by the Court. These Pleadings may not be in sequential order but maybe randomly place so that reader Get a sense of what they have to do if they were to file a lawsuit.

IN CLOSING I HOPE THIS BOOK GIVES YOU A SENSE OF EMPOWERMENT TO PROTECT YOUR RIGHTS UNDER THE FRCA ACT AND OTHER CONSUMER ACTS

WARNING ON FILING A FRIVOLOUS COMPLAINT

DO NOT FILE A FRIVOLOUS, OR MERITLESS COMPLAINT, FOR NOT ONLY WILL YOU LOOK BAD IN THE EYES OF THE COURT, BUT IT CAN HURT YOUR POCKET IF THE COURT ORDERS YOU TO PAY SANCTIONS, SUCH AS COURT COST AND ATTORNEY FEES. ALWAYS BASE YOUR CASE ON THE LAW, CAUSE OF ACTION, AND THE FACTS.

IF THERE IS A PRECEDENT CASE THAT THE COURTS HAVE RULED ON IN YOUR FAVOR WITH SIMILAR FACTS THEN THIS GAVES YOU A GOOD CHANCE OF WINNING.

IMPORTANT SUGGESTIONS

Footnote: before I would file a Complaint I would spend at least 3 hours a day reading anything law pertaining to my case for three months, I suggest you do the same read for example, the FED.RULES.CIV. PROC., FCRA, CASE LAWS, ANY LEGAL TERMS THAT MAY APPLY TO YOUR CASE, as well as your local Court rules WHERE YOU PLAN TO FILE YOUR CASE.

SUGGESTED RECOMMENDED READING AND BOOKS NEEDED

Represent Yourself in Court 2nd Edition; by attorneys Paul Bergman and Sara J. Berman-Barrett a must read at least six months before you start thinking about filing your complaint.

Writing and Analysis in the Law; fourth Edition by Marilyn R. Walter, Helene S. Shapo, and Elizabeth Fajans contain some great insight into the structure on writing a brief as well as the legal grammar

Of course you should also purchase at three different legal Dictionary, such as Barron's Law Dictionary, and Merriam Webster Dictionary.

**IN THE UNITED STATES DISTRICT COURT
FOR THE MIDDLE DISTRICT OF FLORIDA
JACKSONVILLE DIVISION**

JAMES L. WATSON,

Plaintiff, V.

EQUIFAX, EXPERIAN, and TRANSUNION,

Defendants.

DEFENDANTS EXPERIAN INFORMATION SOLUTIONS, INC.'S AND EQUIFAX INFORMATION SERVICES LLC'S JOINT MOTION FOR LEAVE TO FILE COMBINED REPLY IN SUPPORT OF JOINT MOTION FOR SUMMARY JUDGMENT AND OPPOSITION TO PLAINTIFF'S MOTION FOR SUMMARY JUDGMENT

COMES NOW Defendants Experian Information Solutions, Inc. ("Experian"), incorrectly named in Plaintiff's Second Amended Complaint as "Experian," and Equifax Information Services LLC ("Equifax"), incorrectly named in Plaintiff's Second Amended Complaint as "Equifax" (collectively "Defendants"), by and through their undersigned counsel, and respectfully request leave to file a Joint Reply in Support of their Joint Motion for Summary Judgment, combined in one document with a Joint Opposition to Plaintiff's Motion for Summary Judgment. As the basis for this request, the Defendants respectfully show the Court as follows:

Experian and Equifax filed their Joint Motion for Summary Judgment on August 2, 2013. (Doc. 143.)[1] On July 31, 2013, Plaintiff filed a Motion to File More than Twenty-Five Pages (Doc. 134), and a purported "supplementary motion for summary judgment" (Doc. 137). By Order dated August 2, 2013, the Court terminated Plaintiff's Motion to File More than Twenty-

---

1 The Court granted Experian's and Equifax's joint motion for a one-day extension of the dispositive motion period, thereby extending the deadline to August 2, 2013. (Doc. 151.)

Five Pages and directed Plaintiff to file his motion for summary judgment

containing a memorandum of legal authority by August 19, 2013. (Doc. 144.)

On August 19, 2013, Plaintiff filed his "Response Brief Against Defendants Trans Union,

Equifax, and Experian Motion for Summary Judgment" (Doc. 152), and "Plaintiff Refiling

Supplementary Motion for Summary Judgment as Order by This Court to Be Filed On or Before

Aug 19, 2013 During Dispositive and Daubert" ("Plaintiff's Motion for Summary Judgment")

(Doc. 154.) Pursuant to Local Rule 3.01(b) and the Court's Summary Judgment

Notice dated August 20, 2013 (Doc. 155), Experian and Equifax should have until September

3, 2013 to file an opposition to Plaintiff's Motion for Summary Judgment.[2]

After reviewing Plaintiff's Response to their Joint Motion for Summary Judgment,   Experian

and Equifax believe there is good cause to file a Reply in Support of their motion.

Accordingly, pursuant to Local Rule 3.01(c), the Defendants are seeking leave herein to file

a Joint Reply in Support of their Joint Summary Judgment Motion.

In the interest of efficiency and to avoid duplicative arguments in a reply in support of the

Defendants' Joint Motion for Summary Judgment, and in an opposition to Plaintiff's Motion for

Summary Judgment, Experian and Equifax request that they be permitted to file a combined

reply in support of their Joint Motion for Summary Judgment and a joint response to Plaintiff's

Motion for Summary Judgment.

WHEREFORE, Experian and Equifax respectfully request that the Court permit the Defendants

until September 3, 2013, to file a combined reply in support of their Joint Motion for Summary

Judgment and a joint response in opposition to Plaintiff's Motion for Summary Judgment.

---

[2] September 2, 2013 is fourteen days after the filing of Plaintiff's Motion for Summary Judgment, but Labor Day
falls on that date. In light of the holiday, the Defendants understand that the deadline becomes September 3, 2013.

UNITED STATES DISTRICT COURT MIDDLE
DISTRICT OF FLORIDA JACKSONVILLE DIVISION

JAMES WATSON,

Plaintiff,

V.   CASE NO. 3:12-cv-552-J-99MMH-JBT

EQUIFAX, EXPERIAN, and

TRANSUNION,

Defendants

SUA SPONTE ORDER

THIS CAUSE is before the Court *sua sponte.*

A review of the file indicates that Plaintiff is proceeding *pro se.* Because Plaintiff

is proceeding *pro se,* the Court will take the opportunity to inform Plaintiff

of some, but not all, of the procedural rules with which he must comply. The

Court reminds Plaintiff of these obligations because a *prose* litigant is subject

to the same law and rules of court as a litigant who is represented by counsel,

including the Fed.

R. Civ. P. and the Local Rules.[1] *Moon v. Newsome,* 863 F.2d 835, 837 (11th

Cir. 1989).

All documents filed with the Court must be in the form of a pleading, *see* Fed.

---

[1] The parties are hereby reminded that all filings with the Court must be made in accordance with the Federal Rules of Civil Procedure and the Local Rules of the United States District Court for the Middle District of Florida. The Local Rules are available for review on the public website for the Middle District Court of Florida at www.flmd.uscourts.gov and a copy may be obtained by visiting the Clerk's Office. The Federal Rules of Civil Procedure are available for review in the law libraries of the state and federal courthouses.

R.

Fed. R. Civ. P. 7(b).

other paper shall be presented in a

Ciy. P. 7(a), or of a motion, *see*

Each pleading, motion, notice, or

separate document.

Plaintiff must timely respond to the motions filed by other parties in this case, for if he does not timely respond to such a motion, the Court may assume that Plaintiff does not oppose that motion and any relief requested therein.[2] Local Rule 3.1 (b) provides that any brief or legal memorandum in opposition to a motion must be filed within 14 days after Plaintiff is served with that motion by his opponent. If a party has missed a filing deadline, the party must file a motion seeking leave of Court to file the document out of time.

Plaintiff shall not correspond with the Court or any Judge or Magistrate Judge of the Court in letter form. In keeping with their sworn duty to maintain complete impartiality in the exercise of their judicial duties, the Judges of this Court will only deliver their decisions and opinions in response to those documents filed with the Clerk's Office in accordance with the governing rules of procedure. Any correspondence sent to judicial officers will not be responded to, will be stricken from the case file, and will be returned to the sending party.

All documents filed with the Court must include a caption; a brief title that describes the nature of the document; Plaintiffs name and signature; and a Certificate of Service. These last two items are explained below.

---

[2] Motions that Plaintiff must respond to include, but are not limited to, discovery Motions under Fed. R. Civ. P. 37, motions to dismiss under Fed. R. Civ. P. 12(b), and motions for summary judgment Fed. R. Civ. P. 56.

All pleadings, motions, or other papers filed with the Court by Plaintiff must bear an original signature, or they will be rejected by the Court. Among other things, that signature serves as Plaintiff's certification, pursuant to Fed. R. Civ. P. 11(b), that the document is not submitted for any improper purpose; that the claims or defenses presented in it are warranted by existing law; and that there exists reasonable factual support for the allegations or assertions made. Plaintiff is advised to review and become familiar with Fed. R. Civ. P. 11, as the failure to comply with its provisions can result in the imposition of sanctions, including monetary fines or dismissal of Plaintiff's case.

All pleadings, motions, or other papers filed with the Court by Plaintiff must also include a signed Certificate of Service. The Certificate of Service is confirmation that Plaintiff has complied with the requirements of Fed. R. Civ. P. 5 by serving on every other party to the action (or its attorney) a copy of the particular pleading, motion, or other paper filed with the Court. At a minimum, a Certificate of Service must state the date upon which a copy of the particular document was served on the other parties to the action (or their attorneys) and the means by which such service was made (*e.g.,* U.S. Mail, Federal Express, or hand delivery).

As previously mentioned, all requests for relief from, or action by, the Court must be in the form of a motion. If Plaintiff seeks any relief from, or action by, the Court, or seeks the entry of an order of any kind, Plaintiff must file a proper motion requesting that relief. The motion must meet the requirements of all applicable rules, including the Local Rules and the Federal Rules of Civil Procedure. All motions must be accompanied by a legal memorandum with citation of authorities in support of the relief requested. *See* M.D. Fla. R. 3.01 (a). The motion and memorandum shall be filed as one single document, however, and cannot exceed twenty-five pages

(25) in length. *See id.* Further, Plaintiff is advised that prior to filing most motions, Local Rule 3.01 (g) requires that he confer with opposing counsel in a good faith attempt to resolve the issue. Plaintiff must include a certification in the motion that he has complied with this requirement and he shall also notify the Court whether the parties agree on the relief requested. The Court would note that Local Rule 3.01 sets forth several other important requirements and rules governing motions filed with the Court. The failure to comply with these requirements or any other rule may result in the denial of the motion.

Plaintiff is also cautioned that he must abide by and comply with all orders of this Court. Failure to do so may result in sanctions, including dismissal of this case. Lastly, Plaintiff is reminded that, although he is now proceeding *prose,* he is not relieved of all of the obligations that rest upon an attorney. There are still many requirements with which Plaintiff must comply, including those imposed by the Federal Rules of Civil Procedure and the Local Rules of this Court. Plaintiff is warned that the failure to comply with these requirements and obligations can have significant consequences. For example, failure to respond to discovery requests as described in the rules may result in sanctions. *See* Fed. R. Civ. P. 37. In addition, failure to conduct a timely Case Management Conference and submit a

Case Management Report can result in dismissal of this case for lack of prosecution.
See M.D. Fla. R. 3.05 & 3.10.

While the Court has set forth some of the more prominent procedural

obligations and requirements of litigants in this Court, this Order does not

purport to set forth all of those requirements and should not be relied upon

as limiting Plaintiff's duties

and obligations in litigating this case. Upon consideration of the foregoing, it

is hereby ORDERED: Plaintiff shall review and comply with the provisions of this Order, as

well as the Federal Rules of Civil Procedure, the Local Rules of the Middle

District of Florida, and any applicable statutes and regulations.

2. The Clerk of Court is directed to send Plaintiff a copy of the "Step by Step Guide to Filing a Civil Action in the United States District Court, Middle District of Florida, Jacksonville Division."

DONE AND ORDERED at Jacksonville, Florida, on June 20, 2012.

Copies to:
Pro Se Party   United States Magistrate Judge

**UNITED STATES DISTRICT COURT
MIDDLE DISTRICT OF FLORIDA
JACKSONVILLE DIVISION**

JAMES L. WATSON, SR.,

                  Plaintiff,

vs.   Case No. 3:12-cv-552-J-99MMH-JBT

EQUIFAX, EXPERIAN, and TRANSUNION,

                  Defendants.

_____

O R D E R STRIKING DEFENDANT's EVIDENCE

This cause is before the Court on Defendant Trans Union's Objections to Plaintiff's Summary Judgment Evidence and Response in Opposition to Plaintiff's Motion for Summary Judgment (Dkt. No. 159; Objection) filed on September 3, 2013. In the Objection, Defendant Trans Union appears to respond to Plaintiff's Motion for Summary Judgment, but also, in part, addresses the evidence Plaintiff presented in the Plaintiff's response to Defendants Motions for Summary Judgment. <u>See</u>

Dkt. No. 152. To the extent that the Objection Addresses Plaintiff's response to

 Defendants Motions for Summary Judgment it is an improper reply and is due

to be stricken. Accordingly, it is

ORDERED:

Defendant Trans Union's Objections to Plaintiff's Summary Judgment Evidence and Response in Opposition to Plaintiff's Motion for Summary Judgment (Dkt. No. 159) is **STRICKEN** to the extent that it addresses Plaintiff's Motion for Summary Judgment evidence presented in Plaintiff's response to Defendants Motions for Summary Judgment (Dkt. No. 152). The Defendant Trans Union shall have up to and including **September 23, 2013**, to file a response to Plaintiff's Supplemental Motion for Summary Judgment (Dkt. No. 154) which does not separately address issues raised only in Plaintiff's response to Defendants Motions for Summary Judgment.

DONE AND ORDERED at Jacksonville, Florida, this 9th day of September, 2013

UNITED STATES DISTRICT COURT
MIDDLEDISTRICTOFFLORIDA
JACKSONVILLE DIVISION

James Watson
        Plaintiff

        V.   Case No. 3:12-cv-552-J-99MMH-JBT

JURY TRIAL DEMANDED

Equifax, Experian and Transunion
        Defendants

COURT HEARJNG ARGUMENTS AND DOCUMENTARY PROOF

10-29-12

The main reason we are here today is because Equifax fail to have Plaintiff credit file online at

the financial institution as required by FCRA Act when Plaintiff applied for a loan at those

commercial financial institutions, after repeatedly being told over two weeks' period by Plaintiff

that the financial could not retrieved his credit report for a loan he was applying   for.

Most importantly Plaintiff would like to stress the importance that this not a hearing to admonish

or humiliated Equifax with their behavior but to have the Court and God correct or modify their

behavior so this case can move forward to a speedy resolution. My God is a just God of love not

hate. Plaintiff is not stating he is a perfect person, Mr. Olson reminds Plaintiff that is English is

not the best we all have weaknesses but Plaintiff has written and self-published two books, as I

have said we all have our weakness and we all have a past. Pastor Trey Brunson says, "Bitterness

is a choice to respond negatively to a negative wounded situation in your life. "My God is a God

of love and teaches us to love not to hate. Someone once said, "what a person does for himself he

takes to his grave, but what he does for others becomes immortal forever.

The first ti.me Mr. Brian and Plaintiff got into a verbal altercation is when Mr. Brian called me and started casual talking about the case and then mention to me that the Judge is going to dismissing this case so I should go ahead and accept his offer of deleting all the Negative accounts from my file if I would send him a dismissal letter. I told him I would consider it, I had the letter all type up and ready when Mr. Brian said something oddly and my instinct kick in and said you should not send the letter until he sends you one which states he will deleted all those negative accounts. Exhibit (1). When I spoke to Mr. Olson again I told him I like to have   the account deleted but would like to have a letter from him first saying Equifax would delete the negative accounts. I never got that letter from Equifax or Mr. Olson.

I thank God for listening to that little voice inside that Mr. Brian would say one thing and does another thing, e.g. Plaintiff sent Mr. Brian five disputed accounts that Equifax failed to provide Plaintiff a written answer within 30 days from the disputed date, in violation of FCRA 621(i) Mr. Brian initially stated to Plaintiff he did not received the disputed letter but then when Plaintiff told Mr. Brian that the post office verified that the letter was received on 7-18-12 by someone at Equifax he changed his story and said yes I received it. Exhibit (2)

You Honor, in fact the reason why Plaintiff applied for the loans at credit union, Fifth Third Bank, one two One credit Union, and Community credit Union in the first place is because Mr. Olson assured Plaintiff on a call from Mr. Brian Olson dated Oct. 5, 2012 at 3:02 PM asking me who I wanted to be the mediator on the CMC to be submitted to the Court, I inform Mr. Olson that the mediator Defendants selected would be ok with me. Plaintiff then went on to ask Mr. Olson did he have any results from the disputes Plaintiff had submitted to him in Sept. 18, 2012. Mr. Olson proceeded to say yes. Equifax had deleted all of Plaintiff's, "negative accounts or those accounts Plaintiff had disputed to Equifax back in July 14,2012, is it a coincident that

"This conversation with Mr. Olson happened just before Plaintiff turn in his Amended Complaint to the Court on Oct. 9, 2012.

My girlfriend the other day on or about 10-24-12 said after me and Mr. Olson got finished talking that because of our friendly conversation with each, ask me who was that I was talking to I said Mr. Olson from Equifax. She said the way you to where talking to him I thought you were talking to someone you had known for a long time. I sometimes believe Mr. Olson do not distinguish between business talk from cordial friendly talking and forget what the Plaintiff is saying to him. I don't think he knows how to separate the two or is suffering from ADD (attention deficit disorder). Plaintiff has repeatedly asked for score but to this day still has not received a score from Mr. Olson in which Plaintiff knows he has to pay for it under the FCRA Act, as he has done with the other two CRAs.

Under the FCRA Act if a Consumer dispute an account and that dispute is not reported back to the consumer within 30 of days as stated by 611, [15 U.S.C. § 168li](a)(l)(A) of the FCRA, and the CRAs have to provide the consumer with written results concerning the reason for the dispute from the consumer or the CRAs deem the dispute frivolous has to within 5 days as stated   by FCRA 623(F)(ii) notice of determination, that person shall notify the consumer of such determination not later than 5 days after making such determination , by mail or if authorized by the consumer for the purpose, by any other means available to the person.

The fact of the matter all three CRAs has violated all 612, 623 provisions under the FCRA Act. On Thursday at 10:48 AM while talking to Mr. Olson he mentioned to Plaintiff that he did not want Plaintiff taking up his time with these disputes, Plaintiff said to Mr. Olson that he is the gatekeeper for Equifax and that if he does not want to accept my disputes he can ask Equifax to assigned someone else to do it and Plaintiff would gladly talk to them instead. Mr. Olson should consider that Plaintiff is tired of the CRA's negligently making violations like not having Plaintiff

credit file online for financial institution to evaluated Plaintiff credit worthiness as stated by FCRA.

What do they want Plaintiff to do bring a law sue for every violation at the rate of the violations

being made by these CRAs we be in Court for ten years, which in Plaintiff opinion would be a

waste of judicial resources and tax payers money?

The fact that Mr. Olson would say such a thing is a form of waiver of the Equifax FCRA rights and

automatic triggers default Judgment by Equifax and Plaintiff is entitle to default Judgment of

$125,000 dollars as a matter of law., e.g. once a nurse refuse to provide nursing care to a patient

the law said it is considered abandonment and he/she can be sued or lose their license, Plaintiff do

not want that to happen to Mr. Olson but to remind him of his obligations under FCRA as an

attorney, representative the law and Equifax, we all are responsible for our action.

Today is the day for the Defendants to mediate a settlement for money damages in this case and

for the Defendant Equifax presents a fair righteous, and just settlement amount today as it relates

to the issues of harm and wrong done to Plaintiff, concerning Equifax liability and damages to

Plaintiff. In closing we are all responsible for our negative actions and consequences

of those negative actions.

Plaintiff is requesting a Jury trial on disputed facts on the issues of negligence and

Defamation in this action.

If Mr. Olson would now and then take a more concentrated approach and to consider that

his decisions are affecting consumers' lives in a profound way.

In closing, no matter what the outcome of this case, my God has given me a different path to travel

and a new direction to take in life now. For I realize I have only so many nights to sleep and so

many days to open my eyes. End this case today with Justice, Righteousness and fairness for the

sake of all parties involved. Plaintiff certifies that all statements are true to best of his knowledge

and that all parties are served on this date Oct. 29, 2012.

IN THE UNITED STATES DISTRICT COURT
MIDDLE DISTRICT OFFLORIDA

James Watson

Plaintiff

V.   **Case No. 3:12-cv-SS2-J-99MMH-JBT Defendants**

Equifax, Experian, Transunion

PLAINTIFF COUNTERAFFIDAVITCONTROVERTING

ALL THREE DEFENDANTS AFFIDAVITS ATTACHED

TO PLAINTIFF REPLY

For good cause and in keeping with Plaintiff seeking truth and Justice of and from this Court Plaintiff is requesting that the Court Controverting.

1. all documents and statements of these defendants which has no relevancy to this case and the issues at hand in their Summary Judgment against Plaintiff e.g. Trans Union allegation of provocation of trying to not have statement made by these defendants as not admissible evidence and attempting to have Plaintiff affidavit dismiss in this MSJ.

2. Experian and Equifax committing fraud on the Court by stating Plaintiff did not take a deposition on Mar. 19, 2013, the Court has in its possession exhibit#1 for Experian and Equifax; exhibit (EE) for Plaintiff

3. The reason Plaintiff is requesting the Court to controvert Equifax MSJ is because of a false statement in Equifax answers Defenses section page 2#5, exhibit# P, Plaintiff affirms to the fact that he did indeed sent a letter to Equifax on 6-6-11 and it was delivered on 6-8-11 at 10:39 AM as confirmed by the U.S. Postal Service to Equifax. Plaintiff is admitting exhibit# P to this Court as proof and Prima facie Evidence in this action at hand.

4. All other false facts, documents, and statements that these defendants made in their Motion for Summary Judgment that is false toward Plaintiff should be controverted or denied, such those stated above.

5. Overrule Trans Union sustain objection to Plaintiff Motion for Summary Judgment Affidavit and Response Affidavit base the rule o fevidence of relevance.

6. Deny or Controvert Trans Union objections to statements made by employees and lawyers employed by Equifax, Trans Union, and Experian CRA's as inadmissible hearsay but rule that those statements should be admissible non-hearsay base on Business documents and statement made with business relevance as it relates to issues in the case.

7. Claims are not preempted as Defendants are stating and asserts under Florida Law.

Date

Notary   Date

James Leon Watson Sr.
2970 Tall PineLane #8
Jacksonville, FL 32277

CERTIFICATE OF SERVICE

Plaintiff hereby certify that a true and correct copy under penalty of perjury the foregoing was either

email, facsimile, or mailed this ....LL day of Sept, 2013.

A SAMPLE INDEX DEPOSITION PAGE

1   I N D E X

2

WITNESS   PAGE

4   JAMES WATSON

7

8

9   E X H I B I T S

10

11   NUMBER   DESCRIPTION   PAGE

12

25   Exhibit 11, Defendant Trans Union's First Set **98 page 3**
        of Interrogatories,

NEVER WAIVE YOUR RIGHTS TO MAKE CORRECTIONS TO YOUR
DEPOSITION OR TO RECEIVE A COPY OF YOUR DEPOSITION.

EXHIBIT S
(Continued)

3/14/13 Credit Report,   236

1. E X H I B I T S

(Continued)

UNITED STATES DISTRICT COURT
MIDDLE DISTRICT OF FLORIDA
JACKSONVILLE D1VISION

Plaintiff,

vs.

JAMES WATSON,

Defendants

STIIPULATION FOR ORDER DISMISSING MAIN CLAIM WITH
PREJUDICE AND COUNTERCLAIM WITH PREJUDICE

COME NOW the Plaintiff, by and through its undersigned attorney, and the Defendant. JAMES WATSON. and stipulate as follows:

l. On or about July 31, 2013, Plaintiff filed a Complaint for money damages based on Defendant's failure to make payments pursuant to the terms of debt instrument now owned by, and in the possession of, Plaintiff. Suit was filed in the Court Judicial Court in and for Duval, County, Florida.

2.	On or about August 27, 2013, Defendant removed said action to this Court and filed an

Answer, Affirmative Defenses and Counterclaim.

3.	Plaintiff and Defendant have resolved all matters in controversy and request that the Court enter an Order dismissing the main claim with prejudice and the counterclaim with prejudice. with each party bearing their own costs and attorney's fees. The parties also agree to execute a Mutual Release.

4.	The parties agree to the entry of the Order attached hereto.

5.	Defendant acknowledges that he has freely and voluntarily entered into this Stipulation and has not been coerced or unduly influenced to do so.

DATED this 		day of 			,2013

387

EXAMPLE OF COURT'S DOCKETS

BELOW

06/19/2012	26	MOTION for clarification re 20 Order on motion to dismiss, Order on motion for leave to file, Order on motion to strike by James L. Watson, Sr. (MK) (Entered: 06/19/2012)
06/19/2012	27	
06/19/2012	28	SUMMARY JUDGMENT NOTICE re 27 MOTION for summary judgment (MK)(Entered:06/19/2012)
06/20/2012	29	ORDER striking Plaintiff's affidavit, denying as moot 22 Motion to quash, and granting 26 Motion for clarification to the extent stated in the attached Order. Signed by Magistrate Judge Joel B. Toomey on 6/20/2012. (JRW) (Entered: 06/20/2012)
06/20/2012	30	ORDER informing pro se Plaintiff of some procedural rules. The Clerk is directed to send Plaintiff a copy of the Step by Step Guide. Signed by Magistrate Judge Joel B. Toomey on 6/20/2012. (JRW) (Entered: 06/20/2012)
06/22/2012	31	Joint MOTION to extend time to Respond to Plaintiff's Motion for Summary Judgment by Equifax, Experian, Trans Union. (Tierney, Thomas) Motions referred to Magistrate Judge Joel B. Toomey. (Entered: 06/22/2012)
06/22/2012	32	DEFENDANT'S BRIEF re 11 Joint MOTION to extend time to Respond to Plaintiff's Motion for Summary Judgment filed by Equifax, Experian, Trans Union. (Attachments: # Text of Proposed Order) (Tierney, Thomas) Modified on 6/25/2012 notified counsel re: Jacksonville Div. (AMM). (Entered: 06/22/2012)
06/22/2012	33	RESPONSE in opposition re 22 Unopposed MOTION to quash Plaintiffs Request for Disclosure of Credit Accounts by Telephone [Docket No. 18] filed by James L. Watson, Sr. (AMM) (Entered: 06/25/2012)
06/22/2012	34	Plaintiff AFFIDAVIT by James L. Watson, Sr. (AMM) (Entered: 06/25/2012)
06/25/2012	35	Joint MOTION to dismiss Plaintiff's Amended Complaint by Experian, Trans Union. (Tierney, Thomas) Modified on 6/26/2012 notified counsel re: correct case number(AMM). (Entered: 06/25/2012)
06/25	36	MEMORANDUM in support re 35 Motion to dismiss *Plaintiff's Amended Complaint* filed by Experian, Trans Union. (Tierney, Thomas) (Entered: 06/25/20 12)
06/25/2012	37	MOTION to grant ECF filing by James L. Watson, Sr. (AMM) (Entered: 06/26/2012)

MY CASE GENERATED 164 DOCKETS IN ALMOST A TWO YEAR PERIOD.
IMAGINE IF EACH ONE WHERE 10 PAGES EACH, IT WOULD BE ALMOST 1700 PAGES, THE COST WOULD BE EXPENSIVE JUST TO COPY 50 DOCKETS.

KING & SPALDING

June 21, 2013

VIA USMAIL

James Watson 2970 Tall Pine Lane #8

 Jacksonville, FL 3227

King&Spalding LLP

1180 Peachtree Street N.E.

Atlanta, GA 30309-3521

Brian J. Olson

Re: James Watson v. Equifax Information Services LLC, *et al.,* Case No. 12-cv-00552-UAMH-JBT

Dear James:

Enclosed please find Defendant Equifax Information Services LLC's Answer in the above captioned action. If you have any questions, please give me a call.

Sincerely,

BRIAN J. Olson

Enclosure

UNITED STATES DISTRICT COURT
MIDDLE DISTRICT OF FLORIDA
JACKSONVILLE DIVISION

JAMES WATSON,

Plaintiff,

V.

EQUIFAX, EXPERIAN, TRANS UNION
Defendants.

DEFENDANT EQUIFAX INFORMATION SERVICES LLC'S ANSWERS AND DEFENSES TO PLAINTIFF'S SECOND AMENDED COMPLAINT

Defendant Equifax Information Services LLC ("Equifax") by Counsel, hereby files its answers and defenses to Plaintiffs Second Amended Complaint ("Complaint").

ANSWER

In answering the Complaint, Equifax states that it is responding to allegations on behalf of itself only, even where the allegations pertain to alleged conduct by all Defendants. Equifax denies any and all allegations contained in the headings and/or unnumbered paragraphs in the Complaint. In response to the specific allegations in the enumerated paragraphs in the Complaint, Equifax responds as follows:

Unnumbered Paragraph I. Equifax admits the allegations contained in Unnumbered Paragraph I.

Unnumbered Paragraph 2. Equifax admits that Plaintiff purports to bring this Complaint for damages for alleged violations of the FCRA, but denies that it has

violated the FCRA, or any law in its handling of Plaintiffs credit files.

Unnumbered Paragraph 3. Equifax is without knowledge or information sufficient to form a belief as to the truth of the allegations contained in Unnumbered Paragraph 3 and, therefore, denies them.

Unnumbered Paragraph 4. Equifax is without knowledge or information sufficient to form a belief as to the truth of the allegations contained in Unnumbered Paragraph 4 and, therefore, denies them.

Unnumbered Paragraph 5.   Equifax denies the allegations contained in Unnumbered Paragraph 5 as they pertain to Equifax. Equifax is without knowledge or information sufficient to form a belief as to the truth of the remaining allegations contained in Unnumbered

Paragraph 5.

1.   Equifax is without knowledge or information sufficient to form a belief as to the truth of the allegations contained in Paragraph I and, therefore, denies them.

3.   Equifax is without knowledge or information sufficient to form a belief as to the truth of the allegations contained in Paragraph 3 and, therefore, denies them. Equifax denies the allegations contained in Paragraph as they pertain to Equifax. Equifax is without knowledge or information sufficient to form a belief as to the truth of the remain in allegations contained in Paragraph 4.

2.   Equifax denies the allegations contained in Unnumbered Paragraph 2 as they

pertain to Equifax. Equifax is without knowledge or information sufficient to form a belief as

to the truth of the remaining allegations contained in Paragraph 2.

5.   Responding to the allegations contained in Paragraph 5, Equifax states that it did

not receive any dispute communications from Plaintiff in June 2011. Equifax is without knowledge or information sufficient to form a belief as to the truth of the

remaining allegations contained in paragraph 5.

6. Equifax denies the allegations contained in Paragraph 6 as they pertain to Equifax. Equifax is without knowledge or information sufficient to form a belief as to the truth of the remaining allegations contained in Paragraph 6.

7. Equifax is without knowledge or information sufficient to form a belief to the truth of the allegations contained in Paragraph 7 and, therefore, denies them.

8. Equifax denies the allegations contained in Paragraph 8.

Equifax denies the allegations contained in Paragraph 9.

10. In response to the allegations in Paragraph 10, Equifax states that the provisions of the FCRA speak for themselves.

11. Equifax denies the allegations contained in Paragraph 11.

12. Equifax denies the allegations contained in Paragraph 12.

13. Equifax is without knowledge or information sufficient to form a belief as to the truth of the allegations contained in Paragraph 13 and, therefore, denies them.

14. Equifax is without knowledge or information sufficient to form a belief as to the truth of the allegations contained in Paragraph 14 and, therefore, denies them.

15. Equifax is without knowledge or information sufficient to form a belief as to the truth of t he allegations contained in Paragraph 15 and, therefore, denies them.

16. Equifax is without knowledge or information sufficient to form a belief as to the truth of the allegations contained in Paragraph 16.

17. Equifax is without knowledge or information sufficient to form a belief as to the truth of the allegations contained in Paragraph 17 and, therefore, denies them.

18.   Equifax is without knowledge or information sufficient to form a belief as to the truth of the allegations contained in Paragraph 18 and, therefore, denies them.

19.   Equifax is without knowledge or information sufficient to form a belief as to the truth ofthe allegations contained in Paragraph 19 and, therefore, denies them.

20.   Equifax denies the allegations contained in Paragraph 20 as they pertain to Equifax. Equifax is without knowledge or information sufficient to form a belief as to the truth of the remaining allegations contained in Paragraph 20.

Trans Union Defamation

Unnumbered Paragraph 6. Equifax is without knowledge or information sufficient to form a belief as to the truth of the allegations contained in Unnumbered Paragraph 6 and, therefore, denies them.

Unnumbered Paragraph 7. Equifax is without knowledge or information sufficient to form a belief as to the truth of the allegations contained in Unnumbered Paragraph 7 and, therefore, denies them.

Unnumbered Paragraph 8. Equifax is without knowledge or information sufficient to form a belief as to the truth of the allegations contained in unnumbered Paragraph 8 and, therefore, denies them.

Experian Defamation

Unnumbered Paragraph 9. Equifax is without knowledge or information sufficient to form a belief as to the truth of the allegations contained in Unnumbered Paragraph 9 and, therefore, denies them.

Unnumbered Paragraph J 0. Equifax is without knowledge or information sufficient to form a belief as to the truth of the allegations contained in Unnumbered Paragraph 10 and, therefore, denies them.

Unnumbered Paragraph 11. Equifax is without knowledge or information sufficient to form a belief as to the truth of the allegations contained in Unnumbered Paragraph 11 and, therefore, denies them.

Unnumbered Paragraph 12. Equifax is without knowledge or information sufficient to form a belief as to the truth of the allegations contained in Unnumbered Paragraph 12 and, therefore, denies them.

Unnumbered Paragraph 13. Equifax is without knowledge or information sufficient to form a belief as to the truth of the allegations contained in Unnumbered Paragraph 13 and, therefore, denies them.

9 (second). Equifax denies the allegations contained in Paragraph 9 (second) as they pertain to Equifax. Equifax is without knowledge or information sufficient to form a belief as to the truth of the remaining allegations contained in Paragraph 9(second).

There are no paragraphs between 9 (second) and 12 (second).

12(second). Equifax denies the allegations contained in Paragraph 12 (second) as they pertain to Equifax. Equifax is without knowledge or information sufficient to form a belief as to the truth of the remaining allegations contained in Paragraph 12(second).

13(second). Equifax denies the allegations contained in Paragraph 13 (second), including subparts, as they pertain to Equifax. Equifax is without knowledge or information sufficient to form a belief as to the truth of the remaining allegations contained in Paragraph 13 (second).

DEFENSES

Without assuming the burden of *proof* where it otherwise rests with the Plaintiff, Equifax pleads the following defenses to Plaintiff's complaint:

FIRSTDEFENSE

Equifax asserts that Plaintiffs Complaint fails to state a claim against Equifax upon which relief can be granted.

SECOND DEFENSE

At all times relevant herein, Equifax maintained reasonable procedures in its handling of Plaintiffs consume credit file.

THIRD DEFENSE

Equifax has acted in good faith and without malice or intent to injure Plaintiff.

FIFTH DEFENSE

Equifax has complied with the provisions of the Fair Credit Reporting Act, 15 U.S.C. § 1681 *et seq.*, in its handling of Plaintiffs credit file.

SIXTH DEFENSE

Plaintiff's complaint seeks the imposition of punitive damages. Equifax adopts by reference the defenses, criteria, limitations, standards and constitutional protections mandated or provided by the United States Supreme Court in the following cases: BMW v. Gore, 517 U.S. 559 (1996); Cooper Indus, Inc. v.

Leatherman Tool Group, Inc., 532 U.S. 923 (2001) and State

Fann v. Cam2bell, 538 U.S. 408 (20

SEVENTH DEFENSE

Plaintiff's damages, if any, were not caused by Equifax; but rather, they were

caused by another person or entity for whom or for which Equifax is not responsible.

EIGHTH DEFENSE

As defense, Equifax asserts that some or all of plaintiff's claims are barred
by

qualified immunity.

NINTH DEFENSE

Some or all of Plaintiff's claims are pre-empted by the Fair Credit Reporting Act,
15

U.S.C. § 168lh(e).

TENTH DEFENSE

Plaintiff's claims are barred, in whole or in part, by the applicable statute of limitations.

Equifax reserves the right to have additional defenses that it learns of through the course of discovery.

WHEREFORE, having fully answered or otherwise responded to the allegations contained in Plaintiffs Complaint, Equifax prays that:

(1) Plaintiffs Complaint be dismissed in its entirety and with prejudice, with all costs taxed against Plaintiff

(2)   That Equifax have a trial by jury on all issues so triable;

(3)   That Equifax be dismissed as a party to this action;

(4)   That this lawsuit be deemed frivolous and Equifax recover from plaintiff its expenses of litigation, including but not limited to attorneys' fees pursuant to J 5 U.S.C. § 1681n(c) and 15 U.S.C. § 1681o(b); and

UNITED STATES DISTRICTCOURT
MIDDLE DISTRICT OF FLORIDA
JACKSONVILLEDIVISION

James Watson

Plaintiff

V.   Case No. 3:12-cv-552-J-99MMH-JBT

JURY TRIAL DEMANDED

Equifax, Experian

and Trans union

Defendants

Plaintiff Authentication of evidence

IN

Support of Plaintiff Summary Judgment

This CAUSE BEFORE THE COURT, by and through undersigned Pro Se James

Watson, and pursuant to Rule 56(C) summary judgment, Federal Rules of Civil Procedure,

Plaintiff moves for the entry of an Order granting summary judgment *in* his favor and against

Defendants, Equifax information Services, LLC ("Equifax"), Experian information Solutions,

Inc. ("Experian"), and Trans Union LLC ("Trans Union") and bring claims of negligent non-

compliance and common law defamation as stated by this Court, Doc. 124, under federal Fair

Credit Reporting Act, 15U.S.C.§§1681-1681x.

COME NOW Plaintiff files this motion in support of his Summary Judgment and submission of evidence to this Court to respectfully rule and grant Summary Judgment in Plaintiff favor.

About two weeks later the wife sent me a thank you card, sometimes in life it is not how much money you make for the work you do or the service you render to others but the "Thank You" received. The party seeking summary judgment bears "the initial burden to show the district court, by reference to materials on file, that there are no genuine issues of material fact that should be decided at trial." *Clark v. Coats & Clark, Inc.* 929

F.2d 604, 608 (11th Cir.1991). In deciding a motion for summary judgment, the Court must determine whether "the pleadings, depositions, answers to interrogatories, and admissions on file, together with the affidavits, if any, show there is no genuine issue as to any material fact and that the moving party is entitled to judgment as a matter of law." Fed. Rule. Civ. P.56(c); *Celotex Corp. v. Catrett,* 477 U.S. 317, 322. 106 S.Ct. 2548, 91 L.Ed.2d 265 (1986).

I.   CASE **PROCEDURAL**

I. On August 19, 20 13 Plaintiff file his refilling Supplementary Motion for Summary Judgment, as order by this Court to be filed on or before Aug 19, 20 13 during Dispositive and Daubert ("Plaintiff Motion for Summary Judgment") which included Plaintiff Affidavit as it Relates to Plaintiff Supplementary Motion for Summary Judgment, against these three Defendants, ("Plaintiff Summary Judgment Affidavit") with attached exhibits.

2. On August 29, 2013 Trans Union filed its unopposed Motion for leaved to file combined reply in Support of Motion for Summary Judgment, and opposition to Plaintiff S Motion for Summary Judgment. On Sept 3, 2013 Trans Union filed its Response in opposition.

Plaintiff s Motion for Summary Judgment and objection to Plaintiff S Summary

Judgment Evidence.

3. On Sept 10, 2013 Trans Union Response and Objections were struck down by this

Court, and Trans Union had until Sept 23, 2013 to refilled its Response Doc. 168 and

prior to

filing Doc. # 168Trans Union filed Doc. #166, 167 all on 9120/13 objection to Plaintiff

evidence.

II.   PERSUASIVE ARGUMENT

4. Plaintiff affirmative and conclusive evidence exhibits (J) and (p) renders

Equifax with no more defenses to argue i n this Court with exhibit (J)proving that

these defendants and Equifax committed the duplications of Plaintiff s creditors on

or about

June 20 11on Plaintiff credit report which makes them guilty of negligent of

violating 1681 (e) b of the FCRA Act, a Statement of Material F a c t .

5. Experian Rep misrepresented the facts when their employees Teresa Iwanski

made a false declaration as to the duplication of Plaintiff creditor accounts

Doc. 143-12.

Experian Senior legal compliance specialist in inadvertently confess to the

deletion of the wrong ____account of Plaintiffs of Plaintiff consumer

credit report. This false declaration has been reported to Ms. McAneny on or

about 19th of Sept 2013. As evident from the two Redacted account as present to the Court these two Redacted accounts have two different amount

owed, different first report and different date of status.

The Redacted account that was duplicated is located on exhibit G) was The

_____with address ID # 0061663385 as stated on Experian documents

submitted to the Court along with Doc. 143-1 1 and Experian Watson 0117 see

Doc. Exhibit (J).

6. Furthermore, the evidence received from _____ exhibit (i) which

    shows Plaintiff omitted accounts omitted on this credit report from a third

    part _____ provided through _____ date 1 1/281201 1, this undisputed evidence

    shows Experian injured negligent act of 168 l (e)b of the FCRA Act.

7. Most important as to the defendant Equifax the misrepresentation of the fact of

    Equifax explicitly denying to the Court that Equifax (p) in their Answers and

    Defenses, Doc. 133 where Plaintiff has presented enormous amount of

    relevant, material, and competence evidence in Plaintiff exhibits e.g.

    Experian erroneous declaration. Trans Union credit monitoring membership service
    credit report exhibit (a)

(d) E) (t) (r) (z) (AA) (dd) (ff) (gg) (jj) (kk), Plaintiff Experian exhibit (i) (v) (x) (bb)

(Q). Equifax exhibit (c)(b) (i) (v) (p) U), and others not mention herein.

8. All of the above exhibits either shows the duplication of plaintiff c r e d i t

    accounts or are relevant evidence to explicitly proves duplications of plaintiff

    Creditors' accounts, done by these Defend ants.

9. The various unreasonable procedures these three defendants had in place on

June 2011whetherit is operative errors such what happen in plaintiff exhibit(AA) from

Trans Union, computer data as in the duplication of plaintiffcred it Accounts, cross-checking

of personal Identification such as social security or two of same accounts with same account

numbers on Plaintiff consumer credit report are factual issues regarding the unreasonable

procedure that cause Plaintiff creditors accounts to be

duplication in his consumer credit report file for example the recent citing a

recent case miller v. Equifax.

10. Courts have held that the issue of reasonable procedures

under 1681e (b) is a Jury Question. In the overwhelming

majority of case se e.g. Dalton v. Capital Assoc. Indas

lnc. 257 F.3d 409, (416 4th Cir. 2001) (citation

omitted)

Plaintiff moves for Summary Judgment with respect

to his claim under section 168 1 n, 168lh(e), and

16810.

11. 1681n which provides for recovery for willful violation of

FCRA. A willful Violation occurs in the event that a

defendant... knowingly committed an act in conscious

disregard for the rights of other, this is exactly what plaintiff

is Claiming these defendants committed, by denying they

did not duplicate Plaintiff credit accounts.

12. This wrongful act happened in this case when these defendants

made knowingly false Statement e.g. when Trans Union rep

stated, "He only saw one account for each Creditor when in fact

there were two, accounts and when Mr. Lewis and Mr. Tom

Tierney Said, "These things happens sometimes" this statement by

these two people of Experian is a direct disregard for the rights of

others, especially Plaintiff.

13. Exhibit (R) is relevant, material and competent. The

Plaintiff credit report monitoring membership letter sent

to Plaintiff as requested in the ordinary

Course of business by Trans Union and is relevant to the issue is material and

Competent to the cause of action in this case, is admissible under the business

Record exception.

14. The foundation for Exhibit (r) was laid by Trans Union when they stated they had

presented all the affirmative and conclusive evidence to prove their case although

these defendants present evidence dated May 20 2011, they failed and refused to admit this

crucial evidence dated May 26, 2011 in the correct format of Plaintiff creditor accounts because they knew it would weaken their case and prove that duplication took place. Evid. code 210, Fed. Rule Evid. 410, and Evid. code 700, Fed rule. Evid 601, 901 902 and any other applicable Fed. Rule. Evid.

Authentication

15. Evid. Code 1400, Fed Rule Evid 901, 902, 802, 803, 8 0 1

Evidence **irrelevant** when it has atendency in reason to make the facts that is offered to proveor disprove either more or less probable.

Plaintiff proves that Trans Union sent May 26, 201 1 credit monitoring report Plaintiff request by plaintiff because it has Trans Union letterhead and address to plaintiff with his name address exhibit (R).

Evidence Type

16. Relevant- Evid. Code 210, Fed. Rule Evid 401

A. Material- Evid code 210, Fed. Rule evid 410

B. Competent- Evid code 402, 403 and Evid code 700, Fed Rule Evid 601

C. Evidence is material it is offered to prove a fact that is at issue in the case.

The issues in the case are determined by the pleading, any formal stipulation or admission and the applicable law.

While the defendants continue to state that Plaintiff Complaint consist of conclusory speculative allegation but what these defendants are forgetting to mention is that Plaintiff " conclusory allegations are supportive with truthful facts.

When there are well pleaded factual allegations a Court should 1. Assume their veracity

2. Then determine whether they plausibly give rise to an entitlement to relief...

Relief for Plaintiff MSJ to be granted in his favor).

WHY PLAINTIFF EVIDENCE SHOULD BE ACCEPTED

17. Plaintiff Response Affidavit: Plaintiff stated in the beginning

paragraph of his Affidavit that he "Affirms that all statements and

document attach to this Summary Judgment are true to best of his

knowledge ."

Affirm means as a synonym to swear, and when you swear to

something you take an oath which is the same as taking an oath

declared under penalty of perjury. In Addition to having an affidavit

Notarized as to the truth of something being Said or something that is

what is attested to be what it is supposed to be. Notwithstanding,

Plaintiff certified all exhibits and documents in *is* certifying Statement

at the end of his summary before signing it.

18. Most importantly the Court said plaintiff to make sure the affidavit is attached

To his motion for Summary Judgment brief which makes if inclusive and

certified? It is admissible because of its Relevance, Material, and competent

to the issues

Of the cause of action or lawsuit under the provisions of l681(e) b, 168lo,

1681n, 168lh (e) of FCRA Act.

19. Exhibit (R) is admissible under the chain of Custody document as a document

Received from

Trans Union credit monitoring service credit report sent to

Plaintiff from Trans Union in or about the last part of May 2011.

It is unique because it is totally different from the other Trans Union credit

Monitoring service report sent to Plaintiff from June to Aug 2011.

This document exhibit (R) is admissible because it is relevant, Material, and

Competent to the issues at hand rebut that Trans Union failed to present   all

Of the evidence in this case as they stated by Trans Union, "Trans Union affirmatively

and conclusively have presented all the evidence in this case to prove we should be

Granted Summary Judgment." Controverted by Plaintiff.

The statement in exhibit (R) of Plaintiff Trans Union credit monitoring service

Consumer credit report dated May 26 2011 is not hearsay but nonhearsy because

Trans Union failure to produce this Exhibit (R) to this Court.

Beside Trans Union claiming that Plaintiff had not submitted any evidence that

Would disprove that Trans Union credit monitoring service is not part of

Plaintiff consumer credit report, exhibit (R) proves otherwise that it is part of

Plaintiff consumer credit report because of the consumer credit report sent to

Plaintiff by Trans Union credit Monitoring service.

Trans Union failure to admit exhibit (r) proves to this Court the importance of this

evidence and should be Admissible because of its Relevant, Material and Competence

to one of the issues in this case.

20. Exhibit (Z) is admissible because it is Relevant, Material, and Competent.

It is authenticated from Trans Union by continuous claiming and refusing to Admit that Trans

Union did not provide Plaintiff credit report to 3rd parties Such as Lenders, Furnishers

and Public utilities companies, etc.

Trans Union bas no merit and opposition to the admission of Plaintiff

is unfounded because Plaintiff Statement in his SAC on p. 14 FN, "All documents and

exhibits submitted to sic Court and Defendants attorneys in prior motions and submissions

are to apply to This SAC in this claim," as well as what was said and Admitted in his

1st Summary Judgment dated June 19, 2012, p.3, paragraph 11.

21.   Number Paragraph 3 is admissible because of its Relevance, Material, and

Competent under Fed. Rule. Of Evid, and under the FCRA Act. Its no hearsay

Because the foundation was laid upon disagreement of ____

Service account of Plaintiff s, which claims he didn't dispute this account with

Trans Union Attorney Mrs. Reddoch because it already had a paid in full status. It is

Admissible under the business record exception.

22. Number 5 is admissible under the Relevant, Material, and Competent as well

as Admissible under the business Record exception; Present sense

impression and Declaration of state of Mind Fed.Rule. Evid 901, 902 401,

402, 403.

23.   Number 6 as stated above in number 5 plus, the foundation is based

on The FCRA Act and provision 1681(e) b and the right to dispute invalid

Inaccurate, incomplete, and invalid, creditors accounts errors on a

consumer Credit reports.

Admissible as business record exception, the foundation was laid when

Trans Union stated it was an internal document. Authenticated as chain of

custody Under the Fed.Rule. Evid from Trans Union to the law firm

strasburger and

Attorney Reddoch during g. Discovery sending this document as part of discovery

see Case law Miller v. Equifax where Ms. Miller brought suit against Equifax for

Inaccurately reporting her SSN #, Date of birth, see case Miller v. Equifax

24. Document # Number 11 exhibit (R) is Relevant, Material and

Competent to this Case due to the fact Trans Union refuse or

failed to produce to this Court Because they realized it would

prove there where duplication on Plaintiff Credit report. It is

as admissible under the business record exception.

Authenticated by the established chain of custody from Mrs. Reddoch

attorney Representing Trans Union then sending it to Plaintiff during

Discovery. Admissible under the Fed. Rule. Evid of Relevant,

Material, Competent, it is Nonhearsay under the Present sense

impression, Declaration of state of Mind. Undisputed Document

Exhibit (R)

25. Document Number # 12 is Relevant, Material, and Competent

Authenticated from exhibit (J) downloaded from Equifax computer monitoring

Membership credit reporting site and is undisputed by Equifax. ALLEGING A

FALSE DECLARATION by Ms. Iwanski FROM EXPERIAN

26. There is one of Plaintiff Accounts _____which is disputed by Plaintiff

Because Experian erroneously deleted the wrong ___Plaintiff

Creditors account.

This declaration from Ms. Iwanski is falsely stated and is disputed

by Plaintiff as to the truth of this declaration.

27. Document Number # 13 is Relevant, Material, and Competent

The FCRA stated that once an account has been deleted it has to be certified and the

Consumer bas to be notified before it can be reinserted on the consumer credit report.

Change by the FCRA act is base and premise on fairness to consumer; if an account

With a paid in full Status and then change to unpaid without written

consent of Plaintiff, then the CRA I as much obligated for the wrongful act

as the furnisher, 1681i.

28. Document Number #14 is Relevant, Material, and Competent

Base on this Court Rule on the Claim adjudicated by this Court in Plaintiff

SAC Complaint from the facts stated by Plaintiff under the provisional laws of FCRA Act. 1681e (b.

29. The Pawnbroker Contract Exhibit (DD) is Relevant, Material, and Competent. It is a One-page part of the actual damage where Plaintiff is requesting from these Defendants which was authenticated many times in conversations with these Defendant's attorneys on the telephone that Plaintiff had to__ his Jewelry to Finance defending his rights under the FCRA Act when these inaccurately Duplicated his creditor accounts on his credit report.

30. Document exhibit (FF) is Relevant, Material, and Competent which is medical Correspondence which shown the stress of something may have behavior change on Plaintiff and manifest anxiety, depression, sadness, feeling of isolation, anger

More than usual does not want to socialize with others, withdrawn.

31. Document Exhibit t (GG) is relevant, Material, and competent, it is authenticated by the chain of Custody under the Fed. Rule Evid. 901, 902.

This is a central Part of Plaintiff proving his case against these defendants for the __ is a lender which denied credit to Plaintiff and that denial in which. Mr.__said that the omission of Plaintiff creditors accounts on Plaintiff

Credit report by Experian was a cause for being denied credit from

____when Plaintiff applied for credit at ___.

It is admissible as a business record exception.

32. Scan Envelopes from Trans (JJ) that are Relevant, Material, and

Competent. Authenticated by Trans Union stating that Plaintiff did not

received those Documents from June 4, 5,9,13,17,18,26, July 16, 20, Aug 2,

8, 201 credit monitor Membership service to show that the duplication took

place from the account being sent to Plaintiff. It has the zip codes of Trans

Union membership monitor service on i t .

Admissible as a business record exception and chain of custody.

33. Document exhibit kk this is a one-page copy of Trans Union copy of

Plaintiff Consumer credit report date 10/412011 with an Inquires from

asset acceptance Dated 6-11- I I during the inaccurate duplications of

plaintiff creditors accounts.

Authenticate from Trans Union affirmative denying they did not report Plaintiff S Credit

Report to any 3rd parties during that time period during June 2011. Fed.Rule.

Evid 901, 902.

34. Exhibit (R) Trans Union Interactive Letter dated May 27 2011 and attached Plaintiff

May 26, 20 11 Consumer credit report.

35. Exhibit (Z) a page from Plaintiff ____ consumer credit report with the

name of a 3rd party creditor _____ given to Plaintiff after he was denied credit. Date

J 1/28/20 1 I. The page affirmatively states, "Results for Trans Union"

36. For the foregoing reason Plaintiff moves for this Honorable Court to overrule

    Tran Union sustain objection to not allow the admissible o f Plaintiff

  evidence. since defendants are in possession of all digital files in a computer age

  There is no dispute that defendants possess all the documents Plaintiff have

  in

  His possession unless allegation of Defendant Purging the file they are in

  Violation of the FTC. Quoting from Plaintiff First Summary Judgment Date June 19, 2012

  Doc.#27.

37. Purport of Plaintiff evidence exhibit (i), (J), R, and (P) substantiated by Prima

    facie evidence exhibit U) which explicitly show a credit report from Equifax

    CRA date June 8, 2011 duplicated credit accounts on Plaintiff credit

    Report.

  In Equifax and Experian MSJ Doc.#158, p.1 these defendants stated "Plaintiff.

  Proceeding Pro Se has completely failed to Marshall. The evidence required for a

  Grant of Summary Judgment in his favor..."Plaintiff digest that it's Defendants Who

  have not produce evidence to repudiated Plaintiff claims and Summary Judgment?

  And this Court should grant Summary in Plaintiff favor, because these

  defendants failure to Marshal enough evidence to overcome Plaintiff claims in

  his Complaints and his SAC and unable to do the same for Plaintiff MSJ because

  of Plaintiff evidence.

38. Equifax and Experian Statement of Material Factual d i s p u t e d

In Doc. #158 p.3 last paragraph these defendants claim they listed 31 as to which no genuine issues exist and those facts are incorporated herein, but These defendants negated to expressly state Equifax denial in Equifax Answers and Defenses p.2 #5 see evidence exhibit (p) and exhibit (i)'. And all documents in this case that Plaintiff has been admitted included that admission as stated

In the deposition, which is the foundation swore under oath of perjury of the

About two weeks later the wife sent me a thank you card, sometimes in life it is not how much money you make for the work you do or the service you render to others but the "Thank You" received. The party seeking summary judgment bears "the initial burden to show the district court, by reference to materials on file, that there are no genuine issues of material fact that should be decided at trial.

" *Clark v. Coats & Clark, Inc.* 929

G. 2d 604, 608 (11th Cir.1991). In deciding a motion for summary judgment, the Court must determine whether "the pleadings, depositions, answers to interrogatories, and admissions on file, together with the affidavits, if any, show there is no genuine issue as to any material fact and that the moving party is entitled to judgment as a matter of law." Fed. Rule. Civ. P.56(c); *Celotex Corp. v. Catrett,* 477 U.S. 317, 322. 106 S.Ct. 2548, 91 L.Ed.2d 265 (1986).

I.   CASE PROCEDURAL STORY

On August 19, 20 13 Plaintiff file his refilling Supplementary Motion for Summary judgment, as order by this Court to be filed on or before Aug 19, 20 13 during Dispositive and Daubert ("Plaintiff Motion for Summary Judgment") which included Plaintiff Affidavit as it Relates to Plaintiff Supplementary Motion for Summary Judgment,

against these three Defendants, ("Plaintiff Summary Judgment Affidavit") with attached exhibits.

15. On August 29, 2013 Trans Union filed its unopposed Motion for leaved to file combined reply in Support of Motion for Summary Judgment, and opposition to Plaintiff S Motion for Summary Judgment. On Sept 3, 2013 Trans Union filed its Response in opposition

Plaintiff s Motion for Summary Judgment and objection to Plaintiff S Summary Judgment Evidence.

16. On Sept 10, 2013 Trans Union Response and Objections were struck down by this Court, and Trans Union had until Sept 23, 2013 to refilled its Response Doc. 168 and prior to filing Doc. # 168 Trans Union filed Doc. #166, 167 all on 9120/13 objection to Plaintiff evidence.

II. PERSUASIVE ARGUMENT

17. Plaintiff affirmative and conclusive evidence exhibit bits (J) and (p) renders Equifax with no more defenses to argue i n this Court with exhibit (J) proving that these defendants and Equifax committed the duplications of Plaintiff s creditors on or about June 20 11on Plaintiff credit report which makes them guilty of negligent of violating 1681 (e) b of the FCRA Act, a Statement of Material Fact .

18. Experian Rep misrepresented the facts when their employees Teresa Iwanski made a false declaration as to the duplication of Plaintiff creditor accounts _____ Doc. 143-12. Experian Senior legal compliance specialist in inadvertly confess to the deletion of the wrong redacted account of Plaintiffs of Plaintiff consumer credit report. This false declaration has been reported to Mrs. McAneny on or about 19th of Sept 2013.As evident from the two redacted account as present to the Court these two _____ accounts have two different amount owed, different first report and different date of status.

The _____ account that was duplicated is located on exhibit G) was The redacted with address ID # 0061663385 as stated on Experian documents submitted to the Court along with Doc. 143-1 1 and Experian Watson 0117 see Doc. Exhibit (J).

19. Furthermore, the evidence received from _____ exhibit (i) which
shows Plaintiff omitted accounts omitted on this credit report from a third   part
____ provided through ____ date 1 1/281201 1, this undisputed evidence shows Experian
injured negligent act of 168 l (e)b of the FCRA Act

20. Most important as to the defendant Equifax the misrepresentation of the fact of
Equifax explicitly denying to the Court that Equifax (p) in their Answers and
Defenses, Doc. 133 where Plaintiff has presented enormous amount of relevant,
material, and competence evidence in Plaintiff exhibits e.g. Experian erroneous
declaration. Trans Union credit monitoring membership service credit report exhibit (a)
(d) E) (t) (r) (z) (AA) (dd) (ff) (gg) (jj)(kk), Plaintiff Experian exhibit (i) (v) (x) (bb)
(Q). Equifax exhibit (c) (b) (i)(v) (p) U), and others not mention herein.

21. All of the above exhibits either shows the duplication of plaintiff credit
accounts or are relevant evidence to explicitly proves duplications of plaintiff Creditors'
accounts, done by these Defendants.

22. The various unreasonable procedures these three defendants had in place on June
20ll whether it is operative errors such what happen in plaintiff
exhibit(AA) from Trans Union, computer data as in the
duplication of plaintiff credit
Accounts, cross-checking of personal Identification such as social security or two of same
accounts with same account numbers on Plaintiff consumer credit report are factual issues regarding
the unreasonable procedure that cause Plaintiff creditors accounts to be

duplication in his consumer credit report file for example the recent citing a recent case Miller v.Equifax.

23. Courts have held that the issue of reasonable procedures under 1681e (b) is a Jury Question. In the overwhelming majority of case see e.g. Dalton v. Capital Assoc. Indas Inc. 257 F.3d 409, (416 4th Cir. 2001) (citation omitted) Plaintiff moves for Summary Judgment with respect to his claim under section 168 1 n, 168lh(e), and 16810.

24. 1681n which provides for recovery for willful violation of FCRA. A willful Violation occurs in the event that a defendant... knowingly committed an act in conscious disregard for the rights of other, this is exactly what plaintiff is Claiming these defendants committed, by denying they did not duplicate Plaintiff credit accounts.

25. This wrongful act happened in this case when these defendants made knowingly false Statement e.g. when Trans Union rep stated, "He only saw one account for each Creditor when in fact there were two, accounts and when Mr. Lewis and Mr. Tom Tierney Said, "These things happens sometimes" this statement by these two people of Experian is a direct disregard for the rights of others, especially Plaintiff.

26. Exhibit (R) is relevant, material and competent. The Plaintiff credit report monitoring membership letter sent to Plaintiff as requested in the ordinary course of business by Trans Union and is relevant to the issue is material and Competent to the cause of action in this case, is admissible under the business record exception.

27. The foundation for Exhibit (r) was laid by Trans Union when they stated they had presented all the affirmative and conclusive evidence to prove their case although these defendants

present evidence dated May 20 2011, they failed and refused to admit this crucial evidence dated May 26, 2011 in the correct format of Plaintiff c r e d i t o r accounts because they knew it would weaken their case and prove that duplication took place. Evid. code 210, Fed. Rule Evid. 410, and Evid. code 700, Fed rule. Evid 601, 901 902 and any other applicable Fed. Rule. Evid.

Authentication

15. Evid. Code 1400, Fed Rule Evid 901, 902, 802, 803, 8 0 1

Evidence **irrelevant** when it has atendency in reason to make the facts that is offered to prove or disprove it more or less probable.

Plaintiff proves that Trans Union sent May 26, 201 1 credit monitoring report Plaintiff request by plaintiff because it has Trans Union letterhead and address to plaintiff with his name address exhibit (R).

Evidence Type

18. Relevant- Evid. Code 210, Fed. Rule Evid 401

    A. Material- Evid code 210, Fed. Rule evid 4 1 0

    B. Competent- Evid code 402, 403 and Evid code 700, Fed Rule Evid 601

    C. Evidence is material it is offered to prove a fact that is at issue in the case.

The issues in the case are determined by the pleading, any formal stipulation or admission and the applicable law.

While the defendants continue to state that Plaintiff Complaint consist of conclusory

speculative allegation but what these defendants are forgetting to mention is that Plaintiff "

conclusory allegations are supportive with truthful facts.

When there are well pleaded factual allegations a Court should 1. Assume their veracity

2. Then determine whether they plausibly give rise to an entitlement to relief... (Relief

for Plaintiff MSJ to be granted in his favor).

WHY PLAINTIFF EVIDENCE SHOULD BE ACCEPTED

19. Plaintiff Response Affidavit: Plaintiff stated in the beginning paragraph of his

Affidavit that he "Affirms that all statements and document attach to this

Summary Judgment are true to best of his k n o w l e d g e ."

Affirm means as a synonym to swear, and when you swear to something you take an

oath which is the same as taking an oath declared under penalty of perjury. In Addition to

having an affidavit Notarized as to the truth of something being Said or something that is

what is attested to be what it is supposed to be. Notwithstanding, Plaintiff certified all

exhibits and documents in *is* certifying Statement at the end of his summary before signing

it.

21. Most importantly the Court said plaintiff to make sure the affidavit is attached

To his motion for Summary Judgment brief which makes if inclusive and certified? It is

admissible because of its Relevance, Material, and competent to the issues

Of the cause of action or lawsuit under the provisions of l 681(e) b, 168lo,

1681n, 168lh (e) of FCRA Act.

22. Exhibit (R) is admissible under the chain of Custody document as a document

Received from Trans Union credit monitoring service credit report sent to

Plaintiff from Trans Union in or about the last part of May 2011.

It is unique because it is totally different from the other Trans Union credit

Monitoring service report sent to Plaintiff from June to Aug 2011.

This document exhibit (R) is admissible because it is relevant, Material,

and Competent to the issues at hand rebut that Trans Union failed to

present all of the evidence in this case as they stated by Trans Union,

"Trans Union affirmatively and conclusively have presented all the

evidence in this case to prove we should be Granted Summary Judgment."

Controverted by Plaintiff. The statement in exhibit (R) of Plaintiff Trans

Union credit monitoring service Consumer credit report dated May 26

2011 is not hearsay but nonhearsy because Trans Union failure to produce

this Exhibit (R) to this Court.

Beside Trans Union claiming that Plaintiff had not submitted any evidence that

Would disprove that Trans Union credit monitoring service is not part of

Plaintiff consumer credit report, exhibit (R) proves otherwise that it is part of

Plaintiff consumer credit report because of the consumer credit report sent to

Plaintiff by Trans Union credit Monitoring service.

Trans Union failure to admit exhibit (r) proves to this Court the importance of this

evidence and should be Admissible because of its Relevant, Material and Competence

one of the issues in this case.

23. Exhibit (Z) is admissible because it is Relevant, Material, and Competent.

It is authenticated from Trans Union by continuous claiming and refusing to

Admit that Trans Union did not provide Plaintiff credit report to 3rd parties

Such as Lenders, Furnishers and Public utilities companies, etc.

Trans Union bas no merit and opposition to the admission of Plaintiff

is unfounded because Plaintiff Statement in his SAC on p. 14 FN, "All documents and

exhibits submitted to sic Court and Defendants attorneys in prior motions and

submissions are to apply to This SAC in this claim," as well as what was said and

Admitted in his 1st Summary Judgment dated June 19, 2012, p.3, paragraph 11.

31. Number Paragraph 3 is admissible because of its Relevance, Material, and

Competent under Fed. Rule. Of Evid, and under the FCRA Act. Its no hearsay

Because the foundation was laid upon disagreement of _____

Service account of Plaintiff s, which claims he didn't dispute this account with Trans

Union Attorney Mrs. Reddoch because it already had a paid in full status. It is

Admissible under the business record exception.

32. Number 5 is admissible under the Relevant, Material, and Competent as well as

Admissible under the business Record exception; Present sense impression and

Declaration of state of Mind Fed.Rule. Evid 901, 902 401, 402, 403.

33.   Number 6 as stated above in number 5 plus s, the foundation is based on

The FCRA Act and provision 1681(e) b and the right to dispute invalid

Inaccurate, incomplete, and invalid, creditors accounts errors on a consumer Credit

reports. Admissible as business record exception, the foundation was laid when Trans Union

stated it was an internal document. Authenticated as chain of custody Under the

Fed.Rule. Evid from Trans Union to the law firm strasburger and

Attorney Reddoch during. Discovery sending this document as part of discovery see Case

law Miller v. Equifax where Ms. Miller brought suit against Equifax for

Inaccurately reporting her SSN #, Date of birth, see case Miller v. Equifax

34. Document # Number 11 exhibit (R) is Relevant, Material and Competent to

this Case due to the fact Trans Union refuse or failed to produce to this Court

Because they realized it would prove there where duplication on Plaintiff

Credit report.

Authenticated by the established chain of custody from Mrs. Reddoch attorney

Representing Trans Union then sending it to Plaintiff during Discovery.

Admissible under the Fed. Rule. Evid of Relevant, Material, Competent, it is No

hearsay under the Present sense impression, Declaration of state of Mind.

Undisputed Document Exhibit (R)

35. Document Number # 12 is Relevant, Material, and Competent

Authenticated from exhibit (J) downloaded from Equifax computer

monitoring Membership credit reporting site and is undisputed by Equifax.

FALSE DECLARATION by Ms. Iwanski FROM EXPERIAN

36. There is one of Plaintiff Accounts ___ which is disputed by

Plaintiff Because Experian erroneously deleted the wrong ____ Plaintiff

Creditors account.

This declaration from Ms. Iwanski is falsely y stated and is disputed by Plaintiff

as to the truth of this declaration.

37. Document Number # 13 is Relevant, Material, and Competent

The FCRA stated that once an account has been deleted it has to be certified and the

Consumer bas to be notified before it can be reinserted on the consumer credit report.

Change by the FCRA act is base and premise on fairness to consumer; if an   account.

With a paid in full Status and then change to unpaid without written consent of Plaintiff, then the CRA I as much obligated for the wrongful act as the furnisher, 1681i.

38.   Document Number #14 is Relevant, Material, and Competent

Base on this Court Rule on the Claim adjudicated by this Court in Plaintiff SAC Complaint from the facts stated by Plaintiff under the provisional laws of FCRA Act. 1681e (b.

39.   The Pawnbroker Contract Exhibit (DD) is Relevant, Material, and Competent.

It is a One-page part of the actual damage where Plaintiff is requesting from these Defendants which was authenticated many times in conversations with these Defendant's attorneys on the telephone that Plaintiff had to pawn his Jewelry to Finance defending his rights under the FCRA Act when these inaccurately Duplicated his creditor accounts on his credit report.

40.   Document exhibit (FF) is Relevant, Material, and Competent which is medical Correspondence which shown the stress of something may have behavior change on Plaintiff and manifest anxiety, depression, sadness, feeling of isolation, anger More than usual does not want to socialize with others, withdrawn.

31. Document Exhibit t (GG) is relevant, Material, and competent, it is authenticated by the chain of Custody under the Fed. Rule Evid. 901, 902. This is a central Part of Plaintiff proving his case against these defendants for the ____ is a lender which denied credit to Plaintiff and that denial in which. Mr. ___ said that the omission of Plaintiff creditors accounts on Plaintiff Credit report by Experian was a cause for being denied credit from ___ when Plaintiff applied for credit at ____

It is admissible as a business record exception.

39. Scan Envelopes from Trans (JJ) that are Relevant, Material, and Competent.

Authenticated by Trans Union stating that Plaintiff did not received that Document s

from June 4, 5,9,13,17,18,26, July 16, 20, Aug 2, 8, 201 credit monitor

Membership service to show that the duplication took place from the account being sent to

Plaintiff. It has the zip codes of Trans Union membership monitor service on it. Admissible

as a business record exception and chain of custody.

40. Document exhibit kk this is a one-page copy of Trans Union copy of Plaintiff

Consumer credit report date 10/412011 with an Inquires from asset

acceptance Dated 6-11- I I during the inaccurate duplications of plaintiff

creditors accounts. Authenticate from Trans Union affirmative denying

they did not report Plaintiff S Credit Report to any 3rd parties during that

time period during June 2011. Fed.Rule. Evid 901, 902.

41. Exhibit (R) Trans Union Interactive Letter d a t e d M a y 27, 2011 and attached Plaintiff

May 26, 20 11 Consumer credit report.

42. Exhibit (Z) a page from Plaintiff _____ consumer credit report with the name of a 3rd party

creditor _____ given to Plaintiff after he was denied credit.

Date 1/28/20 1 l. The page affirmatively states, "Results for Trans Union"

43. For the foregoing reason Plaintiff moves for this Honorable Court to overrule

Tran Union sustain objection to not allow the admissible of Plaintiff evidence.

since defendants are in possession of all digital files in a computer a g e there is no dispute that defendants possess all the documents Plaintiff have in

His possession unless allegation of Defendant Purging the file they are in

Violation of the FTC. Quoting from Plaintiff First Summary Judgment Date June 19, 2012

Doc.#27.

44. Purport of Plaintiff evidence exhibit (i), (J), R, and (P) substantiated

by Prima facie evidence exhibit U) which explicitly show a credit

report from

Equifax CRA date June 8, 2011 duplicated credit accounts on Plaintiff

Credit Report.

In Equifax and Experian MSJ Doc.#158, p.1 these defendants stated "Plaintiff. Proceeding

Pro Se has completely failed to Marshall. The evidence required for a Grant of Summary

Judgment in his favor..."Plaintiff digest that it's Defendants Who have not produce

evidence to repudiated Plaintiff claims and Summary J u d g m e n t ?

And this Court should grant Summary in Plaintiff favor, because these defendants failure to

Marshal enough evidence to overcome Plaintiff claims in his Complaints and his SAC and

unable to do the same for Plaintiff MSJ because of Plaintiff evidence.

45. Equifax and Experian Statement of Material Factual Disputed in Doc. #158 p.3

last paragraph these defendants claim they listed 31 as to which no

genuine issues exist and those facts are incorporated herein, but These defendants negated

to expressly state Equifax denial in Equifax Answers and Defenses p.2 #5 see evidence

exhibit (p) and exhibit (i)'. And all documents in this case that Plaintiff has been admitted

included that admission as stated

In the deposition, which is the foundation swore under oath of perjury of the

PLAINTIFF AFFIDAVIT

Plaintiff affidavit attests to the fact that Plaintiff was denied credit from __ on June 7, 2011, during which time Plaintiff credit file was duplicated.

Plaintiff is submitting this document as proof of Plaintiff claim against Defendants and the harm cause in this action of economic loss, Lack of trust in others, loss of business revenue, and

Psychological stress all cause by Defendants negligent action of Duplicating Plaintiff credit file. When Plaintiff applied for credit, creditors denied Plaintiff credit as a result of Defendants Negligence and Defamation cause of action which caused Plaintiff financial hardship in this action. Statements made on this affidavit are true to the best of my knowledge.

5/22/2012
_____

Date

James Leon Watson Sr.
Jacksonville, FL 32211

DECLARATION OF CUSTODIAN OF RECORDS

I.   My name is _____ I am competent to testify and have personal knowledge of the facts stated herein.

2.   I am employed by and am the custodian of records for Vital Recovery Services, Inc. Attached hereto are pages of records of Vital Recovery Services, Inc.

3.   The attached records were made at or near the time of the occurrence o fthe matters set forth in the attached records by, or from information transmitted by, a person with knowledgeof those matters. The attached records were kept by Vital Recovery Services, Inc. in the regular course of its business, and as a regularpractice of Vital Recovery Services, Inc. The attached records were made in the course of the regularly conducted business activitiesof Vital Recovery Services, Inc. and as a regular practice of Vital Recovery Services, Inc.

4.   The records attached hereto are exact duplicates of the originals.

5.   I declare under penalty of perjury that the forgoing is true and correct.

Signature

Dated_____

Fair Debt Collection Practices Act

Background

The Fair Debt Collection Practices Act (FDCPA) (15 USC 1692 et seq.) which became effective in March 1978, was designed to eliminate abusive, deceptive, and unfair debt collection practices. It also protects reputable debt collectors from unfair competition and encourages consistent state action to protect consumers from abuses in debt collection.

Coverage

Debt That Is Covered

The FDCPA applies only to the collection of debt incurred by a consumer primarily for personal, family, or household purposes. It does not apply to the collection of corporate debt or debt owed for business or agricultural purposes.

Debt Collectors That Are Covered

The FDCPA defines a *debt collector* as any person who regularly collects, or attempts to collect, consumer debts for another person or institution or uses some name other than its own when collecting its own consumer debts. The definition includes, for example, an institution that regularly collects debts for an unrelated institution, such as an institution that, under a reciprocal service arrangement, solicits the help of another in collecting a defaulted debt from a customer who has moved.

Debt Collectors That Are Not Covered

An institution is not considered a debt collector under the FDCPA when it collects:

- Another institution's debts in isolated instances
- Its own debts under its own name
- Debts it originated and then sold but continues to service (for example, mortgage and student loans)
- Debts that were not in default when they were obtained
- Debts that were obtained as security for a commercial credit transaction (for example, accounts receivable financing)

- Debts incidental to a bona fide fiduciary relationship or escrow arrangement (for example, a debt held in the institution's trust department or mortgage loan escrow for taxes and insurance)
- Debts, regularly, for other institutions to which it is related by common ownership or corporate control

Other debt collectors that are not covered by the FDCPA include:

- Officers or employees of an institution who collect debts owed to the institution in the institution's name
- Legal-process servers

Communication in Connection with Debt Collection

Definition of *Consumer*

For communications with a consumer or third party in connection with the collection of a debt, the term *consumer* is defined to include the borrower's spouse, parent (if the borrower is a minor), guardian, executor, or administrator.

When, Where, and with Whom Communication Is Permitted

Communicating with Consumers

A debt collector may not communicate with a consumer at any unusual time (generally before 8:00 a.m. or after 9:00 p.m. in the consumer's time zone) or at any place that is inconvenient to the consumer, unless the consumer or a court of competent jurisdiction has given permission for such contracts. A debt collector may not contact the consumer at his or her place of employment if the collector has reason to believe the employer prohibits such communications.

If the debt collector knows that the consumer has retained an attorney to handle the debt and can easily ascertain the attorney's name and address, all contacts must be with that attorney, unless the attorney is unresponsive or agrees to allow direct communication with the consumer.

Ceasing Communication with Consumers

When a consumer refuses, in writing, to pay a debt or requests that the debt collector cease further communication, the collector must cease all further communication, except to advise the consumer that:

- The collection effort is being stopped

- Certain specified remedies ordinarily invoked may be pursued or, if appropriate, that a specific remedy will be pursued
- Mailed notices from the consumer are official when they are received by the debt collector

Communicating with Third Parties

The only third parties that a debt collector may contact when trying to collect a debt are:

- The consumer
- The consumer's attorney
- A consumer reporting agency (if permitted by local law)
- The creditor
- The creditor's attorney
- The debt collector's attorney

The consumer or a court of competent jurisdiction may, however, give the debt collector specific permission to contact other third parties. In addition, a debt collector who is unable to locate a consumer may ask a third party for the consumer's home address, telephone number, and place of employment (location information). The debt collector must give his or her name and must state that he or she is confirming or correcting information about the consumer's location. Unless specifically asked, the debt collector may not name the collection firm or agency or reveal that the consumer owes any debt.

No third party may be contacted more than once unless the collector believes that the information from the first contact was wrong or incomplete and that the third party has since received better information, or unless the third party specifically requests additional contact.

Contact with any third party by postcard, letter, or telegram is allowed only if the envelope or content of the communication does not indicate the nature of the collector's business.

Validation of Debts

A debt collector must provide the consumer with certain basic information. If that information was not in the initial communication and if the consumer has not paid the debt five days after the initial communication, all of the following information must be sent to the consumer in written form:

- The amount of the debt
- The name of the creditor to whom the debt is owed
- Notice that the consumer has thirty days to dispute the debt before it is assumed to be valid

- Notice that upon such written dispute, the debt collector will send the consumer a verification of the debt or a copy of any judgment
- If the original creditor is different from the current creditor, notice that if the consumer makes a written request for the name and address of the original creditor within the thirty-day period, the debt collector will provide that information

If, within the thirty-day period, the consumer disputes in writing any portion of the debt or requests the name and address of the original creditor, the collector must stop all collection efforts until he or she mails the consumer a copy of a judgment or verification of the debt, or the name and address of the original creditor, as applicable.

Prohibited Practices

Harassing or Abusive Practices

A debt collector, in collecting a debt, may not harass, oppress, or abuse any person. Specifically, a debt collector may not:

- Use or threaten to use violence or other criminal means to harm the physical person, reputation, or property of any person
- Use obscene, profane, or other language that abuses the hearer or reader
- Publish a list of consumers who allegedly refuse to pay debts, except to a consumer reporting agency or to persons meeting the requirements of section 603(f) or 604(3) of the FDCPA
- Advertise a debt for sale to coerce payment
- Annoy, abuse, or harass persons by repeatedly calling their telephone number or allowing their telephone to ring continually
- Make telephone calls without properly identifying himself or herself, except as allowed to obtain location information

False or Misleading Representations

A debt collector, in collecting a debt, may not use any false, deceptive, or misleading representation. Specifically, a debt collector may not:

- Falsely represent or imply that he or she is vouched for, bonded by, or affiliated with the United States or any state, including the use of any badge, uniform, or similar identification
- Falsely represent the character, amount, or legal status of the debt, or of any services rendered, or compensation he or she may receive for collecting the debt
- Falsely represent or imply that he or she is an attorney or that communications are from an attorney
- Threaten to take any action that is not legal or intended

- Falsely represent or imply that nonpayment of any debt will result in the arrest or imprisonment of any person or the seizure, garnishment, attachment, or sale of any property or wages of any person, unless such action is lawful and intended by the debt collector or creditor
- Falsely represent or imply that the sale, referral, or other transfer of the debt will cause the consumer to lose a claim or a defense to payment, or become subject to any practice prohibited by the FDCPA
- Falsely represent or imply that the consumer committed a crime or other conduct to disgrace the consumer
- Communicate, or threaten to communicate, false credit information or information that should be known to be false, including not identifying disputed debts as such
- Use or distribute written communications made to look like or falsely represent documents authorized, issued, or approved by any court, official, or agency of the United States or any state if the appearance or wording would give a false impression of the document's source, authorization, or approval
- Use any false representation or deceptive means to collect or attempt to collect a debt or to obtain information about a consumer
- Fail to disclose in the initial written communication with the consumer, and the initial oral communication if it precedes the initial written communication, that the debt collector is attempting to collect a debt and that any information obtained will be used for that purpose. In addition, the debt collector must disclose in subsequent communications that the communication is from a debt collector. (These disclosures do not apply to a formal pleading made in connection with legal action.)
- Falsely represent or imply that accounts have been sold to innocent purchasers for value
- Falsely represent or imply that documents are legal process
- Use any name other than the true name of the debt collector's business, company, or organization
- Falsely represent or imply that documents are not legal process forms or do not require action by the consumer
- Falsely represent or imply that the debt collector operates or is employed by a consumer reporting agency

Unfair Practices

A debt collector may not use unfair or unconscionable means to collect or attempt to collect a debt. Specifically, a debt collector may not:

- Collect any interest, fee, charge, or expense incidental to the principal obligation unless it was authorized by the original debt agreement or is otherwise permitted by law
- Accept a check or other instrument postdated by more than five days, unless he or she notifies the consumer, in writing, of any intention to deposit the check or

instrument; the notice must be made no more than ten nor less than three business days before the date of deposit

- Solicit a postdated check or other postdated payment instrument to use as a threat or to institute criminal prosecution
- Deposit or threaten to deposit a postdated check or other postdated payment instrument before the date on the check or instrument
- Cause communication charges; such as charges for collect telephone calls and telegrams, to be made to any person by concealing the true purpose of the communication
- Take or threaten to repossess or disable property when the creditor has no enforceable right to the property or does not intend to do so, or if, under law, the property may not be taken, repossessed, or disabled
- Use a postcard to contact a consumer about a debt

Multiple Debts

If a consumer owes several debts that are being collected by the same debt collector, payments must be applied according to the consumer's instructions. No payment may be applied to a disputed debt.

Legal Actions by Debt Collectors

A debt collector may file a lawsuit to enforce a security interest in real property only in the judicial district in which the real property is located. Other legal actions may be brought only in the judicial district in which the consumer lives or in which the original contract creating the debt was signed.

Furnishing Certain Deceptive Forms

No one may design, compile, or furnish any form that creates the false impression that someone other than the creditor (for example, a debt collector) is participating in the collection of debt.

Civil Liability

A debt collector who fails to comply with any provision of the FDCPA is liable for:

- Any actual damages as allowed by the court:
  - In an individual action, up to $1,000

- In a class action, up to $1,000 for each named plaintiff and an award to be divided among all members of the class of an amount up to $500,000 or 1 percent of the debt collector's net worth, whichever is less

- Costs and a reasonable attorney's fee in any such action

In determining punitive damages, the court must consider the nature, frequency, and persistency of the violations and the extent to which they were intentional. In a class action, the court must also consider the resources of the debt collector and the number of persons adversely affected.

Defenses

A debt collector is not liable for a violation if a preponderance of the evidence shows that the violation was not intentional and was the result of a bona fide error that arose despite procedures reasonably designed to avoid any such error. The collector is also not liable if he or she, in good faith, relied on an advisory opinion of the Federal Trade Commission, even if the ruling is later amended, rescinded, or determined to be invalid for any reason.

Jurisdiction and Statute of Limitations

Action against debt collectors for violations of the FDCPA may be brought in any appropriate U.S district court or other court of competent jurisdiction. The consumer has one year from the date on which the violation occurred to start such an action.

Administrative Enforcement

The Federal Trade Commission (FTC) is the primary enforcement agency for the FDCPA. The various financial regulatory agencies enforce the FDCPA for the institutions they supervise. Neither the FTC nor any other agency may issue regulations governing the collection of consumer debts by debt collectors. The FTC may, however, issue advisory opinions under the Federal Trade Commission Act on the meaning and application of the FDCPA.

Relation to State Law

The FDCPA preempts state law only to the extent that a state law is inconsistent with the FDCPA. A state law that is more protective of the consumer is not considered inconsistent with the FDCPA.

Exemption for State Regulation

The FTC may exempt certain classes of debt collection practices from the requirements of the FDCPA if the FTC has determined that state laws impose substantially similar requirements and that there is adequate provision for enforcement.

Fair Debt Collection Practices Act

Examination Objectives and Procedures

Examination Objectives

1. To determine the adequacy of the institution's internal procedures and controls to ensure consistent compliance with the FDCPA
2. To determine if the institution complies with the requirements of the FDCPA in collecting or attempting to collect third-party consumer debts

Examination Procedures

The following procedures are to be completed through interviews with personnel knowledgeable about and directly engaged in the institution's collection activities and through reviews of any written collection procedures, reciprocal collection agreements, collection letters, dunning notices, envelopes, scripts used by collection personnel, validation notices, individual collection files, complaint files, and other relevant records.

1. Determine if the institution is a debt collector under the FDCPA.
2. Determine if the institution has established internal procedures and controls to ensure compliance with the FDCPA.
3. If the institution has acted or is acting as a debt collector under the FDCPA, determine if the institution has

a) Communicated with the consumer or third parties in any prohibited manner
b) Furnished the written validation notice within the required time period and otherwise complied with applicable validation requirements
c) Used any harassing, abusive, unfair, or deceptive collection practice prohibited by the FDCPA
d) Collected any amount not expressly authorized by the agreement creating the debt or by state law
e) Applied all payments received as instructed and, where no instruction was given, applied payments only to undisputed debts
f) Filed suit in an authorized forum if the institution sued to collect the debt

INQUIRES

I would like to emphasize when you are disputing inquiries with a creditor and that creditor doesn't respond to you within thirty days from the time of the dispute, that inquiry should be deleted from your credit file or report.

There are two types of inquires, one is called a soft inquire and the other one is called a hard inquiry. A soft inquiry does not hurt your credit score for example when are you checking your credit report through a third party say e. g., Walmart has a service where you can check your score because you have their credit card.

In addition inquiries by existing lenders when monitoring your credit accounts for making preapproved credit offers or when these lenders are requesting your personal credit report are only seen by you, they are excluded from credit reports seen by lenders and only appears on your consumer report, but when applying for credit you should ask a lender what type of inquiry it will be soft or hard.

Before a lender or creditor can pull your credit they must have your permission as define by FCRA, "permissible purpose " under this act, if they do not obtain your permission you can dispute it and have it removed.

A credit inquiry is noted on your credit report every time a credit report is accessed by anyone you give permission to, and stays on your report for a period of two years.

Some seems to think that older inquires doesn't effect your score and that only hard inquiries from within the past year can have an impact on your credit score, with older hard and soft inquiries completely ignored entirely.

Hard inquiries are initiated when a lender get access to a consumer credit report and score as part of a credit application as well as hard inquiries can also result from collection agencies using credit reports in their skip tracing efforts.

There are statistical evidence as stated by Fair Isaac (FICO) which is people who add six or more inquiries during a past year can be up to eight times more likely to file for bankruptcy than those with credit reports showing no inquiries.

Since inquiries are updated immediately on your credit report they are an indication that a consumer has applied for credit, and tends to be an indicator of future credit rusk.

Inquiries can also provide early evidence of identity theft when a consumer credit file has been accessed fraudulently.

Finally the main purpose of a credit inquiry is to be used by lenders to determine whether or not a consumer applicant is a high or low risk borrower.

Finally, this book was not written to be vindictive toward CRA's or any organization nor against any individuals or business but as a collection of pleadings, motions etc., for those who contemplates filing a complaint against CRA's or any Defendant in the Courts.

For I realize that most Pro Ses will always have the odds against them but by reading legal cases researching the law and closely following how the Pleadings have been done in this book, those odds perhaps will be decreased and perhaps the tide will turn in their favor for them to get the results they are seeking which is to have those wrongful Creditors errors removed from their credit report or to be compensated for the CRA's not removing those errors on their consumer credit report as required by FCRA Act.

But as you know litigation can sometimes be nasty and dirty so if you don't have the will or stomach nor tenacity, I would advised you to think twice.

www.ingramcontent.com/pod-product-compliance
Lightning Source LLC
Chambersburg PA
CBHW082124210326
41599CB00031B/5863